HOLOCAUST VERSUS WEHRMACHT

HOLOCAUST VERSUS
WEHRMACHT

How Hitler's "Final Solution" Undermined the German War Effort

Yaron Pasher

UNIVERSITY PRESS OF KANSAS

© 2014 by the University Press of Kansas
All rights reserved

Published by the University Press of Kansas (Lawrence, Kansas 66045), which was
organized by the Kansas Board of Regents and is operated and funded by Emporia
State University, Fort Hays State University, Kansas State University, Pittsburg
State University, the University of Kansas, and Wichita State University

Library of Congress Cataloging-in-Publication Data

Pasher, Yaron, author.
  Holocaust versus Wehrmacht : how Hitler's "Final Solution" undermined the German
war effort / Yaron Pasher.
    pages cm -- (Modern war studies)
    Includes bibliographical references and index.
  ISBN 978-0-7006-2006-7 (hardback)
  ISBN 978-0-7006-2037-1 (ebook)
1. Holocaust, Jewish (1939–1945)—Europe, Eastern—Influence. 2. World War, 1939–1945
—Campaigns—Eastern Front—Social aspects. 3. World War, 1939–1945—Atrocities
—Eastern Front. 4. World War, 1939–1945—Campaigns—France—Normandy—Social
aspects. 5. World War, 1939–1945—Transportation--Germany. 6. Europe, Eastern—Ethnic
relations. 7. Germany—Armed Forces—History—World War, 1939–1945. I. Title.
  DS135.E83P37 2014
  940.54′1343—dc23

                              2014029767

British Library Cataloguing-in-Publication Data is available.

Printed in the United States of America
10 9 8 7 6 5 4 3 2 1

For my daughters, Nili and Ruthi

Contents

Map galleries follow pages 77 and 145.

Photo galleries follow pages 94 and 202.

Preface

The present research was a long journey for me—and not just through modern European history of the twentieth century. It was also an opportunity to explore my own family history, to better understand where I came from, and to link this knowledge to the historical narrative. The extraordinary life stories of two people in particular influenced and shaped my way of thinking and point of view: Louis B. Pasher and Aharon Anglister (Agmon). Both men (my grandparents) were forced in midlife to suffer the horrors of World War II, an experience that would haunt them till their last days.

Louis B. Pasher was a British subject born in London in 1905. He was the first of nine children from a Zionist family, which emigrated in 1921 in order to fulfill Theodor Herzl's vision and move to their homeland, Israel, where they resided in a tent in the eleven-year-old city of Tel Aviv. In September 1939, at the age of thirty-four, he joined the British army in its war against European fascism. He would return to Tel Aviv only in mid-1947 after a long period of service that included over two years in Italy and Germany after the Third Reich's unconditional surrender. Back home, he met for the first time a seven-year-old boy, my father, born in March 1940. Louis was one of the first to join the British armed forces and one of the last discharged. During his military service, Louis would fight Erwin Rommel's Panzerarmee Afrika in El Alamein with Bernard Montgomery's 8th Army, and he would be taken prisoner in Sicily and eventually manage to escape the POW camp there with an Australian colonel. In April 1945, he would be present in Milan to see Benito Mussolini and his mistress's bodies hanging upside down, and even manage to capture this historic scene on camera. In 1961, Louis Bernard Pasher was honored with an OBE from Her Majesty Queen Elizabeth II for helping Jewish widows and orphans of the British Legion after the war ended. Until his death ten years later, the war would continue to be the most influential and defining experience of his life.

My other grandfather, Aharon Anglister (Agmon), another Zionist, left the small town of Garwolin, some sixty kilometers southeast of Warsaw, in 1933, and made his home in Tel Aviv too. He married his hometown sweetheart a year later and maintained contact with both families in Garwolin via mail. When the war broke out, Garwolin would be one of the first towns in Poland to suffer under the Nazi boot, and the entire Jewish community was deported to the Warsaw ghetto. Both families—the Anglisters and the Rubins—lived for two years in terrible conditions, but with the hope of a brighter day. This hope, portrayed through letters sneaked out of the ghetto, agonized a helpless young couple in Tel Aviv who had managed by chance to escape the terrible fate of the other members of their families.

In July 1942, one week before the birth of their first baby (my mother), they would receive a devastating letter informing my grandmother that her father had perished in the Warsaw ghetto from starvation. The fate of the others would be no better. From what could be gleaned from letters, the entire family was probably liquidated during the first big *aktion* in the Warsaw ghetto, which began on July 21, 1942, and dispatched them to the gas chambers of Treblinka. No one survived to tell the tale of the two families, leaving two people heartbroken forever. My grandparents lost mothers and fathers, brothers and sisters—a total of twelve close family members, as well as numerous other relatives from both sides. They would never quite get over this tragedy; they lived with feelings of guilt and remorse, and for at least half of their adulthood in agony and despair.

This, then, is the background to my narrative, constructed while searching for answers. That quest guided me through the research for this book, which I dedicate to their memory.

Acknowledgments

Many people helped me complete this journey, whether by suggestions, insights, thoughts, or paths of research—or by ruling out some of my initial assumptions. They made a profound contribution to this research, and I extend my gratitude and appreciation.

My deepest gratitude and appreciation go to my mentor, Gerhard L. Weinberg, for uncompromisingly aiding me in achieving my goals and leading me along the right path while keeping me focused with his immense knowledge and patience. His readings and insights were instrumental in sustaining this project. My deepest thanks also go to Dina Porat, teacher and mentor throughout my academic life, for her support and friendship as well as for her profound influence and faith throughout this project. Without her, it would never have been accomplished.

I would like to thank Matityahu Maizel, who has faithfully supported me since my undergraduate years at Tel Aviv University, then through the advanced stages of this research, teaching me, first and foremost, how to read history and how to ask the right questions. Gabriel Gorodetzky and Shulamit Volkov, through their tutorials, challenged me all the way through my master's thesis and supervised it in a way that gave me deeper insights into my doctoral research, which is the basis for this book. Dan Diner introduced me to unconventional historical thought. Hartmut Pogge von Strandmann, University College, Oxford, lent his enthusiastic support to this complex topic and suggested I widen the scope to include all the major campaigns of the war. Hew Strachan of All Souls College, Oxford, made me sweat with questions concerning military theory, and Azar Gat, Ezer Weizman Chair of National Security at Tel Aviv University, broadened my knowledge of military thought. I would like to thank Aron Shai and Raphael Vago, Tel Aviv University, for focusing my attention on questions arising from my research on the East European and Far East theaters of war. Richard Overy provided valuable insight into the overwhelming amount of archival material I had to go through; in particular, he introduced me to the documentation at Duxford Airfield and at the Liddell Hart Centre for Military Archives, London. Special thanks go to Dan Laor, former dean of the faculty of humanities at Tel Aviv University, for encouraging me to complete my research; Edna Pasher, my mother, for her support, inspiration, and encouragement, as well as for introducing me to the theories of Thomas Kuhn on scientific revolutions, which have helped me over hard times during this research when I had my own doubts.

Warm thanks go to Robert M. Citino, University of North Texas, and Dorris L. Bergan, University of Toronto, for reading the book in manuscript and giving me their wise suggestions, permitting me to strengthen some major points.

I extend many thanks to Major General Jakob Amidror, former Israel Defense Force (IDF) chief of military colleges; Brigadier General Yitzhak Rabin, former IDF chief of the Armored Corps[1]; and Major General Amiaz Sagis, former IDF head of the technology and logistics division, for the interviews they gave me, along with practical insights and suggestions that have helped me consolidate my assumptions.

I am grateful to Stephen Walton for his help at the Imperial War Museum, London and Duxford; Cesrin Schmidt, Bundesarchiv Berlin, for her assistance and patience; and Helga Waib'el and Andrea Meier from the Bundesarchiv Militärarchiv, Freiburg, for their assistance in helping me find archival material during my several visits there. My thanks also go to Sarah Vered, Chaim Rosenberg School of Jewish Studies, Tel Aviv University, for her assistance and friendship—and for helping me keep to a time schedule.

Special thanks go to the photo archives of the Bundesarchiv and to the archives of Stadtarchiv Bielefeld and Yad Vashem for their courtesy in allowing me to use the images for this book. My thanks and gratitude also go to the Trustees of the Liddell Hart Centre for Military Archives, Bundesarchiv Berlin and Bundesarchiv Militärarchiv, Freiburg, Cambridge University Press and Gerhard L. Weinberg, and Martin Gilbert for their courtesy in allowing me to use the maps for this book.

Several institutions and funds have generously helped finance my research. Many thanks to the Yad Vashem International Institute for Holocaust Research (Jerusalem), Alfried Krupp von Bohlen und Halbach Stiftung (Essen), Anglo-Israel Association (London), Minerva Institute for German History (Tel Aviv University), Raul Wallenberg Scholarship Fund (Tel Aviv University), Ignatz Bubis Foundation (Frankfurt), Yoran Schnitzer Foundation for Jewish History, Ovadia Margalit Fund for Holocaust Research, Lisa and Norbert Schechter Foundation, and Scholarship Fund for Holocaust Research Studies in memory of Rachel and Moshe Bialystock.

I am deeply indebted to my father, Yossi Pasher, for all his wise suggestions. He read the book in various versions, when I could no longer tell whether the text was good enough or should undergo a further revision, and gave me his impressions. I would also like to express my warm appreciation to Beryl Belsky for proofreading this work and for patiently and devotedly helping me edit it. I also extend warm thanks to everyone at the University Press of Kansas, particularly to Kelly Chrisman Jacques, Rebecca J. Murray, Michael Kehoe, and Michael Briggs for his patience, advice, and long-lasting support.

Last but not least, my wife, Merav, who stood by me through it all. Thank you.

HOLOCAUST VERSUS WEHRMACHT

Introduction

The Final Solution, which began with organized executions performed by the Einsatzgruppen and certain units of the Wehrmacht in conjunction with the Nazi struggle against the Soviet Union, and which eventually developed into the genocide of European Jewry, was assisted by logistics that were no less ambitious than those used by entire armies. Infrastructure and resources for operational and military needs that were in short supply were exploited in support of the successful perpetration of the Final Solution. Given that such logistics did not help Germany's war effort but rather were a burden on it, the key question is to what extent implementation of the Final Solution affected the operational capabilities and function of the German army during the various campaigns of World War II.

Analysis of the extent of resources and effort the Germans invested in the implementation of the Final Solution during World War II evaluates their influence on the performance of the Wehrmacht during four major campaigns, with the main objective being to examine the relationship between the German war effort and the Final Solution at the tactical level of warfare during World War II. The scope here covers November 1941 to August 1944—that is, from the beginning of organized Jewish train transports to the East, an undertaking that paralleled Operation Typhoon (a direct sequel to the German invasion of the Soviet Union), until the last transports carrying Hungarian Jews left for Auschwitz, paralleling the Allied invasion of Western Europe and the encirclement of the Third Reich. A major share of the logistical problems faced by the German army on the various fronts stemmed from the use of manpower and transportation in favor of objectives that were not part of the military struggle: implementation of the Final Solution, with the aid of Germany's rail company, the Reichsbahn.

Evidence that points specifically toward the utilization of supply lines in favor of mobilizing Jewish transports to death camps and extermination sites indicates a connection between the operational capabilities of the army and the influence that the Final Solution had on them at the level of logistics. Resources were diverted to Jewish transports despite supplies being desperately needed for a Wehrmacht division or an army. For instance, several trains bringing Jews from various parts of Europe to the crematoriums of Auschwitz and Treblinka could have carried the supplies needed to restore the combat capability of an infantry division—perhaps fuel that could move tanks of an armored division trapped in one of the pockets of Soviet resistance in the Caucasus or, in the later phases of the war, on the Western Front. Even if only 10 percent of resources from the entire transportation and military infrastructure were utilized for the deportation of European Jews during any one of the campaigns, the Final Solution must have had a major impact on the German war effort.[1]

After some successful and impressive blitz campaigns, the Wehrmacht seemed invincible. Poland, Scandinavia, the Netherlands, France, and the Balkans were all swiftly conquered, one after the other, with the Germans experiencing only minor casualties. Moreover, Austria and Czechoslovakia were overcome without a shot being fired. However, from June 22, 1941, although it seemed at first that Germany was about to win another successful campaign against the Soviet Union, a countdown had begun toward the collapse of this mighty German military force. Hitler's strategy to bring the Soviet Union to its knees through another swift German blitz failed during that summer. German objectives may have been achieved geographically but not militarily. The bulk of the Russian army west of the Dnieper–Dvina line was not annihilated, and although already in July 1941 it was certain that the original operational program had failed, no concrete steps were taken to prepare a war program that would take into consideration Germany's logistic and economic capabilities under these new circumstances.[2] At approximately the same time, a campaign against a people began—a campaign that eventually ended with the planned genocide of European Jewry.

According to the view most commonly held to this day regarding World War II, Germany had no chance whatsoever of winning the war, especially once the United States had joined and it became evident that the tide had turned in favor of the Allies. On the basis of this assumption, historians up through the 2000s have seen the German attack on the Soviet Union as Hitler's greatest blunder during the war and as a move that determined its fate. June 22, 1941, therefore stands as an important landmark, even more so than September 1939. However, this date, apart from its significance in the military annals of the war, is no less important ideologically. It represented the finding of a solution to the Jewish problem, which had occupied the Nazi leaders of Germany as much as the war itself; that solution was determined physical annihilation.

At the beginning of the campaign against the Red Army, the Wehrmacht's infrastructure and mobility were not based on train supply but on paved roads. However, as the Germans penetrated deeper into Soviet territory, it became increasingly necessary to use trains because there were almost no proper roads. By the end of 1941, 15,000 kilometers of Soviet railway line had been adapted to the standard width of the German tracks (which were three and a half inches narrower), and in September 1942, Hitler announced that within a few weeks, the remaining 10,000 kilometers of rail line out of 25,000 kilometers in the occupied Soviet territory would be adapted.[3]

Germany had entered the war with limited resources, and the Reichsbahn, which linked the front to the rear, with all the logistics that this involved, was no different in that respect. In 1939, Germany had fewer trains and locomotives than in 1914, and its successful conquests left no time for the victorious generals to deal with perceived trivialities such as reorganization of the rail system. Still, the new conquests provided a rail network that was annexed to the German Reichsbahn with no special difficulties because the width of the tracks (except, as noted, in the Soviet Union) was identical throughout Europe.[4] It was only at the beginning of 1942, when Albert Speer succeeded Fritz Todt as minister of armaments and took charge of industrial production, that there were attempts to inquire whether the destination of a particular train was necessary and whether it made any contribution to the war effort.

By examining the historical facts on a parallel timescale to find linkages between the operative events of the war and its ideological aspects, it is possible to assess each test case in each of the geopolitical fighting arenas to determine the influence of the Final Solution on the operative breakdowns of the Wehrmacht. The balance of power between Germany and its opponents, the decision-making process in the German High Command, and the conflicting interests between purely logistical military requisites and priorities versus ideological policy can all be assessed via train allocation.[5] One way to examine the significance of the Jewish transports—which originally left the German Reich for the Soviet Union and later departed from all over Europe for the death camps, using the Wehrmacht's logistical organization—is to compare the weight each train could carry to the front with the weight that a train could carry to one of the extermination camps in Poland.

The SS had no carriages of its own to transport Jews. Instead, SS officers usually arranged to allocate sealed cattle freight cars, which were chosen to prevent the victims from escaping. This is an important aspect because the Wehrmacht's mobility in the USSR was based mainly on horses fastened to wagons. When Germany invaded the Soviet Union, the Wehrmacht was equipped with 600,000 horses[6] (another source puts the number higher, at 750,000 horses[7]). In total, the Germans used about 2,750,000 horses compared to 1,400,000 during World War I.[8] Apart from tanks that moved independently and not always successfully, most of the artillery was loaded onto wagons that were dragged by horses. Because most of the motorized vehicles could not survive the harsh weather conditions, horses proved essential for transferring supplies to the front lines; they were used to carry loads such as heavy artillery and ammunition. Paradoxically, they helped the Wehrmacht survive the war over such a long period.[9] Seventy-seven infantry divisions were used in the first phase of Operation Barbarossa and on the eve of the attack on Moscow, with only freight horses leashed to 200 wagons.[10] The same cars that the Reichsbahn allocated for transporting Jews transferred the main transport vehicles to the Eastern Front. Therefore, when assessing the relationship between the logistical abilities of the Wehrmacht and the logistics involved in transporting thousands of Jews daily to the camps, it is also important to examine the weight of the horses compared to the amount of people forced to board those cars, and to formulate an assumption regarding the logistical effect in numbers on the fighting forces in the East each time another transport departed for the death camps.

Apparently the Final Solution did not pose a strategic challenge to the Reichsbahn because of the relatively small number of trains involved in the plan's execution compared to the numbers the army needed. As a result, Julius Dorpmüller, Reich minister of transportation and head of the Reichsbahn, and Albert Ganzenmüller, his deputy—and in fact everyone in key positions at the Reichsbahn—paid little attention to the trains used for transport.[11] This was perhaps the root of the problem Germany eventually faced.

There is no accurate documentation regarding the number of trains that actually participated in the execution of the Final Solution. On the basis of the number of people deported to the six death camps, Chełmno, Belzec, Sobibor, Treblinka, Majdanek, and Auschwitz-Birkenau—for which it is also difficult to obtain an accurate figure—somewhere between 3.5 and 4 million people were transported by the Reichsbahn to their deaths.[12] The average number of persons compressed into a single car was about 100, which meant the Reichsbahn had to allocate 40,000 train wagons and between 2,500 and 3,000 locomotives. The Reich's Jews were deported to the East in transports of 1,000 people, or ten cars per train; a similar number per transport were deported to Belzec. Transports arrived in Auschwitz with an average of 2,000 people aboard trains of twenty cars each, and Treblinka received transports containing even 3,000 people per train, with an average of 150 to 180 people per car. To this total number of 40,000 cars, one must add another 33,000 carrying the booty looted from the victims to Germany—another 2,000 trains.[13]

In order to get some sense of proportion, consider the following. Transporting an entire infantry division to the Eastern Front required about seventy trains, and transporting an entire new Panzer division took about ninety trains.[14] Seventy trainloads were also all that were needed to transfer the engineering structure for a solid railway bridge across the Don River at Rychkov, not far from Stalingrad, in order to move goods for the 6th Army to the city itself before its encirclement at the end of November 1942—and this should not be on account of supply trains that were indispensable to the 6th Army's existence.[15]

After all, the logistical situation that General Friedrich Paulus faced in summer 1942 before the 6th Army under his command was encircled by Soviet forces was based on a single supply line, which, relatively speaking, was insufficient for the Reichsbahn's capacity.[16] This single line was supposed to supply horses to the front, and from there, these pack animals had to bring supplies to German forces in the battlefield. Thus, had the Germans taken the 3,000 trains that were used during the war for the Final Solution plus 2,000 trains of booty to move troops to the front (whether the Eastern Front or the Western Atlantic Wall), the Wehrmacht could have in general transferred approximately seventy-one divisions—namely, about five armies totaling just about half a million troops with full gear, including the horses and other pack animals on which German logistics were based.[17]

On the eve of the mass evacuations from the concentration camps just before the death marches began in January 1945, a total of 37,674 armed male German guards and another 3,508 armed female German guards were still part of the concentration camps' disposition. They all belonged to the guarding units of the concentration camps, which were apart from the administrative units that ran them under the Gestapo's responsibility. In armed manpower, they were worth at least eight divisions, which could be reconstructed during the critical months of fighting for the Reich's borders.[18] On May 9, 1944, for instance, Hitler put out a decree that authorized Himmler to draft for guarding tasks in the concentration camps soldiers close to age forty (that is, born in 1906 and later). In accordance with this decree, 10,000 Wehrmacht soldiers who returned from the Crimean peninsula as well as soldiers from the Luftwaffe defense units and even the navy served in the concentration camp system.[19]

As Ian Kershaw has demonstrated, Hitler's regime had bought off the German population, securing loyalty through a standard of living sustained by exploiting the occupied territories. Wages and salaries were still being paid in April 1945, and despite mounting difficulties, distribution of food rations was maintained. Until the end of the war, limited forms of entertainment still functioned to sustain morale. For example, a concert by the Berlin Philharmonic took place on April 12, 1945, four days before the Soviet assault on the German capital was launched; cinemas were still open; even football matches were still on. When Goebbels tried to introduce measures to save labor in an effort targeted to providing men to the front, he met resistance from Hitler, who drew the line when Goebbels planned to stop the production of beer and sweets, stating that even the Bolsheviks had never halted the production of sweets, which were thought to be necessary not only for citizens at home but also for the soldiers at the front.[20]

On July 12, 1944, Speer wrote a memorandum to Hitler insisting that it was essential to make total war demands on the population. He claimed people were ready to make the necessary sacrifices to their daily lives. On July 18, Goebbels wrote another memorandum to Hitler, coordinated and maneuvered by Speer: Germany could produce fifty new divisions for the Wehrmacht in just under four months. By working through the figures that Speer provided, they thought it was possible to recruit as many as 4.3 million extra men for the Wehrmacht through an efficiency act.[21] The manpower would translate into military force that could be sent anywhere needed to extend the war even further. They needed only to choose when to draft the men and to calculate the amount of time needed to train them well enough to form an effective military combat division.

By late 1943, when even the Germans were beginning to feel that the tide had turned against them, they began to explore the possibility of utilizing existing World War I positions in the Dolomite Alps of Northern Italy as the basis for a defensive line running east from Bregenz on Lake Constance to Klagenfurt, then along the Yugoslav border toward Hungary. Because many of these fortifications had remained in relatively good condition, the Germans assumed that they could quickly build a strong position. In late July 1944, Swiss intelligence had growing concerns that the Nazis would hold out in the Alps until new secret weapons or a split in the Allied coalition produced a decisive turnaround in the war. These concerns were also expressed to American intelligence agents working in Switzerland; they spoke of monstrous fortifications, with the construction work to improve them beginning in September 1944. It included building underground factories, weapons and ammunition storehouses, and secret airfields, as well as stockpiling supplies. These intelligence reports stated that should the Germans successfully retreat into this fortress, the war could be extended by six to eight months, causing American forces to suffer even more casualties than in Normandy. The Nazis could hold out for two years longer if this last stronghold was not assaulted—a situation that might encourage widespread guerrilla activity throughout occupied Germany. On September 22, an analysis by the American office of strategic services (OSS) concluded that southern Germany was a potential base for the continuance of the war.[22] In March 1945, even General Omar Bradley was beginning to rethink operational goals. He assumed that all indications suggested a trend toward guerrilla warfare as the Germans slowly withdrew into a prepared fortress. The fact that the Allies were aware of strong German mobile reserves in Czechoslovakia added to their anxiety, as did the knowledge that harsh fighting would result if even a fraction of the troops withdrawing from Italy, the Balkans, and southern Germany reached the redoubt area in the Alps.[23] Only in late March 1945 did an SS security service intelligence report describe German popular opinion as doomed. The last remaining hope of avoiding defeat had evaporated.[24]

Finally, an ideological factor kept the wheels of the German resistance moving forward until the bitter end. The Final Solution was perceived by the German leadership as synonymous with the war against the leading powers of the anti-Nazi Allied coalition led by Stalin, Churchill, and Roosevelt. Nazi propaganda saw the coalition members as accomplices and puppets of Jews operating behind the scenes. Hitler and members of his close entourage argued that it was necessary to exterminate the Jews before they were able to exterminate Germany and the Germans.[25] The term *Vernichtungskrieg*, which had a familiar Clausewitzian ring to it, symbolized the complete defeat of the enemy armies. In describing the Jewish people as a whole as the enemy of the Nazis, the German narrative attempted to situate the threats of annihilation and extermination within the language of warfare.[26] In an address to 20,000 young officer candidates on November 30, 1943, Hitler said that Germany had a choice: "Victory or merciless annihilation." In this rare public appearance, Hitler had repeated that the goal of "the Jewish powers standing behind British politics who unleashed this war in alliance with the Soviet Union was first of all to exterminate Germany, in order to hand Europe over to Bolshevism."

The German people and German armies were the "only barrier to our enemies' plans for extermination of Germany dictated by Jewish hatred."[27] This was the essence behind Hitler's operational decisions, and this is what would keep the German war machine fighting in the name of ideology in addition to fighting on behalf of its military objectives.

Part 1

Operation Typhoon and German Deportations to the East

From October 16 to December 15, 1941, forty-three Jewish transports, which also included five Gypsy trains, left the German Reich for Lodz, Minsk, Riga, and Kovno in the East.[1] This operation, which did not take place during the earlier successful blitz campaigns, appeared to have been a logistical burden that was not taken into consideration by Nazi leaders and was to cause major problems. The transports were halted because of protests coming from the Wehrmacht High Command about the waste of trains for missions other than military ones. At that point, the German army had ceased gaining new territory in the Soviet interior but had managed to repel a Soviet counteroffensive launched on December 5, 1941, bringing the blitz era to an end. Operation Typhoon—the sequel to the course of events that began on June 22, 1941, and part of Operation Barbarossa—was allegedly another gamble taken by Hitler. However, if the other side were lucky this time, the course of events on the German side had nothing to do with luck or chance but with decision making.

In this respect, it is worth examining Soviet histories, which for years shaped, at least partially, the perception of war on the Eastern Front. The official approach toward Soviet histories, which viewed 1941 as the beginning of the Great Patriotic War, split this event into to two time periods. The treatment of and amendments to official Soviet history were linked to the ongoing changes in the communist regime over almost fifty years, from the end of the war until communism's collapse. Under Stalin, there was no Soviet history. The Soviet dictator's wartime speeches and essays were compiled into a volume entitled *The Great Patriotic War* and served for years, and certainly until his death in 1953, as the only official Soviet history.[2] At the beginning of the cold war, official Soviet history was rewritten in the context of Soviet propaganda against the West, and it went through several transformations and revisions. In the early postwar years, the aim was to glorify Stalin and credit him with defeating Germany. In addition, there was an attempt to undermine Russia's allies during the war by claiming that their contribution was insignificant.[3]

Throughout the years, the Soviet position was colored by the ideological line of the time. However, historical writing that actually dealt with the war began only in the days of Khrushchev (1953–1964). The historical approach during the eras of Khrushchev and Brezhnev (1964–1982) differed, of course, from that in the days of Stalin. The narrative was revised after Stalin died because the political situation within and the military-strategic situation without demanded changes—this time with the objective of learning from the past, especially concerning assumptions related to surprise attacks in a possible future war.[4] Under Khrushchev, the official approach was characterized by attempts to create a narrative whose central motif was the assumption that the USSR's natural strength, along with the Communist Party's strong leadership, promised certain victory against the Nazi invaders from the outset.[5] Soviet history in the days when Khrushchev was secretary general of the Communist Party was marked by three fallacies. The main one was directed at freeing the Soviet leadership from any responsibility for the initial failures of the war and to explain the Red Army's withdrawal as part of a pre-planned strategy. The second sought to give the Communist Party all the credit for winning the war and to diminish the part of the Red Army High Command and the soldiers and people, who carried the heaviest burden. The third fallacy was underestimation of British and American fighting abilities in the war and an attempt to portray the Japanese surrender as a direct outcome of the Soviet invasion of Manchuria, which allegedly was far more significant than the consequences brought about by the atomic bombs dropped on Hiroshima and Nagasaki.[6] Emphasis during the Khrushchev regime was on the leadership of Stalin and the Communist Party. As the party's secretary general, Khrushchev conducted a struggle against the senior officers of the armed forces, especially Marshal Georgi Zhukov, former chief of the Red Army's High Command and a hero of the Soviet Union. After Khrushchev's resignation, Soviet history underwent another revision.

When Brezhnev became secretary general of the Communist Party, dozens of titles about the war were published, the most important of them being Zhukov's memoirs issued during the marshal's later years. They too appeared only after strict censorship and in an incomplete version.[7] Emphasis during Brezhnev's time was on the Red Army's strength as well as on the Soviet state. It was only in the 1980s, at the peak of Mikhail Gorbachev's glasnost, that the Russians began revising their official history, a process that continued into the 1990s with the fall of the Soviet bloc and that limited access to part of the Russian archives. The myth that had been created in regard to Stalingrad, which symbolized Soviet strength and endurance, was suddenly undermined.[8] Stalingrad remained a Soviet victory, but the price the Russians had to pay turned out to be almost too much: although the 6th Army had been brought to its knees, the superhuman efforts made to drive the German invaders from Soviet soil had involved enormous losses and major military failures.

1

Operation Barbarossa
From Minsk to Moscow

To obtain a swift victory over the Soviet Union, the German High Command initially planned to annihilate the majority of Soviet forces in a series of encirclements close to the new Polish–Soviet border.[1] The scheme presented to Hitler regarding the upcoming campaign in Russia by the German High Command on December 5, 1940, exactly one year before a Russian counteroffensive forced the Germans to move to defense formations, was to concentrate the main forces in the central sector of the Eastern Front. Army Group Center under General Fedor von Bock's command got two Panzer groups; the army groups in the northern and southern flanks got one Panzer group each.

Their initial objective was to encircle Soviet forces gathered around Minsk. After a short pause for reinforcements, the intention was to continue deep into Russian territory toward Moscow and strike a final blow to the enemy formations. Northern Army Group under General Ritter von Leeb was supposed to cleanse the Baltic states of enemy forces and capture Leningrad, while Army Group South under General Gerd von Rundstedt was to conquer the Ukraine, with Kiev as its main objective. Hitler made a few changes in the plan, although they were not conceived until August 1941 in the midst of the campaign. Instead of capturing Moscow, his first priority was to encircle the Russian forces before they could retreat deep into the vast territories of the Soviet state. To gain that advantage, Army Group Center had to turn one of its two Panzer groups toward the northern sector after it had finished encircling the enemy in its own area, help with the annihilation of enemy forces in the Baltic region, and finally capture

Leningrad. The other Panzer group was to turn south and take part in encircling the enemy in the Ukraine.[2] This plan was presented as Directive 21, code-named Barbarossa, issued on December 18, 1940, with the final objective being to build a barrier against Russia in general on the Volga–Archangelsk line.[3]

At the time, there appeared to be no objection to this document from the German High Command, except for General Franz Halder, chief of the Army General Staff, who in his diary referred to its purpose as unclear, "since 'Barbarossa' does not solve the British threat."[4] However, in general, no one argued that it was impossible to destroy Soviet Russia in a swift blitz campaign. On July 22, 1940, the commander in chief of the army, General Field Marshal Walther von Brauchitsch, told Hitler that the German forces would need only four to six weeks of combat to bring the Soviets to their knees, and that eighty to a hundred divisions would be needed against fifty to seventy-five divisions of quality Russian troops. Halder claimed in July 1940 that from his point of view, a victory over the Soviet Union was simply a matter of executing the correct operational approach.[5]

Thus, although the German generals were not convinced at the time of the necessity of a campaign against Russia and thought that Germany should deal first with the British threat on the Western Front before turning toward the East, both Halder and von Brauchitsch[6] believed that an operation such as Barbarossa was feasible if it could be carried out swiftly.[7]

Hitler was especially intent on annihilating the forces of the Red Army. However, he claimed Moscow had no particular significance. The forces deployed in western Russia were to be destroyed in a series of swift operations that would involve penetrating deep into enemy lines and preventing elements capable of fighting from withdrawing to the vast Russian interior. A rapid pursuit would take place, beyond which the Soviet air force would be unable to attack the German territories of the Reich.[8] The German planners hoped that the lack of roads or rail network would be to their advantage: it meant that a Soviet retreat eastward was impossible without falling prey to German encirclement. It later became apparent that German intelligence misinterpreted the amount of forces concentrated on the front line and had no idea of the reserves that were available east of the Dnieper

River. After the initial battles around the border, the planned advance of the German forces led to deployment along the entire Russian front. From the outset, such archaic planning of a linear attack resembling Napoleonic strategy posed the risk of decentralizing efforts in an attempt to achieve all objectives at the same time.[9]

Although preparations for Barbarossa had been made and the generals studied the terrain countless times, there was no concrete objective and no precise definition of an operational approach. Rather, Operation Barbarossa exemplified competing objectives and operational approaches while everyone was convinced that the campaign would move forward in the direction he intended.[10] If one examines the counteroperational opinions — Moscow versus Leningrad and the Ukraine — it is apparent that neither Halder nor Hitler expected to bring the Soviet campaign to a showdown by conquering either of those objectives. In any event, as evidence shows, the decision was cardinal only in mid-July 1941. The only operational aim was the subjugation of the Red Army; the assumption was that the initial blows would pave the way to move forward with the other missions.[11]

When the attack began, the main effort was focused on the Minsk–Smolensk line on the way to Moscow. Both Panzer armies, under the command of generals Hermann Hoth and Heinz Guderian, operated on that front. They attacked on separate routes. On the sixth day of fighting, they met near Minsk, some 200 kilometers from the Russian–German border (created in 1939) while leaving large numbers of encircled Soviet forces behind them in western Belorussia. In the Soviet war scenarios and plans for deployment prepared between February and June 1941, there was no coordination among the Russian forces, and the surprise attack by the Germans did not allow for organized resistance. Each division fought by itself, and operational maneuvers were carried out by local commanders, not always in accordance with orders from the Soviet High Command.[12]

Until mid-July, Guderian and Hoth managed to cover some 450 to 600 kilometers from the border to Smolensk. On the northern front, German forces penetrated as deep as 450 kilometers, conquering Lithuania, Latvia, and part of Estonia, as well as territories in northern Russia, until they reached the outskirts of Leningrad.

In the southern sector, the Germans advanced into the Ukraine, and by mid-July, they had managed to conquer the western part.[13] On July 15, the German armies had to pause for reinforcement and re-deployment. It was then necessary to make decisions regarding the next objectives, in particular for the two Panzer armies in von Bock's Army Group Center. Because they had reached Smolensk and completed the first stage of their advance successfully, the German High Command, including von Bock, Hoth, and Guderian, sought to return to the original plan and annihilate the enemy at the point where they expected it to concentrate before the capital. In contrast to the generals, Hitler preferred to clear the Baltic states of enemy concentrations and conquer Leningrad in the north, as well as renew the advance toward Kiev and the Dnieper in the southeast. This was intended to disengage the Russians from their industrial and agriculture resources in the Ukraine and open the way to the Caucasus.

The dispute within the German High Command between Hitler and his generals lasted for more than a month. The delay in renewing the attack and reaching a decision originated from the savage ongoing battles around Smolensk and Yel'naya as well as along the flanks of the Army Group Center.[14] Among other reasons was perhaps Hitler's poor physical condition during his stay at the Wolf's Lair, his temporary headquarters during Operation Barbarossa, which neutralized him for about three weeks. According to Theo Morell, his personal physician, Hitler had dysentery, which probably had some influence on the timing of the crucial decision.[15] Eventually both parties reached a compromise: it was decided that the push toward Moscow would be renewed but only after a breakthrough in the Ukraine.[16] A halt and a shift to the north and the south were in any event required by the supply situation, which was becoming an obstacle. Apparently the earliest time for a resumption of the offensive on Moscow was October, but it seemed that the attack in the Ukraine was being held up as another factor because of the risk of a Soviet thrust into the southern flank of any bulge toward Moscow.

Although the initial assault was disastrous for the Russians, it still did not break their spirits. At this point, the Germans made a decisive blunder. While Hitler was arguing with his generals over the next objectives, the Soviet High Command was given a blessed delay, which enabled them to renew lines, and redeploy and advance new divisions, even though these divisions were not adequately trained and equipped. After being sent by Stalin to bring the forces concentrated on the western border back to the Moscow area, Marshal Semyon Timoshenko created a defense line that would prevent encirclement of the 16th Army and deep penetration by the German forces eastward. General Konstantin Rokossovsky, who was stationed in the western headquarters of the front as commander of the 16th Army, gathered some dismantled units under him in an attempt to prevent the 3rd Panzer Army from crossing the Dnieper with a few unsuccessful counteroffensives.[17] During this entire period, the Germans did not renew their offensives east of Smolensk, thus encouraging the Russians and giving them enough time to deploy their forces around Moscow.

The momentum of the blitz slipped slowly away—not just because of the German High Command's hesitance but instead as a result of Russian resistance. The remission that began on July 16 finally ended on August 23, when Guderian's Panzer group changed direction southward and joined German forces there on their way to another victory, this time in the Ukraine.[18] Hoth's Panzer group was assigned to capture Leningrad.

Through a major encirclement by Guderian's Panzer group, and with the help of German forces coming from the West, large parts of the Ukraine were conquered, including Kiev, the capital, on September 19, with more than 500,000 Soviet soldiers falling into German captivity. In the northern sector, matters were a bit more difficult with the failure of the German attempt to conquer Leningrad. However, they managed to besiege the city from all sides with the help of the Finns, and on September 13, they decided to starve its residents into surrender.[19]

At this point, Hitler was already interested in an offensive on Moscow and was convinced that in a matter of weeks the Wehrmacht would reach the Kremlin. On October 2, Operation Typhoon (for the conquest of Moscow) was set in motion. The second and crucial stage of the war in the Soviet Union was about to begin.

The Russian Winter and Perception of the Battlefield

In the first few years after the war, there was mystery regarding the Russian winter that originated in the extreme weather and fighting conditions. The winter element is so well rooted in historical awareness since the age of Napoleon that it deserves special reference. The Russian winter was harsh—perhaps too harsh for the infantry and armored corps that were forced to cope with it. However, over the years, this alone became increasingly irrelevant as an explanation for the German failure because the Red Army had to deal with the same hardships and weather conditions.

In this respect, it is important to remember that winters are always difficult in Russia—an unsurprising fact that was certainly in the back of the minds of the planners of Operation Barbarossa.[20] In war, when the weather is extremely bad, it sometimes has an impact, usually by assisting the forces on the defending side. Therefore, whereas in November 1941 the Russians were in a defense layout, in December it was the Germans who were on the defensive. They failed to conquer Moscow because they had reached the limits of their offensive ability.[21] Historians who hold a conservative approach to events argue that the Soviet soldiers were equipped with combat gear for winter weather conditions while the Germans found themselves freezing, without any means of surviving in such extreme temperatures and certainly unprepared to go on fighting. Guderian's memoirs and those of other officers who participated in the Russian campaign describe German tank engines that had to be started by lighting small fires underneath them, machine guns and cannons that failed to function because of the cold, and frostbite that took its toll on the general performance of the German soldiers by early November.[22]

The Germans were certainly not surprised by the weather conditions that awaited them in Russia, and in contrast to Napoleon's army, which experienced similar weather conditions, they were even able to forecast the depth of snow in certain areas with the help of synoptic maps covering the entire eastern territory.[23] Further, the defeat at Stalingrad occurred during the second winter of the Wehrmacht's operations in the Soviet Union. There was thus no element of surprise stemming from the weather conditions in winter 1941.

As some historians have pointed out, in the first Russian counter-offensive that began on December 5, 1941, and that continued throughout the war, the Russian advantage was a result of better winter equipment and gear, which included snowsuits, goggles, skis, and sleds, as well as hardy steppe ponies that could survive extremely low temperatures and carry supplies and ammunition, heated hangars for the air force, and all-weather vehicles.[24] In modern terms, compared to the Wehrmacht, the Red Army would be considered a high-tech military force, armed and equipped with all the most up-to-date technology for combat.

On the basis of these descriptions, as well as the supply shortages the German army faced, the Red Army's troops were more prepared for combat in winter conditions. Although the Russian army had special ski units, thus ostensibly making it a military force fully prepared for winter combat, the soldiers were unable to exploit this advantage—at least not in the first winter. In many cases, recruits drafted to these units came from areas in southern Russia where there was no snow during winter months; skiing techniques were thus foreign to them. Preparations for the battle were superficial, a result of lack of time and in certain cases of the battle program. Soldiers and officers skied unprofessionally, especially on hills and slopes, for their missions were not only on flat terrain. Little attention was given to properly fitting the skis, and many troops found themselves struggling to catch up with their unit. Tactical preparation and shooting were poor and movement was not homogenous, often resulting in exposure to the enemy. The officers' orientation in the field was problematic too, and in most cases, they were unable to lead the units at night. This type of winter warfare was still embryonic. Considering that these units had been established spontaneously, the advantage they gave to the campaign was negligible, at least during the winter of 1941–1942, when they were first used.[25]

The entire Eastern Front was simply frozen during the combat months of Operation Typhoon, until spring 1942: tanks did not start, engine oil turned to dough, fuel froze, and the soldiers suffered from unbearable frostbite. Guderian points to the lack of fuel for trucks and the difficulties faced by supply vehicles in reaching the first line of combat as a result of the muddy roads.[26] However, the same was true for Soviet equipment. Despite the Russians' sophisticated equipment, fighting at a temperature of -25°C in the snow was not easy for them either. Likewise, Russia's rough terrain was experienced by both sides. Memoirs of German generals and the reports they gave after the war lend a perception of the terrain's great expanse and its difficulty. General Günther Blumentritt (Gerd von Rundstedt's deputy as commander of Army Group South) described during his interview with military historian Basil Liddell Hart a land full of great forests, swamps, bad roads, and even worse bridges, all of which hampered the progress of the German Panzers. However, the terrain also affected the motorized vehicles that escorted them. They could not leave the roads when the rain turned the earth into mud. Horses remained the only means of transport able to cope with the terrain, at least temporarily, until they collapsed and were replaced by others, brought from the Reich aboard train wagons. Historian Klaus Schüler indicates that although German locomotives could operate in harsh weather conditions of up to -20°C, in December, the temperature could fall to even -35°C in Russia, rendering logistics almost impossible.[27] On April 29, 1942, Hitler told Mussolini after the fact that they were lucky the winter had started early that year because otherwise the German army would have penetrated 200 to 300 kilometers deeper into Soviet territory. Such a position would have been catastrophic because German trains could not reach that far on the existing rail network.[28] However, the transport problems had begun even before the onset of the winter crisis, in the initial phases of Operation Typhoon.

If paved roads were already in existence, then according to Blumentritt, time and again Wehrmacht headquarters were surprised to learn that what German intelligence had marked as roads often turned out to be muddy paths with no access whatsoever to the battlefield.[29] Guderian emphasized, however, that during the first weeks of the campaign there was still room to maneuver, and even Zhukov paints a similar picture in his memoirs regarding the perception of space. Zhukov describes how until February, while checking, together with the defense commissar, the means of establishing a line of fortifications along the border, they found the road network in appalling condition. The bridges were unfit for tanks and heavy artillery to cross, and the dirt road system was in need of fundamental renovation. Even the railways were in a bad way and were unfit for conveying Russian soldiers.[30] These descriptions demonstrate that both sides suffered from the same limitations under the same conditions. It was true that there were many difficulties, but they did not determine the fate of the war, and they were certainly not inclined to favor the Soviet side. Yet one should not overlook the impressive defense ability of the Russian divisions concentrated along the Smolensk–Moscow line, which revealed, especially to the commander of Army Group Center, that a breakthrough toward the Russian capital was not an easy task.[31]

General Philip Golikov, who headed the Russian intelligence service and was appointed commander of the 10th Army on October 21, 1941, claimed that the divisions under his command were formed mainly from men with no military experience, who were sent to the front after basic training lasting only six weeks. Until mid-November, in terms of clothing and food supplies, not to mention armor, ammunition, and technical gear, the entire Red Army, like the German army, was unprepared for winter warfare. According to Golikov, all these essentials were subject to rationing. Furthermore, the transportation system was under huge pressure, and the reserve armies were all utilized simultaneously. The situation was also exacerbated by the fact that all the General Staff and the commissariats, including the defense commissariat, had been evacuated from Moscow to Kubishev and other cities, making supply extremely difficult. Many provisions were distributed to troops on their way to the front and sometimes even during battle.[32]

Thus the winter was extremely hard for the Wehrmacht.[33] However, it is in the nature of difficulties, in contrast to problems, to be surmounted and creative ways found to deal with them. They could not be eliminated completely. The Russian winter was a fact, and the German army learned to survive it until winter 1944–1945. In contrast to difficulties, problems are solvable, and indeed one of the major problems that occupied the German elite, in parallel to fighting the Bolshevik enemy, was finding a solution to the "Jewish problem." Finding a solution to this problem was a factor that in itself created logistical burdens on the Eastern Front, just as winter did. Dealing with this second factor — which could be controlled to a greater extent than the first factor, winter — became no less significant a parameter in the fighting arena than strategy itself. During the events of 1941, the end of the war was still distant. One may therefore safely conclude that neither the harsh winter nor Soviet technical abilities and strength was the reason for German limitations but rather logistics, which were the essence of fighting the war in the Soviet Union. Was the cause of these problematic logistics an ill-prepared army, or conducting a major ideological operation parallel to military events, with an apparently increasing effect on them?

The German Rail System

Food, fuel, ammunition, spare parts, and other combat needs had to be supplied to over three million German soldiers equipped with some 600,000 motor vehicles and 650,000 horses. All this had to be transferred along a front that stretched over more than 2,500 kilometers, from the northern cape of Russia to the Black Sea. Within a few weeks, the operational size of this front reached 1,500 kilometers into the heart of the conquered territory from the initial point of the assault.[34] Each one of the 166 divisions involved in Barbarossa depended on at least sixty trains. However, it was generally assumed before the operation that there would never be a need for so many supply trains in order to overcome the Red Army.[35] In addition, about 40 percent of the infantry divisions recruited for the invasion were unprepared because of a lack of supplies and equipment.[36]

The blitz campaign in the Soviet Union forced the Germans to rely more than ever on motor vehicles, creating a further burden of maintenance expenses, wear and tear, and fuel supply. To cope initially with the problem of the width of the Russian tracks, 1,600 trucks were required as a supplement for the front, but there still were not enough vehicles for all the forces. Seventy-seven divisions out of 166 were equipped with freight horses only, tied to 200 wagons.[37] In 1941 the German army still depended on infantry divisions to do the hard work. This meant that troops walked, or at best were driven on vehicles dragged by horses. The motorized divisions were still a small part of the entire system.[38]

The plan was to use trucks for the first 500 kilometers in the first stage of the attack and in the second to use trains. The trucks could transfer 10,000 tons of supplies per day to the front, meaning about seventy tons per division. However, because the assumption was that the motorized divisions needed about 300 tons per day each, the quartermaster general, Lieutenant General Eduard Wagner, who was responsible for all motor transport in the communications zone behind the lines, made sure that for each army group there would be reserve supplies with trucking capacity of at least 20,000 tons.[39] The basic problem was that only one million out of three million troops were equipped for combat, and they were still 500 men short in each division.[40]

Operationally, in order to continue the war in the Soviet Union after the invasion in June 1941, it was necessary that all transport vehicles at the Russian front, without exception, transfer supplies required for combat only. Accordingly, strict orders were given to all Wehrmacht forces in the occupied Soviet territories to keep the vehicles in working condition and to prevent unnecessary use because of an increasing lack of spare parts.[41] Trains, therefore, were a crucial part of operations Barbarossa and Typhoon. First the Germans had to deal with many problems having to do with connecting the railways under their jurisdiction with those conquered outside the Reich's borders. The problem in the Soviet Union was that the railway infrastructure was different, with the Russian rail gauge three and a half inches wider than the European gauge. Nevertheless, the Germans proved skillful in carrying out the necessary repairs and changes. On October 3, 1941, Hitler declared that out of 25,000 kilometers of conquered railway, 15,000 kilometers had been changed by widening the gauge to fit them to German trains.[42]

The military unit responsible for the rail network in the Soviet Union operated as part of Army Group Center and was in charge of more than 2,000 kilometers of railways, which included 261 locomotives and 1,599 cars. It also oversaw 11,000 Germans operating in teams and more than 22,000 Russian workers and officials.[43] They worked on repairs and on fitting the tracks to the German trains. On a good day, they managed to convert twenty kilometers of Soviet tracks to the width of the German ones.[44] Because the Soviet rail system had only limited capacity, it was determined that the trains would carry supplies only.

The shortage in trains was felt as early as July 20, when twenty-five troop trains were driven from Riga to Rujene for deployment before the resumption of fighting in the direction of Leningrad. At the same time, Army Group North asked for another division to be deployed in the sector north of Riga, but this turned out to be impossible because of a lack of train cars and locomotives.[45] Only in October 1941 could fresh divisions from France be transferred, which meant a total of six trains per day. At that pace, it was possible to transfer one division every three days, excluding supplies—in other words, troops only.[46] According to the original plan for the Soviet invasion, which was based on a swift showdown in a blitz strike, the army received food supplies for only twenty days of combat. Any food supplies that extended beyond this time frame were already dependent on looting and exploiting the Soviet Union's local resources.[47] Attempts to overcome the food shortage by shipments from the Reich were rebuffed, and transport was limited to the transfer of ammunition and fuel to the front. Under no circumstances was food to be moved there—an extraordinary fact considering that ninety days later, entire ethnic communities would be transferred to the Soviet Union.[48]

2

Operation Typhoon
The Battle for Moscow

The objective of the second German operation in the Soviet Union, Operation Typhoon, which began where Barbarossa ended, was to conquer the Soviet capital. It began on October 2 and lasted until late December, when a Soviet counterattack struck a blow to the morale of the top German command. As noted, it is customary to attribute the German failure outside of Moscow to the weather, in particular to the winter of 1941, which began relatively early, by October 6. (The first snowflakes fell only four days after Operation Typhoon launched.) Even at this point, Hitler's plan, after the flanks had been captured and the troops were advancing toward the gates of Moscow, still had a reasonable probability of success, although a sense of defeatism could be sensed among the higher-ranking officers. Already at the beginning of July, skeptics had begun to reassess the entire situation. General Halder understood that they had underestimated the Soviet colossus; where he had expected 200 Russian divisions, the German Field Army (OKH) headquarters had counted some 360. In terms of both equipment and professional preparation, they were not always equal to the Wehrmacht, but the Soviets were able to form a dozen new divisions for every dozen the Germans liquidated. Thus, the objective of annihilating the Red Army eventually seemed unrealistic.[1] A German Armed Forces (OKW) memorandum from August 27, 1941, the same day on which the offensive was resumed, reflected skepticism regarding the chances of subduing the Soviet Union that year; the memo also recognized that the campaign in the East would continue into 1942.[2] In October, Heinz Guderian noted in his diary that Soviet resistance had taken a heavy toll on the German side, morally rather than physically.[3]

There is no doubt the Russians demonstrated fanatic and stubborn steadfastness until they launched their counteroffensive on December 5. However, it is hard to say that the battle against the Germans was close to a showdown. On October 5, Stalin ordered Zhukov to return to Moscow and reorganize the front line. Zhukov had already gone there to check the defense around the city and had found the Soviet army in chaos. In addition to the massive retreat eastward behind the encircling German lines, entire armies had lost contact with one another, and as a result of a lack of intelligence, no one knew for sure where the Germans were situated. Zhukov had in formation only 90,000 men separating Moscow from the Germans, out of 800,000 Red Army soldiers who had fought against the renewed German offensive from the beginning of October. There were almost no forces defending the main road leading to Moscow.[4]

The battle at Bryansk, located 379 kilometers southwest of Moscow, reflects in particular the danger the Russians themselves recognized if Moscow were to fall. A successful ending for the Germans depended not just on encircling the Soviets but also on a fast advance eastward while cutting off the Russians from their escape routes and simultaneously preparing for the occupation of the city of Tula, 193 kilometers south of Moscow. Tula, which was important for the production of armaments, became the target of a German offensive to break Soviet resistance in the Moscow area.[5]

The winter was almost unbearable for the German soldiers, who were ill-prepared for winter warfare and found it extremely difficult to move to the front. However, the mud of the *Rasputitza* season in Russia also slowed down Zhukov's redeployment, and it hindered the swift movement of manpower and Soviet tanks.[6] It seemed, therefore, that during October luck was actually on the German side. The Wehrmacht units continued to advance toward Moscow, capturing Kaluga (188 kilometers southwest of Moscow) on October 12 and the city of Kalinin on October 14.[7] With the Germany army located at the northern and southern flanks of the Russian capital, it looked as though they were about to encircle Moscow. Zhukov's forces were outflanked. He was forced to make a major retreat, all the while urging Stalin to send more forces to face the Germans in order to slow them down and disrupt their plans. A Mongolian cavalry division, which began an offensive in the open snowy steppes, was simply mowed down by machine guns. Two thousand soldiers on horseback were killed while the Germans had no casualties at all.[8] Thus, although the Germans were coming to a halt toward the end of October, the Russians still had no immediate answer because they too had to wait some time until the mud froze again, thus hardening the roads so they could move vehicles over them. At the beginning of November, the ground was finally hard enough, and the Wehrmacht could resume the offensive.

Two Panzer groups attacked to the north of Moscow toward the town of Klin, which fell on October 24, and on October 28, German forces crossed the Volga. The leading forces were now just 18 kilometers from the center of the Russian capital. At this point, Zhukov had very little manpower to stop the attack. His front line numbered only 240,000 men, who had been gathered from fragments of defeated units, some of them not even fit for battle, combined with clerks who were not trained for battle at all.[9] The other divisions set up by the Russians served as immediate replacements for the ones already destroyed, but they were neither well equipped nor well trained.

At the end of November, it was evident that the German offensive was weakening. The last assault required a struggle for which the exhausted troops were in no shape. The lack of tanks and ammunition all began to take their toll, and casualties began to rise. Still, for every German soldier killed, the Russians lost twenty men.[10] Moreover, out of a total of 3.8 million Wehrmacht soldiers, 3.2 million invaded the Soviet Union on June 22, 1941, facing an army of 4.5 million Red Army soldiers. In fact, in the first stage of Operation Barbarossa, only 2.5 million were there to withstand the invading army, leaving the advantage in numbers on the German side.[11] The Germans were eventually contained by the Red Army; however, this happened at the last minute —and in fact at the last trench before Moscow.[12]

Deportation of Jews

During the period of debate between Hitler and his generals regarding forthcoming moves and further operational strategy, a clear order was given on July 17, 1941, that was understood as coming from the Führer himself alone: for the execution of Jews living within the borders of the Soviet Union. Parallel to this directive, other avenues for solving the "Jewish problem" were explored by Hitler's subordinates in the territories of the extended Reich, and primarily in Germany.

This is the context in which the memorandum issued by Hermann Göring on July 31, 1941, to Reinhard Heydrich, chief of the Reich Main Security Office (RSHA), should be understood. According to this document, which was based on a previous memorandum from January 24, 1939, dealing with Jewish emigration from Germany or their deportation as part of the Four Year Plan for which Göring was responsible, Heydrich was to prepare and organize technical and matériel issues before taking action toward finally solving the Jewish question in all the territories under German rule.[13] In keeping with these orders, the SS began to organize transports of Jewish populations deported from the greater German Reich to the newly occupied territories in the Soviet Union.

After deportations to the General Government (the official name for Nazi-occupied Poland)[14] ceased on March 15, 1941, in the framework of so-called Program No. 3 for a short-term solution, and in light of the planned operation in the Soviet Union, an alternative program was organized similar to the Madagascar Plan—that is, the deportation of over four million Jews from Europe aboard vessels to the island of Madagascar—for the mass deportation of European Jewry to Soviet territory. The figures involved in this program were the basis for those examined during the Wannsee conference in January 1942. The program was supposed to be implemented only after the war of annihilation against the Soviet Union and not during it, in order to prevent clashes with the Wehrmacht's needs of the hour. The intention was to wait patiently until autumn 1941 for a clear victory.[15]

Five days after the deportations of Polish Jews to the General Government ceased, Adolf Eichmann declared on March 20, 1941, before representatives of the Propaganda Ministry, that Heydrich had been appointed by the Führer to execute the final evacuation of Jews from the territories under German influence.[16] In a meeting at Hitler's headquarters on September 23, Heydrich told Goebbels that as soon as it became possible, and in accordance with the situation, the Jews would be moved to camps that the Communists would build along the

White Sea and Baltic Channel.[17] The plan included deportations of all European Jewry—eleven million people—excluding the Jews of the Soviet Union.

An intriguing fact regarding this figure is that the number of Jews about to be deported from the Reich and protectorate territories, as well as from the General Government, stood at 3,120,000.[18] This number, taken from the protocols of the Wannsee conference and that presumably was updated there, point to planning that corresponded to strategic opportunities that the Germans had pinpointed, as well as the anticipation in June–July 1941 of a swift victory. Accordingly, it might be assumed that Reichsführer-SS Heinrich Himmler and Reinhard Heydrich, his subordinate, planned to transfer Jews to the East aboard trains that would be driven there empty in order to transport to the Reich millions of tons of wheat from the Soviet territories, as well as three million Wehrmacht soldiers from Operation Barbarossa, whose next task would be to prepare for the upcoming campaign against Britain.[19]

Hans Frank, the governor general of occupied Poland, in his interrogation after the war, claimed, as expected, that he had no control over the trains but that to his knowledge, train traffic to the East was bilateral: that is, the trains that transferred Jews to the East were the same ones used to return soldiers to Germany and send back fresh troops to fight the Soviets.[20] Thus, Frank strengthens the argument that the trains and railways used by the SS for transporting Jews to the East also served the Wehrmacht for transporting troops and war supplies.

Eichmann claimed that the idea regarding the transports to the East was first brought up by Dr. Carltheo Zeitschel, who was responsible for German diplomatic staff in Paris. According to Eichmann, in late August 1941, Zeitschel suggested that the German ambassador in Paris, Otto Abetz, discuss the Jewish issue with Himmler and Alfred Rosenberg, Reich minister for the occupied eastern territories from July 17, 1941. Zeitschel said that if the conquest in the East continued, it would be possible to quickly solve Europe's Jewish problem. It was advisable to close off a certain area in the newly occupied territories and to arrange, by military order, mass transports there of all Jewry from Holland, Belgium, Norway, Yugoslavia, and Greece. Zeitschel emphasized that there were not enough camps to lodge Jews in France; he recommended sorting out this issue with Göring, who already had experience in the East and could assist in carrying out the program.

Zeitschel's idea received an enthusiastic response, and Himmler told him that as soon as appropriate approval for the transports was received, it would be possible to deport all French Jews to the East as well.[21] Because officials in Paris were eager to rush things, Eichmann's office began work on authorizing these transports. In addition, the Gestapo head, Heinrich Müller, began negotiating with the transport ministry regarding this issue. Eichmann argued that on the basis of these negotiations, it was also possible to send transports to the East in October 1941, as actually happened.[22] Apparently Zeitschel's idea was quickly embraced among the higher echelons, and Nicolaus von Below, Hitler's Luftwaffe adjutant, confirmed that in August 1941, Goebbels had arrived at the Führer's office to discuss the Jewish issue and to press him and Heydrich to reach a firm decision. Goebbels in particular wanted Hitler's approval for giving priority to the deportation of the 70,000 Jews still living in Berlin, even before the French Jews. Because at this stage Hitler had still not given permission for their deportation, all that Goebbels's stay at the Wolf's Lair (Hitler's headquarters at Rastenburg in eastern Prussia) achieved was an order from the security police for the Berlin Jewish community to wear a yellow Star of David on their clothing.[23]

On September 18, Himmler sent a memorandum to Arthur Greiser, an SS officer and the governor of the Warthegau district in Poland, explaining that the Führer's wish was that the Altreich (Germany and the protectorate territories) be cleansed of Jews and that this should be done by transferring them eastward as soon as possible. Later, Himmler asked Greiser to be patient and show understanding because they intended to move some 60,000 Jews that year to the Lodz ghetto for the winter, and to transfer them further east in the spring.

Between September 22 and 24, 1941, Himmler and Heydrich were at the Wolf's Lair; Goebbels joined them on September 23. Heydrich's position at the time was strengthening. In addition to his other roles, Hitler put him in charge of Reich issues in the protectorates of Bohemia and Moravia. About a month after their almost fruitless previous meeting, this time, there was a breakthrough, and for the first time, deportations of Jews to the East were discussed in a concrete way. It was noted that such an operation constituted an unprecedented transportation problem. Moreover, the German advance at the front was not going as anticipated. Nevertheless, it was decided to move forward with the program. On September 23, Heydrich told Goebbels, "It can be executed as soon as the situation at the front stabilizes and clears. Likewise, the Führer's opinion is that the Jews should be evacuated from Germany in total."[24]

Accordingly, on October 14 and 24, Kurt Daluege, chief of the SS Ordnungspolizei under Himmler, issued the appropriate orders for the deportations. Eichmann recalled in his memoirs that from October 1941 (without indicating a specific date, although it is apparent that he meant the October 24), the deportation programs to the General Government, which had been halted before the invasion, were renewed to the occupied territories in the Soviet Union. Eichmann was the chief expert responsible for the transports at the Reich Main Security Office. While preparing the program and referring to the transports, he was talking only about European Jews. Soviet Jewry were not part of the equation because there was no need to allocate trains for them, and therefore, they were not under his area of responsibility.

In October, Eichmann received an order to deport 50,000 Jews from the Reich, including Jews from the protectorates of Bohemia and Moravia, to the area around Riga and Minsk. In the first phase, between mid-October and mid-November, twenty-one Jewish train transports left for the East. Eichmann managed to transfer 20,000 Jews from Berlin, Vienna, Cologne, Hamburg, Frankfurt, Düsseldorf, Munich, Nuremberg, Prague, and Luxemburg, a process that took place parallel to Operation Typhoon, which had already been launched.[25] This huge undertaking continued until the end of November but was immediately delayed because of transportation difficulties created by the military situation. Only 30,000 Jews were transferred, mostly from the big cities that served also as gathering points.[26] The decision to deport the Reich's Jews to the occupied territories in the East and its timing was influenced, among other things, by appeals from mayors and heads of districts in the Reich interested in the thousands of apartments that the German Jews would evacuate, so that German civilians, whose homes were damaged by British bombers, could use them. The governor of Hamburg, Karl Kaufmann, appealed to Göring and through him to Hitler regarding this matter.[27]

As early as September 18, 1941, Julius Dorpmüller, Reich minister of transport and chief executive of the Reichsbahn, sent a letter related to deportation issues, with an attached form for completion, to all governors and heads of departments at the ministry. This meant that before the actual deportation took place, there would be accurate registration of every Jew or Jewish family that had evacuated a home in order to learn where it was located, whether it was still empty, and whether it had already been confiscated.[28] On September 30, immediately after the first Jewish deportation to Lodz, Alois Brunner, one of Eichmann's assistants who was then in charge of the center for Jewish immigration in Vienna, informed Dr. Joseph Löwenhertz, head of the Jewish community in the Austrian capital (who progressed from coordinating the deportations with Eichmann to full cooperation in the deportations themselves) that, "due to the need to change the Aryan population's residences, as a result of air attacks, some of the Jews from the old Reich, Vienna, and the protectorate areas are to be moved to Lodz."[29]

This order conformed to a policy—one retained until 1944—to try and prevent the German people from bearing the brunt of the war. A memorandum written by Heydrich from December 15 deals with the issue of Jews transferred to ghettoes in Litzmanstadt, Minsk, Riga, and Theresienstadt after being evacuated from their apartments in Prague and the city of Brünn for the benefit of ethnic Germans in Bohemia and Moravia.[30] Accordingly, the Reich finance ministry had to deal with Gestapo reports on vacant assets that become available to the town authorities for renting, so that the Reich could be freed from paying rent to landlords whose apartments had been vacated by Jews hastily deported to the East.[31]

On October 6, one day before the completion of the double encirclement of Vyazma and Bryansk, and despite Hitler's talk about deportations and his belief that the Jews should be evacuated from the protectorate not just to the General Government but further east, Hitler finally admitted that the main obstacle to implementation of this complex operation was lack of transport. Despite these difficulties and the need for the military situation to become clearer, a matter that Hitler and Heydrich had discussed, the preparations for the deportations began, presumably uncoordinated with the army. A Nazi functionary in Prague later commented that the first transport from that city, which had departed on October 16, needed lengthy advance preparations lasting until mid-September.[32]

On October 9, just before the fall of Kalinin and Kaluga, the Western Front, which defended the Soviet capital, was about 165 kilometers long, but only 105 kilometers were manned by the Russians, thus leaving the flanks exposed to enemy attacks. Losses on the Soviet side were so heavy that when Zhukov was recalled from Leningrad to the Western Front in order to defend Moscow, all he had at his disposal were fragments of units that together amounted to a mere 90,000 troops.[33] Yet that same month, between October 16 and 31, 16,000 Jews were sent aboard sixteen trains to the East. It would have been possible to instead transfer three fresh infantry divisions from France (excluding supplies and horses) to use against the defense forces covering the Russian capital in addition to the troops already manning the front line. Even at the beginning of December 1941, when the race between Stalin and Hitler concerned who could draft more manpower, the Western Front defending Moscow consisted of three armies (the 10th, 13th, and 3rd), amounting to a combined force of some 140,000 soldiers. This followed great efforts to rebuild all the divisions, some of which numbered fewer than 2,900 soldiers. In December, the number of Soviet soldiers defending the Russian capital was equal to the diluted combat power of General von Bock's Army Group Center.[34] The situation was so delicate that every train counted.

The Reich's Train Transport

Between October and mid-December 1941, the SS used a total of forty-eight trains for transporting German Jews to the Soviet territories, including five Gypsy trains.[35] Had these trains been used for military needs, by December 18, they could have transferred five or six infantry divisions, amounting to 36,000 fresh Wehrmacht troops, based on a calculation of 750 soldiers per train, which was the standard for military transportation. In addition, another twenty-seven trains were assigned to carry those who carried out the killing operations in the Soviet Union. They consisted of some 20,000 men working under direct orders from Himmler: 3,000 belonged to the Einsatzgruppen and another eleven battalions to the Order Police (5,500 to 6,000 men); an additional 11,000 were from two SS brigades, one destined to reinforce Erich von dem Bach Zelewski's central killing squads and the other to reinforce Friedrich Jeckeln's in the south.[36] Like any other unit in the Wehrmacht, these forces were equipped with supplies, including food, warm clothing, and ammunition, increasing the amount of trains needed. However, if these factors are overlooked and we concentrate only on the numbers used to transport these special units to the Soviet territories, we are still looking at a manpower total that could have been replaced by two to three infantry divisions. When we add together the number of cars bearing Jews to the number of cars carrying guards and executioners, it would have been possible to send ten German divisions to the front, or a total of about 56,000 troops—a chilling figure, and one close to the number of Jews planned for deportation to the East (50,000) by the end of 1941.[37]

During a meeting Heydrich organized in Prague on October 10 in the presence of Eichmann, the cities of Riga and Minsk were discussed as possible destinations for deportations, in addition to Lodz. Heydrich summarized the issue as follows: "Since the Führer would like to see the Jews leave the German sphere by the end of the year, the questions that are still open should be resolved immediately. Nor should the transportation question cause difficulty in this matter."[38]

Hans Frank also confirmed that Wilhelm Keitel, Wehrmacht chief of staff, had passed him Hitler's message concerning his interest in transferring the Jews to the East at any cost.[39] In a conversation Hitler had with Himmler and Heydrich on October 25, 1941 (one day after Kurt Daluege issued the deportation decrees for the Reich's Jews to Kovno and Riga), Frank said:

> This same race of criminals holds on its conscience the death of two million that died in the First World War and now is already responsible for the death of hundred of thousands more. Let no one stand up and tell me that in the same manner we cannot resettle them in the swampy areas of Russia! Who takes care of our soldiers?

It is not a bad idea, by the way, that rumors attribute to us programs to exterminate Jews; terror is a useful measure.[40]

A memorandum dated September 9, 1941, directed to Army Group Center and signed by General Halder, indicates that the preparations needed for the new operation, Operation Typhoon, were for 200 tanks that would be supplied by the Krupp factory at Magdeburg: ninety-five Panzers type III, fifty Panzers type IV, and fifty-six Panzers type T-38. Those same tanks were to be transferred aboard trains to the city of Orscha on the Minsk–Smolensk route. From there they were to be deployed for the forthcoming operation.[41] In total, only thirteen trains, which could travel 600 kilometers in twenty-four hours, were allocated to transfer these tanks. Yet in October alone, the SS used sixteen trains for Jewish transports departing the Reich. Some 50,000 Jews from the Reich and the protectorates were planned to be transferred by fifty trains, although only forty-three trains actually left.[42] In comparison, an infantry division with all its equipment, including supplies, fuel, ammunition, and horses, used thirty-three trains, a cavalry division twenty-nine trains, and a fully armed Panzer division about fifty trains.[43]

On November 3, 1941, Göring wrote a letter to the transport minister, Julius Dorpmüller, proposing that the rail network be reorganized to deal with special requirements and broadened to conform to the Four Year Plan, which he was in charge of.[44] On that day, the last transport of Prague Jews in the first wave of deportations departed the Reich and the protectorates for the Lodz ghetto; this was also five days before the beginning of the second wave, whose destinations were Minsk, Kovno, and Riga.[45]

The Wehrmacht commanders were apparently aware of these activities and protested more than once. On November 8, 1941, Rudolf Lange, chief of Einsatzkommando A in the Baltic States and the person responsible for the murder of Jews in Latvia in particular, sent a letter to Hinrich Lohse, the Reich commissar for the Baltic States and Belorussia, noting that 50,000 German Jews were on their way from Germany, half to Minsk and the other half to Riga. A transit camp was built in Salasphils next to Riga in order to receive them. When the trains reached Minsk, there were more protests from Army Group

Center because of the waste of trains for transporting civilians instead of troops. The frustration among the army commanders was great, especially after they demanded that all trains be used solely for the transportation of military supply needs for combat.

On November 12, 1941, von Bock, commander of Army Group Center responsible for the offensive on Moscow, indicated that he had received an oral message stating that it was possible to supply his army group with a minimal amount of trains for the upcoming attack on Kalinin, which was only seventy kilometers north of the Russian capital. In addition, he received another report saying that several trains were carrying Jews from Germany to the rear areas of his army group. Von Bock informed General Halder that he would do everything in his power to oppose this because "the arrival of these trains must result in the loss of an equal number of trains vital for supplying the attack." The attack on Kalinin was planned for November 15 and the attack on Moscow on November 18.[46] In order to ensure that the assault forces had sufficient supplies for encircling Moscow, there was a need to defend the Ryazan–Vladimir–Kalyazin line and strive for a screening front on the main Kolomna–Oreckhovo–Zagorsk–Dimitrov line. The German attack executed by Army Group Center could receive supplies for conquering Moscow up to that crucial line on one condition: that there be enough trains for the task.[47]

On November 17, Heinz Guderian, commander of the 2nd Panzer Army in von Bock's Army Group Center, complained that he was short of fuel for his tanks; this turned out to be one of the most severe supply problems. Although it was possible to bring fuel to the front directly from Romania, one of Hitler's stronger arguments in favor of the division of forces in late August was capturing the oil fields of Baku in the Caucasus. However, the assets that would be captured by the Germans were unusable because Soviet fuel had a lower octane than that used by the Germans and could not be converted without reprocessing it or modifying it to work with more than 2,000 different types of German vehicles. This caused a severe shortage in spare parts for all vehicles and reestablished the Reich's position as the main source for fuel supply to the front, based on logistics supplied by the Reichsbahn's trains.[48]

On November 17, the same day that Guderian complained about the fuel shortage, Halder discussed the supply situation with the senior quartermaster at OKH, Friedrich Paulus; Lieutenant General Adolf Heusinger, chief of operations of the Army High Command;[49] Colonel Alfred Baentsch from the quartermaster general's branch; and Staff Officer Colonel Bork. At the meeting, it was determined that steps would be taken to confirm that supply trains passing through the General Government would have priority over all other traffic activities, and that the weight of the burden would be on military logistics. It was clear at this point that whatever passed through this region was also bound to be exploited by the SS to transfer Jews to the East—hence the sharpness of the warning from General Halder.[50] Hitler must have been aware of the supply situation at the front and about the meeting at OKH. However, he had other priorities. He finally made it clear to Heydrich at the end of November that he was expecting all Jews, without exception, to be deported from the German Reich by the end of the year, if possible. A solution should be found, he said, to all questions related to this matter, and transportation problems could not serve as a reason for delays. Because there were no death camps yet in the General Government, Hitler's demand nevertheless concealed a swift transfer of Jews to the death areas in the East.[51]

The same cars that the Reichsbahn allocated for transporting Jews transferred the main transport vehicles to the Eastern Front. Some 625,000 horses—comparable to the number used in Napoleon's huge army—were brought to the front aboard trains. However, in contrast to Napoleon's army, which did not depend on supply logistics but on local granaries, the Wehrmacht relied, at least in 1941, on provisions from the Reich.[52] Poland was an additional source for livestock, horses, and particularly freight wagons. About 15,000 Polish peasant wagons reinforced infantry divisions in their transport formation. Wagons were requisitioned by the General Government of Poland, with each division getting about 200.[53] The number of horses allocated to each division was 3,000, and the reserves amounted to no more than 150 horses per division, if all went well. However, according to veterinarian reports, there were no more than forty-five horses to fill the ranks at the beginning of the campaign. Again, a single train could have solved the problem of reserve freight transportation within Soviet territory for one to three divisions.[54] State secretary Herbert Backe, an expert on agrarian politics, and who as of May 1942 was also minister for food affairs, refused to supply fodder for the pack animals and horses used by the army at the Eastern Front. As a result, there was no choice but to feed the horses with thatch taken from the locals' rooftops in the villages of the occupied areas. Conditions continued to deteriorate, and in December 1941, reports from the Kalinin sector revealed that the horses that served the fighting units had not received grain stocks for more than two months.[55] The death toll among the animals during the winter was also high because of frost and famine. By mid-February, 5,000 horses serving the 17th Army died as a result of famine—not because there were no food reserves but because there were no trains available for sending them.[56] In August, the 12th Infantry Division, which was part of Army Group North, gathered about 760 tons of hay for its horses in the environs of the town of Kholm (on the Leningrad–Moscow route).[57] This weight was equivalent to seven freight trains, which could have supplied hay for an entire division.

The Jewish deportees aboard the trains were allowed to take along a suitcase weighing up to fifty kilograms, which had to be marked clearly with their evacuation number.[58] That made the average weight of every transport approximately 100 tons—the average weight of the deportees (about fifty kilograms per person) together with their luggage. This odd list of priorities lacked any operational logic. State secretary Backe refused to supply fodder for the pack animals for political reasons, along with other reasons related to the morale of the German people. However, this does not mean there was no way of transferring food. Each transport of Jews from the Reich could have been replaced by 100 tons of hay or fuel.

3

The German War Economy

The Wehrmacht's ability to confront the Red Army depended on the German economy, industrial production, emergency stocks, and supplies arriving from Germany to the troops at the front. Although it is true that Germany's industrial production and capacity could not match that of its opponents, not to mention the superiority of Russian T-34 tanks over the German Panzers, new perspectives on the economic issue paint a different picture. Train allocation for transporting German Jews to the East had to be balanced with trains carrying ammunition, fuel, food, and other requisites. This is the key to understanding the symbiotic relationship between the Final Solution and the war effort.

In July 1941, the Balkan states were the economic rear upon which Germany depended for its requirements.[1] If one considers that according to the original program, Operation Barbarossa should not have lasted more than seventeen weeks, there was still no need for the Soviet resources Hitler was speaking of so passionately. These assets could be used, if at all, only for the administration of the German civil government and *Lebensraum* after the campaign ended. Although the Balkans provided an answer to German needs, especially during peacetime, and were perhaps insufficient for a bloody war such as that in the East proved to be, when the German forces halted their advance in mid-July, the war on the Eastern Front seemed to be going well for the Wehrmacht. The campaign was in its initial phase, and there seemed to be no complications on the horizon. Had Hitler accepted his generals' views and suggestions, he would not have needed the resources of the Ukraine and the Leningrad area in the summer of 1941. The Romanian oil fields were sufficient for Operation Barbarossa. In a speech delivered in Berlin on April 29, 1941, Erich Neumann, who worked for the German foreign office, summarized the achievements of the Four Year Plan. As of late April 1941, the information Hitler received, which was stated in Neumann's report, was that there were sufficient raw materials and oil supplies for the military needs of fighting the war.[2]

By the end of January 1940, Hitler himself assessed that conquering Belgium, Holland, and northern France would make the industrial areas of Duoai and Lens, as well as Luxembourg, Longwy, and Briey, accessible, and these would replace the supply of raw materials from Sweden. Hitler decided to exploit the stock of Swedish raw materials in 1940, taking into account that the war would last for a few years. This decision resulted from a view that the best way to produce war supplies was not by creating a stock of raw materials but by manufacturing arms ready for immediate warfare.[3] That was what Nazi rearmament in the mid-1930s was all about.

If Hitler argued that it was preferable to prepare arms supplies in advance and knew that the planned campaign should take no more than seventeen weeks, perhaps even less, then it was certainly clear to him that raw materials from the Soviet territories could not yet be exploited for that period. Capturing economic resources and exploiting them for long-term warfare still did not mean that they could be utilized immediately. Ukrainian oil fields and the Ukrainian granary were resources for the long term. When the German armies invaded these territories, the villagers did not greet them by showing them the way to parking lots or gasoline stations with pumps ready to fill up the Panzer fuel tanks. Nor did the troops find warehouses full of food supplies with the compliments of the Ukrainian motherland, ready for distribution among the exhausted newcomers.[4]

Soviet fuel, which was supposedly worth fighting for, was of a different octane than that used for Panzers and other German vehicles. As for food supplies, the Soviets did not leave any in storage but cleared most of them when their forces withdrew deep into Soviet territory. Although they would have made an important contribution to the German economy, the German occupiers in summer 1941 found that exploiting resources in the Russian territories would not answer their immediate needs, either of the German economy or the

German army.[5] However, this fact did not prevent the main office of the Reich for food supply from refusing to allocate regular provisions for the forces and forcing the troops to survive on what they could find within the Soviet Union, mainly by looting the local population.[6]

The German war industry depended largely on foreign resources. During World War II, and particularly in the Russian sector, the Soviet Union was the main source of supply for German warfare. However, the most important resource for the German war economy was in Western Europe. Economic relations with West European countries and exploitation of their resources after the blitz conquests were much more relevant for preservation of an active German war machine.[7] Furthermore, although a major part of the European continent's resources was by the summer of 1941 in German hands, the Germans still did not succeed in maximizing and exploiting them enough in the short term, partly as a result of a shortage of manpower.[8]

The brutal policy of the German occupiers in the Soviet Union, as well as in the General Government, created a chaotic economic situation that prevented reasonable economic exploitation of these territories for military needs, as Hitler saw it, or rational economic planning for future rule.[9] Thus, it seems that the policy of annihilating populations entailed unnecessary effort and waste: when Einsatzgruppen units liquidated Soviet Jews, they actually eradicated a workforce of about one million people, including Communist commissars and excluding children and those deemed unfit.[10] Economic exploitation in slave conditions of this population would surely have been more worthwhile for the German war effort. According to documents relating to the German civil administration in the occupied Soviet territories, a picture arises of conflicts between the treasury, the SS, the security police, and the Wehrmacht. The SS, it was argued, was killing the Jewish labor force in the Soviet Union when it could be usefully employed, especially when professional and skilled manpower in industry and agriculture were not always immediately replaceable.[11]

In spite of the strong will of the SS to liquidate the 6,000 Jews in the ghetto of Schaulen in Latvia, on September 10, Herman Gevke, the senior commissar in the area, described a situation in which the SS "hardly" managed to kill 1,000 Jews because of the demand for professional labor. Their extermination or deportation further to the East would be enabled only after each Jewish worker was attached to a Latvian worker who would learn his craft and serve as a substitute.[12]

In late August, Hitler still believed he could achieve victory over the Soviet Union. Only at the end of October did he begin to grasp that the war would take longer than he initially expected and would extend even after winter 1941–1942.[13] What convinced Hitler to go ahead with an operation on such a large scale as Barbarossa, followed by Typhoon, was the immense success of the German victories in the two years of war against enemies whose matériel capacity (military industry, economy, and resources) was much larger than Germany's. These successes had nothing to do with advance economic planning for the blitz campaigns but rather with teamwork, leadership, and the Germans' combat ability, in contrast to weakness, defective leadership, and problematic intelligence on the enemy side.[14] Similar conditions were present in the first two months of the war in the East as well, and this is what convinced Hitler that the gamble he took was fairly reasonable and did not demand an economic effort greater than that already undertaken.[15]

Hitler knew that German industry faced a manpower problem and an increasing economic crisis. In February 1941, he stated that he would not let economic problems interfere with his upcoming military programs. Of course, an invasion of the Soviet Union promised economic benefits. Soviet food, manpower, and natural resources would serve the German war effort. However, Hitler was apparently aware of the fact that an invasion would not immediately benefit German armaments consumption. Like General Georg Thomas, head of the War Economy Office at the headquarters of the supreme command of the Wehrmacht (OKW), in spring 1941, Hitler reached the conclusion that only reorganization would increase production in the military industry. Therefore, on May 18, he invited the armaments minister, Fritz Todt, along with Thomas, to meet him at Berchtesgaden, where he presented the two with his plans to make the war economy more efficient. As a starting point, Hitler claimed that the armed forces were placing too many technical demands on the industry, hampering mass production. The army's insistence on extremely high-quality equipment created an extra burden on the industry and endangered armaments production where the use of labor was concerned. Hitler called for a return to more basic and less sophisticated manufacturing processes in order to facilitate mass production. After the meeting, Wehrmacht chief of staff Keitel issued a directive calling on all three High Command branch officers of the Wehrmacht to reduce the number of orders for armaments and complex weapons in order to encourage the production of new models that would decrease the use of manpower and raw materials.[16]

Until July 1941, there was no order canceling Keitel's directive. What Hitler told his generals was one side of the coin. The other was not then revealed to them. The fact is, he did not invite any of his senior generals to the meeting with Todt and Thomas so they could hear what they had to say regarding the matter. The implications of liquidating Soviet Jewry at that time were not considered, including the fact that it would have been possible to use this population as forced labor in the arms industry, which suffered from a shortage of manpower, as Keitel's memorandum implies.

The blitzkrieg against Russia was an attempt to push the German economy to its limits before the abandonment of ideas upon which the National Socialist economy was based and the shift to a full war economy. Only during the Russian campaign did it become apparent that the resources Germany had allocated for the war in the East were insufficient for a decisive military success. The ill-prepared planning of the operation became clear only after five months of heavy fighting, on November 26, when the Russians began their counteroffensives and recaptured Rostov on the banks of the Don River.[17]

Stocks and Supplies

At a certain point, even Stalin thought the Germans had enough reserves of food, fuel, and resources to bring the war to a showdown. He claimed that British and American estimates regarding the German fuel supply were erroneous. Stalin's new assumption was based on the fact that in the framework of the Nazi–Soviet pact, which lasted for almost two years, the Germans demanded less fuel than the pact permitted them during 1940–1941. He assumed the German army was prepared to fight a winter campaign in Russia in terms of manpower, food stocks, and fuel in order to threaten the Soviet capital.[18] Stalin revealed these thoughts to Harry Hopkins, President Roosevelt's private envoy, who held a series of meetings with him in Moscow in late July 1941. Allegedly, Stalin had a clear interest in presenting Hopkins with these pessimistic estimates in order to win American support. However, at the same time, he had to maintain a balanced perspective and be careful not to overdo it and risk a cease-fire agreement between Hitler and the Western powers.

Many of President Roosevelt's advisors wanted to see the Russians defeat the Nazi invaders, but they preferred not to be involved with direct aid. The objection originated not only from antipathy toward Soviet rule and American reluctance to continue preventing the British from receiving supplies for the Russians, but also from a strong belief that the Soviet Union would not be able to hold on much longer and repulse the German assault effectively.[19] Because this consideration held some truth, and in light of the constant fear among the Allies that the Russians would strive for an agreement like the Brest–Litovsk pact in World War I, or just another sequel to the Ribbentrop–Molotov pact, the assessments that Stalin presented to Hopkins seem to have been relatively reliable.

Unlike most of his close consultants, President Roosevelt believed that the Soviet Union would not collapse. Nevertheless, he too needed some reassurance. This came only after Hopkins reported on his meetings with Stalin.[20] Stalin also pointed out that the most important thing was to produce tanks during the winter. Tank losses, he claimed, were heavy on both sides, but for winter 1941–1942, Germany was able to produce more tanks per month than the Soviet Union.[21] In addition, Stalin urged the British Royal Air Force to bomb the oil fields in Romania as quickly as possible.[22] This request proves that Stalin was aware of the fact that the Romanian oil fields were a huge resource and in fact were all the Germans needed for the time being.

On August 25, 1941, Hitler updated Mussolini regarding the situation on the Eastern Front. According to the conversation between the two, all the arguments he gave to his generals regarding the strategy he had chosen were irrelevant and stood in strong contrast to whatever he reported to the Duce. Hitler told Mussolini that he had no doubt about the outcome of the campaign in the East and that he thought the Red Army would collapse by October, if not earlier, under the continuous blows from the Wehrmacht: "The tools for victory are in German hands now."[23] Hitler said that despite the bitter battles, the Germans had suffered only 68,000 losses, while the Soviets had lost hundreds of thousands. The Germans had captured so many weapons that they exceeded the needs of the Reich's armed forces. Therefore, he told Mussolini his decision was to concentrate on building U-boats, tanks, and artillery against air offensives. Finally, he concluded that when the campaign in Russia was over, he intended to strike a fatal blow to Britain with an invasion. His forces were thus preparing themselves by obtaining sea and land equipment necessary for an amphibian landing. Among other things, he proclaimed that most of the Ukrainian grain crops, if not all, would be taken by the Germans, but in the following year, Russian crops would meet the needs of the occupied countries in particular.[24] Considering that apart from focusing on arms production alone, Hitler refused to cancel the Autobahn project and construction of new party buildings in Berlin until July 1942 (only then did he give into Speer's plea to transfer all the materials for these projects to the military industry), the discussion with Mussolini appears to have authentically reflected Hitler's perspective as of late August 1941. Overall, it seems that resources for continuing the war, which Hitler argued that Germany needed desperately, were certainly within reach.

September 1941, however, left no room for further speculation. At a meeting that took place on September 29, Rosenberg reported to Hitler, in the presence of Martin Bormann, on the political and economic state of the territories conquered so far. Among other issues, Rosenberg described the condition of the "Ukrainian granary." According to Rosenberg, only 60 percent of the crops found were usable; all the rest had been destroyed by the Russians either during the campaign or in the course of the scorched-earth policy the Soviets were executing. What became apparent from his report, however, was that for agricultural and seasonal reasons, Hitler could expect to exploit his gains only in the summer of 1942. Thus, his economic basis for diverting forces to the various sectors proved impractical.[25]

The entry from July 1941 in the war diary of the chief quartermaster of the 6th Army—the same army that eighteen months later would be completely annihilated at Stalingrad—confirms this point. It was already evident in 1941 that supplies for the Wehrmacht from Soviet sources were not accessible. At the end of September, rationing was introduced. The only alternative the army was left with was to loot from local inhabitants because the Red Army either took food supplies along during its retreat or destroyed them.[26]

As early as June–July, little remained in the territories the Soviets had evacuated. Most of the economic potential of these areas had been wiped out by the Russians by moving heavy industry as far east as possible, using the workers and engineers employed there to rebuild them, or destroying full stocks of supplies they could not move because they were pressed for time and were adamant about not letting them fall into the enemy's hands. Supplies in any form, as well as mines and entire industrial plants, were burned, excluding cases where the Russians simply abandoned their positions because of the swift German advance.[27] The scorched-earth doctrine was highly relevant to the territories Hitler was referring to as being necessary for his war economy and was another indication that accusing his generals of ignorance in war economics had nothing to do with military strategy but with ideology. These resources, important as they might have been, would not help Germany's war effort in winter 1941–1942, and if at all only in winter 1942–1943, which was not part of the German plan in the Eastern Campaign. Because Hitler must have known about the condition of the territories abandoned by the Soviets as well as the scorched-earth policy, his economic arguments can simply be rejected.

In September 1941, Julius Klausen, deputy chief of the agriculture and food department of the Reich, who in May 1941 had claimed it would be possible to supply twenty-five tons of wheat, found out that no crops had been sown in the spring, as he had assumed, and those sown in the autumn covered only 20 percent of the fields of the Ukraine. Thus, in December, the Wehrmacht could use very little of the Soviet territories' potential, and most food supplies were delivered from the Reich.[28]

According to a document from May 23, 1941, regarding economic policy and agrarian industry in the East, great significance was given to meat consumption by the army and within the Reich itself. Belorussia in particular, as well as the main industrial areas around Moscow, were to be exploited for meat. The livestock concentrated in these areas reached a total of sixty-three million heads of cattle and thirty million hogs. The document states that these areas were top priority for conquest in order to supply the needs of the army as well as the inhabitants of the Reich. It specifically indicates that any delay in reaching this objective could result in the entire livestock herds being butchered for the needs of the local population.[29]

When Hitler claimed it was necessary to divide German forces in order to capture the Ukrainian granary for a continuous war effort, in theory, he was right. However, Belorussian livestock was more available for German needs. The use of grain and wheat was possible only after the winter of 1941–1942. The livestock, on the other hand, could have served two-thirds of the entire Wehrmacht for a whole year. Various methods for preserving the meat, such as freezing, smoking, and canning, were also discussed, as well as the use of food plants and packing factories located in those areas.[30]

In a series of discussions that took place on September 15–16 at the office of Hermann Göring, who was also commander of the Luftwaffe, regarding exploitation of the land conquered in the East, the Reichsmarschall said that the army appeared to be demanding far too much, especially in regard to preserved food from home. Except for tobacco, chocolate, and dried vegetables, all food supplies for the troops should come solely from exploiting the conquered territory:

> I shall not approve food supplies apart from the ones specified for transferal from the Reich to the East, especially meat supply, which could lead to shortages in supplies for the civil population in Germany. By no means will I allow that. . . . The morale at home would be damaged and become fragile. It is enough that the home front is bearing continuous bombings, slow achievements in the East, and the fact that this is the second war within the same generation. This could serve as ideal propaganda for the enemy.[31]

While the conflict over food supplies continued, surely Göring's hypocrisy did not extend to Jewish transports sent by the SS to the East from October. The Jewish deportations could hardly boost civil or military morale when German troops at the front were freezing or starving to death because of the lack of trains supplied by the Reichsbahn.

On the eve of November 5, in the presence of SS colonel Hugo Blaschke, mayor of Vienna, and Richard Richter, a Nazi physician and party member well acquainted with Hitler, Hitler mentioned a document dating from the time of Julius Caesar, indicating that "soldiers of that time lived on a vegetarian diet. According to the same source, it was only in times of shortage that soldiers had recourse to meat." It was known, he continued, that

> the ancient philosophers already regarded the change from black gruel to bread as a sign of decadence. The Vikings would have not undertaken their now legendary expeditions if they'd depended on a meat diet, for they had no method of preserving meat. The fact that the smallest military unit was the section is explained by the fact that each man had a mill for grain. The purveyor of vitamins was the onion.[32]

Hitler continued in this vein while the German soldiers he had sent to battle were already suffering from the bitter winter as well as from a serious shortage in food supplies. The only thing he did not forget to mention in his table talks was the fact that in November, the Jewish deportations from the Reich had reached a height, and that the Nordic Vikings did not have to cope with the logistics of conveying populations on such a large scale during their legendary expeditions. The German soldiers could settle for the Ukrainian granary, but around the outskirts of Moscow in winter 1941, they were not equipped with personal mills like the Vikings were, and what they desperately needed was cultivated and processed food, not raw ingredients.

The Reichsbahn and Train Supplies

Until the beginning of the war—and, in fact, during the actual campaigns—the Reichsbahn was a commercial for-profit organization. During the war, the company continued to supply trains on a commercial basis; however, timetables and coordination were dictated by the needs of war. The transport ministry worked with a representative from each military organization, one from the SS and one from the Wehrmacht. Adolf Eichmann's office B4-IV fulfilled this function on behalf of the SS security police. The office did not coordinate trains within the General Government or the Soviet territories.[33] Most of the work was in locating deportees in the countries to be cleansed and transferring them aboard trains to the East or to the General Government. This was a discordant process that created a conflict of interests between the needs of the SS and those of the German army fighting at the front lines.

Eichmann and his assistants worked with the rail company, which supplied them with train wagons. It was extremely difficult to coordinate timetables and tracks, find the right cars, concentrate the deportees from many train stations across Germany and the protectorates, and prepare the transports. The cars for these transports varied from regular freight wagons to cattle wagons and third-class passenger carriages, such as those used for the Kassel transports to Riga. The latter had separate compartments with eight seats each. The journey from Kassel to Riga lasted more than seventy hours, with the deportees traveling via Berlin, Breslau, Posen, Konigsberg, and Tilsit—the same route used by the Wehrmacht to provision its units from the supply centers along the Minsk–Moscow route.[34]

The logistics connected to arranging a transport could take a few days. The growing complexity of train coordination required great skill; Franz Novak, Eichmann's assistant, became an expert.[35] In accordance with the agreement made with the commander of the security police—the Gestapo—it was decided that the German Ordnungspolizei would take over security on the trains. The security police comprised twelve men and a commander, which meant one security guard per car.[36]

Within the army two major departments of the High Command—the General Staff and elements that were under the army's maintenance division, as well as the Reserve Army under General Friedrich Fromm—played a major part in finding the trains required for the army. The General Staff presented its demands, and the maintenance division obeyed orders.[37] More specifically, there were four departments involved in the process: the General Army Headquarters, under the command of the chief of Army Reserves, and at the General Staff (the transport and organization branches), and the general quartermaster's office. The process was as follows: General Halder would discuss the military situation of the day on a regular basis with the head quartermaster, Walter Bouhle, and with the chief of organization and planning, Eduard Wagner. Both men and their delegates were present at Halder's morning briefings. In accordance with the needs of the day, each department would make immediate preparations, including provisions for the army at the front with all that this involved: transportation, equipment, ammunition, food, fodder, and fuel, as well as fresh combat troops. In the next phase, responsibility would move to Brigadier General Rudolf Gercke, who was in charge of sending armed forces to the front. Where the railway line came to an end, responsibility would be transferred to Wagner, who oversaw the dispatch of motorized convoys, horses and carriages, and equipment for the troops. The main requirements for such an operation were coordination and synchronization.[38]

However, in another not particularly big office outside the military quarter, a clerk named Adolf Eichmann manned a position parallel to that of Gercke in the army, except that he was stationed at one of the departments belonging to the Reichssicherheitshauptamt (the Reich main security office) under Reinhard Heydrich's command and was not present at Halder's daily briefings regarding the situation at the front. There was no coordination between these two bodies because they were independent of one another. Each received trains for its needs from the Reichsbahn, but eventually Eichmann's activity became a burden on the entire transportation system. When it became apparent that there was a shortage in locomotives and that the army was unable to receive supplies, Gercke accused the Reichsbahn of losing count of the number of trains they had been sending to the East. On November 20, in an attempt to overcome the upcoming crisis, he met with Dorpmüller to discuss transportation matters. Dorpmüller agreed to dispatch a personal representative with extraordinary powers to the Wehrmacht's operations office in Warsaw, but after a bitter argument with Gercke, this measure failed. Gercke demanded that the representative be subordinated to him and be considered a member of the military; Dorpmüller refused.[39]

Lack of coordination, disorder, and confusion were part of the SS organization system. According to a letter sent by the chief of the Ordnungspolizei in Berlin, Kurt Daluege, to the commanders of the security police in the Reich, Vienna, Prague, and Riga, between November 1 and December 4, 1941, the security police had deported 50,000 Jews from the old Reich, Austria, and the protectorates to the East, around the areas of Minsk and Riga.[40] Although Daluege's account was correct, no one knew the actual dates the trains had departed. Even after those dates, the local municipality of Düsseldorf informed Eichmann's department as well as Heydrich—in a letter dated December 11, 1941, with a copy to the chief of security police and Einsatzgruppe A in Riga—that a train carrying some 1,007 Jews had left the station at Düsseldorf for Riga, and that storm troopers should be waiting for them there.[41] Actually, the last transport that year left Hannover on December 15, and deportations were resumed on January 9, 1942. Clearly there was no coordination between the commanders of the security police and Eichmann, and even less so with the army.

Beyond the border, all tasks involving the conversion of rail tracks to the German gauge, as well as rail traffic, were under military supervision. Train employees were organized in rail divisions operating parallel to the advancing forces and were attached to an army group transportation officer. This officer was the link between the civil train system to which the cars and locomotives belonged and the army. The military command passed on all tactical and logistical requests involving train traffic to the transportation officer. The latter was dependent on the civil train agency's goodwill because the civil agencies were not subordinated to the army but to Dorpmüller, the transport minister, who also wore another hat as executive director of the Reichsbahn. This situation led to friction and conflicts.[42]

The most severe supply problems were located at the northern sector of the Soviet–German front. Although the rail teams managed to convert 500 kilometers of tracks to the desired gauge, the city of Daugavpils—where Supply District North had been set up in the first stage of the advance—received only one train per day instead of the ten needed for the offensive on Leningrad. In the second half of July, the supply troops were engaged in moving the supply base from Daugavpils to Riga. Army Group North, which counted on thirty-four trains per day in order to furnish its needs, settled for eighteen a day at most, and even this figure was seldom achieved.[43]

Instead of the twenty-four trains per day that were supposed to reach Army Group South, General von Rundstedt received an average of 14.5 trains per day—less than half those that reached Army Group Center. From October 13, the forces reached a deadlock in supply matters.[44] During October 1941, only 195 trains out of 724 that were supposed to reach the base on the Dnieper River arrived at their destiny.[45]

According to Halder, within a time frame of two weeks, the railways could carry only one division to the front. Thus, all that remained for the OKW to decide were the most urgent tasks of the moment.[46] On November 14, von Bock noted in his diary that the army commanders were complaining of severe supply problems in all areas, including fuel, ammunition, and winter clothes: "With a small number of trains, it is hard to do anything regarding this matter, and it certainly projects onto the preparations for the assault." General von Kluge, commander of the 4th Army, portrayed a gloomy picture of the 13th Corps, whose troops could barely hold onto the existing line. With no regular train traffic, he said, it was impossible to think about preparations for the upcoming attack.[47]

On November 14, 1941, four transports left Berlin for Minsk, and on November 16, one transport departed from the city of Brünn and another from Hamburg. However, out of the 25,000 Jews headed originally for Minsk, only 7,000 reached their destination; the others were forwarded to Theresienstadt, partly because of the objection of Wilhelm Kube, general commissar of Belorussia headquartered in Minsk, who claimed that the transports were being initiated behind his back and were bypassing his authority. On December 16, Kube sent Heydrich a letter of protest. He said that although some of the train cars used for transporting Jews were originally cattle wagons, they could be used for transferring soldiers to the front and returning the dead and wounded to Germany.[48]

On November 15, the Germans resumed their attack on the right flank and on November 17 on the left flank, after waiting for the muddy soil to freeze and become passable again.[49] It was their last assault before the Russian counteroffensive began in December. It is therefore hard to understand why only a day or two before, it was considered important to transfer Jewish deportees to the East when there were clear demands for more fuel, winter equipment, and food supplies at a critical stage of the war. On October 26, the army command had already ordered that all transport vehicles carry only provisions necessary for the battles.[50] Apparently, after receiving complaints from the Wehrmacht, a phone conversation took place between Himmler, who was at the Führer's headquarters, and Heydrich, who was in Prague. In this conversation, which took place on November 30, Himmler belatedly asked Heydrich to cancel an earlier directive and not send another transport from Berlin in order to assuage the fury of the troops fighting at the front lines.[51]

On November 16, Oberst (Colonel) Görltz, who was charged with restoring order to railway operations, came to von Bock's bureau. The conclusion reached at that meeting was that the biggest problem appeared to be the great confusion at the General Government. Because a portion of the Reich's Jews were being sent to the Lodz ghetto, train traffic there had become a heavy burden. That same morning, after the meeting with Görltz, a telex message was sent to von Bock's armies informing them that because Army Group Center had only one reserve division, they had to manage with the forces they already had and could expect no more support. When on November 19 Hitler suggested encircling the enemy northwest of Moscow by turning the northern wing of the attack south, the only obstacle to this action was the train problem. Only one division behind the front was able to attack. This well demonstrates the significant impact the Jewish transports had on the fighting behind the lines. Every train counted. On December 1, Army Group Center was spread over a 1,000-kilometer front, with only a single weak reserve division at the rear and a major supply problem. However, this did not interfere with another planned transport of Jews, which departed from Stuttgart to Kovno that same day.[52]

On November 29, Hitler explained to Count Galeazzo Ciano, the Italian foreign minister, that military operations were dependent on the supply of trains to the battlefields. "The problems in conducting the operation are particularly related to transport," he said.[53] On April 29, 1942, Hitler told Mussolini, after the fact, that the German army had not penetrated deeper into Soviet territory in October because the long railway lines, combined with the harsh winter, would have created even greater transport problems, resulting in a total catastrophe. Fortunately, he said, the winter began early, for if not, "We would be 200–300 kilometers deeper and then the passage of supplies and military forces by train would have been absolutely impossible." However, evidence suggests that the transportation problem began even before the onset of winter, in the critical stages of Operation Typhoon.[54] Although Hitler did not then see a major logistical problem in transferring the Jews of the Reich to the Soviet Union, the operation actually had an unpredictable influence because of the difficulties it created.

On December 2, the Waffen-SS Das Reich division reached the outskirts of Moscow, just fifteen kilometers from the city center. Otto Skorzeny, who was in the division's commando unit, claimed that he could see the Kremlin through his binoculars.[55] Skorzeny argued that despite the mud, ice, lack of paved roads, confusion, and logistical problems, it was possible, even in December, to conquer Moscow. However, Army Group Center did not receive a single reserve division as a backup or substitute for the forces that had been lost. At the same time, Stalin moved thirty Siberian infantry divisions to the front, six tank divisions, and three cavalry divisions.[56] This progress on the Russian side was achieved when at the beginning of November the Russians had only 90,000 troops standing between Moscow and von Bock's army.

In a directive dated December 8, 1941, ordering the retreat of the army in the East because of winter, Walther von Brauchitsch, commander in chief of the armed forces until that day, when Hitler dismissed him and appointed himself to the position, explained that Army Group Center could reach Moscow if it were not for the problems of supplies and reserves.[57] On December 3, Halder noted in his diary that General Paulus and General Gercke had again reported transport problems in bringing reserve forces for the relief and replacement of the exhausted troops at the front. However, again, these reports seemed to have had no impact in Berlin: on the same day, another Jewish transport left the station from Vienna to Kovno.

4

Soviet Capabilities

The balance of power between Germany and the Soviet Union, particularly in the initial stages of the war in Russia, is a key factor in examining the relationship between the German war effort and the Final Solution. Despite their quantitative advantage and alleged tremendous fighting spirit, the Soviets were revealed mostly as an opponent equal to the Germans, although at times inferior to them. Because during the initial period of the war there was doubt as to whether the Russians could hold on much longer, German strategy during the second half of 1941 influenced the outcome of the campaign more than anything else.

The strongest indictment of Stalin on the eve of the Great Patriotic War and in its initial phase (apart from the fact that he kept ignoring warnings from his own General Staff and the Allies about the imminent Nazi invasion) was his liquidation of the Red Army High Command during the Great Purge of the late 1930s, which resulted in the army being ill-prepared for such an event. Because among the executed officers were engineers and industrial plant executives, military manufacturing capability was damaged, causing weakness in the Soviet defense configuration. After the Great Purge, with its arrests and mass executions, new and inexperienced officers were recruited to high positions, leaving many ranks unmanned and an army with a serious morale problem among both men and officers.[1] The catastrophic situation in summer 1941 is illustrated by the fact that close to 75 percent of the top military leadership and about 70 percent of all political officials had held their positions for less than a year. Many of the Red Army professionals who had been executed had been graduates of military academies and had accumulated military experience after active service in the civil war. All had been willing to apply their skills but were not given the opportunity to do so.

After their liquidation, a new military leadership was appointed: low-ranking officers located on the third or fourth rungs of the ladder were promoted to vacant senior positions. Most of those promoted were reliable and loyal to the party but had no experience in combat. They thus had to pay a heavy price when they came up against Hitler's forces.[2] In the first six months of fighting, the Soviet Union lost more than 50 percent of its combat-ready military strength. Afterward, the Soviet nation was forced to face the task of managing operations with a big, only partly trained army that suffered from a shortage of military supplies. There was also a need to build a new power base for the Red Army.[3] Ultimately, the commanding officers of the army in 1942 would bring victory in 1945; in 1941, however, these officers did not number in the Red Army's ranks.

In his summary the Soviet Union's situation on the eve of war, Zhukov noted in his memoirs that the weakness of the Soviet side in the initial months of the operation originated primarily from misleading assessments regarding the date of the German invasion: "It looks like the defense of our country was managed properly in regard to its basic tendencies. For many years everything was done in the social and economic fields in order to strengthen our defense ability. . . . The people and the Party have made an exceptional effort."[4] Regarding the army itself, Zhukov paints a picture of a force ready for war from the point of view of infantry, armor, artillery, antiaircraft, and naval forces, but one that displayed weakness in communications and the engineering corps. As for the air force, Zhukov says that its aircraft were outdated, although when war broke out, it was in the midst of a broad process of reorganization. Nevertheless, "History has given us too short a period, not enough for us to organize everything as needed. . . . There were many things that we didn't have time to complete."[5] The affirmative elements on the Soviet side that Zhukov mentions eventually became stronger during the war and finally prevailed, but he adds: "Miscalculation of the time the Germans would attack worked severely against us and emphasized the impartial advantages of the enemy. In addition, it gave them temporary advantages, thus creating the difficult situation we were forced into at the beginning of the war."[6] Zhukov thus admitted that even if the military leaders had taken urgent measures concerning fulfillment of the operational plan and the recruitment program, "these means would not assure us full success in repelling the German assault, since there was no balance of forces between the two sides."[7]

Although Marshal Zhukov's memoirs should be treated critically, because when he wrote them he was engaged in closing accounts with Stalin and he was trying to whitewash himself of responsibility for the omissions of June 22, it should not be overlooked that Zhukov attaches great importance to the rare momentum the Germans had at the beginning of the operation and to their offensive strategy. Although the Soviets prevailed over the Germans in the long run, in terms of resources for resumption of the war, even the Russian chief of staff admitted that in certain cases, and particularly in the initial months of Operation Barbarossa, German strength was superior to that of the Soviets. Therefore, strategy and logistics were decisive for the outcome of the campaign. Mistakes in a situation like this in the German conduct of war were crucial.

Zhukov's memoirs deal with the Red Army's counterattack. According to Zhukov, in the first days of combat, the Red Army retaliated against the Wehrmacht, although many of the soldiers were new recruits and everyone was in a state of shock and confusion. The first counterattacks were conducted at the border on June 24 and 28, 1941, and seriously hampered the Wehrmacht's advance.[8] Although the counterattacks at the beginning of the war were not successful, in the case of the Southern Army Group, they caused a week's delay in its advance. Moreover, the counterattacks helped Hitler come to his decision at the end of August to turn a part of Army Group Center to the south instead of toward Moscow in order to secure the Ukraine. According to this same line of reasoning, the fighting along the Ukrainian border exposed German armor as vulnerable.[9] Yet the Soviet counterattacks were criticized for being senseless and for causing a great many casualties on the way to stopping the Germans in an attempt to convince the Soviet nation that it could halt the invaders. Zhukov was sincere enough to admit that "the attacks were badly organized, the command wasn't operating on the basis of hard-headed decisions, but mostly because they wanted to do something no matter what the consequences were, regardless of the ability of the corps and their condition. . . . Therefore they did not achieve their objective."[10] The bottom line was that the Soviets were helpless during the first days of Barbarossa, with no suitable defensive or offensive possibilities. On the night of July 11–12, 1941, during one of his wearying conversations, Hitler said,

> Soviet propaganda—in spite of its criticism of us, always operates within certain lines. It looks like Stalin, this cunning Caucasian, is ready enough to give up European Russia, if he thinks that failing to solve the situation will cause him to lose everything. Let nobody think that Stalin is likely to re-conquer Europe from the Ural! It's just as if I was situated in Slovakia and from there went out to re-conquer the Reich. This is the catastrophe that will cause the loss of the Soviet Empire.[11]

Thus, on the basis of the enemy's situation, in mid-July, Hitler seemed quite confident of victory. In the strategic crisis that dominated the German command during July and August 1941, Hitler emerged the undisputed victor. His strategic choice was certainly the wiser alternative, given both German logistical constraints and the dreadful Soviet strategic deployment in the south. However, unlike the German army, the Red Army did not have to win the war in 1941; it only had to survive long enough for Germany's offensive power to disappear. The Red Army was undoubtedly weak in the summer of 1941, but it was entirely successful in one fundamental respect, which apparently the Nazi leaders failed to recognize: it confounded the plan to conquer the Soviet Union in a blitz-style campaign in the early weeks of the war. Indeed, the Nazi regime's search for a solution to its Jewish problem in the same early period of the war in the East was not seen as a distraction from it; on the contrary, it was an integral element of the war itself.[12]

One of the problems the Soviets faced, particularly because Stalin, who, like Hitler and Churchill, was a military dilettante with combat experience only from the outdated battles of the civil war, was that almost instinctively, he made the Red Army fight for every square meter of Soviet soil instead of extracting tactical possibilities from controlled retreat that would enable his forces to refresh their lines and redeploy against the advancing enemy.[13] Although the fighting was hard and also involved casualties on the German side, the Wehrmacht managed to surprise the mass Soviet forces (air and land), gaining a huge advantage over the Red Army—an advantage that could not even be compared to that achieved in the struggle against British forces. Attacking at daybreak June 22, 1941, the Germans surprised the Red Army soldiers while they were asleep in their barracks outside the bunkers and without ammunition for combat. Even as they awoke and began to retaliate, the level of proficiency of Soviet soldiers in the early stages of the campaign remained the same throughout the entire war. Nevertheless, it was the Germans who initially prevailed. Thus, in spite of the Soviets' bitter, persistent defense and determination not to surrender to the barbaric invaders, the German army still managed to reach some fifty kilometers west of Moscow by the end of the summer.[14] The Red Army's defeat had apparently nothing to do with Stalin's morale boosters—remarks such as, "Cowards should be shot and POW's should be treated as deserters whose families should be arrested," a call that caused the Russian soldier to literally continue fighting until death. This was in addition to the false report that Russian commissars spread among the divisions fighting at the front: that the Germans would kill every POW who fell into their hands.

As for the Soviet air force, Colonel Pyotr Grigorenko, a highly respected Red Army officer, claimed the reason Soviet foreign minister Vyacheslav Molotov, standing in for Stalin, who was in a state of shock in the first few days of the invasion, did not mention Soviet air activity in his speech to the nation, had to do with the fact that the Germans had destroyed the entire air force: "Molotov did not comment about it because there was already nothing much to say."[15]

Another point in favor of the Germans was the collapse of the command system, including the control and communications systems. In his memoirs, Zhukov admits that communications were the Achilles' heel of the Red Army and that serious defects had appeared early on in the networks. When they were severed by the Germans, it was very hard to control the units.[16]

The British were more careful than the Germans in their assessments regarding the outcome of the war; nevertheless, during these days, it was said in Whitehall that the Germans would cut through Russia like a warm knife through butter. Although the pessimists estimated that Hitler would become master of Russia within six weeks, the optimists among the British gave him three months to accomplish his task. It was not surprising, then, that Lord Beaverbrook, a member of the British war cabinet to whom Soviet ambassador to Britain, Ivan Maisky, first appealed for aid in the hope that he would show more empathy than foreign minister Anthony Eden and Churchill, asked Maisky, "Are you really going to fight? Are you sure that what happened in France won't happen in Russia?"[17]

Churchill himself wrote that Russia's entry into the war was blessed by the British; nevertheless, this did not really help Britain in 1941, nor in the year after the invasion. The German armies, he wrote, were so strong that it almost seemed they would continue to threaten the British Isles for many months to come while simultaneously continuing to penetrate deeper and deeper into Soviet territory. The opinion among the high-ranking military in Britain was that the Russian armies would quickly be defeated and liquidated. Churchill summarized it well:

> In spite of heroic resistance, competent despotic war direction, total disregard of human life, and the opening of ruthless guerilla warfare in the rear of the German advance, a general retirement took place on the whole twelve hundred–mile Russian front south of Leningrad for about four or five hundred miles. The strength of the Soviet Government, the fortitude of the Russian people, their immeasurable reserves of man-power, the vast size of their country, the rigours of the Russian winter, were the factors which ultimately ruined Hitler's armies. But none of these made themselves apparent in 1941.[18]

German Strategy and Logistics

Germany's timetable for crushing the Russian colossus—a rapid blitz campaign of up to ten weeks—relied on Hitler's and the German generals' underestimating the strength and spirit of the Red Army. Hitler believed the campaign would continue for no more than a few weeks, mainly because of the German army's superiority over the inferior Soviet forces that made up the ranks of the Red Army, but also because another revolution would break out in Russia and bring down the Soviet Union from within. Several comments seem to indicate the disregard and misconception of German evaluations of the enemy. One is Hitler's remark to General Alfred Jodl, chief of the Wehrmacht Operations Division: "All we should do is kick the door and the whole rotten structure will collapse into fragments."[19] Another is a famous entry in General Franz Halder's diary dated July 3, 1941: "On the whole, then, it may be said even now that the objective to shatter the bulk of the Russian army this side of the Dvina and Dnieper has been accomplished. . . . It is thus probably no overstatement to say that the Russian Campaign has been won in the space of two weeks."[20] Yet another is Hitler's declaration from July 4, 1941, to Jodl and Walther von Brauchitsch: "Practically speaking, he—the Russian—has already lost the war."[21]

Halder's remark in particular is worth discussing. It indicates contempt for Russian strength, and it provides evidence for the fact that in the early stages of the operation, the picture portrayed to Hitler as the sole decision maker was that there was a reasonable possibility of overcoming the Soviets. This assessment was based on reports from German generals, including well-substantiated professional evaluations and desires that had no connection to reality. In one of his conversations with Heinz Guderian in July 1941, the Führer noted that had he listened to the former's briefings from the end of the 1930s regarding the existence of some 10,000 Soviet tanks, he would not have attacked Russia in the first place[22]; against this force, Hitler assembled only 4,000 German Panzers.[23]

A deficiency in the Germans' planning of the operation became evident during the campaign itself, and in October, it was clear that the odds in favor of Germany for a successful end to the war were slim. The lack of manpower and raw materials, coupled with the limits of the German armaments industry, would not allow a sequel to the campaign in Russia as it was run until July 1941.[24] In addition, stubborn Soviet resistance had caused the halt at Smolensk and curbed the Germans for the first time during World War II.[25] In any event, the question as to whether Hitler's and the generals' assessments were wrong does not change the fact that until December 1941, the Wehrmacht was fighting with great success against the Red Army.

With the exception of 4th Army commander general Günther von Kluge, consensus briefly existed among the German generals in July–August 1941 regarding the aims and next objectives. General Jodl and Major General Walter Warlimont, together with General Wilhelm Keitel, remained loyal to Hitler until the end of the war, while von Brauchitsch, Halder, Fedor von Bock, Guderian, and Hermann Hoth all held the view that the next step should be conquering Moscow, and most importantly, that it was feasible in the summer of 1941. Their line of thought was based on that of military theorist Carl Y. P. von Clausewitz: they would concentrate on annihilating the enemy's forces, which in this particular case were around the outskirts of Moscow—in other words, the major portion of the Red Army.[26] However, was this possible in terms of logistics, time frame, and German morale? Moreover, would such a move eventually bring a German victory?

By examining the months of June until September, it is clear that despite the logistical failures resulting from the harsh winter, the turning point of Operation Barbarossa had more to do with operational objectives. Guderian's offensive on Roslavl is probably one of the best examples. When Basil Liddell Hart interviewed General Günther Blumentritt, commander of the 4th Army in von Runstedt's Army Group South, after the war, Blumentritt revealed that Guderian's view was to move forward as fast as possible and leave the encirclement of the enemy to infantry forces that would follow the Panzers. Guderian emphasized the importance of a rapid advance toward the capital while pushing back the Russians without allowing them to redeploy.[27]

Without considering Hitler's reaction and his hesitance; in the hope that he would change his mind when he recognized a realistic opportunity and give the green light to attack Moscow; and with von Bock's support, Guderian launched a short eight-day campaign against Roslavl on August 1. In one of the best and swiftest victories the Wehrmacht had seen in the East, the Germans gained full control of the entire southern part of the Army Group Center sector. This provided an opportunity to move forward toward Moscow until about August 18. During this battle, 38,000 Russian soldiers were taken prisoner and 250 tanks were captured. The battle of Roslavl can serve as evidence of the logistical and military capabilities the Germans still had in the first half of August while they were moving toward Moscow.[28] It was thus possible to transfer supplies to the front lines. From a morale perspective (according to Guderian's description of his soldiers in his particular Panzer division), it seems that everyone was prepared for a final showdown.[29]

On September 4, a meeting was held at Army Group Center headquarters in Novi Borisov, whose purpose was to report to Hitler for the first time about the forces' advance directly from the officers in the battlefield. Present at the meeting were Hitler; his chief military adjutant, Rudolf Schmundt; generals von Bock, Hoth, and Guderian; and High Command delegate Colonel Adolf Heusinger, chief of the Operations Division. One by one, they were interrogated by the commander of the Army Group and both of his deputies, who were commanders of the Panzer groups. Once again, the same arguments came up regarding the next objectives of the operation. However, this time Guderian (who had just won the battle of Roslavl), out of sincere concern and undoubtedly with the intention of thwarting the program according to which the Panzers would be turned to outflank and encircle the enemy in the south, described the condition of German machinery and warned that if more major operations were planned for the next year, a significant number of Panzers should be replaced because 70 percent of them needed new engines.[30]

Logistical capabilities were problematic as early as summer 1941, without connection to logistical problems related to winter. Guderian's assumptions regarding the logistical capabilities of the Wehrmacht of reaching Moscow were relevant for August. When he saw that the intention was to move with the same tanks to the flanks and only afterward to move toward Moscow, he warned that the condition of the Panzers would not allow an attack on such a scale. Thus, logistical capabilities after August 1941 were already based on transportation and renewed supplies from the Reich, not just on forces and tanks that were already within the Soviet Union.

The resemblance between what happened in 1941 and the Napoleonic campaign of 1812 seems to underline the axiom that Russia's border is invulnerable to any assault that comes from the West. Hitler's approach, therefore, conformed to the theory of Antoine-Henri Jomini,

Napoleon's military philosopher, a contemporary of von Clausewitz, although Jomini developed his military theories before him. The aggressor, according to Jomini, can break through the enemy line or, if the enemy is divided into several parts, penetrate them. In the case of Operation Barbarossa, the Germans indeed penetrated the Minsk area and advanced up to Smolensk while most of the Russian army was concentrated on the same line in the Moscow area. The issue of flanks—Kiev in the south and Leningrad in the north—is also part of this theory, while the aggressor—in this case the Germans—was concentrated in a central position around Smolensk and was operating along inner lines against a divided enemy, which functioned along several external lines. As a result, the aggressor could defeat each and every part of the enemy army separately. Jomini developed the concept of the "center position and inner lines" as one of most important lessons from his studies on the Seven Years' War, verified in Napoleonic strategy.[31] This strategy failed twice in Russia, first in 1812 and again in 1941. However, some generals had rather different blueprints for Hitler's campaign in Russia. One of them was General Erich Marks, who was an influential and respected officer in the German High Command before Hitler took over. Marks died in 1944 as commander of a corps on the Western Front. The plan that carried his name was no more than an operational study conducted in the High Command. Nevertheless, it served as a blueprint for the generals of the old school serving in the Wehrmacht, such as Gerd von Rundstedt and von Bock—army group commanders of the center and southern part of the front.

Marks's plan was divided into three stages. The first consisted of a strategic defense alignment along the relatively short Baltic line between Riga and the Pripet marshes, and an assault using all forces to the south of the marshes in Rostov, on the lower part of the Don River. The second phase would consist of an attack on Moscow from south to north, and finally an assault toward the west on enemy forces in the hinterland. The latter would be concentrated in accordance with the Baltic states Pripet marshes plan. This transformed it into a huge Cannae battle, when during the Second Punic War between Carthage and Rome, a Roman army that numbered close to 90,000 soldiers and cavalry was defeated by Hannibal's army of 35,000 troops and 10,000 cavalry—or half the Roman army.

It was not easy to maintain a 900-kilometer-long defense line that connected the Dnieper and the Don rivers, but it could serve the Wehrmacht by giving it both tactical and technological superiority. If this was the plan for Barbarossa, the enemy would turn all its forces in the south against the assault and thus weaken its own line of attack in the northwestern part of the sector, leaving the German forces in a strategically defensive position. A German assault on Moscow from the south was probably easier for the Reich army because of the terrain. The assault launched by Guderian's 2nd Panzer Army at the end of autumn 1941, conquering more territory than any other operation, notwithstanding the quantitative disadvantage and relatively low number of operational tanks, is an example of the opportunities that existed.[32]

In spite of his alleged objection to the invasion plan of the Soviet Union, Guderian participated in the strategic debates for Barbarossa in spring 1941 while believing that the correct strategy for approaching the campaign was to target the Russian capital and thus neutralize the Soviet colossus.[33] Finally, in mid-September, when Hitler gave the order to renew the advance toward Moscow, the 2nd Panzer Army, like the other forces of Army Group Center, were already exhausted and lacking supplies. Some responsible voices like von Bock asked for a temporary halt in the advance during autumn and winter. They also claimed that the German army in the East had to move into defensive positions until spring 1942, when it would be possible to move forward again to Moscow. Guderian, who was not among that group of generals, omitted to note in his memoirs that it was primarily he who urged Hitler to make a final gamble to take Moscow before the winter and that he was the one who convinced Hitler to renew the attack.[34]

Although the amount of forces the Germans used during the 1941 Balkan campaign was small in relation to Barbarossa, the number of tanks was large. Most of the tanks in von Kleist's 1st Panzer Army, under the command of von Rundstedt's Army Group South, participated in the Balkan campaign, and when Operation Barbarossa began, there were only 600 tanks in it. Most had driven all the way from the Peloponnesus without undergoing any repairs. At the front, facing von Kleist were some 2,400 tanks, a ratio of 1:4 in favor of the Russians, making the German success a result of superiority in quality of forces and skill.[35]

On July 23, Walther von Brauchitsch and Halder presented Hitler with figures regarding the concentration of Soviet divisions at the front and their personal opinion on further objectives. Halder claimed that the goal was to eliminate the possibility of future Soviet rearmament by the destruction of weapons and ammunition factories that were also located around Moscow. Looking at the Soviet force formations at the end of July, Halder assessed that the German soldiers could reach Moscow and Leningrad, as well as the line between the Urals and the Crimean peninsula, on about August 25. Accordingly, it was possible to reach the Volga by the beginning of October, and Baku and Batum at the beginning of November.[36]

Just by examining the deployment of forces, Hitler's decision appears tactically odd. In mid-July, after conquering Smolensk, they found fifty Russian formations confronting Army Group South with its own fifty divisions. Twenty-three enemy formations faced twenty-six divisions belonging to Army Group North, and opposing Army Group Center's sixty divisions were about seventy Russian ones. In other words, the largest concentration of enemy forces was deployed along the central sector, so transferring forces elsewhere from that part of the front seems unreasonable.[37] Halder confirmed this in his diary on July 16, when he wrote that the meaning of such a plan was "removal of strategy from the operational level to the tactical level." He claimed that if the operation's objective turned out to be a series of assaults on small and local enemy formations, the front would expand and the German army would advance eastward only several more meters. Therefore, even if they managed to encircle Russian forces, all these achievements would be negligible.[38]

Impact of the Jewish Transports

Thus, in total, the Germans managed to deport in the action that took place from October until December 1941 some 48,000 people from the territories belonging to the Reich all the way to the Eastern Front. A more detailed examination reveals that on the basis of 1,000 people compressed into one train in each of these transports, the Germans used for this task some forty-eight trains, each consisting of ten to twenty cars. Alternatively, it would have been possible to transfer on the same trains, based on the same numbers, 3,300–6,700 horses—a sufficiently large quantity to serve one or two infantry divisions.

In order to make sense of the supply situation, it is important to concretize the figures. The daily schedule was based on 122 trains, divided across the Soviet front's three sectors: thirty-five trains to the northern sector, fifty-two to the central sector, and thirty-five to the southern sector. Apart from trains used for transporting troops, another three trains were available for the northern sector, another six for the central sector, and another four for the southern sector. In practice, however, Army Group Center sought to receive no more than twenty-four trains.[39] Nonetheless, von Bock claims that his army group received no more than fourteen daily.

However, in order to transfer new reserve forces, at least one more train was needed in the north, two in the center, and another in the south. In other words, all that was required was another four trains in order to transfer 3,000 troops daily, or 90,000 a month. Thus, the transfer of 320,000 reserve soldiers was a task that could be achieved in a period of three and a half months. Narrowing this down even further, each train carried 750 soldiers with full gear.[40] Therefore, 1,000 Jews per train and 50,000 of the Reich's Jews transported to the Soviet territories were more than half of the monthly quantity of reserve forces that should have reached the front. It was not surprising, then, that Wehrmacht chiefs called to halt the deportations immediately.

On December 9, it was revealed that about 1,000 men belonging to the 3rd Panzer Group were being held up at Vitebsk, near the prewar Latvian border, while their commanders complained that they were short of combat troops.[41] As a result, von Bock gave strict orders that every man who could bear firearms be sent to the front the following day. All that was needed was a single train to transfer those troops to the line facing Moscow. On the other hand, on the same day, December 9, a train packed with 1,000 Jews left the city of Kassel in Germany for Riga, and the day before, another train had departed Cologne, also for Riga. Apparently, because of von Bock's request on December 10, a train with combat troops was sent to the front, and indeed, on that day there were no Jewish transports from the Reich. However, on December 11, another transport from Düsseldorf was sent to the Riga district.[42]

Ultimately, each train that did not carry combat forces or supplies to the front was at the expense of available reserve troops, speed of action, and quality of combat. Combining these parameters was a setback for the struggling German army as it tried to gain another military victory. Logistically, it was possible to supply the German soldiers with winter clothing, boots, skis, and other winter equipment, which at this point of the war in the Soviet Union the Russian soldiers still possessed. If it was possible logistically during November and December to move thousands of Jews from Germany to Riga and Kovno at the height of the confrontation with the Russians and to meticulously organize an execution system by using the Einsatzgruppen companies, then it was certainly possible to equip the troops with supplies for winter warfare. Thus, the order of priorities and the fact that the war effort was not focused entirely on operational and logistical issues so necessary for a successful campaign seem odd if the ideological aspect is not also considered to be a prime factor in the entire military aspect.

On November 18, 1941, Joseph Goebbels referred to the issue of winter supplies for the front. He claimed it was known to him that essential winter clothing for the troops at the front had been organized in advance in the summer, and indeed, by August 18, more than ten million reichsmarks had been raised from the German people through donations. This sum also included payment to the Reichsbahn for every train used for military purposes. Thus, every train the Wehrmacht used entailed payment to the rail company.[43]

As for the Jews or any other population using the trains, in general, the Reichsbahn was prepared to transport Jews as long as the transport ministry was paying. The invoice was simply handed to anyone who ordered the train service (Eichmann in this case) and was calculated according to the number of "passengers" and the destination. As a basis for payment, a third-class tariff of four pfennigs per kilometer per person was set, while children under the age of four traveled free of charge. Later the transport ministry added a communal rate of half price on the condition that there were at least 400 people per train. The minimum payment was set for 200 reichsmarks, and there was a penalty for returning the car empty.[44] Ironically, the SS collected money from the Jews shoved onto the trains because somebody had to pay the bill for these transports. After registering them for the deportation transports, the Jews were left with fifty reichsmarks for paying for the train ride east, the sum demanded by the Gestapo to be exchanged for Reich credit notes that circulated in the Reichskommissariat Ostland. However, in practice, the money taken from the deportees was given to the head of transportation, who handed it to the local security police representative at the destination point. Therefore, each transport of 1,000 Jews made a sum of 50,000 reichsmarks—more than enough to pay the Reichsbahn for the journey.[45] On the Stuttgart train leaving for Riga, the deportees were asked to pay an extra 7.65 reichsmarks for food and drink. But the most profitable transports came from Cologne, where the deportees had to produce 100 reichsmarks for the train ride to the East.[46]

The appeal from Goebbels in mid-November to the German people for donations in order to supply the troops at the Russian front with winter clothing shocked officers at the front lines, because even if everything worked out according to plan and the Wehrmacht marched into Moscow, there still was need for warm clothing for the occupying forces.[47] Goebbels commented,

> The equipment is stored at train stations and ready for distribution to the forces. Up to a certain point, such distribution was indeed done. Right now there is a certain unavoidable delay because of transportation conditions . . . therefore it is advisable not to reflect on the winter equipment issue in order that the public's trust in the German information system not go through turmoil. One should be careful not to display in public pictures Soviet POWs wearing winter coats while being led by their captors—German soldiers without winter coats.[48]

Significantly, at this point in November, Jewish transports were already arriving from Germany. This, then, is a clear example of the odd list of priorities made in favor of ideology instead of supplies for the troops. Moreover, if already in August so much money was being raised for winter equipment, it might be concluded that the Russian winter did not catch the Germans ill-prepared or off-guard, and indeed that it was only logistical problems that eventually caused the tide to turn.

Even for the Germans, the difficulties of winter could be dealt with because they were known to be a part of life in the Russian steppes. However, the "Jewish problem" had an answer—a solution by definition of the term "problem." The Jewish problem was something that could be resolved by immigration, by deporting the Jewish communities to the East, or by the ultimate solution: extermination. An alternative was to send German Jews to the East in spring 1942 after conquering Moscow—a solution that would not pose an additional logistical burden on Germany.

In mid-July, when von Bock reported that his chances of capturing Moscow in a swift assault were good, the Soviets had no tanks at their disposal to defend the Yartsevo–Vyazma–Moscow passage, while their divisions consisted of an average of 6,000 men each. At the time, no more than 50,000 Soviet soldiers were defending the city—almost the number of Jews from the Reich and the protectorates deported to the occupied territories. In October, the situation changed dramatically: facing von Bock's army group were 800,000 Soviet soldiers and 770 tanks, or half of the entire Soviet army in the western sector. In addition, three defense lines that were not present in August were now formed around the capital. Regardless of the change in balance, Operation Typhoon should be regarded as a success because it managed to strike this huge Soviet deployment until mid-November. After 700,000 losses, the Russians remained with only 90,000 men defending Moscow.[49]

Could the logistical situation in which the Germans found themselves have enabled Army Group Center to advance toward Moscow in any event at the end of August 1941? No. The absence of a strategic supply base did not permit an attack on Moscow even if Hitler had decided in late August not to divide the forces and continue with a linear offensive across the entire Soviet front. The proponents of this argument claim that Operation Typhoon had problems with the fuel supply to the seventy divisions concentrated at the front. There were few paved roads, and the limited railway network would not be sufficient for such a military force to receive adequate supplies. Accordingly, supplies for a force twice as big in late August were clearly impossible.[50] The mud of the *Rasputitza* season was not the reason the Germans did not enter Moscow; the transportation crisis was. During October, it very hard to transfer supplies, including fuel, which was in extremely short supply, to the front via rail. Only in November 1941 did the army receive priority for anything connected to the train system.[51]

It was clear from the outset that a deportation effort involving mass populations on such a large scale would create an unprecedented challenge. Moreover, the German advance was not moving forward as anticipated—a fact that did not prevent Hitler from insisting that the Jews be deported from the territory of Germany without further delay.[52] General von Bock pointed explicitly to the lack of carriages and locomotives as the reason for the winter crisis in 1941, as well as the muddy terrain and stubborn Soviet resistance. The Minsk route, which was supposed to bring supplies to his army group, was the same route that until November operated smoothly, carrying Jewish transports from Germany to the East with no special difficulties. Indeed, when the trains reached Minsk, officers of all ranks at Army Group Center, including von Bock himself, protested strongly that trains to the occupied Soviet territory were wasted on transporting Jews and demanded that the railways serve the army alone in order to fulfill its combat needs.[53]

The 1st Panzer Army's headquarters, under General von Kleist's command, were in a forest to the east of Zamosch, southeast of Lublin. Army Group South headquarters, under the command of General von Rundstedt, were at Bochnia, to the east of Krakov. Therefore, the train supply lines for the German divisions, including the remaining armored ones, were the same ones used by the SS for Jewish transports to the East. The problem of refreshing and relieving forces was primarily a supply one—and one already known to the planners even before the blitz in the West began.[54] The military supply center built in the area around Warsaw and Suwalkic is a good example of the extent to which these routes served two operational systems. The supply center established small bases in order to shorten the lines to the front and included fuel and food storage, spare parts, field hospitals, workshops, and garages for repairing weapons and vehicles.[55] With a supply center in the Warsaw area, there is no doubt that between October and December the same trains that were supposed to transfer supplies to the front brought the Reich's Jews to the newly occupied territories of the Soviet Union.

During operations in Russia, it was quickly revealed that the distance between the German front lines and the supply bases in Germany had become so great that if it was possible to transfer supplies by train, it would turn out to be an expensive business economically; therefore, the rail net had to be exploited to the greatest extent possible. A few train lines were available in East Prussia that could carry supplies for the army. However, all the supplies for Army Group North and apparently also for Army Group Center had to move along the double track going through Konigsberg–Walenstein and all the way to Riga. This line carried the lion's share of shipments, as well as regular passenger traffic from Riga to the port city of Tallinn. Train lines in the Soviet Union had a capacity of between three to six trains per day in each direction. In other words, no more than six trains brought supplies to the troops every day. The 18th Army, for example, received its supplies from the Riga line.[56] If one considers that between November 27 and December 15, 1941, eleven Jewish transports from the Reich traveled the same line, sometimes one transport comprised one-third of the supply of an entire army, or a minimum of one train out of six supply trains per day. Thus, the effect in such a case was destructive.

The question that arises, therefore, is why, precisely, when the Wehrmacht received priority over the SS in everything connected to the train system, the transports from the Reich and protectorates began. The answer lies in the fact that in November the odds to win the campaign in 1941 already seemed unrealistic. Dark clouds hinting that the war was going to be a long one, like those that began to loom in 1914 and that Hitler remembered so well, were in the air. In this context, transport of the Reich's Jews to the Soviet Union could be seen as a short-term, although essential, attempt to find a temporary solution for the Jews of the Reich. The fact is that until October, no transports were sent to the East, apparently because of an awareness that it would interfere with the army's logistics. At this point, the outcome of the war was unpredictable even to Hitler, although it cannot be said that he lost his will to fight. It should be assumed that ridding the Reich of Jews was an attempt to achieve an objective, even if only partially: to cleanse the Reich of all elements that burdened the purity of race. Clearly, these deportations ended relatively quickly, although in November and December it was already obvious that the entire population of European Jewry was intended for extermination. A homicidal process that began in the East and moved slowly westward, with all the camps dealing with the extermination of the Jews of Europe concentrated within the territories of the General Government, marked the beginning of the Final Solution to the Jewish problem.

Regarding the war in the Soviet Union, it seems that even Goebbels was impressed by the way Hitler managed to pull all the strings together. On December 17, just before a meeting with Reichsführer-SS Himmler the next morning and one day before the departure of the last transport from Hannover before their resumption on January 9, 1942, the Führer raised the Jewish issue again before his minister of propaganda, and together they discussed the deportation of Jews from the Reich to the territories in the East. That evening, Goebbels wrote in his diary that "he was encouraged by the fact that in spite of the heavy military burden that was inflicted upon the Führer's shoulders at that moment, he still found time to deal with these issues and has a strong opinion about them."[57] It is not surprising that Goebbels described matters in that manner, when only a day before, on December 16, General von Bock had asked permission to withdraw his forces and redeploy them after the Soviet counterattack. That same night, von Brauchitsch and Halder also tried to convince Hitler that a withdrawal at this point was essential in order to prevent disaster. Thus, on December 18, Hitler relieved von Brauchitsch from his position as commander of the armed forces, taking over the high command himself.[58] That same day, Hitler met with Himmler, and in a document in a secret archive in Moscow bearing the date December 18, he gave an order concerning the Jewish question: "They [the Jews] should be exterminated as partisans." At this stage, the term *partisans* no longer referred to the Jews in Soviet territory who for the past six months were being murdered by the Einsatzgruppen, but to the Jews from the German Reich.[59]

Strong protests from the officers of the Wehrmacht received concrete expression only on November 20, when Major General Walther Brehmer informed Hinrich Lohse, Reich commissioner of the Baltic states and Belorussia, that the forces of Army Group Center had ordered the cessation of all deportation actions immediately because the railways and all other transportation vehicles were to be put at the army's disposal for transferring supplies to the front. Only in late November did the army receive priority over the SS in all that concerned trains, but in spite of Brehmer's objection, the deportations to Minsk and Riga continued. Eventually the SS gave in and agreed to halt the deportations in mid-December.[60] Einsatzgruppe B, which operated in Belorussia, was forced to admit that the execution of Jews in Belorussia was hampered by more than a few logistical problems. After the killing of Belorussian Jews on November 20, the harsh winter conditions made the ground too hard for digging pits to bury the victims—a fact that helped most of the German Jews deported to the Russian territory survive until mid-1942. This was another reason for turning to extermination by gas in the death camps in the territory of the General Government.[61]

The deportations continued until December 18, 1941, when the last transport departed Hannover for Riga. The deportations to Riga, Kovno, and Minsk stopped, but not necessarily because of the army's protests.[62] There was a general freeze on transports imposed on account of the use of holiday trains for the Wehrmacht during the Christmas period,[63] but in addition, the beginning of December saw the first of the extermination camps operating with gassing facilities—systematic mass killings at the village of Chełmno in Poland.[64] The Jewish transports to the Soviet territories were therefore unnecessary, regardless of logistical problems.[65] By chance, this moment in the history of the Holocaust coincided with global events. On the same day, December 8, just after the Japanese attacked Pearl Harbor, Ribbentrop sent a draft for the tripartite declaration of war on the United States to Foreign Minister Tōgō.[66] The beginning of the war with the Americans turned the conflict into a world war. It marked a physiological moment in the history of the war that caused the Nazi regime to rethink its deepest objectives. It also meant a prolonged struggle for the survival of the Third Reich. The vicious extermination of the Jews was rationalized as a requirement of that struggle.[67]

On December 1, von Bock admitted that if the intentions of the High Command were for his army group to ride out the winter on the defensive, it was essential for his forces to recuperate. For that purpose, he needed twelve new divisions on the condition that order and dependability in running the trains would be restored, together with well-regulated stockpiling and supply. The entire operation of moving the Jews, as well as accessories from the various SS departments, to the East came to a total of seventy-five trains, or thirteen or fourteen divisions, and von Bock had at his disposal only one weak division.[68] The Reichsbahn operated some 20,000 trains daily; one could claim that the Jewish transports were a drop in the ocean. However, this number refers to the continental military and civilian disposition covering the entire train layout of occupied Europe and the German Reich.[69]

It should be recalled that Army Group Center received all its needs from a rail company that controlled a fleet of only 261 locomotives and 1,599 cars.[70] Therefore, Army Group Center could receive supplies from just 261 trains—or actually half of that, 130 trains per day, because each train moved in two directions, from the Reich or the General Government to the East and back. If one considers that they were not serving the needs of Army Group Center alone but also civilian needs, the forty-eight trains used for ideological actions related to the Jews comprised a large percentage of the logistical burden of the army group that had conducted the most significant battle of the war until then.

Two hundred years before, Benjamin Franklin had coined an axiom that is relevant to this day, and certainly for the Wehrmacht fighting on the Eastern Front: "For want of a nail, the shoe was lost, for want of a shoe, the horse was lost, for want of a horse the rider was lost, for want of a rider the battle was lost."[71] The Final Solution could be termed the nail.

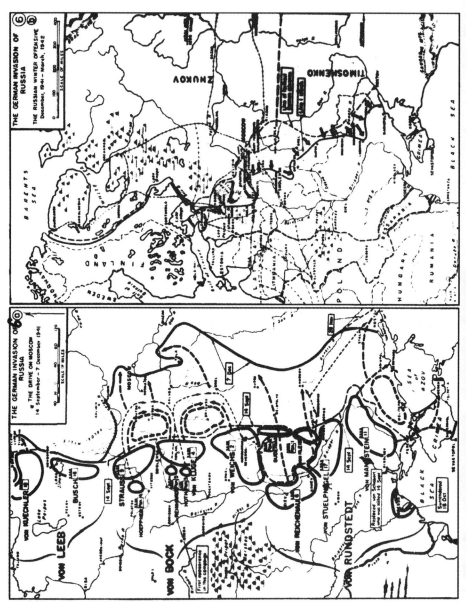

Deployment of the German Army groups during the advance towards
Moscow and the Russian winter offensive. September 1941–March 1942.
(Courtesy of Liddell Hart Centre for Military Archives, ref: von Manstein 9).

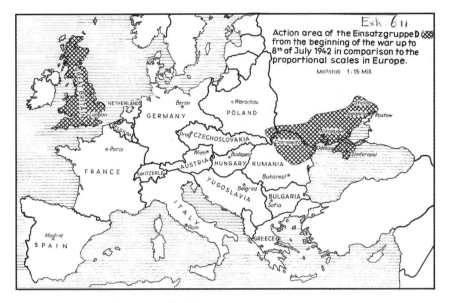

Action Area of Einsatzgruppe D under command of Otto Ohlendorf. It took a total of more than 53,000 men to support the actual killing squads, equivalent to ten Wehrmacht divisions. (Courtesy of Liddell Hart Centre for Military Archives, ref: von Manstein 6/12)

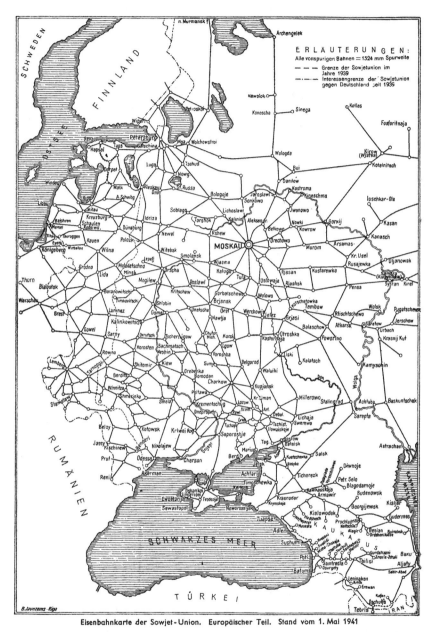

Eisenbahnkarte der Sowjet-Union. Europäischer Teil. Stand vom 1. Mai 1941

Railway Map of the Soviet Union's European Part, May 1941. (Courtesy of Bundesarchiv-Militärarchiv/Freiburg, RH4/725)

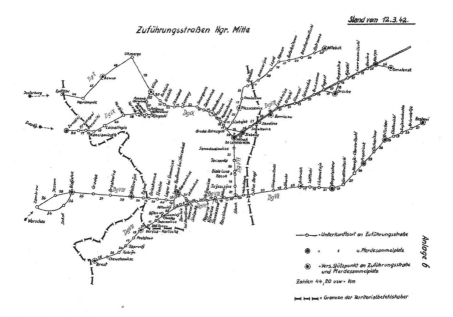

German Army Group Center advance routes and bases as of December 3, 1942. (Courtesy of Bundesarchiv-Militärarchiv/Freiburg, N119/13)

Part 2

Operation Reinhard and the
Downfall at Stalingrad

The 6th Army suffered logistical problems during the campaign at Stalingrad until their encirclement by Soviet forces in November 1942. These hardships resulted from the misuse of resources and the effort that the Germans invested in Operation Reinhard, which consisted of the establishment of three new death camps, Belzec, Sobibor, and Treblinka, and which concentrated mostly on the annihilation of Jews living within the borders of the General Government. The process that the German army underwent during this period, from the invasion of the Soviet Union until the downfall at Stalingrad, demonstrates the burden a large-scale operation such as the Final Solution had on military logistics.

The campaign at Stalingrad ought not be interpreted as a "turning of the tide" or "the beginning of the end," two phrases often attributed to the Stalingrad campaign—but unjustly, because of the battle of Kharkov that followed immediately after General Paulus's capitulation. Seldom during the war was the turmoil as dramatic as during the last two weeks of February and the first two weeks of March 1943. After Stalingrad, the German army managed to perform a miraculous recovery, proving their superiority over its enemy on every tactical level. In a series of swift armored blows from south of the Donets area, the two Panzer armies of Army Group South smashed into the Soviet spearheads, retaking Kharkov and Belgorod, following a pincer movement of General Hermann Hoth's tanks and SS tanks to the south of Kharkov. The Tiger tank, with its 88mm gun, with which the Waffen-SS units Das Reich and Gross Deutschland were already armed, brought the hegemony of the Russian T-34 to its end. Because the Germans were short of infantry soldiers, the pocket created could not be sealed, and many Russian troops simply abandoned their gear and crossed the frozen Dnieper by foot or on horseback. The Germans claimed they counted some 23,000 losses for the enemy and captured 615 tanks, 354 guns, and 9,000 Soviet POWs.[1] Germany was comparable to a man holding a hungry wolf by its ears with no possibility of releasing it.

Even at the beginning of the cold war, some claims were heard that differed completely from the official Soviet version. Vladislav Anders, a Polish general who fought the Germans alongside the Allies and who represented the anti-Soviet approach, wrote his account of the war in Russia during a period when no one in the West dealt with it, and he was therefore the first to raise doubts about the abilities of the Russian colossus. In contrast to the version the Russian leadership tried to establish—that the victory over Germany was due exclusively to the impressive abilities of the Red Army and the Soviet system—Anders held that the Russian victory was primarily thanks to the military supplies that their allies, the Americans and the British, pumped into the campaign. True, the Soviet economy did not crumble during the war and resources were poured into the military effort, but at the same time, there was a shortage of basic commodities, which caused famine and death. Anders noted that the German army was capable of felling its greatest rival under two conditions. The first was that the Wehrmacht would fight without Hitler interfering with the normal conduct of the war and without his making any strategic decisions; the other was that the USSR fight the war on its own, without the help of its Western allies.[2]

In general, Western historians who wrote about the war tended to adopt the basic Soviet approach, while pointing out additional elements that influenced the German downfall, such as fighting on two fronts and failing to estimate Soviet strength and power. Western historians began examining the Soviet Union's part in the war only during the Brezhnev era, but even the monumental works of Earl Ziemke and John Erickson focus mainly on military operations.

Western historians do not deal with transportation and logistics—and certainly not with the murder of Jews and Communist commissars in the Soviet territories occupied by the Nazis, a lacuna that exists also in Manfred Kehrig's comprehensive research on Stalingrad. Kehrig, a West German historian, describes in detail the campaign at Stalingrad from a tactical point of view. However, like Ziemke and Erickson, he does not mention the extensive resources invested parallel to that campaign in the Final Solution.[3] In his examination of the war, Mark Harrison, a contemporary Western historian, representing a more up-to-date approach on the post-Communist age in Russia, raised a logistic-economic element that was not present in any discourse during the regimes of Stalin's heirs. Harrison claims there was no economic program and that the Russians were counting on help from the Allies much more than Soviet historians were prepared to admit; still, this does not undermine the great Russian military-economic achievement. Ultimately, Harrison claims that the Axis powers were forced to a showdown because of the Allies' superiority in economic resources, which translated to a definite numerical advantage over the military power Stalin's regime supplied.[4]

Western historians have emphasized more than once the illpreparedness of the Wehrmacht in the Soviet Union. According to them, no resources were allocated for the war and no concrete objectives defined. Hence, they conclude, lack of preparation for the war was the main element that brought about operational failure. On the basis of these assumptions, a German victory on the Eastern Front was beyond the Wehrmacht's ability in the first place. The German invasion of the Soviet Union in the summer of 1941 was Hitler's biggest blunder of the war, and the formation of the Grand Alliance left no room for doubt regarding the final outcome.[5]

5

The Wehrmacht and the SS
Operating on Parallel Lines

To understand the personnel and cooperation between SS officials and Wehrmacht leaders, it is important to understand the profiles of the decision makers who found themselves in the midst of the turmoil of the Battle at Stalingrad and who at the same time were aware of activities that would stain their military careers; for these, they would have to provide excuses until the end of their days. The year 1942 was a juncture for the personnel conducting the war against the Soviets and those conducting the war against the Jews in Europe. Many high-ranking officials were replaced—an action that would set the stage for the events to come. The Wehrmacht took part in exterminating Jews in the Soviet Union; further, a significant number of army units participated in the murderous activity of the Einsatzgruppen against Jewish Bolshevists, partisans, and the inhabitants of surrounding towns and villages to help the SS carry out its tasks.[1] It would be unreasonable to assume that the Einsatzgruppen units, which amounted to a mere 3,000 men, could have undertaken this job alone; they had to have had considerable assistance from regular German armed forces. From the outset, the army cooperated much more with the security police and the Sicherheitsdienst (security service) in the extermination of Jews than even the agreements between Reinhard Heydrich and army quartermaster, Eduard Wagner, had allowed for.[2] When Jewish transports were involved in the logistics of the Reichsbahn, there were complaints from the army—which only goes to show that there was definitely some knowledge of what was going on behind the front lines.

On July 19, 1941, Himmler allocated a full SS cavalry brigade to Erich von dem Bach Zelewski, the head of the SS Einsatzgruppe center, and on July 22, a full SS brigade was allocated to the southern command. A week later, an additional 11,640 SS men of the Ordnungspolizei and over 400 police officers who operated behind the Wehrmacht lines were assigned by the Reichsführer-SS as an additional supplement to the Einsatzgruppen units in the first weeks of Operation Barbarossa. In addition, there were eleven battalions of security police, each consisting of 500 men, who were initially part of the invading forces and which Himmler allocated to the three commanding officers of the security police in the north, center, and southern parts of Russia. This amounted to 5,500 to 6,000 extra troops.[3] By the end of 1941, the number of SS battalions was raised to twenty-six.

However, this was not the end of reinforcements. A few days later, toward the end of July, while visiting one of his brigades on the front, Himmler declared that he was about to set up a new police formation that would be based on the local population, namely Lithuanians, Latvians, Estonians, and Ukrainians. The local population had already participated in pogroms and even murder, but not in an organized way. At the end of 1941, the number of collaborators serving the Reich within the units Himmler had formed had reached 33,000 men.[4] Similarly, it was possible to recruit collaborators to take part in operations—if not fully, then at least for regional defense purposes or by replacing exhausted forces encircling the Soviet divisions. In total, by the end of 1941, over 65,000 men were dealing with occupation and mass execution activities in the Soviet Union, excluding Wehrmacht troops that also participated in the actual killings and encircled cities and villages in order to allow the Einsatzgruppen to carry out the *aktionen*. Additional companies of the Waffen-SS also operated as part of the invading forces (although not very successfully, as General Field Marshal Erich von Manstein testified); they participated in the killing operations that were becoming a fact on the Eastern Front, whether planned or not. It is on record that in July, parallel to the debates between Hitler and Walther von Brauchitsch, Franz Halder, Heinz Guderian, and von Manstein, Himmler recruited 25,000 men, including Waffen-SS troops that were under his command, for activities that had nothing to do with face-to-face combat with Red Army troops.[5]

Overall, some 160,000 Waffen-SS men were sent to the front to fight along with Wehrmacht troops, all under Reichsführer-SS Heinrich Himmler's command.

Over the years, however, there was a growing assumption, for which Liddell Hart was responsible as a result of his interviews with German generals, that they were all outstanding professionals unaware of what was happening at the rear of the front lines and, of course, had nothing to do with it. Von Manstein is a good example of such men, but eventually he too was tried in Hamburg for crimes against humanity. One obvious issue that arises from the documents relating to his trial is that von Manstein, the so-called tank genius and strategist, knew everything that was happening in the territories under his command, especially in the area of Simferopol in the Crimea.[6] When asked by psychiatrist Leon Goldensohn at Nuremberg whether he had heard of the Einsatzgruppen who operated under his jurisdiction, he said that Commandant SS Major General Otto Ohlendorf's Einsatzgruppe was in his district, and that he had heard of them for the first time as field marshal responsible for all operations in the district. Naturally, he said, he had heard that these commando units existed, but he was told that they were SS formations whose job was to maintain strict order:

> What they did I never knew, all I know is that they were active in other army group areas as well. Perhaps someone told me by coincidence that something not quite right happened around September when I just arrived, however, I was sent there as a military commander and most of my time was spent at the front. Never have I seen or heard of reliable testimony about these Einsatzkommando shooting Jews en masse. Such activities did not happen under my command and in reality I couldn't have done anything about them.[7]

The truth was, immediately behind the front, there was an area for combating partisans for which only the Wehrmacht was trained. The depths of these areas varied from thirty to fifty kilometers behind the front. The commander of the rear army territories was located beyond that area, and the Wehrmacht operated there too, as did the police authorities directly subordinate to the Wehrmacht. Then there was the real territory of the Reich commissioners, where a civilian administration was already established. Here the situation was reversed. The higher SS and police chiefs were responsible for fighting the partisan movements, and the Wehrmacht units that participated were subordinate to them. In the areas where the Wehrmacht had control, the Waffen-SS units became part of the Wehrmacht for the purpose of fighting partisan activities and were actually subsidiary to it.[8]

Antipartisan action included some six front line divisions that were moved to the rear in order to deal with the problem. Occasionally the Germans took a division from the front and replaced it with a new one. Cooperation with the offices of the Wehrmacht was sometimes so close that in the offices of the commanders of Einsatzgruppe A, which operated around Leningrad, discussions took place regularly with local commanders and other interested officers of the Wehrmacht on questions of local importance.[9] One of the most striking aspects of the war in the East was the delicate planning process run by Himmler to prepare the SS and the police forces for the campaign. To avoid clashes between the Wehrmacht and the SS during the Polish campaign, Hitler and his senior SS police chiefs drafted detailed policy guidelines and military orders outlining the duties and responsibilities of military and SS police battalions as early as spring 1941. On May 6, the Army High Command sent a letter to Himmler, Heydrich, and Kurt Daluege (chief of the Ordnungspolizei) calling a meeting between the SS and commanding officers of the military rear areas, as well as the army security divisions, presumably to discuss command relations, and the duties and responsibilities of the two branches in the next campaign. After final negotiations with the Wehrmacht on May 21, Himmler issued a top-secret decree entitled "Special Order from the Führer" describing the command relationship between the SS and the police forces and their military equivalents.[10] There is every reason to believe that the military commanders were well acquainted with the Jewish situation.

When in October 1941 the German High Command realized that the campaign against Russia would tax the strength of the Reich far beyond what was first contemplated, especially after it seemed certain that within a short period America would join in the war, a plan for mobilizing all inactive reserves of men and matériel was hastily drawn up by Fritz Todt, minister of armaments, and General Friedrich Fromm, commander in chief of the reserve army. Todt and Fromm differed on certain points, but both were convinced that because the war was not likely to end soon, it was necessary to preserve staying power and keep industrial potential unimpaired.

Albert Speer, who soon succeeded Todt and whose views at that time did not carry decisive weight, held a different opinion. Speer argued that Germany must win the war by the end of October, before the Russian winter set in, or the war would conclusively be lost. It was therefore necessary to reinforce the front by using men and matériel from the war industry.[11] Apprehensive about the immensity of Russia and the impact of new armies from the United States, Speer urged that the war be ended in the shortest possible time, lest not only Germany lose the war but the Nazi Party be swept out of existence. His view won the support of Hitler and the party. Speer drew up his own plan for bringing the war to a rapid closure. Todt rejected the plan, and for a brief time it was forgotten.[12]

In February 1942, when Todt's death was revealed,[13] Speer, a highly respected architect-engineer and the man responsible for repairing the railways in southern Russia, was personally appointed by Hitler to replace him. Hitler's choice of Speer only goes to show how Hitler was determined to make changes even in the war economy.[14] Speer was a young technocrat, only thirty-seven years old at the time, and willingly or not, he was dragged into involvement in the Final Solution—although he concealed this fact well all the way to Spandau prison, thus escaping the hangman.

Speer's appointment implied the adoption of his plan. He used the phrase coined by Rathenau in 1918 to explain a similar policy to meet a similar situation. The *lev'ee en masse*—mobilization of all available men and matériel—the term Speer used to describe what he intended should take place by the end of May, indicates that Nazi high officials were influenced by the military philosophy of Antoine-Henri Jomini rather than by Carl von Clausewitz. Speer saw that saving on transport was crucial for the war effort. He argued that booty taken from the Russian front should not be used immediately for steelmaking because it could not be transported to the blast furnaces in Germany; therefore, only scrap collected in Germany could be depended on, and here too it was transported by empty trucks or by waterways.[15] Although a network of committees dealing with specific transport questions was established, there was no central control of transport with ultimate authority over wagon loading. Measures such as loading trains efficiently to avoid intermediate remarshaling, or even a query such as, "Is this journey really necessary?," appeared relatively late in the war.[16]

In mid-July 1942, after a series of disputes between von Bock and the German High Command, the former was unsurprisingly replaced by General Field Marshal Maximilian von Weichs as commander of Army Group Center. This change was a result of a direct order from the Führer after von Bock deemed the forced advance of all available forces in the direction of Kamensk, demanded by the Army High Command, unfeasible because of the road conditions. The fact that the mobility of certain formations, such as the 24th Armored Division and the Gross Deutschland infantry division, which was at that time greatly reduced as a result of fuel shortages, confirmed von Bock's doubts about the success of the entire operation, which, in view of the enemy's withdrawal both east and south, he considered fundamentally mistaken in concept.[17]

The Führer's desire to turn the younger generation of officers into his willing tools was finally fulfilled when General Halder was relieved in autumn 1942 from his post as chief of staff of the High Command. He referred in his diary to the farewell meeting with Hitler as being extremely tense: "We must part," Halder said. The message he received from Hitler was that it was necessary "to educate the General Staff in fanatical faith in The Idea. He (Hitler) is determined to enforce his will onto the army as well."[18]

According to Speer, in 1942, criticism of operations practically ceased when Halder left his position as chief of the High Command. The movement of each division was discussed with Hitler personally in daily conferences; even the most irrelevant details had to be reported. Both Hermann Göring and Wilhelm Keitel accepted Hitler's point of view unreservedly.[19] At this point, all aspects of the war, including economic ones, appeared to be run by the Führer's yes-men. These were the grounds for Kurt Zeitzler's appointment as chief of staff of the High Command, replacing Halder. Zeitzler, an inconspicuous officer advanced to the highest position in the army, came, surprisingly, without resentment. The fact that he was promoted to brigadier general only on April 1 was not held against him. Nor did it bother anyone that he was not part of the Army High Command but was a field staff member, with little experience of command in the East. On the contrary, Hitler saw this to be in his favor. The Führer wanted a relatively young, optimistic officer who would be compliant and politically weak, unlike the traditional generals who by right should have been candidates for the position of chief of staff. Ironically, in dismissing Halder, Hitler got rid of one of the most fundamentally optimistic military leaders surrounding him. Even at this relatively late period of the war, Halder was unable to grasp the seriousness of Germany's position.[20]

Known for his ambition and dedication, Zeitzler also had a reputation for brutality toward subordinates and subservience to superiors. The fact that Zeitzler was reputed to be a true Nazi probably made Hitler's choice even easier.[21] When Zeitzler first met with the officers of the General Staff, immediately after Halder's farewell address, he opened the meeting with a loud "Heil Hitler" and went on from there to demand a new atmosphere in the headquarters. Organization, improvisation, and faith in the Führer would be the keys to victory, he declared.[22] Zeitzler, so it appeared, was a friend of Himmler and an ideal party member — at least, this was the information published by a Swiss newspaper just after his appointment. After the war, Zeitzler denied the claims made against him during his interrogation at a British interment hospital in Hannover.[23]

Interestingly, on December 19, the day von Manstein launched his relief operation to rescue the 6th Army from encirclement at Stalingrad, Himmler informed Oswald Trucks, chief of the SS main economic and administrative office, that Ernst Kaltenbrunner would take over the Reich main security office, the Reichssicherheitshauptamt, in place of Heydrich, who had been assassinated on June 4, 1942, by Czech agents parachuted into Bohemia from Britain.

For six months, the top spot in the Reich's main office for security remained vacant, until December 10, when Himmler received Hitler's approval for taking over the position. However, it took more than a month, until January 30, for the appointment to be made official because apparently Kaltenbrunner did not agree with the centralized police structure that the Reichssicherheitshauptamt represented because Himmler also took charge of the Gestapo and the Kripo, the criminal police, leaving Kaltenbrunner solely responsible for the Sicherheitsdienst.[24] Coincidently, on November 10, the day he approved Kaltenbrunner's appointment, Hitler decided to invade Vichy France the next morning because on November 8, the Allied forces of British and American troops had landed on the Atlantic and Mediterranean coasts of French North Africa.[25] Within days of his appointment, Kaltenbrunner sought eagerly to demonstrate his willingness and ability to aid in the difficult but necessary task of evacuating Jews to the East. Throughout occupied Europe, Kaltenbrunner supported the deportation teams in their efforts to round up and ship European Jews to the death camps. Wherever Eichmann's team ran into difficulties, Kaltenbrunner jumped into the breach.[26]

Overall, the changes that took place in the German High Command, and that were completed with Halder's replacement by Zeitzler, were significant, especially because of their connection to ideology. National Socialist principles were key elements for these men, above and beyond any emphasis on quality and performance at the front. General Keitel had already released a decree on March 2, 1942, stating that the war effort required much closer cooperation and collaboration between the Wehrmacht and the party, noting, "Full trust and an exchange of ideas were necessary." Above all, however, on October 10, 1942, the personnel office issued an order declaring that an officer's views toward Jewry must be a decisive part of their National Socialist attitudes. In light of this new atmosphere, Hitler insisted that adherence to Nazi ideals be a prerequisite for a troop command post. National Socialist beliefs played a central role in their selection from then on.[27]

USSR, September 1941. Scene from the *Rasputitza* season: German soldiers extricating a car stuck in the mud. (Courtesy of Yad Vashem Archives)

Ukraine, 1942. Horses pulling the 116th Gendarm unit's truck that was stuck in the mud. The horse became an essential element for the German logistics on the eastern front; without it, the entire supply system would collapse. Consequently each division, whether infantry or armored, had to have at least 3,000 horses on hand at any time. (Courtesy of Yad Vashem Archives)

August/September 1942. Southern Soviet Union, German Soldiers loading horses on a ramp to a train. (Courtesy of Bundesarchiv)

Lodz Deportation Poland. Jewish women boarding cattle cars on a ramp; these were the exact same cars used for transporting horses. (Courtesy of Yad Vashem Archives)

German soldiers being transported in cattle wagons either on their way to the front or coming back from it. (Courtesy of Yad Vashem Archives)

USSR, 1941. German infantry on the march with horse-drawn wagons for supplies. (Courtesy of Yad Vashem Archives)

Latvia, 1943. Wehrmacht officers examining potato crops. Due to extreme weather conditions in the Eastern Front and Stalin's scorched-earth policy, most crops, which were used for feeding the German troops, were supplied from the Reich by trains. (Courtesy of Yad Vashem Archives)

Hungary, summer 1941. Transport of Italian troops loading on to freight cars, looking stressed and exhausted. The scene is very similar to a Jewish deportation image, and the troops used the same means of transportation. (Courtesy of Bundesarchiv)

Westerbork, Holland, 1942–1943. Jews boarding a deportation train to Auschwitz. Note that not all wagons are identical. The two wagons on the far right are regular passenger wagons and the others are cattle cars. (Courtesy of Yad Vashem Archives)

Orel, Central Soviet Union, December 1941/January 1942. Unloading of wagons with provisions and frozen pieces of pork. Inscription on the left wagon: "Wehrmacht-AK Kursk." (Courtesy of Bundesarchiv)

Southern Ukraine, November/December 1943. New supply of winter clothing, including boots for Wehrmacht soldiers, is issued and tried. (Courtesy of Bundesarchiv)

Tula, Russia. A Soviet soldier next to corpses in the snow and a destroyed German train with the same wagons that were used for deportations, indicating just how deep into Russian combat front the Reichsbahn trains reached and during extreme weather conditions. (Courtesy of Yad Vashem Archives)

General Fieldmarshal Fedor von Bock, Commander-in-Chief of Army Group Center during the offensive against the Soviet Union. Von Bock was among the first to complain about the German transport situation. (Courtesy of Yad Vashem Archives)

Soviet Union, Ukraine, Berdichev, August 26, 1941. Central rail station. Fuel replenishment from train to truck by Soviet POWs. Fuel barrels such as the ones in the image were transported from the Reich in open cars also used for coal, Panzers, troops, and Jewish deportations. (Courtesy of Bundesarchiv)

Volkhov, Soviet Union, 1942. German troop transport over a wooden bridge. Contrary to the myth created by Speer after the war that the *"Sonderzüge"*(special trains) were combined of only sealed freight or cattle cars, these same open wagons were also used for transporting Jews to the death camps, as well as the transport of oil barrels, hay for the horses, and coal. (Courtesy of Bundesarchiv)

Jews being deported to Theresienstadt on a train car almost identical to the ones used for troop transport in the above image. Among them, the submitter of the photo, Haim Judkewicz. (Courtesy of Yad Vashem Archives)

6

From German Blue to Russian Uranus

The two exhausted titans, Germany and the Soviet Union, had been fighting one another for almost a full year. The second half of 1942 and the beginning of 1943 demonstrated their equal abilities, the result of their balance of forces, which shaped perhaps one of the most important clashes of World War II. Both sides' choices and strategies profoundly affected military decision making regarding the southern sector of the Eastern Front around the Stalingrad area, between the Don and Volga rivers. The Battle of Stalingrad is a case where military logistics were a factor for victory—or defeat—in all that had to do with the German configuration of forces before the 6th Army's siege of Stalingrad in November 1942.

From January 1942 until May, nothing significant happened on the operational level. On the Eastern Front, all the Germans did was hold the positions won in 1941 and wait until winter passed. On May 12, the Russians broke this stalemate with an attack aimed at disconnecting Kharkov,[1] although in the first ten days of 1942 they had launched a series of offensives. In the north, an attack by the 2nd Assault Army, with two fresh Siberian divisions, opened a narrow corridor through the German line along the Volkhov River. However, after being cut off twice, this army could not be effectively reinforced, and even the distinguished general Andrei Vlasov, who fought bravely during the battle for Moscow, could not save it from destruction by the Germans. The Red Army managed to tear open the junction between Army Group North and Army Group Center to the south of Leningrad, penetrating the rear of Army Group Center and isolating a small portion of German forces around Cholm and a larger one around Demyansk. Still the Germans managed to hold both garrisons in bitter fighting until the spring of 1942 with supplies flown in by the Luftwaffe.[2]

Contrary to what is believed from December 1941—that the German army would only be able to win decisive victories if it had the advantage of a surprise attack—in 1942, after the front had stabilized as a result of winter operations, and when surprise was no longer a factor, the Wehrmacht was still strong, with the entire arsenal of Europe working for Hitler. As of spring 1942, the war became even more bitter for the Russians, who continued to wage it alone because the British and Americans had opened a second front that year in the European sector in addition to the one that they were already fighting by sea, land, and air in North Africa.[3]

The weather conditions were of course the same for both sides. The temperatures never fell to –40°C or –50°C, as Heinz Guderian and Günther Blumentritt claimed, so as to blame for their failures on the weather. Nevertheless, fighting during the spring of 1943 and 1944 did not save the Germans in the Ukraine either. It was not frostbite at the gates of Moscow or on the banks of the Volga that prevented them from defeating the Red Army.[4]

On February 12, it was reported that each sector on the Eastern Front would be allocated another half a million extra troops: Army Group South would receive 140,000 soldiers, Army Group Center 260,000, and Army Group North 100,000.[5] The fact that Army Group South, where the Stalingrad sector was located, was given fewer than Army Group Center only goes to show that in early 1942, Hitler and his High Command had no idea they were about to be entangled in a bloody battle that would necessitate the concentration of almost all military efforts in order to overcome the enemy. Perhaps one of the reasons for their error in judgment was that according to their meteorological data, the snow in the Rostov area usually began to melt on March 1. The process took an average of forty days, and the ground was dry again from April 10. Perhaps Hitler wanted the 6th Army to hold on a bit longer so that it would be easier to transport supplies and reserves and reach Stalingrad.[6] However, there is no evidence that Hitler actually halted the 6th Army because of the weather. Moreover, because it was impossible to move anything on the roads until mid-April, the weather ultimately made no difference.

The Soviet counterattack of 1941–1942 was launched during severe winter conditions and without the Red Army having an advantage in numbers over the enemy. In addition, according to Georgi Zhukov, they lacked quality armored and mechanized units to fight the Wehrmacht.[7] Hence, by the beginning of April 1942, the condition of the Russian forces that had attacked the German 5th Armored Division on February 10 had deteriorated. The slush in late April 1942 restricted the mobility of the Russian forces, as well as their communication with the areas under the control of guerilla forces, through which they received supplies and fodder for their pack animals.[8] This is not to suggest that the Russian forces were inferior in combat ability to the Wehrmacht, as Zhukov tried to portray in his memoirs; still, he must bear the brunt of the enormous casualties that followed.[9]

Despite the superior military level of the High Command of the German armed forces, their planning and skill in managing the first assaults and the forces they had, including their satellites, were still insufficient for conducting strategic operations in three sectors along the Soviet front—not to mention the other major operational effort, the Final Solution. The battle, as would become evident in the case of Normandy, was about who could mobilize more forces to the battlegrounds. Zhukov was proud of the Red Army's support services, which worked nonstop and transported, in 1942 alone, 2.7 million soldiers via the train services of the Soviet Union.[10] Himmler ensured that almost the same amount of Jews would reach the camps in the General Government that same year. The proportions were comparable to the other broad military operational effort that the Germans were conducting at the time and that served as another front as far as logistical capabilities were concerned.

Stalin, the Stavka, and Marshal Semyon Timoshenko all assumed that the German task force was the one they had immobilized the previous winter. Convinced that the main German effort would take place in the Moscow area, they seriously misjudged the Wehrmacht's strength and mobility.[11] Stalin, for his part, believed that in summer 1942, the Germans would conduct major operations in two strategic directions: around Moscow especially, and in the south. As for his own forces, Stalin presumed that they had neither sufficient means nor the capability to conduct offensive operations, and therefore, he considered it best to maintain a strategically active defense posture. In contrast, Zhukov thought they should prefer a strategic breakthrough in the West in order to defeat the enemy in the Vyasma–Rz'ev sector. According to him, such a victor would shake up the entire enemy layout because they would be forced to abandon their offensives against the Soviets—at least in the near future. At the end of March 1942, however, during a meeting of the Russian National Defense Committee, the view of General Boris Shaposhnikov—then still chief of the General Staff—was the one accepted by generals Voroshilov, Timoshenko, Begermin, Zhukov, and Stalin. This was similar to Stalin's proposal, which took into consideration the German advantage in numbers and the absence of a second front in Western Europe. It was decided to limit Russian operations to active defense only and to concentrate strategic reserves closer to the central sector.[12]

When the German counteroffensive began on May 17, 1942, Timoshenko, Stalin, and the Stavka remained optimistic about their strength relative to that of their opponents. It was not until May 19 that the 21st and 23rd tank corps were redirected to the southeast, but they were unable to stop the Germans. By May 22, the Germans had completed encircling four Russian armies: the 23rd, 6th, 57th, part of the 9th, and a task force under the command of General L. V. Bobkin. A few managed to fight their way out, but the Red Army lost the equivalent of three rifle armies and a tank army, together with a host of senior commanders and General Staff members, including three generals: General Fyodor Kostenko, deputy commander of the front; Lieutenant General K. P. Podlas, commander of the Russian 6th Army; and Bobkin.[13]

An examination of the balance of power, therefore, between the Wehrmacht and the Red Army, which was Germany's main opponent in Europe for most of the war, reveals a less gloomy picture than is usually thought regarding the abilities of the German army in 1942. By the beginning of March 1942, the Wehrmacht had suffered some one million casualties; this amounted to 35 percent of the initial force that had invaded the Soviet Union in June 1941, and only 450,000 soldiers had replaced them. Before the summer offensive of 1942, another 740,000 had been deployed, with great effort, so that the final total force available on all sectors of the Eastern Front comprised 143 divisions, with 3,050,000 men.[14]

In spring 1942, the argument that took place at the German High Command headquarters dealt with the question of whether Germany should move from an aggressive strategy to a defensive one. According to Halder, Hitler's ideas were creating opposition from the Army General Staff because of the discrepancy between objectives and available forces. As a result, an alternative concept was developed in the form of a provisional strategic defensive approach; however, no documentary evidence for this argument exists. The German generals did not support an offensive in the Caucasus and Stalingrad, but at the same time, they raised no new ideas that could serve as an alternative to fulfill the grand objective in whose name Hitler launched the war in the East: the destruction of the Soviet Empire.[15] Speer claimed that he tried to convince his field commanders that an immediate loss of the war would ensue from the abandonment of manganese deposits in the Ukraine and nickel deposits in Finland, although, as he well knew, stocks were available for many months to come.[16]

Finally, when the weather and terrain allowed the Wermacht to take action, it was time to decide where to go. Because Hitler was the one making the decisions, the main objective was to seize the areas most important to the military economy, above all Leningrad in the north and the Caucasus in the south. The decision eventually made was based on the limited availability of forces and transport, which forced the Wehrmacht to take each goal one at a time, leaving no room for ambiguity. All available forces were about to unite for the main operation in the southern sector, with the aim of destroying the enemy facing the Don.[17]

One thing is certain: Even by mid-January 1943, after almost two months, the 6th Army had been encircled at Stalingrad. The general view among the Wehrmacht leaders, as well as among the staff at the Führer's headquarters and Hitler himself, was that all that had been achieved up to that point had not been in vain, and even if not all of them shared Hitler's confidence in victory (expressed in a New Year's speech), they still did not believe that Germany would actually lose the war.[18]

On the eve of Operation Blue (Fall Blau), the German summer offensive that began on June 28, 1942,[19] the most complex problem was the planned destination. In the Führer's original directive, Directive 41, Stalingrad was no more or less important than Voronezh or Rostov or half a dozen other key centers in the region. It certainly did not appear to be any sort of Nazi obsession of Hitler's. The operational language did not even call for taking the city. The first reference to it mentioned the Stalingrad area as a meeting point for German forces coming from the northwest down the River Don and those advancing from the Donets Basin and the lower Don.[20] The balance of power on the Southern Front was significantly in favor of the aggressor—the Wehrmacht. The Germans placed 250,000 troops, including those of their allies, 740 tanks, and 1,200 aircraft against a Soviet force of only 187,000 Red Army troops, 360 tanks, and 330 aircraft.[21] When matters at Stalingrad turned increasingly more complex, the balance changed in favor of the Red Army, which demonstrated a growing ability to fight impressive mobile operations. However, this fact does not suffice to explain the German downfall, because in 1941, Soviet forces were allegedly superior in numbers, and yet they were the ones torn to pieces, enabling the Germans to gain huge territorial gains. The Russians had a small advantage in equipment, but the gap was too small for the Wehrmacht's defeat to be attributed to the Soviet masses.[22]

When the German High Command planned assault operations for summer 1942, the generals realized they could not repeat the strategy they used during Operation Barbarossa in 1941, when they launched an attack in all directions. Although they still had far more forces and means of combat than the Soviets, strategically, this was not what they now sought. Directive 41, which Hitler put out on April 5, 1942, foresaw the disconnection of areas rich in agriculture and industry from the Soviet Union, the fall of more strategic resources into German hands, including oil in the Caucasus, and above all, holding these areas in order to fulfill the military and political needs and objectives of National Socialism.[23] This was the strategy chosen because the Germans were still inferior to the Soviets and therefore strove to capture the oil resources in the south.

When the spring offensive of 1942 began, Hitler called it "the greatest victory in world history," but obviously the Russian strategic withdrawal had been planned. Even in July 1942, army replacements covered only what was necessary.[24] In summer 1942, however, the Germans launched another offensive in the Soviet territories, code named Operation Blue. As a result of an unnecessary scattering of forces during this campaign, in addition to the call in autumn 1942 to allocate resources to deal with the Allies' Operation Torch (the invasion of North Africa), the Germans were eventually forced to face a stubborn Soviet enemy in a bloody battle that ended with the humiliating act of capitulation of General Friedrich Paulus's 6th Army. It should be noted that as of November 1942, Hitler ordered a rapid and massive buildup of Axis forces in Tunisia, as well as sending a large air force contingent from the Eastern Front, including most of the bombers that until then had been engaged in fighting convoys on the route to Murmansk, and a squadron of ninety bombers that had supported the German offensive in the Caucasus. More than 50,000 German troops were rushed to Tunisia, and another 100,000 were sent there at the beginning of 1943. In addition, vast quantities of equipment were flown or shipped in and hundreds of fighters were assigned to the new front, leaving Army Group Don with a deficit in military resources that were already wearing out.[25]

Under orders from Hitler to take Stalingrad by August 25, the Germans tore toward the Volga, regardless of losses. August 23 turned out to be a tragic day for the city, when, with only several infantry divisions and one Panzer division, and at the cost of enormous losses, the Germans managed to break through the 62nd Army's defenses between Vertyachi and Peskovatka. With just 100 tanks, the Germans reached the Volga north of the village of Rynok.[26]

One might ask whether the siege of the German 6th Army under General Paulus should still be seen as the biggest defeat — the one that actually turned the tide on the Eastern Front. The answer remains unclear. However, if in May 1942 the Germans had managed to apply the same strategy to four Russian divisions as the Russians had done to them in November of that same year, Stalingrad would have had a more symbolic significance for both sides than actually determining the outcome of the war.

The result of the loss of the Crimea and the defeat of Soviet forces in early July 1942 in the Brovenkovo sector, the Donets basin, and Boroniz was that the Germans took the strategic initiative. While activating new and fresh reserves, they launched a swift advance toward the Volga and the Caucasus.[27] However, after the initial success of Operation Blue in early July with the capture of Voronezh on July 6, a shortage of fuel forced the motorized units to wait several days for the arrival of supplies.[28] The reserves participated in every battle and were the ones that determined the outcome. By mid-July, the Germans had already captured the richest areas in the coal basin territories of the Don and Donets, and there was a great risk that the Kuban sector, with all the roads leading to the Caucasus, would be lost. Hence, the most economically valuable region of the Soviet Union, which supplied oil to the military and the war industry, was about to fall into German hands.[29]

Soviet forces on the southwestern front suffered heavy losses during their retreat from Rostov (the gateway to the Caucasus) and could not halt the German advance toward the Caucasus. During their withdrawal, the southern Russian front suffered irreplaceable losses, and all of its four armies were left with a total of no more than 100,000 men. In late July 1942, the front at Stalingrad had thirty-eight divisions, but only eighteen of them were combat ready, while six numbered between 4,500 and 6,000 men; fifteen more divisions had 300 to 1,000 men each. These ill-prepared and weak corps had to spread along a 530-kilometer-long front line. The forces there amounted to 187,000 men, 360 tanks, 337 planes, and 7,900 guns and mortars. The Germans, on the other hand, had 250,000 soldiers, 740 tanks, 1,200 planes, and 7,500 guns and mortars, giving them a clear advantage over Soviet forces. In July 1942, there were no indications of what was about to happen in the winter. All that occurred over the next months may be attributed to decision making regarding supplies and logistics. The problem began when, in September, German operational reserves between the Don and the Volga had no more than six divisions, and even these were scattered along an extended front.[30]

On another front, and in a different kind of war than Germany was conducting, a place called Treblinka received 5,000 passengers a day. The question why the High Command did not send a new reserve division daily to reinforce the forces aligned in the area between the Don and the Volga remains unanswered, but explaining that it was due to a lack of rail transport seems irrational in light of the rail system in the General Government. The Russians moved their troops along the front from the Volga to the Don River in layers. They also used troop trains, but like the Germans, they had a shortage of carriages. It was not until late 1944 that the Russians would improve their mobility; in fact, at the end of July 1942, the rearmost parts of the army and army supplies were still in the Tula region, awaiting rail transport.[31]

Early on the morning of September 13, 1942, German assault units attacked the central sector of Stalingrad, determined to break through into the streets of the city. Some twenty German divisions, including Allied forces, fought their way through the ruins, literally block by block, against severe Soviet resistance. The city that bore Stalin's name had become a site of destruction and annihilation along the banks of the Volga and had sucked the German forces into a limited geographical space, while in the Caucasus, a few greatly overstretched formations operated over vast areas. One of the reasons the Germans were able to continue was that the Russians fed just enough troops into Stalingrad to prevent the Wehrmacht from capturing the city, but not enough to stop their advance.[32]

It appeared to the German High Command that by mid-November, their summer offensive had achieved its objectives; however, an exhausted German force was now inside the city without even imagining what the enemy was preparing as a surprise. Between July and November 1942, German losses rose to 862,700 men (dead, missing, wounded, and sick removed from the military areas), who were replaced by only 417,792 men; 1,000 tanks, more than 2,000 guns and mortars, and some 1,400 fighter planes between the Don and the Volga at Stalingrad. Still, from June 1941 until November 1942, the Germans conquered a huge amount of territory in the Soviet Union. A total 1.8 million square kilometers of Soviet soil, where before the war almost eighty million Soviet citizens resided, was now under the Nazi boot.[33] In his report to Hitler on the situation on the Eastern Front at the end of September 1942, Kurt Zeitzler said that as a result of the summer offensive, the territory occupied in the East no longer corresponded to the size of the occupying army. Briefly, "there were too few soldiers for too much ground."[34]

The entire plan for Operation Uranus—the vast Soviet counterattack against the 6th Army—was based entirely on deception. The plan, which was given full support by Stalin on the eve of September

13, only proves that what turned the tide was not Russian superiority of forces but strategy. The strategy was to let the Germans concentrate on capturing the city of Stalingrad, while the Stavka would secretly prepare fresh armies behind the lines for a massive encirclement by deep penetration attacks far from the center of the fighting.[35] Before the Soviet counterattacks on the Volga and the Don, it appeared that the Soviet command had skillfully maneuvered its troops and resources, bringing about a position of substantial superiority in the main areas of military operations.[36] Out of the forty-one new divisions Germany allocated in the south for Operation Blue, twenty-one were not actually part of the Wehrmacht but were insufficiently trained Axis divisions — six Italian, ten Hungarian, and five Romanian.[37]

The race between the two colossuses was about which one had the better logistical layout that would be able to mobilize troops, tanks, and ammunition more effectively. A report from the Supreme Command from June dealing with German war potential in 1942 went so far as to warn that the army's mobility would be seriously affected in the upcoming campaign and that a measure of demotorization was inevitable.[38] As part of the operation, several trains were dispatched on the new Saratov–Astrachan railway line to stations in the Soviet steppes, where reserve units of the Stavka unloaded the trains in the deep rear for transport to the areas of troop concentrations. The pressure on the Russian railway system, which transported 1,300 wagons daily — about twenty trains per day — was huge.[39] The fact that these trains were conveying troops to three fronts puts the Reichsbahn's numbers into perspective as well.

On November 4, the French found themselves fighting with the Allies on the beaches of Tunisia as Operation Torch began. Taking advantage of the situation, Hitler decided on the eve of November 10 to occupy Vichy, France. Despite the pleas of Count Ciano and the French prime minister, Pierre Laval, to reconsider the issue, the next day, November 11, an invasion of the unoccupied southern part of France took place. Although it proceeded swiftly and without incident, it still took a few days to capture Toulon, while at Stalingrad matters had come to a head.[40] German forces entered the free zone of Vichy on the same day that Paulus launched his final attack on Stalingrad. Needless to say, this gave the green light for Eichmann to prepare Jewish transports from Vichy to Auschwitz, which until then had been technically impossible because Vichy was still considered an independent state. This was followed by mass deportations of French Jews to the East, and by the end of 1942, some 15,000 of them had been sent to Auschwitz.

In the city of Abganerovo, the Russian infantry learned on November 26 that the railway crossings were full of abandoned freight cars. According to the marks on them, they had been taken from various countries around occupied Europe—France, Belgium, and Poland—and decorated with the black eagle and the swastika of the Third Reich.[41] It is clear that these freight cars were also used to transport Jews to the General Government and were part of the arrangement with the Reichsbahn to supply both the SS and the Wehrmacht with trains.

The Red Army launched its counteroffensive, code named Operation Uranus, on November 19 after penetrating deep into the German rear. On November 21 and the following days, General Paulus realized that his forces, together with elements of the 4th Panzer Army, stood in danger of being trapped between the Volga and the Don. The formations involved were four army corps, one Panzer corps, fourteen infantry divisions, three armored divisions, one Romanian infantry division, and one Romanian cavalry division.[42] On Sunday morning, November 22, 1942, word spread on the German side that the 6th Army was being surrounded by enemy forces. On the afternoon of November 23, the 26th Russian Tank Corps completed the encirclement. The Nazi command was in desperate need of reserves to try and improve the situation in the Stalingrad area and the Caucasus. According to most German accounts, General Paulus could have broken out of the siege had he acted promptly. However, apart from disobeying Hitler's orders, this argument assumes a logistical strength that Paulus did not possess. His troops lacked fuel, ammunition, and transport to break out without the assistance of additional forces. These were not in reach because of the logistical problem of moving them to the front.[43]

To try and save the encircled forces in Stalingrad, on November 24, General Fritz Erich von Manstein, who was recalled from Leningrad, undertook the formation of a new army group named Don, consisting of troops taken from other sectors of the German Soviet front, some brought all the way from France and Germany. The idea was to organize two storm forces near Kotelnikovo and Termosin. Von Manstein was ordered to establish communications between Army Group Don and the 4th Panzer Army, which had managed to escape the siege. Von Manstein had to operate mainly with this army and other divisions brought from other fronts. Realizing the difficulties Hitler made for him, he frequently threatened to resign. Because he could not start the operation before December 10, he proposed retreating to the Mius River and then to the Dnieper. However, Hitler raged at this proposal and refused to accept it. Everything depended now on the provision of additional forces. The plan was to cut a corridor to the 6th Army through which to supply its fuel and ammunition stocks and thereby restore its mobility and enable it to move out of the pocket. However, once again, luck turned against von Manstein and Paulus's besieged forces. The Wehrmacht suffered from a severe shortage of reserves, and even when the German command did manage to gather some, they were moved too slowly along the transport lines. Because most of von Manstein's troops were situated in Tunisia at the time, it was almost impossible to move them to the Don front.[44] Von Manstein simply did not have the men.

The relief attack, which was aimed at creating a strategic corridor for the 6th Army, finally began on December 12, 1942. At the beginning, all went well for the forces of General Hermann Hoth. On December 21, the 4th Panzer Army was only about 48 kilometers from Stalingrad, and there the attack came to a halt. Its momentum was exhausted. The troops, which were inadequate in numbers and desperately overtired, could only be supplied with great difficulty.[45] The last occasion for the 6th Army to break through was from December 18 to 22. Nevertheless, Hitler permitted Paulus to join the operation at the earliest on December 21, on the condition that he not surrender Stalingrad.[46] Hitler agreed to an attack by the 6th Army in a southwest direction. However, he continued to reject all pleas to consider a breakout. His demand was simply unfeasible: the 6th Army could not simultaneously mobilize all its remaining offensive power for a breakthrough to the southwest and at the same time still hold the fronts around Stalingrad. In any event, military information indicated that the 6th Army, greatly weakened and surrounded by mighty Soviet forces, would be able to advance a maximum of thirty kilometers to the southwest—not far enough to meet up with Hoth's relief Panzer army.[47]

The morale of the German troops on the Stalingrad front was down because of the extreme conditions they had to bear, including hunger and lack of sleep. Amazingly, at the beginning of December, although the soldiers within the *Kessel* (encirclement) were getting increasingly weaker, according to Lieutenant General Schmidt, who was inside the Stalingrad cauldron, they were still confident of victory. The concept of taking Stalingrad and establishing the Wehrmacht's hold on the Volga was not far-fetched; the only problem was that of supplies, which simply were not enough.[48] When the Soviet counterattack began, the Germans had in the Don area more than one million soldiers, 675 tanks, and over 10,000 guns and mortars. In numerical terms, the rival forces were equal in strength; however, the Soviet side had a small advantage in tanks.[49]

Historian Antony Beevor, in his book about Stalingrad, managed to portray, tangibly and graphically, the daily difficulties the Wehrmacht soldiers had to face. However, Beevor does not even mention one of the biggest Soviet operational flops at the time, Operation Mars. Beevor is not the only historian who chose to ignore it. Operation Mars, under the command of Marshal Zhukov, was eclipsed by the shadow of Operation Uranus, the Soviet counteroffensive that led to the turning of the tide in the war. In Operation Mars, which continued for less than a month in late November 1942, German soldiers who were on the edge of exhaustion managed to cause more than 335,000 losses to the Red Army. The Soviet victory, which took another two and a half months, was won at the expense of another 485,000 deaths, amounting to total losses of 820,000.[50] The possibility of subjection by the Soviet Union was surely connected to the questions as to whether Hermann Göring's Four Year Plan prepared Germany economically for a war on such a huge scale as the one in the Soviet Union, and why the Germans moved toward a war economy only in the spring of 1942. The general assumption was that the confrontation with the Soviet Union would quickly come to an end, and therefore Göring was not the one to blame.

Nevertheless, until the defeat in Stalingrad, Germany managed to prove exceptional operative ability. In a letter Stalin sent to Churchill on September 4, 1941, the Soviet dictator made it clear that without opening a second front and without a supply of aluminum, tanks, and airplanes, the Soviet Union would be defeated and would lose the ability to continue being part of the struggle against the Germans.[51] Almost a year later, during Operation Blue in August 1942 and after Churchill's visit to Moscow, General Alan Brooke, chief of the Imperial General Staff, argued that the Germans were about to cross the Caucasus, and the Caspian Sea would be under their hegemony.[52] The lost victories that von Manstein wrote about after the war and historian Mark Harrison's "Soviet defeated victor" raise questions about the real reason for the outcome of these events.[53] The significance of the equivalence in the balance of power is that whatever took place on the Soviet front was unforeseen from the outset on both the German and Russian sides. If the German army had no chance whatsoever against the Soviet colossus, then the Russians could have reached a possible showdown in the war by 1943—a goal that they missed or that was not within their capabilities.[54] Zhukov admitted, "Now that I look with critical observation on the events of 1942, I see we weren't wise enough to consider the situation in the Wyasma area. We overestimated the power of our own corps and underestimated the enemy's. It turned out that the enemy was a tougher nut to crack than we thought." At the time, Soviet resources were being exploited and stretched to their limit. It was impossible to fulfill the requirements of the armed forces in accordance with the demands of the situation and with regular assignments. This was especially felt in regard to the lack of ammunition. As Zhukov noted, "It sounds unbelievable, but we approved only one or two gun shells to be fired by every piece of artillery, and this was in the middle of an assault campaign!"[55]

As for the beginning of November 1942, only nineteen days before the 6th Army was encircled, the Germans stationed on the Eastern Front comprised 266 divisions made up of 5,750,000 troops, over 70,000 guns and mortars, 6,675 tanks and other combat vehicles, 8,500 front-line aircraft, and 194 battleships. Against this impressive force, the Soviet Union drafted and positioned 6.1 million troops, 72,500 guns and mortars, 6,014 tanks, and 3,088 front-line aircraft. In addition, the Soviet High Command had twenty-five divisions, thirteen armored corps, and seven independent infantry and tank divisions in strategic reserve.[56]

Yet the balance of power remained in favor of the Wehrmacht in troops, aircraft, and tanks. It is not surprising, then, that Marshal Vasily Chuikov, commander of the 62nd Army, which was to hold Stalingrad, said in his 1959 war memoirs that it seemed to him that General Paulus had more than enough battalions to split his army and reach the Volga. He concluded that this had not happened because of the courage of the Russian troops.[57] Yet another German battalion would do the job. Therefore, the question of transports of "Jewish battalions" moving to the "front" in the General Government remains critical for the outcome of the battle of Stalingrad, just as the outcome at the gates of Moscow a year before was so significant for future events.

The encircled German forces amounted to fewer than twenty-two divisions, totaling about 300,000 men. They were surrounded by seven Russian armies. Six divisions out of the twenty-two remained to fight against the 62nd Army. The question is why Paulus kept one-third of his forces to face the 62nd Army, although they were weakened and exhausted by five months of fighting a nonstop battle. Even when he found himself surrounded, he ensured that a powerful force was at hand to withstand it.[58] The siege can thus be perceived as a tactical blunder, primarily on the part of the German High Command, rather than as a failure of the Wehrmacht to continue fighting on the Don front and advance to the Volga.

The 62nd Army was constantly short of men and tanks. Paradoxically, after encircling the Germans, Chuikov's men were placed on short rations; he was refused more men or tanks, and he received only limited supplies of shells, mortars, and small arms ammunition. Ammunition and tank reinforcements were something they could only dream of. Ferrying cargos across the Volga continued to be extremely difficult. The period of drifting ice on the Volga lasted from November 12 to December 17. As a result, communications with the left bank were completely cut off, reinforcements were not ferried across, and the units suffered from an acute shortage of ammunition and rations.[59]

However, the numbers of German troops trapped within the *Kessel* were exaggerated. At first it was claimed that some 400,000

Wehrmacht soldiers were captured at Stalingrad. Then General Andrei Yeremenko, whose forces helped surround the German 6th Army, revised this figure downward, first to 330,000 and then to 300,000, the number also quoted by Chuikov. However, over the years, several figures have been given, sparking a debate over this issue. According to Manfred Kehrig in 1974, 249,000 men were caught in the *Kessel*.[60] Anthony Beevor quotes several other assessments, the most recent from Peter Hilde, who puts the number at 268,900, including 13,000 Romanian and Italian troops, as well as 19,300 Russian troops who crossed the lines to the German side and fought against the Red Army alongside the Wehrmacht.[61]

7

Jewish and Military Proportions
Reinhard versus Stalingrad

The Germans' military and civil logistics for the campaign in the Soviet Union and by the Wehrmacht, as well as for the death camps at
the General Government and for the Final Solution, which was approaching its apogee, involved handling the transportation of fuel,
tanks, livestock, fodder, winter clothing, ammunition, and humans. At
least 10 percent of every activity performed by the SS security police
had a profound influence on the war effort. New death camps were
established and laid out as part of Operation Reinhard, named after
Reinhard Heydrich, the assassinated chief of the Reich Main Security
Office. The question that arises in regard to the downfall at Stalingrad is whether the logistical problems of the 6th Army, until their
encirclement by Soviet forces in November 1942, were linked to the
resources the Germans used for Operation Reinhard, the code name
for full-scale SS activities within the borders of the General Government against the Jewish population. It was a direct sequel to the policy that began in Chełmno and Auschwitz with gas vans and included
the establishment of three new death centers: Belzec, Sobibor, and
Treblinka.

There is evidence that Chełmno was not the only place where gas
vehicles were used. SS Lieutenant Doctor August Becker, who was
apparently responsible for inspecting how this killing method worked,
made a tour in the Kiev area of the Ukraine as early as May 16, 1942.
Becker reported to SS Lieutenant Colonel Walter Rauff in Berlin
about the condition of the vehicles used by Einsatzgruppen D and C,
whose men complained that the winter conditions were sabotaging

the task. Because rainy weather completely stranded these vehicles, Hecker suggested that instead of driving the victims ten to fifteen kilometers off the main roads, which was difficult enough but almost impossible in damp or wet conditions, they could instead remain stationary and be used as the execution site.[1]

Oswald Trucks, who in addition to his function as head of the SS main economic-administrative office was in charge of the concentration camp inspectorate, reported to Himmler on April 30, 1942, about the situation in the camps. The war had brought about a marked alteration in the structure of the fifteen concentration camps and changed their mission with regard to the employment of prisoners. Auschwitz and Lublin (the Majdanek death camp) were included on this list. Although previously the concentration camps were used for political purposes, circumstances dictated that they be converted into sites more suitable for economic tasks — although long before the war, they did fulfill such tasks.[2]

The Germans apparently did everything within their power to ease the logistical difficulties connected to combat deep behind enemy lines on Soviet soil. In Warsaw, a head office dealing with transportation for the Wehrmacht to Soviet territories was set up, led by an official named Friedrich Kuzbach.[3] This office served as the main coordinating organization between all bodies responsible for the transport issue. Although formally the army enjoyed top priority, Hans Frank, governor of the General Government under whose jurisdiction all six death camps functioned, was in conflict with the army over responsibility and control of the rail network (Ostbahn[4]) operating in his territory. Ultimately the same railways that transported the German Panzers and other military requisites to the front, including the troops themselves, also carried some two million Polish Jews to the death camps in 1942 and 1943.

In order to simplify the evacuation procedure to the death camps, Frank issued a memorandum within the framework of Operation Reinhard on June 3, 1942, transferring all authority regarding Jewish issues in the General Government from the civil management to the SS and the security police. In mid-July 1942, after a visit to the three Operation Reinhard camps, Himmler sent an order to Obergruppenführer Friedrich Krieger, the top senior officer of the SS and security police in the General Government, stating that the Jewish population should be evacuated from the district by December 31, 1942, and that it should be cleansed completely.

From June 1942 until November 10, 1942, a total of 254,989 Jews were transported to the Belzec death camp. Although it formally operated until mid-December 1942,[5] another 100,000 Jews were shot dead in that location until February 1943, the time when the 6th Army capitulated at Stalingrad. During the period the camp was operating, from March to December 1942, a total of 600,000 Jews were transported to their deaths there.[6] A woman from Lubaczów related that all summer long, transports of Jews passed twice a day with seventy or eighty railroad cars each. With 100 people packed into each freight car, the total came to some 10,000 people transported a day. The trip to Belzec would last up to five days, although it was only about ten kilometers from Wieliczka to Belzec.[7] Therefore, not only did the transports use up precious military logistical resources, but they also neutralized locomotives and trains for much more time than was necessary.

Operation Reinhard, and particularly the mass murder of Jews from the Galicia district who were all sent to Belzec, met with a certain reluctance on the part of the army. On September 18, 1942, in the middle of the operation, General Kurt von Gienanth, chief of the Wehrmacht in the General Government of Poland, sent a memorandum to the Army High Command claiming, "The immediate deportation of Jews would cause a substantial blow to the military potential of the Reich and to a halt in supplies to the front and to military forces stationed in the General Government. In order to prevent jobs which are crucial to the war effort from being adversely affected, Jews working in professional tasks should be removed only after suitable replacements are trained."[8] The army was not opposed to the annihilation of Jews, only to annihilation of those who worked for the Wehrmacht or in plants that served the war industry. Himmler, however, did not give in and answered Gienanth in a memorandum dated October 9. He stated that he had given an order to continue operating without regard to opponents of the evacuations. Nevertheless, he assured him he was committed to supplying the Wehrmacht with its needs after the SS received orders regarding the army's military requisites.[9]

As of July 16, 1942, during the time the Germans launched Operation Blue, two trains left for Belzec twice a week. From July 23, three trains headed daily toward Treblinka with a human freight of 5,000 people from Warsaw. During his interrogation after the war, however, Rudolf Höss, the commandant of Auschwitz, stated that when he visited Treblinka, the average number of Jews packed into each train was greater—around 2,000 people—which raises the number of deportees to 6,000 daily.[10]

Treblinka, which was located eighty kilometers from Warsaw, operated for one year, from July 1942 until August 2, 1943, when a revolt broke out that gradually put it out of action. According to assumptions made by a postwar Polish government committee, over 700,000 Jews perished in Treblinka, but other estimates put the number as high as one million. They reached Treblinka in about 7,800 train wagons. This means that on average, there was at least one train destined for Treblinka each day between summer 1942 and summer 1943. Most of the Jews were from central Poland, Białystok, and surrounding areas, as well as from Germany, Austria, Czechoslovakia, and Greece.[11] As noted, the Russian rail service, working nonstop, carried within the Soviet Union some 2.7 million Soviet soldiers in 1942.[12] Therefore, transporting between 700,000 and over one million people to Treblinka alone was an impressive task, but a costly one as well.

Over 250,000 Warsaw Jews were deported to Treblinka between July 22 and September 21, 1942.[13] During the first three weeks of the death operations at Treblinka, it was mainly Jews from Warsaw who reached the camp, but from mid-August, more transports from nearby Polish counties arrived as well. These transports continued until mid-November and included the vast majority of Jews from the ghettos in the General Government. (The Warsaw Ghetto was liquidated during the days of the well-known revolt between April and mid-May 1943.) It is obvious that the period of these mass transports coincided with Operation Blue and ended virtually when the 6th Army found itself surrounded between the Don and the Volga by Russian troops. Surprisingly, the mass deportations from the General Government took place without any special logistical problems.

The headquarters of the Ostbahn, located in Kraków, organized the transports and their schedules, including the trains needed for this task. The traffic along the railways was arranged by special decrees issued by the Kraków office, showing the exact timetable for every station, number, and type of wagon for each train, as well as the arrival time at Treblinka and the train's departure, empty, from the camp to the next destination. Because these trains were not included in the regular movement of freight and passenger transport, they were not subject to military demands; in fact, the armed forces transport chief, Rudolf Gercke, apparently did not even know about them.[14]

The only time that some sort of coordination took place was in late 1942. When two-thirds of Polish Jews had already been sent to their deaths, the train service to the Ukraine collapsed, and the SS was forced to halt the deportations to the death camps for more than a month, from December 15, 1942, until January 20, 1943. Himmler attempted to prevent this cessation in deportations by trying to convince Reichsbahn officials that the Jews had sabotaged the tracks, and because they were the ones responsible for the collapse of the lines in the East, the Reichsbahn should consider their annihilation a main interest.[15]

If this was all that could be done to enhance the volume of military transports to the Don front, where the 6th Army was fighting for its existence at Stalingrad, and possibly support Fritz Erich von Manstein's relief offensive, which began on December 19, the halt in SS deportations in mid-December was too little and too late for helping Paulus and his men. However, it certainly raises the question of the part played by Jewish transports in the logistical problems up to the eve of the Soviet siege.

The Wehrmacht's logistics were brutally exploited by the SS for racial transportation. It is thus useful to conduct a quantitative comparison of the load each train could carry to the front and the weight a train bore to Treblinka, or any other death camp. If during the fighting at Stalingrad the minimum requirements of the 6th Army were 350 to 500 tons of supplies each day,[16] comparing this to the average weight of each individual sent to the death camps should give us a clear picture of the military provisions that could have been dispatched for gaining some substantial achievements at the front. Assuming that the average weight of a person loaded onto the death trains was about fifty kilograms (based on the combined average weight of men, women, and children, and taking into account that some suffered from malnutrition), on days when 10,000 people were sent to the camps, this was equivalent to a human cargo of at least 500 tons.[17] The trains that reached the Treblinka death camp, which in some cases totaled sixty railcars per train, weighed 600 tons without anything loaded onto it. The weight of the passengers was another 300 tons (fifty kilograms per person multiplied by 100 people packed into one wagon equals five tons multiplied by sixty railcars). Every day, three full transports reached Treblinka. Thus, about 900 tons of human weight traveled by rail for seventeen hours to Treblinka, a distance of 375 kilometers—a ride that should have taken no more than two and a half hours.[18] According to several testimonies given in 1987 during John Demjanjuk's trial in Jerusalem, the average number of people packed into one railcar was 150, and at times even 200. There were two escort railcars and fifty-eight freight wagons onto which 6,000 and even 7,000 people were compressed, and not 5,000, as German documents claim. A train that left Warsaw actually took one or two days, or even more, to reach Małkinia, a station three or four kilometers from Treblinka. From there, twenty cars at a time would be uncoupled and moved by a different locomotive to the Treblinka camp, as this was the capacity of the platform at the extermination camp.[19] These 900 tons of human freight, which first had to be assembled, loaded aboard trains, and then deported hundreds, even thousands, of kilometers, occupied, among other things, precious space for new tanks that could have been sent aboard those trains to the East, as well as ammunition, food, winter clothing, and fresh reserves of fighting troops to help penetrate the *Kessel*. The 6th Army at Stalingrad needed only 500 tons of supplies per day. The actual figure asked for by its high command was 700 tons. However, Göring presented his transport officers with the figure of 600. In fact, the Luftwaffe could fly no more than 300 tons daily, and this happened only once.[20] The average division numbered 3,500 to 5,000 troops, amounting to a weight of 255 tons.[21]

The numbers varied according to the freight carried on each train. For instance, one train car could carry fifteen tons: a dozen cows or forty pigs, or possibly sixty sheep. If not livestock, than one car could carry eighty barrels of fuel (200 liters each), amounting to 22,000 to 26,500 liters—that is, 20 tons. Thus, one train with thirty-five cars could supply the army with 25,000 barrels of fuel. Alternatively, one train loaded with thirty cars of flour could make 83,300 loaves of bread, or the train could contain 90,000 rations of oats or 90,000 rations of hay for the horses.[22] Fuel and ammunition supplies, which should have amounted to 200 tons a day according to the needs stipulated by the Army High Command, amounted in practice to only 16.4 tons a day until December 2, when, during the next ten days, it increased to an average of 53.4 tons.[23]

Panzer III and Panzer VI tanks produced in the Krupp factory at Magdeburg, central Germany, could have reached almost any destination on the extended front. The northern lines included the train line to Minsk and Riga. The southern line reached Kiev in the Ukraine up to Rostov on the banks of the Don (southwest of Stalingrad). The significance of Rostov was its strategic location north of the Caucasus, only sixty-five kilometers away from the banks of the Volga at Stalingrad—a distance coverable by infantry troops, and certainly for horses and other pack animals,[24] in eight days. In September 1942, the mountain corps was short 2,000 pack animals for carrying artillery and mortar ammunition.[25] To bring this amount of horses to the front would take between five and ten trains, depending on the number of wagons in each. The same number of trains, most likely with similar wagons fit for horses, was sent in less than two days to Treblinka. This was the distance needed for Paulus to break out of the siege at the end of December 1942. Because the 6th Army had fewer than seventy tanks left, this was all they could do. On the other hand, a mere five trains could have doubled the amount of tanks Paulus had if they had been supplied to von Manstein so that he could open a corridor from within the besieged city. Some 6th Army units were left with only a dozen men fit for combat.[26] Every train the Reichsbahn used at this stage was critical, no matter how far it got without being demolished by Soviet partisans. As the German forces moved deeper into Soviet territory toward Stalingrad during Operation Blue, the only line converted to the width of the German tracks was that of Gorlovka–Lichovskoj–Morozovsk–Stalingrad, up to Chir station.[27]

In 1941, the Panzer III was the backbone of the German armored divisions. Its weight was nineteen to twenty-six tons, depending on the gun's diameter. In 1942, it was replaced by the Panzer IV, which responded better, but still not well enough, to the Russian T-34 tank.[28] The Germans had to wait until 1943 for the Panzer V and VI (Tiger) tanks, each weighing about forty-three tons, which were used until the end of the war. Still, based on the needs of the 6th Army, and taking into account what the German Reichsbahn could supply in the way of locomotives and railcars, it would have been possible to send between twenty and twenty-five tanks per day to the front. In fact, at the end of 1942, the Krupp factories at Magdeburg produced sixty to eighty tanks per month, and in January 1943, the number was doubled to 150.[29] In total, Germany was able to produce 500 tanks per month.[30] For every train that transported supplies, eight to ten Panzers were loaded. Thus, every day, it was possible to send two trains loaded with armored vehicles to the East.[31] In order to grasp the proportions, on November 3, 1942, for instance, the 6th Army and the 3rd Romanian Army had only forty-five Panzers altogether in the northeastern part of Stalingrad.[32] Later, when the 6th Army was completely encircled at Stalingrad, all that General Paulus had left under his command from December 7, 1942, were sixty to eighty tanks.[33] These numbers were confirmed by Paulus himself in a phone conversation he had with Field Marshal von Manstein on December 19.[34] General Hermann Hoth, who was assigned to break through the *Kessel* with two extra Panzer divisions, had at his disposal only 190 tanks.[35] With quantities such as these, every extra weapon of destruction could extend the German forces' ability to withstand the Soviet war machine for longer and force a war of attrition on the Red Army that would make it extremely hard for the Russians to survive over a long period.

It should be noted, however, that the 6th Army did not lose as many tanks as it appeared. If after the siege the numbers of tanks lay between sixty and eighty, then just before the Russian attack on November 19, it had a total of 107, including the 1st Romanian Panzer division. Soviet armored forces that were advancing from north and south, meeting in the area of Mrinkovka–Kalach, had an estimated 100 tanks when the first tank brigade entered the city. The balance was thus still more or less equal between the fighting forces.[36] In any event, from mid-September, the use of at least tanks en masse was ruled out. Stalingrad became an infantry battle of squads dominated by machine guns and small arms.[37] Therefore, it was even easier to send an infantry division as reinforcement by rail rather than another Panzer division.

Because the death toll among animals during the winter was high as a result of frost and famine,[38] the German army demanded that as part of Operation Blue 3,000 horses be available at any time for transportation in freight cars to the front.[39] In a letter sent from the *Kessel* at Stalingrad to the Army Group Don chief of staff, General Friedrich Schulz, on December 22, 1942, the 6th Army chief of staff, General Arthur Schmidt, reported that the number of horses per division was only about 800,[40] compared to the 3,000 horses allocated to an infantry division. The SS, on the other hand, tried to pack 1,000 to 2,000 Jews onto each train—and on trains traveling within the Polish borders even 5,000 per train—for an average of at least 100 people per railcar.[41] Therefore, 3,000 horses that were not sent to the front because of a lack of freight cars, which instead were being used to dispatch Jews to their death, could have made the difference between victory and defeat in a battle, or between falling into captivity and retreating to a new defense line.

The average weight of a freight horse was 550 to 600 kilograms. The saddle and extra equipment added another thirty kilograms. Average food consumption for a mature freight horse over five years old was another four kilograms of grain and four kilograms of hay.[42] Six to eight horses could be fitted into each train car. Thus, in a train with sixty cars carrying Jews, it was possible to transport about 480 horses.[43] The major source for horse supply was not confiscated herds and stables from the conquered countries, as was generally assumed, but the German Reich itself. Thus, the German army really did depend on the Reichsbahn for all that was connected to the supply of pack animals.[44]

The 25,000 horses trapped by the siege of Stalingrad in November represented two different things to the soldiers there. Because of the rapid decline of fodder supplies, the horses that could otherwise become a liability could be used instead for food. By slaughtering the horses for meat, food supplies could be extended, and some horses were indeed actually butchered in late November. On the other hand, the relief attempt involving a breakout by the 6th Army would include the horses for transport. Army Group Don noted that the 6th

Army had some 7,300 troop horses and 15,000 other horses in the city. Saving the troop horses was regarded as vital because they would be needed to save at least some of the artillery. As of mid-January 1943, after von Manstein's relief effort failed, most of the horses in Stalingrad were slaughtered for meat.[45]

To get a sense of proportion, transporting a whole infantry division to the Eastern Front needed about seventy trains, and transporting an entire new Panzer division required around ninety trains.[46] Seventy trainloads were also all that was needed to transfer the engineering structure for a solid railway bridge across the Don River at Rychkov, not far from Stalingrad, to move goods for the 6th Army up to the city itself before the siege, and not on account of supply trains indispensable for the 6th Army's existence.[47] After all, the logistical situation that Paulus faced in summer 1942 before the 6th Army was encircled by Soviet forces was based on a single supply line, which was relatively slight for the Reichsbahn's capacity.[48]

In order to save the 6th Army from encirclement, there was a plan to transfer a single Panzer division from the Caucasus to Stalingrad, a task that would take at least a fortnight. Hitler agreed but demanded that two divisions be sent from the Caucasus (a distance of 350 to 400 kilometers), which was, of course, impossible because rail communications were such that a second division could only be moved after the first division had been unloaded.[49] Moving a Panzer division was a task that demanded the service of ninety trains, yet ninety-two trains were supplied by the Reichsbahn for transporting Jews to Treblinka (a distance of 375 kilometers) and Belzec alone during a period of one month—that is, three trains daily to Treblinka and two trains weekly to Belzec.

In October 1942, there were serious shortages of fodder for the 6th Army's horses, which numbered over 100,000, as well as potatoes and vegetables for the troops. The increasing demand for supplies naturally put pressure on the German transportation system. The wider area of Stalingrad was linked to the German occupied countries by only three single-track railway lines, mostly converted to the German gauge. The result was that despite its priority, the 6th Army was receiving an average of only 4.5 trainloads per day, instead of the planned eight to ten trains.[50] The constant supply difficulties in the rail transport of provisions—including aviation fuel to the airfields, from which the

6th Army was to receive its supplies—and the repeated delays and planning mistakes all resulted in the 6th Army receiving too little of what it urgently needed—ammunition, fuel, and food—which inevitably led to a progressive decline of its ability to fight and survive.[51]

In late October, the Führer's headquarters decided to send most of the 6th Army's pack animals at least 150 kilometers to the rear of the front. This should have spared the Reichsbahn supply trains that were needed to bring large amounts of fodder to the front. Some 150,000 horses, a large number of oxen, and even camels were assembled between the Don and the Volga. Although this step made sense logistically, it had a profound effect on the 6th Army in the future because most of its artillery and medical units were almost entirely dependent on horses.[52]

On November 23, 1942, Gruppe Hollidt was formed from the XVII Army Corps under Karl-Adolf Hollidt, who was to command the northern flank of Army Group Don in response to the Soviet offensive that isolated the 6th Army at Stalingrad. From December 27, 1942, to January 23, 1943, the unit was designated Army Group Hollidt. During this period, it controlled several major Panzer and infantry formations, eventually succeeding Paulus's army and forming the new 6th Army on March 6, 1943. Although in January it demanded a total of 100 trains for the supply of troops and ammunition, only fifty-one trains reached Rostov from Lichaja, and nineteen trains were missing. In other words, Gruppe Hollidt received an average of fewer than two trains a day.[53]

On December 19, the 4th Panzer Army of Army Group Don reported that its 57th corps was some 48 kilometers away from the southern part of the siege. If the 6th Army within the pocket began its breakthrough while the 4th Panzer Army continued to attack northward, the Russians would find themselves caught between German crossfire, enabling sufficient contact between the two German armies to provide the 6th Army with the fuel, ammunition, and food it needed for continuing its advance. For this purpose, Army Group Don prepared convoys loaded with 3,000 tons of supplies behind the 4th Panzer Army in order to help the 6th Army get out.[54] This was the equivalent of the human freight transported to Treblinka in fewer than three and half days.

In the period between September and November 1942, just before the 6th Army was encircled by the Russians, 77,682 Jews were deported to Auschwitz from all over Europe: Poland, France, Holland, Bohemia and Moravia, Slovakia, Belgium, Germany, Austria, Yugoslavia, and Norway. The trains used for transporting this load of people was more than the equivalent of another fully equipped infantry division to help the 6th Army's effort. In December alone, while von Manstein was on his relief mission, another 18,025 people were dispatched to Auschwitz.[55]

On December 27, Army Group Don sent a message to the High Command for the special attention of Hitler, indicating that, on the basis of comparative strength, it was possible for three divisions to be transferred from Army Group A to Army Group Don. The figures provided showed a more favorable ratio of German soldiers to those of the enemy at Army Group A, but Hitler still did not accept this suggestion because of his fundamental unwillingness to surrender anything. Hitler evidently believed he could relieve the 6th Army by transferring the SS Panzer corps from the western to the eastern theater, including the Death's Head division. The corps should have concentrated around Kharkov and from there developed a relief offensive against Stalingrad. The problem was that because of the limited rail capacity, its deployment in the Kharkov area could not be achieved before mid-February 1943.[56] In other words, the amount of time needed to move three SS divisions would have taken almost three months. At the same time, the SS managed to move to Treblinka an amount of people equivalent to three divisions in two days. When one considers the entire load, including freight horses, as well as fuel and ammunition, there is no reason why these divisions could not be moved to Kharkov in a week unless the locomotives and cars were being used for transporting human freight to the General Government. In January 1942, a total of 57,605 people were transported to Auschwitz, and in February, when the 6th Army surrendered at Stalingrad, another 21,039 people, which brought the total number of deportees to 78,644, were transported on trains that could have brought more than one infantry division to the relief effort at the Don front. This support could have been critical because most of the German divisions were engaged at that time in Tunisia on the North African front.[57]

The German army lacked in particular armor and artillery ammunition. Although the High Command had requested the delivery of some 200 tons per day to the 6th Army within the *Kessel*, the actual amount of supplies up to December 2 reached no more than a daily average of 16.4 tons.[58] Over the next ten days, it rose to an average of 53.4 tons per day—a mere three to ten cars in a train headed for one of the Operation Reinhard death camps. It should be remembered that every day, a minimum of three to five trains were transporting Jews from around Europe to camps in the General Government. Therefore, when speaking of supplies needed for the 6th Army in December, one can point to the fact that well over 10 percent of all military efforts were deployed for executing the Final Solution.

A decree from November 4, 1942, dealing with winter clothing for the troops at the front and signed by the general quartermaster, Eduard Wagner, demonstrates this well. It spoke of 150,000 sets of clothing, including hoods, felt boots, mittens, and warm winter suits. This gear would be enough to warm more than ten divisions. Ironically, in order to supply that amount of gear, all that was needed were six trains—25,000 sets of winter clothing per train. The fact that only 150,000 sets were in reserve indicates that this supply was perhaps intended for the 6th Army troops fighting at Stalingrad and that 90,000 soldiers would have to wait for an additional order to be put out by the end of November.[59]

Of the sixty-three reserve trains with winter supplies that were supposed to reach Army Group Don during the four months between July and the end of November 1942, only eleven arrived at the Don front. On the other hand, during this period, Treblinka received some ninety-six trains, with enough human stock to keep its crematorium operating without a break.[60]

8

The State of the Reichsbahn in Winter, 1942–1943

It is doubtful whether Hitler would have launched a campaign against the Soviet Union without the Reichsbahn or whether Himmler would have moved ahead with his demonic program to exterminate European Jewry in its entirety without having some knowledge regarding the capacity of available trains for the mission to be successful. What influence did the Jewish deportations have on the Battle of Stalingrad? The war on the Eastern Front demonstrates that in spite of all the peacetime efforts of the Reichsbahn to maintain the traffic system at a high level, the demands made on the lines of communication increased considerably and eventually could not be fulfilled. Although up to 1942 the Reichsbahn had invested great efforts in the development of its network, these were not sufficient to solve the traffic problems that began to arise. It was evident that the bulk of transport and supply, as well as guarantees of armaments supplies, rested with the Reichsbahn, and heavier demands were being made upon rolling stock than had been anticipated. The great distances in Russia placed new demands on the company that could not fail to affect conditions in Germany and the other occupied countries. Until 1942, arms producers had been given priority in the allocation of quotas among the various users, to the detriment of the remainder, and the extreme importance of the Reichsbahn as a critical system did not receive the attention it deserved. Only at the beginning of February 1942 were all necessary measures taken to include the locomotive and wagon industry in the list of priority programs, and for the first time, it was given preference in the allocation of labor.[1]

Speer introduced a new era in the German armaments industry whose expansion was an urgent necessity under the existing military conditions. Until 1942, the procedure of producing arms had been a time-honored and traditional one: the armed forces specified what they wanted, how they wanted it, and the quantity. An adjustment of programs should have taken place within the armed forces only, but in practice, it did not take place at all. At the time, an officer was requisitioned to the industry, where he organized production to the best of his ability and knowledge; this was determined by military rather than economic factors. Here an important change was made in two important sectors. The armed forces were to continue to say what their requirements were. After all, they were responsible for equipment and for the combat efficiency of the troops once the industrial tasks had been set. However, after the armed forces had submitted a coordinated and clear list of their demands, this was passed onto the Speer ministry. The armaments ministry would decide in which factories and by what methods production would take place. The ministry would be responsible to the armed forces only for the delivery of the equipment in time, in accordance with the quality and quantity ordered. Speer was not required to get the equipment to the front.[2]

The occupied territories also played an important part. They participated in the production of many important raw materials, amounting to over 20 percent of the total. As long as the occupied territories were available, this was a considerable help. After the beginning of 1942, the focus was on production of armaments only. More tanks, planes, and weapons were demanded. The capacity of the component parts industries soon reached their limits. When the main tank committee demanded more engines, chains, turrets, optical instruments, and guns, this was still feasible. However, as soon as other committees came with demands, the component parts industries could no longer cope.[3] Nevertheless, despite mismanagement in the organization and manifold difficulties in the smooth cooperation between the supply industry and the final producers, arms production from 1942 to mid-1944 was extremely successful.[4] The system began to show signs of inadequacy when the SS made demands for its death industry in the General Government, including a Jewish labor force for building the death camps, and when they used the same railway system that the armaments industry needed to get its supplies to the front lines.

On September 16, the Ostbahn president, Adolf Gerteis, wrote a letter to Julius Dorpmüller regarding Jewish craftsmen working for the company in the Kraków district. According to Gerteis, it was in the interest of the rail company to keep these people from falling into the hands of Himmler and being sent to Auschwitz or Lublin (Majdanek) in the actions that were taking place at the time. Altogether, the Ostbahn employed 23,951 Jews in the rail industry, producing thirty locomotives per month for the Wehrmacht to get its supplies to the front.[5]

On July 19, 1942, Himmler wrote to Obergruppenführer Wilhelm Kruger of the Waffen-SS that by December 31 the evacuation of Jews from the General Government should come to an end. Apparently, 300,000 Jews were working in the war industry in 1942; 100,000 of them were professional craftsmen. Some 25 percent produced winter clothes for the Wehrmacht in the textile industry, mostly in private firms, and 25 percent worked in the arms industry. However, they were on Himmler's list for deportation although they were an important part of the Reich war effort. Field Marshal Keitel, who cooperated fully with the SS on these matters, issued a decree to the military district commander on September 5, 1942, in which he stated that all Jewish workers serving the Wehrmacht were to be replaced by Polish labor immediately—although it was already known from the experience in the Ukraine during Operation Typhoon that it took several months to train replacements.[6]

The German defensive layout during 1942 on the northern and central sectors of the front was supplied by the Ostbahn, which took care of the railway in the General Government and served the traffic flow to and from the front. The traffic was dominated by the military operations that took place in the East. The result was heavy traffic in the southern part of the front where trains passed daily by the border at Brest–Litovsk and east at Małkinia.[7] However, moving freight became increasingly difficult during December 1942 as a result of the drain of rolling stock eastward to supply and reinforce the besieged 6th Army at Stalingrad. Despite that emergency, the freight traffic situation in Germany was generally satisfactory, and there was no hint of the disaster that would hit the German army and the Reichsbahn in 1941, nor of what else was about to happen.[8]

Dorpmüller, who through his previous work in the technical development of the railways and rail transportation had earned unique credit for himself, was in old age and no longer equal to the task at hand in 1941. He fondly believed that the simplest solution lay in the golden middle way and in constant subservience to the party and the army. Dorpmüller was too old to rise to the demands of the moment; he lacked clear-sighted and single-minded leadership to guide such a powerful weapon as the Reichsbahn through the pressures of the battlefront and arms supply in the face of enormous handicaps and disruptions. Dorpmüller's assistant, Albert Ganzenmüller, who had always been a loyal party man and who was on good terms with Hitler from an early stage, had been moved to the Ostbahn as a result of his limited capabilities, which had been clearly apparent in his previous positions. However, in the eyes of the party, everything was in order politically. Yet there was no sign at all of economically sound work methods. No attempt was made to curb outside interference in the transport system, a factor that was of valuable assistance to the enemy. In addition, new ways and methods more suited to the war situation were never contemplated.[9]

On May 24, 1942, a conference at the Führer's headquarters took place in the presence of Hitler, Speer, Dorpmüller, Erhard Milch (Göring's deputy as head of the Luftwaffe), and Ganzenmüller. Hitler raised the issue of transport as being critical and said that an answer must be found to the problems that awaited the following winter. He believed that the German army would fight a battle around Charkow and encircle 250,000 to 400,000 Russian soldiers. They were in acute need of coal and iron, he said, and no effort should be spared in getting them the amounts required for the war. No beer should be transported from Munich to Berlin or in the opposite direction, nor vegetables from Styria to Hamburg or from Holland to Vienna. No rolling stock should be moved unless it was essential for the German war effort.[10] Military rail transport was directed with a marked lack of inspiration, and the supply lines to the front were controlled by weak, bureaucratic officers, or, as Speer's associate, Kurt Weissenborn, put it, "in a primitive and stupid manner."[11]

Soon after taking his first steps as armaments minister, Speer turned his attention in early April 1942 to the transport situation. At a crisis meeting held on May 21, Speer forced Reich transport minister Dorpmüller to declare organizational bankruptcy. Together with Milch, Göring's deputy who was put in charge of transport issues in the armaments ministry, Speer's first concern was to overcome the most urgent bottlenecks, and therefore, he made sure for the first time that the manufacturing program for the Reichsbahn would receive top priority. Because Hitler had deemed the transport problem to be strategically important, he made it his business to be personally involved, even in meetings between Speer and Dorpmüller. The war was becoming increasingly locomotive and wagon dependent because enemy air attacks and partisan sabotage were wrecking a large proportion of the German rail capacity. Therefore, it all came down to how fast repairs could be completed.[12]

It is this fact that makes the Final Solution so peculiar and illogical under any reasonable strategic-military circumstances. It could be claimed that compared to the total numbers of locomotives and wagons manufactured during the war, another three to ten trains a day for transporting Jews were negligible. However, as can be seen time and again, for every relief operation, whether for supplies of food, fodder, ammunition, or simply fresh manpower, no more than a few trains were needed daily, particularly in the case of Stalingrad, when even one train could give a breath of fresh air to an entire German division.

From the beginning of 1942, it was settled that Transport Minister Dorpmüller would report daily to Hitler himself on the number of trainloads he had turned over to the chief of military transport, General Rudolf Gercke. The army needed 120 trainloads of supplies every twenty-four hours, but even with supreme effort, the railway's capacity could be raised to only 100 trains per day, and even this was only possible for brief periods.[13] Combining all the trains operating to each camp, including Auschwitz, Belzec, Treblinka, and Sobibor during Operation Reinhard, at least ten trains per day transported Jews to their deaths—that is, roughly 10 percent of the entire logistical effort demanded by the army.[14]

Conditions in the East had caused an unusual shortage of locomotives and rolling stock, which led to Hitler's demand at the end of May

1942 for a special bill to reduce the number of locomotives awaiting repair by 1,500 per month in the shortest possible time. This was the first time an attempt was made to transfer repair work to industrial firms instead of being carried out exclusively by the Reichsbahn in their own repair shops, as had previously been the case. Up to then, the average monthly output of locomotives was 117. Hitler then ordered that a far-reaching construction program be drawn up for the Reichsbahn, with priority over all other production, and aimed for a target of 500 locomotives a month by the end of 1944. Progress resulted in an average of 185 locomotives per month in 1942 and a total of 2,220 that year.[15] These numbers may seem high, but based on a figure of 22,000 locomotives in running order, which the Reichsbahn reportedly operated, and considering the damage caused by partisans and bombings on the German rail net, the numbers are actually quite low.[16] Richard Fiebig, who was head of the main committee for railway vehicles in the Speer ministry, reported after the war that attacks by enemy aircraft resulted in an average of 1,200 locomotives per month being either completely destroyed or requiring repair. Between 1942 and 1945, the workshops repaired an average of 6,000 locomotives per month, leaving the number of trains running per military sector even lower than the optimum 100 trains per day for the entire army. Because of the overall matériel situation toward the end of the war, the construction of new locomotives was practically impossible because production gradually came to a standstill. Eighty locomotives per month had been planned, using the matériel already prepared by the component suppliers. After this, production was to be lowered to fifty vehicles a month, and if the situation demanded, new construction was to cease entirely for the benefit of the repair sector.[17] All repairs were carried out by the Reichsbahn under its own management. The Reichsbahn repair plants were distributed over the entire communications network according to the size of the Reichsbahn directorate districts concerned. Interestingly, in Holland, there were three train workshops, all stationed at principal centers of communications. Because in 1942 and 1943 no operational front in the Netherlands existed, these were trains operating under the SS transporting Jews from France, Belgium, and Holland to Poland. Therefore, if during Operation Reinhard the average monthly transport supply of Jews to the death camps was thirty trains, the influence on the military effort is clear.

The condition of the train wagons was another issue the Reichsbahn head office had to deal with. A decree from July 20, 1942, provided by the Reichsbahn and concerning "special trains," related to the damage to and soiling of passenger coaches. The special trains were the ones used for the transportation of Jews; the term was a code name used by Eichmann and his department. According to reports of the transportation commanders, the special trains were frequently in poor condition. Part of the damage resulted from the wagons being overpacked, sometimes for several days on end. Because officially the SS transported Jews to labor camps and not to death camps, the Reichsbahn referred to these trains as "special labor trains" and to the behavior of "foreign workers." It was therefore decided that the "careless or malicious behavior" of those passengers, which resulted in costly repairs, would be charged to the authorities responsible for their transportation. For example, numerous windows were missing in the coaches. Old French coaches without lavatories were damaged when passengers used compartments as lavatories. In other cases where lavatories existed, they quickly became unusable because the water system was frozen and the flushing apparatus did not work. These problems were apparently the reason why the coaches allocated later were freight cars used mainly for livestock.[18] In agreement with Dorpmüller, it was decided to obtain reliable records on the condition of the special trains at the time of provision and to direct the transportation commanders, together with a representative of the departure station, to determine in writing before departure of a special train "the deficiencies existing in the interior fittings of the railway coaches and, simultaneously, to give particular attention during the journey to the prevention of damage and soiling of the railway carriages."[19]

On September 30, 1942, Goebbels spoke with Ganzenmüller about the transport problem. Apparently there were transport reserves available, and it was obvious that in the coming weeks the demand for them would grow. Goebbels expressed his anger that no one at the transport ministry had the initiative and imagination to overcome the transport problem, including Dorpmüller, whose performance as Reich transport minister displeased Hitler's entourage.[20]

On October 8, 1942, Chief of Staff Kurt Zeitzler put out a memorandum to the High Command noting that 10 percent of supplies to troops would be reduced. This was an extraordinary step because the trains that carried Jews to the death camps were about 10 percent of the military effort. The fact that Zeitzler was the one who issued the decree is significant considering his background and connections to Himmler.[21] A day later, he ordered that the only transports to be sent aboard trains were to be combat units of infantry and artillery. No supplies or reserves were even considered at this point, and the number of trains that would be used for the upcoming battle—which would take place in four or five days—was not to exceed sixty-five.[22]

In 1942, the Reichsbahn was exposed to countless attacks by the British Royal Air Force, which found this sort of strike against Nazi Germany to be quite effective. The damage caused by light planes that made low-level daylight attacks on locomotives paralyzed the train engines. Building a new engine in Germany in those days represented the equivalent of 8,000 to 12,000 workdays. For the sake of comparison, the much heavier American freight engines cost $240,000 each and took seven to eight months to build. German engines cost the equivalent of half that of an American heavy engine. It was therefore worthwhile for the British to risk aircraft in daylight attacks on railroads because the value of one German train engine was much higher than that of a light British bomber. Because the boiler of the engine was under 200 to 300 pounds of pressure per square inch, it carried its own explosive charge of steam, making it easy for a single small shell or bomb bursting anywhere near the boiler or firebox to wreck the engine. Even partial damage was worthwhile because the repairs cost half the labor and the materials of building a new one. In 1942, the RAF reportedly bombed more locomotives than the German and French workshops could build in two years. Many train wrecks were caused this way in France, Belgium, and Holland.[23]

The use of trains for the Jewish deportations was irrational because in addition to the cost of every locomotive, many steps were taken to prevent the threat of a partial collapse of German transportation services. More power was given to the inspector general of transportation, Jakob Werlin, who was also head of Daimler-Benz Corporation. Passenger traffic was cut to the bone, and strict priority schemes were enforced on the entire system, including greater efficiency in the utilization of freight cars.[24] Risking locomotives and freight cars on their way to and from the General Government was thus extremely expensive.

Capacity of Available Trains

In a 1979 interview to the National Press Office in Hamburg, Speer stated that as far as he knew, the Reich had a daily capacity of 130,000 train cars.[25] Accordingly, the average daily capacity of trains was about 4,000, depending on the number of cars each locomotive could carry, which could reach sixty in the case of trains heading for Treblinka. In comparison, the Russian railway system operated some 1,300 cars daily, amounting to only about twenty trains per day for transporting Red Army troops to three different sectors on the Eastern Front.

This puts the number of trains used in much more reasonable proportions than the 20,000 trains daily presented by Raul Hilberg over thirty years ago.[26] In June 1942, the army and the Luftwaffe used 947 trains altogether for transporting supplies, troops, and ammunition to the Eastern Front.[27] Therefore, whether the Reichsbahn used another 5,000 trains in North Africa or in the western sector is irrelevant to the case of Stalingrad. When it came down to the level of regiments and platoons, every train counted.

Eichmann explained that after the Wannsee conference, the number of people deported to the death camps was determined by the simple fact that it was too complex to register 25,000 people or to deport them at the same time. The same rule, according to Eichmann, applied to the transportation of 25,000 animals. Ten thousand, on the other hand, was a more convenient amount, demanding approximately five transports with no more than 3,000 people per transport.[28] The number of cars varied according to the weight each train could carry, but in general, it was forty-six to fifty-two cars per train in 1942. Treblinka received three trains daily, with sixty cars each—almost equivalent to the number of wagons the army supply trains had.[29]

Wehrmacht transport tickets handed out and dated between August 22 and September 14, 1942, shed light on the strong connection between the two German state apparatuses, the military one fighting the war in the East and the ideological one conducted by the SS and the security police. A horse transport left from Treblinka to Lublin and from Treblinka to the Travniki labor camp near Lublin (which, among others, received Soviet POWs), indicating that the number of horses aged over one year that were to be permitted in each car was between six and eight. The weight of each would not have exceeded 2,500 kilograms (2.5 tons). The trains traveling from Treblinka to Lublin were empty. On arrival in Lublin, they were to be loaded with freight horses. The standard limit for freight carts transporting livestock was sixty to eight horses per car — that is, a weight of fifteen to twenty-two tons.[30]

The significance is that trains were being supplied to the Wehrmacht from Treblinka, which in mid-1942 was maintained as a secret camp in a location just off the northeastern sector of the General Government. The signature on the bottom of this series of documents is the SS command of Treblinka *Sonderkommando*. Apparently, this detachment of Jews, whose main task was body disposal in Treblinka, also cleaned and prepared the train cars for their next Wehrmacht mission. Thus, the trains going to Treblinka were not extras in the Reichsbahn apparatus but had a dual purpose.[31]

Until April 1943, the average number of trains operating on the Eastern Front was eighty trains per day. From April this number dropped almost by half, to forty-three to forty-four trains daily. These numbers covered the entire layout of the Reichsbahn in the Soviet Union, and every sector received fewer trains.[32] Until November 19, the number of trains planned for daily allocation to the 6th Army was eight to ten,[33] but despite its priority, it received only an average of 4.5 trainloads per day.[34] Moreover, as of November 14, 1942, the number of trains assigned to an infantry division for transport to the front dropped from seventy-seven to thirty-two, and the number of trains used to transport a Panzer division fell from ninety-five to forty. These decrees show that more than 10 percent of military transport capacity was reduced in 1942.[35]

The daily amount of provisions for a division of 15,000 men with 6,000 horses was around fifty tons, although divisions were increasingly being reduced to an average of 10,000 men. Numerically, this amounted to 1.5 kilograms of bread, including packaging (750 grams per actual portion) per person, and five kilograms of either hay or oats per horse. One train carrying Jews thus took the place of two to six daily provisions for the troops, depending on the number of cars. For example, the trains that left for the Soviet territories carrying a mere 1,000 people were bearing 100 tons of human supplies for the Einsatzgruppen awaiting them in Riga and Kovno.[36] Just before the 6th Army was trapped within the *Kessel* at Stalingrad in late November, the daily amount of bread per soldier went down to 300 grams, by mid-July to 100 grams, and by January 22 to fifty grams and five grams of noodles.[37]

In 1941, the train lines used for transportation to the Eastern Front began at Brussels, then passed through Cologne, Wuppertal, Kassel, Hannover, Berlin, Frankfurt/Oder, Posen, Danzig, Konigsberg, Riga, and Minsk. Another route that bypassed Riga went to Smolensk. However, the Wjasma station was even closer to Moscow. This was also the route that went via the Krupp factory at Magdeburg for the supply of new Panzers. According to Friedrich Kuzbach,[38] in mid-1942, Wehrmacht supply transports were already passing through the General Government via Kraków. This was apparently in order to collect the empty cars sent to Auschwitz, because Kraków was the closest industrial center the Wehrmacht supply trains could pass through without getting too close to the boundaries of Birkenau.[39] Army Group South had a train route that began at Warsaw and ended at Rostov, some 100 kilometers southwest of Stalingrad, while Woronesh was the closest from the northwestern part of the city.[40]

The area of the General Government was about 140,000 square kilometers, while the distance from east to west was about 600 kilometers (the distance from Munich to Berlin), and from north to south it was about 500 kilometers.[41] Horses brought to Warsaw on April 25, 1942, and to Kraków on May 27 were assembled in groups of 250 to 300—the amount that fit on one freight train.[42] Warsaw was the center closest to Treblinka and Kraków the center closest to Auschwitz. Therefore, it is only logical that the reason the horses were sent to those two centers was that the same freight trains that had been emptied of their last transport could be used for carrying them to the front.

Stalingrad: The Final Verdict

Stalingrad had a profound effect on German industry and the economy in general. The closing down of trade, handicrafts, and catering enterprises decreed by the Reichsmarschall of economics obviously had a considerable impact, as did the compulsory registration of men between sixteen and sixty-five and women between seventeen and forty-five. German propaganda made great play of the slogan of "total war."[43]

Although Reich propaganda minister Dr. Joseph Goebbels must have been aware of the situation, he chose to blame Jewish riffraff for what was happening on the Soviet front and in the General Government. On December 14, 1942, he justified the intense operations against the Jews: "The Jewish race has prepared this war; it is the spiritual originator of the whole misfortune that has overtaken humanity. Jewry must pay for its crime just as our Führer prophesized in his speech in the Reichstag when he said that the Jewish race would be wiped out of Europe and possibly throughout the entire world."[44] On December 18, one day before the failure of the relief attack to save the 6th Army, he wrote that there was only one answer to the attempt by the Jews to incite public opinion against the Reich, and that was to continue what they were doing, rigorously and without compromise: "It is fatal to give the slightest indication of weakness."[45]

Speer claimed during his interrogation at Nuremberg that from 1942 onward, Hitler and his military colleagues only seldom went to the front. They thought they could conduct operations solely from their situation maps. They knew nothing of the Russian winter and the road conditions, or of the hardships of the soldiers who had to suffer in the open for weeks. Moreover, they knew nothing of the supply difficulties, the inadequate equipment, and the lack of motor fuel and ammunition. The good, battle-hardened units the Wehrmacht possessed bled to death because they were given no replacements for weapons or personnel.[46] This explains why no one stopped Himmler or Eichmann from carrying out their own operations, which demanded logistics that apparently had a profound influence on the soldiers at the front—much more so than is usually attributed to the transports that were denied them.

If the transport command of the Wehrmacht were to impose an effective veto on the Jewish trains, it could only last as long as the Wehrmacht was advancing, and consequently getting some support from Hitler. This was the case, although only for two weeks, when the German summer offensive toward Stalingrad and the Caucasus began on the Kharkov front on June 28, 1942. At the beginning of the offensive, all nonmilitary traffic on the railways was suspended. However, from July 22, a daily transport of 5,000 Jews left Warsaw for Treblinka via Małkinia, as well as two trains weekly with 10,000 Jews from Przemyśl to Belzec.[47]

General Government governor Hans Frank claimed during his interrogation at Nuremberg that in his opinion (he had argued strongly that he knew nothing of the camps administered by the SS directly from the Reich, and therefore he had no idea where they were taken):

> Transportation of Jews from Poland to different places was very bad for the economy. I got in touch with Himmler, Keitel as chief Oberkommando of the Wehrmacht and Reichsminister Göring to prevent Jews being transported from Warsaw when they worked so well producing uniforms. My point of view was that it was crazy to do such a thing in the middle of the war when one must have every button on every uniform. We had armaments officials that came to us and begged us to leave the Jews because their factories would have to stop.[48]

A letter sent on December 9 by an infantry soldier to his family caught within the siege indicates the hunger and despair from which the troops of the 6th Army were suffering:

> We eat 200 grams of bread a day. Two thin slices in the morning and two in the evening, at noon we get a bit of soup with no potatoes. And beyond that, we live day and night step by step in the snow and stormy weather. Hopefully, we can get out of the 'Kessel' before we starve to death or the ammunition will be gone . . . today was a much better day, we ate some horse meat.[49]

The 1942 summer offensive represented an attempt to achieve by further offensive action what the Germans had failed to do in the late autumn of 1941—bring the eastern campaign to a swift and victorious conclusion. In the minds of the military commanders, this purely military aspect was predominant.[50] Stalingrad was admittedly not the military turning point of the eastern campaign, which came with the German defeat at Kursk and Belgorod in the summer of 1943, but in both German and Soviet eyes, it constituted the political-psychological defining moment of the entire war.[51] The odds of actually defeating the Russians were slim. However, the outcome could be different, at least in the opening moves of the next phase of the war. However, the psychological impact that Stalingrad had on the Germans in particular—the fact that they were vulnerable and not absolutely invincible as they had begun to believe during the blitz campaigns—finally sank in.

Before committing suicide in his cell at Nuremberg, Dr. Robert Ley, one of Hitler's loyalists until the end and head of the German labor front, wrote his political testament to the German people. In it he revealed his thoughts on the situation Germany found itself in at the end of the war:

> Our will converted to obstinacy and our anti-Semitic policy became our dominating force. Looking back upon all this today, I know I could recount dozens of examples of how paralyzing and actually disastrous these two factors influenced us. Consequently, our attitude was wrong; we misjudged situations and missed opportunities that could have become our destiny. The anti-Semitic spectacles upon the nose of defiant and bold men were a disaster. This for once should be courageously admitted. There is a reason for everything, even for this catastrophe. National Socialism in all its positive aspects was correct, great and powerful. . . . Anti-Semitism was correct only insofar as it concerned necessary protection against flooding by Jews, especially from the East and as long as it was necessary, also during the war this defense was necessary. Everything else was wrong and finally led to those blinders that prevented us from seeing.[52]

"Operation Blue"–Stalingrad Campaign, June–November 1942. (Courtesy of Liddell Hart Centre for Military Archives, ref: von Manstein 9)

The Eastern Front, 1943–1944. (Reprinted with permission and courtesy of Cambridge University Press. Copyright © 1994, 2005 Cambridge University Press. Gerhard L. Weinberg, *A World At Arms*, 2nd Edition, p. 1134, Map 8.)

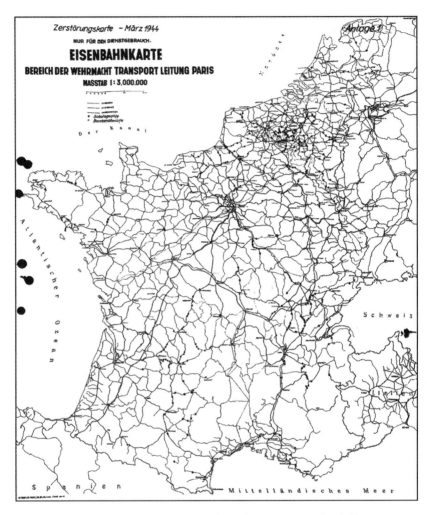

Railway map of Wehrmacht transport lines from Paris to the different parts of France. Black dots exemplify acts of sabotage and air bombardment on the German Railways, but clearly shows that in fact the routes to the Normandy sector, especially between Le Havre and Cherbourg were almost unharmed for military transport, March 1944. (Courtesy of Bundesarchiv/Berlin)

Transports from Hungary. "Jews assembled for deportation 16 April 1944–23 May 1944," Reprinted with permission and courtesy of Sir Martin Gilbert. (© 2009, *The Routledge Atlas of the Holocaust 4th ed.*, by Sir Martin Gilbert 9780415484862 published by Routledge 2009)

Part 3

The Battle of Kursk and the Height of the Final Solution

The Nazi war machine moved forward in investing all its powers, again risking its military campaigns in order to accomplish its ideological missions. The facts of the campaign at Kursk demonstrate that all the Germans succeeded in doing in the summer of 1943 was to use a defensive strategy and hope that a war of attrition against the Soviet enemy would eventually lead to a political-territorial agreement between Germany and the Soviet Union. Or did they actually believe they had a chance of regaining the initiative and forcing the Soviets to their knees?

When the Battle of Kursk began, the Germans did not have sufficient resources and manpower to face an enemy that was demonstrating a growing ability to fight major mobile operations. The proportions in manpower were four Soviet soldiers to a single German one.[1] However, these numbers still do not provide a clear answer for the German downfall.

In this respect, it is important to remember that until the end of 1943, the Germans operated six extermination camps simultaneously and were also fighting on three fronts. By the end of 1943, Treblinka, Chełmno, Belzec, and Sobibor no longer operated as death camps. The significance of examining the influence of the logistical organization of the Final Solution on the German army's operative abilities lies in the fact that in the cases of Kursk and Stalingrad, the limits of German logistical capacity were reached. This was the only period during the war when the logistical operation was exploited to its limits.

9

On the Road to Another Disaster

In spring 1943, the two major players in this colossal war game were reinforcing their armies and getting ready for the next challenges that awaited them. As in the previous campaigns, opportunities were again numerous, as were the debates and arguments within the German and Soviet high commands. It was also a period of assessment and analysis in order to check whether the parallel operations of the SS regarding the Final Solution were taking the correct course and whether Germany could afford to continue with it logistically. By mid-March 1943, the war had changed entirely in the Soviets' favor on all fronts. The Germans suffered terrible losses following the collapse of their forces, as did the Italians, Romanians, and Hungarians in the Volga areas, the Don, and the northern Caucasus in the pullback. From the launch of the counterattack at Stalingrad from November 1942 until March 1943, the Soviet armies destroyed over 100 enemy divisions. The Soviet Union and its people paid a huge price for these victories; there was thus a pause in fighting on most fronts.[1]

The Battle of Stalingrad symbolized a change in each army's fortunes. Still, it was not decisive. The Soviet victory was won in harsh winter conditions against an overstretched, weakened, and demoralized Wehrmacht. However, the counteroffensives in March 1943 around Kharkov were a timely reminder that the Red Army faced a formidable enemy; they might have lost one battle, but because German forces were still deep in Soviet territory, they had not yet lost the war. The Wehrmacht remained unbeaten in summer campaigns. Although Stalingrad was considered a turning point, between June 28 and July 24, 1942, German forces stationed between Kursk and Rostov inflicted 586,834 casualties on the Russians. To lose close to 600,000 men within a month on what amounted to less than one-third of the front line between Leningrad and the Black Sea was hard even for the Red Army to endure. However, the German offensive gradually ran out of steam, leading to the disaster at Stalingrad. Nevertheless, in 1943, the Wehrmacht was actually stronger than it had been the previous summer. In terms of manpower, the German army in the East had grown by nearly 20 percent.[2]

By mid-1943, Germans and Russians alike realized that the Red Army's battlefield performance was validating the General Staff's war experience. Despite the appalling defeats and its suffering in 1941, 1942, and 1943, the Red Army graduated from its harrowing education to defeat the most professional and competent army in the world at both Stalingrad and Kursk. By mid-1943, with victories at Moscow, Stalingrad, and Kursk behind them, few in the Soviet leadership doubted the war's ultimate outcome. Victory was ensured, but no one could say how long it would take or what price the Red Army and the Soviet state would have to pay.[3]

The military and political consequences of the Soviet victory at Stalingrad had such a devastating impact on the morale of the German armed forces' High Command that Hitler was forced to make a statement at a conference that took place at Wehrmacht general headquarters on February 5, 1943: "I can say only one thing regarding the campaign. There is no longer any possibility of ending the war in the East by an offensive. We must realize that clearly."[4] Nevertheless, despite this admission, and in defiance of the facts, Hitler and his close associates thought the war was far from lost and that there was a way out of the situation. A counteroffensive was therefore launched by General von Manstein in the area of Kharkov and Donbas on February 19, which continued well into March 1943. The political aim of this attack, for which large armored forces were committed, was to score a major military victory and thus enhance the morale of the German army and people. The strategic task was to halt Soviet troops that were advancing successfully in the south (after the battle of Stalingrad) and that already had a foothold west of Kursk and Kharkov by mid-February as they moved rapidly toward the Dnieper.

The German plan was to regain the strategic initiative and if possible to encircle and destroy the large Soviet forces west of Kursk. In the course of heavy fighting, von Manstein's troops weakened the Soviets' Voronezh front, and on March 4, when the second leg of the counteroffensive that followed Stalingrad began, the Soviets suffered a powerful blow from concentrated Panzer forces in the area south-west of Kharkov. Marshal Aleksandr Vasilevsky, chief of the General Staff of the Soviet army during the battle of Kursk, admitted that at the time, March 1943, the Germans were considerably superior in strength, particularly in armor and aircraft, and had succeeded in breaking down the heroic Russian resistance of the left wing on the Voronezh front, forcing them to retreat toward Kharkov on March 7.[5] The question now was how the Wehrmacht should continue its struggle in the upcoming summer.

Germany was visibly losing the initiative in the war after Stalin-grad, and its allies began looking for graceful exits. Under these cir-cumstances, it was politically impossible for Germany to surrender the initiative on the Eastern Front. Although only fanatics believed that the Soviets could be decisively defeated, most senior German leaders recognized the necessity for a renewed offensive. Given von Manstein's brilliant success in mobile, mechanized defense, some members of the German leadership considered deferring a renewed offensive. Yet there was no guarantee that the Red Army would oblig-ingly attack when and where the Germans wanted. In fact, the general impression among commanders like von Manstein was that the Ger-mans had ended the winter campaign with a relative advantage over the Soviets—an advantage that should be exploited by an immediate offensive as soon as the *Rasputitza* ended in April or early May. Thus, the concept of an immediate "forehand" offensive became common among German commanders and staff officers.[6]

Although the Kursk offensive subsequently acquired the character of a desperate and tragic gamble, it was conceived as part of a coherent and not unpromising strategy that envisioned a series of limited of-fensives to consolidate German defenses. A victory in the Kursk bulge would straighten the German front and could be expected to keep the Russians off-balance a while longer.[7] As a result of this situation, any strategic move Germany made during the coming weeks connected to the Wehrmacht or resources the Wehrmacht needed would have a profound impact on the upcoming campaign, turning the tide once again in its favor, regardless of Stalingrad.

The Russians had their own plans for an offensive, which was to begin on February 15, 1943. However, first, the Russian front command had to move troops, weapons, and supply trains to the area of concentration quickly and in an organized manner. It was the same game the Germans were playing, and the winner would be the first one to mobilize forces. For the Russians, this task entailed tremendous difficulties from the outset, with inadequate transportation facilities being the main problem. There was only one single-track railway line between Kastornoye and Kursk, with a short branch between Livny and Marmyzhi by which the mass of troops and matériel could be sent to the front. The plans concerning the transfer of combat units and logistical services could not fully be met, and the railway cars obtained for the troops were not suited to this purpose.[8]

The sharp deterioration of the situation in the southwestern strategic sector forced Soviet general headquarters to take emergency steps. On March 15, 1943, Marshal Vasilevsky phoned Stalin to say that the situation in the Kharkov area was becoming increasingly difficult for the Red Army, although four days before, two field armies and one tank army were sent into the Kursk–Belgorod sector in order to reinforce it and prevent a German breakthrough. During this conversation, Stalin informed Vasilevsky that Zhukov was being recalled from the northwestern front to discuss plans for further action to repulse the German offensive. After many days of heavy fighting against German forces that outnumbered them, the Soviet troops on the Voronezh front were compelled to abandon Kharkov and Belgorod on March 18 because they could no longer hold back the powerful German thrust. The Germans had achieved success, halting the advance of the Soviet forces even after Stalingrad and reoccupying a small part of the newly liberated territory of Donbas, Kharkov, and Belgorod. The ensuing strategic lull, which lasted from April to June, was used by both sides to draw up fresh strategic plans and prepare for a new summer campaign.[9]

To overcome the military and political crisis, Hitler decided to carry out a total mobilization program and expand war production. These steps, undertaken in January 1943, yielded definite results. That year, the German war industry produced more than twice as many tanks, field guns, and mortars, as well as 1.7 times as many war planes, as in 1942. However, in contrast to 1941 and 1942, when Stalin and his generals repeatedly misinterpreted the Germans' offensive plans and concentrated their forces in the wrong areas, during the spring of 1943, the obvious threat to the Kursk salient allowed the Soviets, for the first time in the war, to reduce their defenses on secondary fronts and concentrate them at all potentially critical ones. It was this concentration more than any overall strategic superiority that allowed the Soviets to outnumber the Germans in the Orel–Kursk region by 2.7 to 1 in troops (2,226,000 to 900,00), 3.3 to 1 in gun tubes (33,000 to 10,000), and 2.6 to 1 (4,800 to 1,800) in armored vehicles.[10]

In 1943, General Guderian, the inveterate optimist, though worried by the deteriorating strategic situation, still believed that even after the horrific downfall of Stalingrad, Germany was in a position to win the war, if only he himself ran things and effectively contained the damage Hitler was causing. However, he proved to be as strategically incompetent as his Führer. Because Hitler repeatedly directed mechanized forces into strategically senseless situations, Guderian's efforts to rebuild the Panzer arm were hampered. Guderian opposed Hitler's planned summer offensive at Kursk because he believed that even success would bring substantial losses, which would set back his efforts to rebuild the armed forces. Instead, he advocated maintaining a strategic defensive throughout 1943, ignoring the strategic situation at sea, in the air, and on land.[11]

In February 1943, Paul Pleiger, minister of coal and managing director of the Reichswerke "Hermann Göring" (the state-run iron and steel complex), met Albert Speer in Linz and accompanied Hitler on his tour of the Panzer factories. Pleiger had achieved a substantial increase in production in the Reichswerke, and the new Panzer Mark III and IV models were beginning to roll off the production line. Hitler was pleased by the news, which he had long awaited. Accordingly, he immediately decided to postpone his next assault in order to enable strengthening the Panzer force. Yet surprisingly, on March 13, when the Führer returned by air to Rastenburg, making an intermediate stop at Army Group Center headquarters in Smolensk, he had an optimistic talk with Günther von Kluge. Hitler said that one never knew whether the Russians might not be near the end of their strength, and in fact he was now planning an offensive in the East. The first objective was to retake a prominent bulge around the city of Kursk (450 kilometers south of Moscow), which earned the code name Citadel (Zitadelle). However, it was the muddy season on the Eastern Front, and neither side could mount a major attack. Instead, a tense stalemate prevailed that offered no clue as to where or in what direction the opening moves would be made. On March 22, Hitler decided to retire to the Obersalzberg for a few weeks.[12]

Hitler delayed the start of Operation Citadel several times. The question is which side benefited more. The Red Army was better able to prepare their field defenses because their arms production was much greater than Germany's in 1943. The Soviets clearly had the advantage of the delay in more fieldwork and the possibility of creating reserves. Furthermore, the Red Army gained more time to prepare for its own offensive operations, not only around Kursk but also for offensives against the 6th Army and the 1st Panzer Army.[13]

The decision to postpone Operation Citadel was not understood among Hitler's personal entourage because the initial delay of six weeks was of greater benefit to the Russians than to the Germans. If they were not planning an attack, the Soviets would reinforce their defenses so strongly that a German offensive would be much less likely to succeed. As always, however, Hitler could not be dissuaded. The chiefs of the General Staff were reluctant to accept a postponement and pressed for an attack as early as possible. However, Guderian, who since the end of February had been inspector general of the Panzer troops, supported Hitler's view, and the attack was deferred until June. Because so much was at stake, hesitations and doubts were bound to arise. Hitler kept postponing Operation Citadel, partly in order to assemble stronger forces and partly because he had the gravest doubts about the prospects of success. Early in May he held a conference at Munich at which he sought the views of his senior commanders. Von Kluge, commander of Army Group Center at the time, was strongly in favor; Manstein was dubious, and General Walther Model, commander of the 9th Army, produced air photographs showing that the Russians were constructing strong positions at the shoulders of the salient and had withdrawn their mobile forces from the area west of

Kursk. This showed that they were aware of the impending attack and were making adequate preparations to deal with it.[14]

Even the optimistic Hitler had to recognize the limits of German combat power, especially if the new attacks were launched after only six weeks of rest. Operation Citadel emerged as the most important in a series of limited offensives designed to consolidate German defenses while inflicting sufficient damage on the Red Army to delay any Soviet offensive. In particular, Operation Citadel was expected to destroy two Soviet fronts while shortening the German defensive line by 120 kilometers.[15]

In the spring of 1943, intelligence concerning the size and deployment of the Soviets indicated that the Red Army was obtaining arms and ammunition more rapidly than the Wehrmacht and was therefore further increasing its matériel superiority. At the end of March, Intelligence Department East calculated total enemy strength on the European front to be 5.7 million men in sixty-two armies. For this reason alone, it was considered paramount to preempt the enemy with an attack and deal them a costly defeat, drawing as many of their operational reserves as possible into battle while shortening the front drastically by 220 kilometers. It was believed that the successful execution of Operation Citadel could lead to the destruction of no fewer than sixty Soviet divisions and five to six armored corps, as well as free many German divisions that could be made available as reserves for other theaters of war.

The general assumption among the German High Command was that the hope of achieving a Soviet setback represented a considerable overestimation of the possibilities remaining to the Reich.[16] Because the German deployment for Operation Citadel was not concealed from Soviet eyes, there were constant partisan attacks on Wehrmacht transport. Between April and July 1943, some 298 locomotives and 1,222 train wagons were damaged as a consequence of partisan attacks. This in itself postponed the German attack to July, leaving the military transport capacity at thirty-six trains daily.[17]

Whether or not the Kursk operation, as originally proposed by von Manstein and Zeitzler, ever had any prospect of success can be answered only hypothetically. Von Manstein and Zeitzler certainly thought so, as did von Kluge. After the war, General Ewald von Kleist said that if Operation Citadel had been launched six weeks earlier, it might have been a great success, although, as he admitted, they no longer had the resources to make it decisive.[18] Time was of the essence, and it was vital to try to destroy the Soviet reserves in the Kursk salient before the Red Army could recover from its winter losses. The best month von Manstein suggested would be April, when the enemy was still refitting its units and the ground had dried out sufficiently for the passage of armor. April 1943, however, turned out to be a busy time for the Reichsbahn, and with only one railway line to the Kursk area, there was further delay of two months.[19]

Ideology before Objectives

As the war turned remorselessly against Germany, the beleaguered Hitler returned even more to his obsession with Jewish responsibility for the mess they were in. According to his Manichean worldview, the fight to the finish between the forces of good and evil—the Aryan race and the Jews—was reaching a climax. There could be no relenting in the struggle to wipe out the Jews.[20]

In less than eighteen months, from October 1941, when the first deportations departed the Old Reich for the newly occupied Soviet territories, the Reichsbahn simply conveyed another Wehrmacht around Europe, exploiting its entire reserves of trains to the limit. When Operation Barbarossa began, three million German soldiers were deployed along the Soviet border, awaiting Hitler's order to invade. By the time Operation Citadel began in July 1943, some 3,000,000 Jews had been transported aboard Reichsbahn trains to their deaths.

Hans Frank was sure that the transports used for the Jewish deportations were also used by the army: "The transports went east and came from the east." The same trains that sent Jews to the East in 1941 and later in 1942 and 1943 from the West to the General Government transported German soldiers from the front lines and back again to fight against the Russians.[21] In February 1944, at the Führer's headquarters, Frank told Hitler that "the removal of the Jews from the General Government" had been an enormous burden on the country's general situation. He then added, "At the moment all that is left is manpower that is absolutely indispensable, employed in work that it would be impossible to carry out without them."²²

On January 20, 1943, Himmler wrote a brief letter to Albert Ganzenmüller, deputy general manager of the Reichsbahn, with copies to Gestapo chief Heinrich Müller as well as to SS general Oswald Pohl, head of the concentration camps administration system, and Karl Wolff, Himmler's deputy and SS liaison officer to Hitler, asking him to send him monthly statistics of train transports after two cases of sabotage by partisans, which apparently delayed the Jewish trains. Himmler urged Ganzenmüller to supply him with more trains for the deportation of Jews from the West to the General Government and from the occupied Russian territories: "Here I need your help and assistance if I want to do things quickly and get more transports assigned. I know very well how tense the ground is and what demands are placed upon the Reichsbahn. I still need more trains assigned to me."²³ After all, Himmler was still responsible for executing the Final Solution without delay.

On May 13, 1943, Hitler met Goebbels at noon. In the past days, the minister of propaganda had been devoting exhaustive study to *The Protocols of the Elders of Zion*.²⁴ He told Hitler that contrary to previous objections that the *Protocols* were unsuitable for contemporary propaganda, he had found that after rereading them, they could be of great use and were as timely now as when they were first published. Hitler believed that the *Protocols* were absolutely authentic and that the Jewish question would play a decisive role in the war against England. Referring to the *Protocols*, he said,

> Throughout the world the Jews are alike, whether they live in a ghetto of the east or in the banker's palaces of the city or Wall Street, they always pursue the same aims without previous agreement, they even use the same methods. . . . Nature is dominated by the law of Struggle. The principle of Struggle also dominates human life. One merely needs to know the laws of this Struggle in order to face it. In nature, life always takes measures against parasites, in the life of nations that is not always the case. It is from this fact that the Jewish peril actually stems. There is therefore no other recourse for modern nations than to exterminate the Jew.²⁵

This conversation with Goebbels is interesting not because of its content but because of its timing. Instead of examining operational maps with the supreme command of the Wehrmacht, he found time to talk to Goebbels about the *Protocols* and was therefore showing signs of poor judgment. Only three days later, Jürgen Stroop, SS commander of the force that demolished the Warsaw ghetto, wrote a report to Himmler stating that "the Jewish quarter of Warsaw is no more."[26]

On the eve of September 23, Goebbels dined alone with Hitler. The propaganda minister asked the Führer whether he was ready to negotiate with Churchill or whether he rejected such an action on principle. Hitler replied that he did not believe that negotiations with Churchill would avail, as the latter was too deeply entrenched in his hostile views. Besides, he said, Churchill was guided by hatred, not by reason. Hitler said he would prefer negotiations with Stalin but did not believe they would be successful because Stalin could not cede what Hitler demanded in the East. At this point, Goebbels became worried. He advised Hitler that they must come to an arrangement with one side or the other because the Third Reich had never yet won a war on two fronts. He told Hitler frankly, "We must see how we can somehow or other get out of a two front war."[27]

However, neither Goebbels nor Hitler seemed to internalize the fact that Germany was conducting a war on more than two fronts. In addition to the time and resources the Third Reich was investing in perpetrating the Final Solution during the spring and summer of 1943, there was the front at the Kursk salient with the Soviets and the southern European front with the British and Americans, as well as the imminent invasion of mainland Italy. Germany was also engaged in defending itself in the air and conducting a war at sea in which each U-boat built meant giving up thirty tanks. By far the greatest losses inflicted by the Axis and suffered by the Allies were the result of submarine action.[28] By the spring of 1943, over 110 U-boats were operating simultaneously in the Atlantic, with an average monthly production of twenty-five new vessels.[29] Finally, there was the Auschwitz front, the Warsaw ghetto front, the Sobibor front, and the Treblinka and Majdanek fronts. All these ensured that the Wehrmacht's logistical program could not possibly meet Hitler's expectations.

Logistics before the Battle of Kursk

The transport option available to the Germans to maintain a strong, efficient military operation was a railway net divided into three sectors, north, central, and south, with a total receiving capacity of 260 trains a day. This rules out the simplified argument claiming that the Reichsbahn operated 20,000 trains daily and that the special trains used for transporting Jews were a drop in the ocean compared to the entire Reichsbahn layout.[30] Two hundred sixty trains spread throughout the Eastern Front constituted 1.3 percent of the total Reichsbahn capacity. Because of partisan action, the northern sector could expect to receive an average of forty-five out of seventy trains; the central sector, forty out of 100; and the ninety trains scheduled for the southern sector probably reached their destination because there was weak partisan activity there. Therefore, eighty to ninety divisions received supplies daily.[31]

Of the four railway lines connecting the Reich and the Soviet territories, as of May 1941, two began in the Charlotenbourg borough of Berlin, then ran to Warsaw and Małkinia, or directly to Małkinia, Białystok, and Niegdrelodje. From Niegdrelodje there was another line to Minsk, Smolensk, and then to Moscow. Małkinia was the departure station for all the trains destined for the Treblinka death camp.[32] This is another indication that the same trains and wagons used to supply the Soviet front were also used for transport to the death camps in the General Government. Otherwise, why would a rail line have a station in a small town like Małkinia when there was a station in Warsaw just sixty kilometers away?

On March 1, 1943, Fedor von Bock noted in his diary that although he had already been dismissed from his position as commander of Army Group Center,

> there was one thing for certain: the war can not be waged without reserves! They must be created, and in all areas. Only when we have succeeded, with the inevitable loss of space and time, can we hope to be equal to the tasks that lie before us. Until then we must keep our nerve and the Supreme Command must not attempt a

third time, following deceitful temptation and based on inadequate information, to fulfill great, decisive missions with insufficient forces.[33]

The importance of the occupied territories for supplies of consumer goods in 1943 was immense. However, the German consumer benefited only partly from these supplies and reserves because of transport difficulties. Between 1939 and 1944, the volume of consumer goods production (not including foodstuffs, the production of which hardly changed at all) fell by 25 percent. Supplies per head of the population declined by about a third, taking into consideration that the armed forces used up a substantial part. It can be assumed that the part available for distribution to the civilian population was no more than about 40 to 50 percent of the prewar level—that is, about a tenth less than during the nadir of the most serious economic crisis in mid-1932. On the other hand, demand rose continuously, chiefly as a result of the bomb damage, which expanded over time. The situation grew somewhat easier thanks to increasing production in the occupied western territories, under the motto "Shifting the Contract." Consumer goods contracts in particular were shifted to the West because fewer production secrets needed to be revealed than those of the complex iron and metal industries. Moreover, it was assumed that air raids on French and Belgian industrial facilities would probably not destroy the plants. Goods included twill for occupational clothing, uniform cloth, rugs and blankets, heavy leather, work and occupational shoes made from leather, clogs, bedsteads, linen, and wardrobes.[34]

From mid-1944 onward, the absence of supplies was strongly felt. The occupied territories played an important part in the supply process, contributing more than 20 percent of raw materials. As long as the occupied territories were available, this was a considerable help; however, things got increasingly difficult. When Speer entered the armaments ministry, the output of finished products reached a peak and tripled within a period of two and a half years through a flexible system of priorities. There were considerable increases in the production of tanks, weapons, and fighter aircraft. By carrying out its planned expansion program with great energy, industries producing basic materials reached a capacity that would have permitted the war to continue for a long period, independent of imports. This was true for all basic materials, including Buna textiles and fuel.[35]

The Soviet army's logistical services also performed well in the Battle of Kursk. In the course of defensive operations, the central front used up more than 780 railway carloads of ammunition and the Voronezh front 730 carloads. In the same period, the two fronts required 23,900 tons of fuel.[36]

As for fuel supplies for the Wehrmacht, the German government had taken precautionary measures, first by extensive construction within the Four Year Plan, then by storing reserves and also by exploiting the Romanian oil fields. In 1943, German fuel production reached roughly 7.5 million tons, of which 5.7 million tons were obtained by hydrogenation, synthesis, and carbonization. Another two million tons were imported as refined fuel, and six million tons came from the occupied territories. It was only after concentrated air attacks over Germany began in May 1944 that the crucial home production of hydrogenated fuel received a fatal blow. Thus, even after the Germans lost Stalingrad along with the oil supply from the Caucasus, the German war machine was still capable of initiating major campaigns, such as the Battle of Kursk within the Soviet Union.[37]

The closing of trade, handicrafts, and catering firms, decreed by Reich minister of economics Walther Funk after Stalingrad (February 4, 1943), had adverse industrial effects as well as a negative impact on the overall economy, as did compulsory registration for men aged sixteen to sixty-five and for women aged seventeen to forty-five. Whereas German propaganda made great play of the slogan "total war," the economic effect of the measures taken and the severity of the law were in inverse proportion to the volume of propaganda put out by the press, the wireless, and party speakers. In 1943, the German Reich employed 7.1 million foreign workers and prisoners who had to be transported by train, whether they were Soviet POWs or forced labor from the western occupied states. A large proportion of them were brought to Germany before 1943 on a huge scale. For instance, according to the plenipotentiary general for labor deployment from 1942 onward, Fritz Sauckel, who was responsible for organizing the systematic enslavement of millions from lands occupied by Nazi Germany, between April and November 1942, 1,375,567 workers from the occupied eastern territories were recruited for forced labor. By August 1944, 7,651,970 foreign workers would be used as forced labor in Germany, 5.7 million of them civilians and the rest POWs.[38]

This in itself was a burden on the transport system and the Reichsbahn, for the Jewish deportees could have filled this task if they had been used as forced labor.[39] Already in the summer of 1940 it was evident that the Germans could not continue the war without foreign labor, nor could they manage without it afterward. Moreover, because similar manhunt methods were used, with police and army forces surrounding entire villages, the Jewish deportations seem even more pointless. When the foreign workers traveled aboard trains, there were complaints by the rail service about an insufferable stench in the cars and compartments; the seats were frequently so littered with fruit peelings, paper, and cigarette ash that a German passenger could not be expected to use one vacated by a foreign worker.[40]

The Soviets apparently faced logistical difficulties that were similar to those of the Wehrmacht. Because there was a shortage of trucks as well as horses, the troops often had to carry heavy machine guns, anti-tank rifles, and mortars themselves. The artillery lagged behind while the supply trains and bases were still far from the areas of concentration, making it difficult to supply the forces in the field with ammunition, fuel, and food.[41]

The significance of Western supplies for the Soviet war effort was admitted by Khrushchev in his memoirs, but a specific passage published only in the 1990s reveals that Stalin acknowledged lend-lease within his small entourage. He said that if the Soviet Union had had to deal with Germany on a one-to-one basis, it would not have been able to cope because it lost so much of its industry. Marshal Zhukov himself confirmed that without aid, the Soviet Union could not have continued the war. Remarkably, the United States supplied more than half a million vehicles to the Soviet Union, comprising one-third of all Soviet mobility. US aid included some 78,000 jeeps, over 200,000 Studebaker army trucks, and 150,000 light trucks. Without Western aid of even railway equipment, the Soviet war effort would almost certainly have foundered on poor mobility and an anemic transport system.[42]

As a result of the expansion of the railway gauge to fifteen centimeters to fit the European gauge, the Soviets produced train wagons that were bigger and wider, enabling a capacity of up to sixty men per wagon, compared to the German capacity of forty. In the summer of 1943, it took the Red Army thirty-three trains instead of the fifty to sixty trains it took the Germans to transport a full infantry division to the German–Soviet front; fifty trains instead of 100 German trains to transport a full armored division; and eighteen to thirty trains for a cavalry division compared to 100 for the Germans. An infantry battalion needed only one train and a cavalry regiment nine trains. It seemed that even in the field of wagons and locomotives, the Soviets widened the gap between the two countries.[43]

The complex situation that had developed in the Kursk area by the spring of 1943 required great effort on the part of the Soviets in all rear-line operations concerning the organization of supplies as well as evacuation of the wounded and repair of damaged equipment. The Kursk salient was 200 kilometers wide and about 150 kilometers deep and included parts of the Orel, Kursk, and Belgorod regions. This southern part of the central Russian highlands, crisscrossed by ravines and the wide valleys of the Seim, Psyol, Tim, and Oskol rivers, lies in the Black Earth Forest steppe zone. For the Red Army, then, the Kastronoye railway junction was crucial because trains left from there for Kursk and Lgov to supply troops at the central front and for Stary Oskol and Novy Oskol to supply the Voronezh front.[44] The capacity of the Russian railway lines increased from six trains per day to eighteen and then twenty-four. From April to June 1943, some 3,572 trains (171,789 cars) were sent into the Kursk bulge; out of these, 1,400 trains carried heavy weapons, reserve troops, and about 150,000 cars of supplies.[45]

As of early June 1943, the Soviets maintained a rail network of 37,000 to 40,000 kilometers, of which the Germans converted about 35,000 kilometers to the European gauge. As a result of partisan action, they had reconverted some 4,000 kilometers of railway lines for use by horse-drawn vehicles and other traffic. The total capacity of this rail net was 250 trains per day, but as a result of the lack of rolling stock, the Soviets could not fully exploit this. There was thus a two-way traffic of some 170 trains daily — eighty-five trains that could supply the troops on a front that stretched from Leningrad in the north to Kiev in the Ukraine. During 1943, the German locomotive industry could supply 190 new locomotives per month out of a total of 5,000, as well as 175,000 wagons. The partisan movement, however, managed to destroy 230 locomotives per month—more than the entire rail industry could produce at all German plants—leaving the Wehrmacht only forty new locomotives per month for supplying the front.[46]

The overall image of the German economy held by the Allies—its output, organization, and division of labor, as well as the implications of these factors for strategic air offensive—was greatly flawed. Until mid-1943, the Allies emphasized that the German economy was stretched to the limit and that neither reallocation of resources nor expansion of armaments output was possible. They repeatedly predicted its collapse and consistently exaggerated the effects of strategic bombing. The Allies even argued that industrial capacity was being shifted from armaments production to manufacture of civilian goods. The Allies' Enemy Objectives Unit never examined transportation, let alone the Reichsbahn. It took into account only purely military traffic, and its rejection of a general attack on the German railways stemmed from the assumption that disrupting economic traffic would be irrelevant because of the delayed effect it would have on the Wehrmacht. In light of the frantic hunt for every ton of coal and steel in Germany, this view is astonishing.[47]

The German conduct of war and the war economy thus underwent a continuing loss of mobility and vigor as the conflict went on. In early May 1943, the 800-acre Krupp armament plant in Essen was bombed for the fifty-fifth time.[48] There was an inexorable deterioration in the transport system, especially from the end of 1942, as the area of German rule gradually shrank. This was expressed in shipping, inland waterways, traffic, road transport, local public transport, and above all the railway system. The effects were felt first in the occupied territories, in supplies to the population, and in exploitation of these countries for the Reich's purposes. In mid-1943, then, the special trains and the Final Solution did not contribute to the military efforts and the challenges Germany was facing.

At first the Wehrmacht itself was little aware of what was happening. Other than in major operations, its mobility was limited more as a result of fuel shortages than lack of vehicles. In mid-1943, the army, and particularly the Waffen-SS, still relied on horsepower for mobilization. Herds were bought from breeding farms in Hannover for the price of 300 to 500 reichsmarks per animal.[49] Within the Reich itself, military transport needs had absolute priority, and the Wehrmacht as well as the reserve army and military authorities enjoyed transport privileges. The Jewish transports were an exception in this matter. Even in regard to the home army, the shortage of vehicles led to an increasing lack of mobility that dangerously limited its combat readiness. The civilian population was the hardest hit: a great deal of mobility was being demanded of them so that they would be available to the regime and serve the war economy. On the other hand, they were being expected to put up with so many restrictions on local transport services, the railways, and other modes of transport that very soon even trams were needed for carrying goods.[50]

The special trains and their profound impact on the struggle for transport means should not be underestimated. The transport privileges enjoyed by the army were shared by Kaltenbrunner's agencies, especially Section IV-B4, headed by Eichmann. As of 1943, the air war was the main reason for the disruption of the transport system, such as the shortening of wagon turnaround times. The destruction of track and equipment reached dramatic proportions: in 1943 alone, Allied bombers destroyed 1,512 locomotives and 12,430 wagons, while the partisans also accounted for many damaging attacks. Increasingly it was becoming a transport war, and as such, every train counted.[51]

10

The Warsaw Ghetto Uprising
Footnote or Major Operation?

While the supreme command of the Wehrmacht (OKW) was searching for the right place and the right time to continue its next maneuvers across the Voronezh and the central fronts, the SS was busy with its own front. The Warsaw ghetto, which in the spring of 1943 housed more than 56,000 Jews, was destined for liquidation by another big *aktzia* that would transport most of its inhabitants to the Treblinka death camp in the General Government. Actions in the streets of Warsaw turned into a full-fledged military operation. Meanwhile, preparations for Operation Citadel, which may or may not have been the Wehrmacht's top priority at that point, were delayed for logistical reasons, although it finally launched on July 5. When the final liquidation of the Warsaw ghetto began on April 19, 1943, the Germans were well prepared for a fight but were unprepared for a drawn-out one; indeed, the struggle lasted for nearly one month, until May 16, 1943. The earlier street battles continued until April 28, at which point the Jewish combatants who led the uprising were compelled to retreat to underground bunkers.[1] On May 1, Goebbels referred for the first time to the Warsaw uprising in his diary:

> Reports from the occupied areas contain no sensational news. The only noteworthy item is the exceedingly serious fighting in Warsaw between, on the one hand, the police and part of our Wehrmacht, and the rebellious Jews on the other. The Jews have actually succeeded in taking up a defensive position in the ghetto. Heavy engagements are being fought there which even led to the Jewish

supreme command's issue of daily communiqués. Of course, this fun won't last long. But it shows what is to be expected of the Jews when they are in possession of arms. Unfortunately, some of their weapons are good German ones, especially machine guns. Heaven only knows how they got them. Attempts at assassination and acts of sabotage are occurring in the General Government at far beyond the normal rate.[2]

An official report submitted on April 19, at 0800 hours by Jürgen Stroop, commander of the German forces from the beginning of the uprising until the end of the extermination operation on May 16, 1943, speaks of 2,100 troops, including forty commanders fighting 750 Jewish underground combatants daily. Stroop's forces included about 1,000 armored Waffen-SS units, some 1,000 SS cavalry battalions, SS police squads, and Ukrainian regiments. About half of these forces were regular Wehrmacht units allocated by Generalleutnant Fritz Rossum, commander of the military district of Warsaw during the mass deportations of 1942 and the subsequent Warsaw ghetto battle in 1943. The vast majority of these units used tanks and armored vehicles. These forces included Panzergrenadier units, engineering corps, antiaircraft guns, howitzers, and heavy machine guns. During his imprisonment, General Stroop confessed to his interrogators that the units that participated in the Warsaw ghetto operation were equipped with weapons and ammunition similar to those used by combat units fighting in parallel on the Eastern Front with armored vehicles and even some French tanks.[3] It is estimated today that Stroop had an even a larger force of 3,000 men.[4]

According to various reports, on April 18, several army units had been concentrated in Warsaw, and it seemed likely that the Germans were about to launch another action against the Jewish ghetto.[5] Logistically, these forces in Warsaw were equivalent to an entire army division (during the period before the Battle of Kursk), which needed at least four trains for moving equipment and personnel, plus trains carrying supplies daily.

German numbers participating in the Kursk campaign were relatively lower than those of the Soviets. Thus, any extra military force would have carried substantial weight in the battlefield. On July 1,

1943, the German strength in the Kursk area was around 777,000 men. The Wehrmacht had a total of forty-four divisions, including nine Panzer divisions, five Panzergrenadier divisions, and twenty-eight infantry divisions. Because the campaign at Kursk was divided into three battles and sections, the actual number of divisions per army was lower. For instance, the 4th Panzer Army had only four divisions, and the Kempf army detachment only three.[6] In comparison, the Warsaw ghetto received "honorary" treatment of an entire division—namely, one-third of that which a full-scale army preparing for an offensive on the Kursk salient had. The active strength of the grenadier regiment of the 106th Infantry Division of Army Group Center was down to fifty men in November 1943. The mountain corps commander, General Ferdinand Schörner, reported that one division that should have had 5,000 men had only 500.[7]

Perhaps coincidently, on the same day that Stroop's forces entered the Warsaw ghetto to begin the demolition operation, Rudolf Brandt, Himmler's personal administrative officer, received a six-page report marked Top Secret from Richard Korherr, chief inspector of statistics. Regarding the Final Solution to the Jewish question, it comprised an abstract from a more extensive sixteen-page document prepared for Himmler by the statistics department in the Reich Main Security Office with Gestapo chief Heinrich Müller, as a balance sheet to present to Hitler.[8] Up to that point, the Third Reich had managed to deport and evacuate 3,977,541 Jews. This excluded the final *Grossaktion* of the Warsaw ghetto and the deportation of Hungarian Jewry in June 1944, Romanian Jewry, Greek Jewry, and Jewish communities in the General Government. Another 110,360 Jews, according to Korherr, were sent to sixteen concentration camps as forced laborers, the majority to Lublin (Majdanek), Auschwitz, Buchenwald, Sachsenhausen, Dachau, Mauthausen, and Ravensbruck.[9] The next morning, April 20, Korherr received a letter from Brandt on behalf of Reichsführer-SS Himmler asking him to refrain from using the term *Sonderbehandlung* (special treatment) in all that related to the Jews and stick to the euphemism *Transportatierung* (transportation) as the subject was beginning to gain significant attention.[10]

From the beginning of the clashes, the SS assigned the forces concentrated outside Warsaw the task of literally exterminating the ghetto of its Jewish habitants in no more than three days. On the fifth day of the uprising, Stroop was convinced it was extinguished. However, this was only the beginning of a hard struggle that descended from the ghetto streets to the underground bunkers. Still, whatever means the German forces used, from burning down buildings to waiting for the rebellious Jews to emerge from the bunkers or gassing the passages with chlorine, did not help. The battle of the bunkers became a long campaign in which the Germans progressed only gradually. Even on May 16, when Stroop reported that the *Grossaktion* was completed, there were still groups of Jewish fighters hiding in the sewage system, bunkers, and improvised shelters who refused to surrender.[11]

The bunker action extended the uprising and forced the Germans to take much longer to liquidate the Warsaw ghetto than they needed to defeat entire countries during the blitz campaigns. When Goebbels referred to it after the first two weeks of fighting, it was clear that beyond the logistical burden it created by pinning down so much manpower and ammunition in a nonstrategic battlefield, it was a political propaganda embarrassment in general. Also embarrassing was the non-Jewish Polish population witnessing how a few rebels succeeded in forcing a persistent and uncompromising battle on extensive German forces. There is no doubt that the Warsaw ghetto uprising had an effect on the Polish population, which, a year later, in August 1944, began its own uprising against the German occupation. On May 23, 1943, Goebbels again referred to it in his diary:

> The Battle of the Warsaw Ghetto continues. The Jews are still resisting. On the whole, however, resistance is no longer dangerous and has been virtually broken. Within the area of the General Government, assassinations, acts of sabotage and raids by bandits are on the increase. Conditions there are in some respects quite chaotic. "Frank" is to be given one more chance to prove his worth. I should have thought it better to kick Frank right out. When you are once convinced that a man is in no way up to his job, the necessary conclusion should be drawn.[12]

Although formally Stroop reported that the ghetto was liquidated and that the *Grossaktion* had come to an end on May 16, 1943, clashes in the bunkers continued even into September. It is hard to determine when the heavy units were withdrawn from Warsaw because Stroop was interested in a report that showed he had fulfilled his task in the shortest possible time. We know from Jewish participants in the uprising that nobody on the Jewish side of the campaign knew anything about Stroop's report from May 16, and that in fact they continued fighting as if nothing has changed from April 19. On June 2, the Polish Blue Police even reported that the situation had allegedly worsened and that the ghetto walls were encircled by strong SS units with armored cars entering the area.[13]

In early April, the Germans revealed some incriminating information concerning the Red Army that served as fuel for propaganda by Goebbels's ministry. In May and June 1943, Goebbels used the Katyn massacres as propaganda against the "Judeo-Bolshevik" government in the Soviet Union and as a counter to the information coming out of Warsaw in the Polish and international press. The Soviet massacre of Polish POWs in the Katyn forest was revealed, coincidently, in early April 1943. The propaganda campaign that Goebbels unleashed in its wake, however, was not coincidental at all.

The Wehrmacht discovered a mass grave of 4,243 Polish military reserve officers in the forest on Goat Hill near Katyn. This discovery gave Goebbels a wealth of propaganda material, and because this campaign was unleashed during the fighting in the Warsaw ghetto, it also served as a tool to balance German Soviet atrocities in Poland with the ones the Soviets had committed not long before. Goebbels saw this as an excellent way to drive a wedge between Poland, the Western Allies, and the Soviet Union. On April 13, Berlin Radio broadcast to the world that German military forces in the Katyn forest near Smolensk had uncovered "a ditch . . . 28 meters long and 16 meters wide, in which the bodies of 3,000 Polish officers were piled up 12 deep." The broadcast went on to charge the Soviets with carrying out the massacre in 1940. On April 14, Goebbels referred to the Katyn massacres in his diary:

We are now using the discovery of 12,000 Polish officers, murdered by the GPU (the NKVD) for anti-Bolshevik propaganda in a grand manner. We sent neutral journalists and Polish intellectuals to the spot where they were found. Their reports now coming back to us from abroad are gruesome. The Führer has also given permission for us to hand out a dramatic news release to the German press. I gave instructions that the widest possible use should be made of this propaganda material. It will keep us going for a couple of weeks.[14]

Indeed, Goebbels used the Katyn discoveries until the end of June, always linking them to the propaganda campaign against the Jewish Bolshevik system. This was not without reason.[15] The final action against the Jews of Warsaw, which Goebbels would have been happy to cover up, included 56,065 people: 13,136 of them had died in the ghetto, 7,000 were executed on the spot, and the rest perished during the fighting and explosions. Another 42,929 were transported to Treblinka by the Reichsbahn, using at least forty-three trains, which could have instead carried another infantry division to the Voronezh front. This puts the entire operation in Warsaw in a problematic light. It is hard to believe how this action could possibly correlate with the armed forces' buildup of manpower and armaments before the upcoming battle at Kursk, but apparently there was more to these figures.

The Ghetto Uprising and Use of Manpower

On June 11, 1943, Himmler had to reissue the order that "the city area of the former ghetto should be totally flattened, every cellar and every sewer should be filled in."[16] In a letter to Himmler sent on July 23 referring to that order, Oswald Pohl reported that on July 19, a new concentration camp was being built on the ruins of the former Warsaw ghetto. It already housed some 300 prisoners, with SS-Obersturmbannführer Wilhelm Goecke, who had previously served at Mauthausen concentration camp, as commander.[17] Pohl reported that this was being done in coordination with General Stroop. Thus, there is every reason to believe that Stroop's forces remained in the ghetto area, at least until July 19, 1943, when Goecke became commander of the new camp. This puts the entire operation of the Warsaw ghetto in a task frame that occupied Stroop's forces for three months, from April 19, 1943, and the mission of liquidating the Warsaw ghetto an operation that lasted close to two months. The exact date when the heavy units completed their part is irrelevant to the fact that this entire operation turned out to be extremely time-consuming when all attention should have been focused on concentrating forces at the Kursk salient in order to prevent the Red Army from building its strategic layout without interference. The ghetto operation appears irrational, especially considering that Warsaw was already occupied by the Germans. Allocating a full division for combat in the same manner of street fighting as the Wehrmacht had used in Stalingrad, with house-to-house and face-to-face combat, was a huge waste of manpower, ammunition, and particularly precious time. There was no strategic significance in such an operation. It was neither a military maneuver nor a tactical deception to gain advantage over the enemy, which—even though Himmler and Goebbels believed that the enemy was the Jew—was actually increasing its might around Kursk.

One way to grasp the complexity of a military force the size of an army division is by examining the combined manpower invested in liquidating the ghetto in terms of war time. An average of 3,000 men per day employed in the Warsaw ghetto operation is equivalent to the number that could have gained extra territory or positions around Kursk, enabling an earlier deployment for Operation Citadel. Therefore, we are actually looking at a waste of a military force equivalent to 180,000 men, which is more than substantial enough to influence a military operation and territorial gains.[18]

According to the initial plan, the German forces assigned to the ghetto operation were to raze 1,800 of the 3,200 acres of its area. It was decided that twelve million square meters of built-up area, or 2.64 million square meters of building material, would be destroyed. However, according to a report sent by Pohl to Himmler on October 29, 1943, this task was still ongoing. It took months and was disrupted because of the Polish uprising in Warsaw, which began in August 1944. For this task, he said, 1,372 cubic meters of building debris would be removed on a daily basis, using twenty trains a day, 400 trucks, ten excavators, and a fifteen-kilometer normal-gauge railway.[19]

In regard to the Voronezh front of the Kursk bulge, Zhukov reported to Stalin on May 22, 1943, that the Germans had only fifteen divisions on the front line and thirteen more in reserve, including three Panzer divisions. The Germans had 232 divisions along the entire Soviet German front; however, battles sometimes came to a showdown that could be decided by as few as a dozen fighters.[20] In the case of the Okhtyrka sector in the Ukraine, for instance, where on August 18 the Germans encountered a counteroffensive from Okhtyrka toward the outskirts of Kharkov, the 53rd Army tried to repulse the attack, particularly with the 89th and the 105th divisions, which had almost reached a state of exhaustion. Especially harsh fighting took place on Hill 207.1. In the end, it took only sixteen Red Army infantry to conquer the hill from remnants of the German forces that were holding Kharkov. Out of the sixteen, only seven made it to the top, and instead of retreating, they stayed there until Russian backup forces came to their rescue.[21] This example is not to suggest that a dozen fighters can decide the fate of an entire campaign. One can not ignore the size of the Red Army in numbers as one of the reasons for the German failure at Kursk.[22] However, the case of Hill 207.1, if considered by the German High Command, could have changed combat mentality concerning logistical decision making.

After the initial three days planned for the Warsaw ghetto operation, whether General Stroop's forces would have been assigned to Sicily to help halt the Allied invasion of southwest Europe or sent east to stiffen the buildup at Kursk, they were a full military division, fighting a harsh battle with losses of men and ammunition, and with logistical needs such as food, armaments, and other military requisites in order to accomplish its mission. Daily supplies for the troops fighting at the Warsaw ghetto meant more trains and locomotives, which were diverted from other strategic tasks. Therefore, the number of Reichsbahn trains far exceeded the four trains for transporting the troops, as Stroop's report noted.[23] In the rear area of Army Group Center, partisan activity against the German assembly of forces was increasing, exacerbating the difficulties. The Germans reported 1,092 partisan attacks against the railways in June, making Stroop's division fighting in Warsaw look even more pointless.[24]

One might ask whether, instead of wasting two months in Warsaw, an extra division, deployed even as a reserve force, would have changed the outcome of this huge battle. The common view is that the magnitude of the battle itself was enough to show that one Panzer corps or one division was too small as a reinforcement. It is also true that Soviet forces, which had at this time begun their counteroffensive, had been reinforced by two tank armies and five combined armies from their strategic reserves. However, according to von Manstein, there was one German reserve division that could have been used in Operation Citadel, the 14th Panzer Corps. According to von Manstein, this was the only card left in the hands of Army Group South when the battle reached its climax on July 13, 1943. Manstein was referring to two divisions, the 17th Panzer Division with sixty-seven operational tanks and 5th Wicking SS-Panzergrenadier division with fifty-one tanks. In comparison in Warsaw, Stroop was using SS-Panzergrenadier training and Reserve Battalion 3 and an SS cavalry reserve division. They may not have been ideally trained or configured for high-intensity assault combat, but neither were the Russian defense battalions, considering that the Soviet casualties were three times higher than German losses. According to von Manstein, this was perhaps the amount of force needed to turn the scales in the Germans' favor. However, the army group did not get approval from Hitler to use it. Instead, he ordered that the offensive be postponed. By perhaps shifting the main point of attack, Manstein could have taken some ground initially and gained momentum in the attack, allowing him to enhance the possibilities of continuing the offensive before the Soviets had moved forces to counterstrike, or at least continue the offensive as a battle of attrition.[25] The historical record is clear, however: the initial inspiration for an attack at Kursk came from Manstein himself and not from Hitler. He therefore bears responsibility for its failure.[26]

When Governor Hans Frank was asked after the war by his interrogators if he remembered being in Warsaw at any time during the period April 19 to May 16, 1943, and if he recalled the Warsaw ghetto being razed, all he said was that he knew of a report stating there had been fighting in the Warsaw ghetto, the police and the Wehrmacht had been involved in major battles, and they had suffered heavy losses. Frank claimed he had asked at the time for reports from the Wehrmacht and the police, and they informed him that there had been a major uprising with small arms, canons, and machine guns of all kinds, and that it was an internal civil war. Because Frank wanted to save his neck at Nuremberg, he saw the ghetto uprising as part of the war and not just rather "another fight and big uprising that we had last summer in December 1944," referring to the Polish civilian uprising in Warsaw connected to the advance of the Soviets.[27]

In a letter dated February 2, 1943, sent by SS and police head of Poland's Warsaw district, Ferdinand von Sammern-Frankenegg, to Himmler in Berlin, he practically begged the Reichsführer to let him use 20,000 Jews from the Warsaw district for labor in eight textile plants, which had to be removed to the Lublin district by Odilo Globocnik. As a result of massive arrests, the Polish population had fled to other districts, and it was hard to draft new workers. Von Sammern-Frankenegg was therefore asking Himmler to use Jewish labor instead of transporting the Jews to Treblinka. These measures were actually the first to be taken before the offensive on and liquidation of the Warsaw ghetto. Von Sammern-Frankenegg was also the commander of the military force that began the assault on the ghetto on April 19, but he was replaced the next day by Stroop after the unsuccessful morning offensive. He was court-martialed on April 24, 1943, and was found guilty of defending Jews even though he was the one responsible for the *aktzia* that took place on January 18, 1943.[28]

On October 6, 1943, Himmler would refer to the destruction of the Warsaw ghetto in a speech he gave to Nazi officials in Posen, including Minister Speer:

> You will believe me when I tell you that I had great difficulties with economic enterprises. I have cleared many Jewish ghettos in the rear front. In one ghetto in Warsaw we had four weeks of house-to-house fighting; in four weeks we cleared seven hundred bunkers. This whole ghetto produced fur coats, clothing and the like. Earlier when we wanted to get it we were told: stop! You're disrupting the war economy! Stop! Defense enterprise! Of course all this has nothing to do with Comrade Speer. You cannot do anything about it. It is those alleged defense enterprises that Comrade Speer and I will cleanse jointly during the coming weeks and months.[29]

Himmler's audience was stunned—not by the news of the Final Solution, which they all knew about by now, but by Himmler's admission. They had regarded it as a delicate subject of which one spoke quietly and circumspectly, not as a matter to bring up in a semipublic speech.

They felt that Himmler had made them officially privy to the killing of the Jews in order to rope them into his circle of accomplices, and awareness of this stirred their latent fears of the punishment that awaited them if Germany lost the war. According to one witness at Nuremberg, the subject of killing Jews "cropped up" in the German army on the Eastern Front in almost every conversation that lasted longer than three minutes. Not a single person said, "This is completely new to me" or "I don't know anything about it." The transports and killing centers were an established fact for everybody.[30]

Operation Citadel

After the date for Operation Citadel was repeatedly postponed, it became increasingly probable that it would overlap with the anticipated start of the Allied offensive in the Mediterranean. Therefore, on June 18, the OKW operations staff submitted a strategic assessment to Hitler. This led to a proposal stating that until the situation had been clarified, Operation Citadel should be canceled and a strong operational reserve be placed at the disposal of the Supreme Command for use both in the East and in Germany—in the latter by the formation of new units. Although Hitler appreciated their point of view, he decided that same day that the operation should definitely go ahead. He set the date of the attack initially for July 3, then subsequently for July 5. The result was that Operation Citadel was launched just five days before the beginning of the Allied landing in Sicily. The forces employed in the attack, which at the time were the most important reserves at the disposal of the Supreme Command, were mostly reduced to remnants.[31] In a conference that took place at the Wolf's Lair on July 1 with all his senior commanders, Hitler had stated just four days before Operation Citadel that he did not believe that the Russians had the strength to strike a blow against the Wehrmacht. He seemed confident and expected nothing short of victory at Kursk. His only fear was that the Italians would lose Sicily.[32]

As a result of the pointed shape of the Kursk pocket, the German operational plan was obvious to both sides: two massive armies aimed at the northern and southern sides of the bulge would seek to meet in the middle, surround all the Soviet forces, and make a fatal tear in the Soviet defensive front. Fifty divisions, including nineteen Panzer and motorized divisions, with 2,700 tanks and assault guns, would be supported by over 2,600 aircraft.[33]

According to official Soviet history, the Battle of Kursk began on July 5 and ended on August 23, 1943. The campaign was divided into three parts: the defensive phase, the offensive against Orel, and the offensive against Belgorod–Kharkov. For the Germans, the Battle of Kursk actually derived from three different operations, beginning with Operation Citadel, the summer fighting around Orel, and the fourth battle of Kharkov. The main reason for this division was that Army Group South had to shift forces from Operation Citadel to fight along the Mius River far to the south and then react to another Soviet offensive directed against Belgorod–Kharkov. The Battle of Kursk, including Operation Citadel and the two Soviet counteroffensives, involved a total of more than four million troops, 69,000 artillery pieces, 1,300 tanks and self-propelled guns, and nearly 12,000 combat aircraft. In the initial assault, the Red Army outnumbered German forces by a factor of almost three to one (1,426,353 men against roughly 518,000). Nevertheless, the heavy German Tiger tanks proved strongly resistant to Soviet attempts to destroy them, and even the Panzers soon proved their superiority over the Russian T-34s, shooting them to pieces at distances well in excess of 2,000 meters. Von Manstein's and Hoth's forces advanced steadily, and the Soviet generals began to panic. However, as during the months before Operation Citadel, the problem derived mainly from the overworked railway system, which was hard-pressed to get reinforcements to the front.[34] By August 20, 1943, only one railway line and one road running from Kharkov to Merefa and Kransnograd were left in German hands.[35]

The forty-four divisions assembled for Operation Citadel amounted to almost 24 percent of all the divisions on the Eastern Front. These included all men that the unit had to provide with food and other necessities—civilians and even POWs, men belonging to the unit and others attached to it, and the sick and wounded, who were expected to return to duty within eight weeks. In addition, men detached from their units and men on leave were part of the ration strength amount of a division in the Kursk salient. However, examination of combat strength refers to the number of soldiers employed as rifle men or in direct support of rifle men. If a division had 1,000 infantry left, for example, it might still have to supply rations to over 10,000 men. This was the origin of the range of figures accorded to the Battle of Kursk by postwar Soviet and Western historians.[36] Soviet historians always tended to exaggerate the numbers on the German side for propaganda purposes; the number of battalions in a division could differ as well. At the beginning of Operation Barbarossa, an infantry division had three regiments each with three battalions. As losses mounted, the Germans experienced difficulties keeping the units at their prescribed strength. These were further compounded by the raising of new divisions. Consequently, several divisions had to make alterations to their structure. One common change was to reduce the number of infantry battalions in such regiments from three to two. For instance, as of July 2, 1943, the combat strength of battalions of the 6th Infantry Division was 3,121 men and by July 10 was down to 1,851, with an average of 310 men per battalion. On July 3, 1943, the 31st Infantry Division had 3,068 men, which had diminished by July 10 to 1,983, with an average of 362 men per battalion. Also on July 3, the 20th Panzer Division had a total combat strength of 2,837 men, which was reduced by July 10 to 1,751, with an average of 382 men per battalion.[37] For the sake of comparison, from April 19, 1943, and for the next two months, until the beginning of July 1943, General Stroop's forces in charge of the demolition of the Warsaw ghetto operation had six battalions, with an average of 330 men each and a total of almost 3,000 men daily, excluding casualties.[38]

By July 11, six days after the German assault began, von Manstein's forces broke thorough Soviet defenses and were within reach of their first major objective, the town of Prokhorovka. Here the Soviet generals launched their counterattack with the aim of encircling and destroying the German forces. However, they failed to notice a massive four-and-a-half-meter-deep antitank trench dug not long before by Soviet prisoners as part of Zhukov's preparations for the battle. The first lines of T-34s fell straight into the ditch, and when those following finally saw the danger, they veered in panic, crashed into one another, and burst into flames as the Germans opened fire. By midday, the Germans reported 190 wrecked or deserted Soviet tanks on the battlefield, with a few still in flames. To make up for this fiasco, which enraged Stalin, the senior political commissar in the area, Nikita Khrushchev, agreed with Marshal Pavel Rotmistrov, the leading Soviet tank general of the Red Army, that the report would state that the Russian tanks had been lost in a fierce battle in which more than 400 German tanks had been destroyed by heroic Soviet forces. Stalin accepted this report, and it became the source of a legend that marked Prokhorovka as the greatest tank battle in history. In reality, it was a military disgrace. The Soviet forces lost a total of 235 tanks, the Germans only three. Nevertheless, Rotmistrov became a hero of the Soviet Union.[39]

For the Germans, though, there were two battles, one in the north and one in the south. Soviet reinforcements for an offensive against Orel had no effect on von Manstein's options to continue his offensive, as long as his resources were not removed for use in the Orel sector. In addition, in the southern sector, the Red Army had used all the reserves at the Voronezh front and was forced to reinforce it. Consequently, the Soviets had already committed large forces to halt the southern attack, but again, von Manstein could have changed the direction of the main attack. By keeping the offensive going, von Manstein would still have had the initiative, and the troops at the Voronezh front would have had to react to his moves. What the consequences of such a deployment might have been is impossible to determine. It could hardly have turned Operation Citadel into a success, yet it might have enabled von Manstein to destroy parts of the Soviet 38th and 40th armies and inflict further losses.[40]

The Soviet offensive, which continued until August 23, marked the end of the German attacks in the East with the fall of Kharkov. From that point on, the initiative would belong to the Red Army, and the Soviets would command the entire Eastern Front. However, far from being the graveyard of the German army, as the Soviets would have it,[41] the Battle of Kursk had only a relatively minor impact. Undoubtedly, it demonstrated that the Tiger and Panzer tanks were far superior to the Russian T-34s and even the KV-S1 heavy tanks, and at least equal to the IS-1 tanks. The German Panzers were upgraded after 1941, with more effective guns and additional armor, yet both machines could destroy one another at typical battle ranges, and therefore the outcome was determined by tactics, training, and circumstances more than by technical features.[42] However, this made little difference because the German tanks were still too few in number compared to their Soviet counterparts. Although the tanks were left behind in an apocalyptic scene of devastation after they withdrew from the Kursk battlefield, the outcome was unequivocal. For the first time in the war, a German summer offensive had been repulsed.[43]

One month after the fall of Kharkov on September 25, 1943, the Germans were pushed back some 483 kilometers to the northwestern part of the front. They were even repelled from Smolensk, which they had entered so confidently on their way to Moscow during the first few months of the war, in 1941. By the end of September 1943, the German forces had withdrawn to the Dnieper line. The Donets Basin was lost, and the Wehrmacht forces in the Crimean peninsula were in danger of being completely cut off.[44] The old battlefields of 1941 suddenly reappeared, but faith in revising the situation had faded.

11

The Allied Invasion of Sicily

The Allied landings in Sicily on July 10, which might be said to have determined the outcome of Operation Citadel, left no room for mistakes in regard to future events. The balance of war turned against Germany, but surprisingly, and almost correspondingly, the eagerness of high-ranking SS officers to finish the ideological job relating to the Jewish question escalated a step further. Unlike the Stalingrad campaign, however, the Battle of Kursk was not a fiasco, and the myths concerning it fed by Soviet propaganda turned out to be grossly exaggerated. The rapidly deteriorating situation in the Mediterranean, and above all the Allied landings in Sicily on July 10, 1943, convinced Hitler that it was necessary to immediately withdraw key forces from the Eastern Front—in particular, tank divisions that were taking part in Operation Citadel—and transport them to the Italian peninsula in order to prepare a defense against the looming Allied invasion. At that time, von Manstein still believed it would be possible to pull a limited success out of the Kursk offensive, particularly in view of the heavy Soviet losses, but on July 17, 1943, the tank commanders received an order to withdraw their forces.[1]

While Hitler's message of July 1 to the commanders on the Eastern Front that the battle in Tunisia had postponed the invasion of Europe for half a year was basically true, the Germans had done little to increase defensive power in Italy, Sicily, Sardinia, or Corsica. The decision to withdraw six to eight armored divisions and other forces from the Eastern Front and deploy them to fight for the southern fringe of Europe was shelved in favor of Operation Citadel. There was no intention of withdrawing forces from the East other than in an emergency, but it was important for the supreme command of the Wehrmacht (OKW) that the divisions selected should not be otherwise committed or even used until further orders. The problem was that the army formations that were being held ready for the Mediterranean theater—that is, for Sicily—were at the same time the core of the attacking forces for the only major offensive operation of 1943 in the East. Three newly formed divisions from remnants of German formations that had not crossed to Tunisia, in addition to two armored divisions and two Panzergrenadier divisions from the West, were moved to Italy, but all were lacking in equipment and training, which could not be completed before August.[2] Sicily was invaded on July 10 by the 7th and 8th armies, amounting to a total of thirteen Allied divisions against a force of thirteen Axis divisions, including four German and nine Italian divisions. Some 90,000 German troops helped their Italian allies defend a coastline of 966 kilometers and a 16,000 square kilometer area.[3]

Four German divisions were all the Wehrmacht managed to deploy in southern Italy by transporting troops from the eastern formations. This low number requires special attention at the logistical level. In parallel with the fighting in the eastern and southern European theaters of war, between the end of February and the end of August 1943, the SS was successfully struggling against near-impossible logistical circumstances on a front within the borders of the General Government. During these months, the Reichsbahn was operating the special trains continually. Some 120 trains deported Jews during this period aboard SS trains from the German Reich, France, Holland, and Belgium to Auschwitz, Majdanek, Sobibor, and Theresienstadt. Eighty-two trains left during this period from the German Reich, twenty-two headed for Auschwitz and sixty for Theresienstadt. Ten trains left from France, all from Drancy camp: two trains for Sobibor, two for Majdanek, and six for Auschwitz. Another twenty-four trains departed the Netherlands, all from Westerbork camp: three trains to Auschwitz, two to Theresienstadt, and nineteen to Sobibor. Another two trains from Mechelen, Belgium, left for Auschwitz.[4] To transfer a military force to southern Italy that was as large as the forces assembled there—namely, another 90,000 German soldiers—would have required the same amount of trains used by the SS—that is, 120 with

750 combat troops per train, including full combat gear and equipment. The fact that this was not done only strengthens the argument that the Reichsbahn's first priority was to deal with the special trains before even moving reserves to southern Italy.

On August 1, the OKW demanded fuel supplies for operational control of the Alpine passes and a supply base to provide upper Italy. The initial amount was for 40,000 cubic meters (CBMs), but this was reduced to 24,000 CBMs with 10,000 CBMs in reserve. Translating this into Reichsbahn resources, for reserves alone, the supreme command was asking for 100 trains and a total of approximately 340 transports. These, of course, could not be supplied, especially in light of the Jewish transports during these months, which amounted to sixty trains from the beginning of April alone.[5]

On May 2, General Montgomery presented the Joint Allied Chiefs of Staff with his plan for the landing in Sicily. At the meeting, which took place in Algiers in the presence of General Dwight Eisenhower, Montgomery declared in his opening remarks that the conquest of Sicily would eventually be determined by action taken by the ground forces. These forces would have to reach Sicily with the help of the navy, which would be responsible for sustaining them after the landings too. Montgomery was certain that in order for the landing to succeed, they needed an extra two divisions that would be ready to invade Gela Bay.[6] What is clear from Montgomery's report is that again, the operation would be determined by which side would be faster in mobilizing its forces and supplying them throughout the conflict. Just as the Germans were unprepared to defend Sicily, the British were unprepared for an invasion. For the Germans, it was easy to bring forces through mainland Italy and then transfer them on the five train ferries that operated across the Strait of Messina.

The invasion of Sicily came as no surprise to anyone in the German High Command, except they believed it would come from Sardinia, a possibility briefly considered by Hitler, who was influenced by Alfred Jodl's view.[7] On the other hand, Albert Kesselring, commander in chief in southern Europe, believed it more probable that the next Allied step would be a landing in Sicily. Benito Mussolini and the Italian command agreed with his view because the only existing German force left there was the 15th Panzergrenadier division, which had been improvised from conscripts. Although the Hermann Göring Panzer division had been dispatched, German support for the ten shaky Italian divisions was not enough to defend Sicily. While reviewing the event with Basil Liddell Hart after the war, Kesselring considered that the Allied landings could have been repulsed decisively if the two additional German divisions that were hurriedly dispatched to Sicily after the Allies were firmly ashore had been moved there earlier to become, along with the two divisions already there, a powerful, mobile counterattack force under a single German command.[8]

One might ask why the deployment across the southern border of the European fortress was not better organized. From Sicily, it was obvious that the British and Americans would cross the Strait of Messina to southern Italy. All the information received indicated that Italian forces were fighting unwillingly. The German formations in Italy comprised a small minority because it was hoped that the Italians would defend their own country uncompromisingly.[9] The Germans, however, seemed more eager to get rid of the Italian Jews than repulse the Allied landings. After the Italian army capitulated on September 9, 1943, and the incompetent government of Pietro Badoglio negotiated Italy's exit from the war, the Italian boot was divided into three parts. The southern part was occupied by the Allies while the central and northern parts were occupied by the Germans, who quickly seized Albania and the Italian islands of the Aegean Sea, as well as the Italian-occupied zones in France, Yugoslavia, and Greece. The Germans finally found the opportunity to exercise effective authority and were free to act as they wished. They thus invested efforts in rounding up Jews for deportation to the killing centers, always giving this task first priority. These desires were realized after continuing difficulties raised by the Italians to their allies in all three zones of occupation. The Germans agreed to let the Italian government protect the Jews under their sphere of influence until March 31, 1943, after which their fate was sealed, even at the price of friction with the Italians.[10] The Italian Jews were the source of endless disagreement as a result of the reluctance of the Italian occupation authorities to hand over the Jews to be murdered. Most Italian officers simply could not comprehend the German insistence on killing Jews and saw it as merely another indication of their ally's barbaric inclinations.[11]

Overall, by far the most important impact of the landings in Sicily was on the German direction of the war. Just as the Battle of Kursk became a critical turning point, Sicily contributed to the German decision to end all offensive operations on the Eastern Front so that reinforcements of both troops and planes could be sent to Italy and the Balkans. It was expected that three SS divisions could be removed from the Eastern Front, but this did not happen because of lack of transport. It was only in the last days of July and early August that the Germans withdrew SS units from the Eastern Front and sent them to central Italy.[12] However, although it was already too late—Sicily had already fallen into Allied hands—the move was linked to the opportunity that opened up for the exposure of Italian Jews to SS persecution. On May 20, Hitler held a conference in the presence of Wilhelm Keitel, Erwin Rommel, Konstantin von Neurath,[13] and several other officials. Von Neurath, who came from Sicily, reported that every day the British were firing at the rail engines so that movement and supply of locomotive spare parts was virtually impossible.[14]

In the initial assault of the invasion of Sicily, code named Operation Husky, nearly 3,000 ships and landing craft, carrying 160,000 men, 14,000 vehicles, 600 tanks, and 1,800 guns took part. The British 8th Army that invaded Sicily comprised seven divisions, with an infantry brigade from the Malta Garrison, two armored brigades, and commando units. The American 7th Army had six divisions under its command. The Axis garrison in Sicily, originally under the Italian general Mario Roatta, consisted of two German divisions (one of which was armored), four Italian infantry divisions, and six Italian coast defense divisions of poor quality. The German divisions were divided into battle groups to reinforce their allies and counterattack.[15] Allied reinforcements were dispatched to Sardinia, and what Montgomery grandly called the "Sicilian campaign" lasted only from July 10 until August 17.

Although Italian units fought bravely, the other Axis troops, poorly armed and badly led, surrendered quickly. It is almost certain that Charles "Lucky" Luciano, the head of the New York underworld syndicate, who at the time was serving a thirty-year prison sentence, was called upon to use his influence to have the Sicilian Mafia work for Allied objectives. US military intelligence knew that Luciano maintained good relations with the Sicilian and Italian Mafias, which Mussolini had relentlessly pursued. Luciano's help was sought in providing Mafia assistance to counter possible Axis infiltration of US waterfronts during Operation Avalanche (the invasion of Italy), and his connections in Italy and Sicily were tapped to furnish intelligence and ensure an easy passage for US forces involved in the Italian campaign. Albert Anastasia, another New York mobster who controlled the docks, promised that no dockworkers' strike would break out. Both during and after the war, US military and intelligence agencies reportedly also used Luciano's Mafia connections to root out communist influence in labor groups and local governments. In return for his cooperation, Luciano was permitted to run his crime empire unhindered from his jail cell. In 1946, as a reward for his wartime cooperation, Luciano was paroled on condition that he depart the United States and return to Sicily. He was released from prison that same year for the "extraordinary services he had rendered."[16] The Luciano case illustrates how fragile the entire situation was. If the Allies needed the Sicilian Mafia's assistance in order to invade, surely one or two extra German divisions could have repulsed the attack on July 10, 1943.

A comparison between the strength of the eastern army in April and October 1943 shows that numbers rose sharply at first. However, after the Allied landings in Sicily and subsequently on the Italian mainland, it became impossible to transfer substantial forces from the theaters of war in the West. On the contrary, with the threat of an Allied landing in Belgium or northern France, only a few hundred kilometers from the Ruhr, the eastern theater had to relinquish its monopoly over manpower for the first time in the war. The OKW decided to adopt a defensive strategy on the Eastern Front. Only after Operation Husky did this change.

Even before winter set in on October 14, 1943, German forces in the East numbered 2,568,500 men, the lowest level since 1941. Between July and October 1943, the army in the East lost more than 900,000 men and had received only 411,000 replacements transported by the Reichsbahn.[17] This is remarkable considering that six months later, in summer 1944, the SS managed to send some 438,000 Hungarian Jews to Auschwitz. In July 1943, the OKW decided it was time to recruit more men; it was planned to supply units with 700,000 troops that month, but little was done. A first batch of 120,000 men was ordered for September, and the remainder was to follow only at the end of 1943.

Transports during the Critical Months

Because the Waffen-SS was a military force that, like the OKW, carried out combat missions, SS units under the direct command of Himmler fought alongside regular Wehrmacht forces. Around the village of Prokhorovka, for instance, the Germans committed the 2nd SS Panzer Corps, with its three divisions, Totenkopf, Leibstandarte, and Das Reich. Himmler had the power to control the number of combat SS forces wherever and whenever he wished.

The Reichsbahn supplied the SS during April 1943 alone with some forty-three special trains, which included trains from the German Reich (Berlin and Vienna), Belgium, and the Netherlands, as well as trains carrying Warsaw Jews to Treblinka during the *Grossaktion* of April 1943.[18] The routes all led east, but the final destination was not the center or the Voronezh front but the General Government. Had these trains been carrying tanks, an extra 516 Panzers and Tigers could have been sent to Kursk in April, enabling the German assault to begin as von Manstein had proposed. This was also the amount of tanks the Krupp factories in Essen and Magdeburg could produce per month, despite the Allied air attacks.

The difficulties in conducting Operation Reinhard, which was carried out largely in 1942 but ended officially in November 1943, came as no surprise to Adolf Eichmann and his circle. According to a report written during the yearly meeting with his specialists and representatives from each of the occupied countries in August 1942, he had hoped to end the Jewish deportations by June 1943 because of expected transport difficulties in the autumn and winter of 1943–1944. As in the previous deportations, each transport carried 1,000 Jews crammed into carriages and freight cars originally intended to carry no more than 750 soldiers to the front. Eichmann justified this number by comparing it to soldiers traveling with their packs and equipment, while the Jews placed their luggage in the baggage car.

This issue—of Jewish transports being part of the general logistics —is essential for understanding the reciprocation between executing Eichmann's task and the OKW's efforts to build efficient formations at the Kursk salient. The *Sonderzüge*, the term used in official correspondence, were proper trains that would otherwise be transporting combat reserves to the front. Eichmann's "specialist" forum also discussed the difficulties arising from the nationality of Jews slated for deportation. Because the Italian, Portuguese, Spanish, and Swiss governments were prone to intervene, it was decided to concentrate on "stateless Jews."[19] If June 1943 was the targeted date for completion of the task, perhaps this at least partially explains the delays in Operation Citadel, which began in early July 1943. It is not possible to determine whether Hitler was aware of this timetable when he postponed Operation Citadel, but it was certainly known to Rudolf Gercke, who was Eichmann's counterpart in the Wehrmacht, as well as to Albert Ganzenmüller, who supplied the trains on behalf of the Reichsbahn.

Meanwhile, during the spring of 1943, Auschwitz was running at full capacity, murdering 53,000 Jews transported from Salonika in Greece. Of these, 46,000 were deported between March and August 1943, although the route was extremely long and had already proven to be logistically difficult to operate in spring 1941, when Greece was occupied. Still, the SS insisted on using it to transport Greek Jewry from Salonika, Athens, Macedonia, and even the island of Rhodes in July 1944 all the way to Auschwitz.[20] In addition, between March and July 1943, another nineteen trains carrying 32,000 Dutch Jews were sent to Sobibor. During the critical months between March and July 1943, when the German army should have been preparing the necessary military layout for launching Operation Citadel before the decisive battle at Kursk, sixty-five trains were used instead for deportations carrying Jews from the southern part of Europe all the way to central Poland, rather than transporting more arms to the Soviet front, thus enabling the German attack to be launched earlier than July 1943 and preempting the buildup of a huge number of Russian forces.[21]

A report of a police lieutenant by the name of Karl speaks of a transport of 2,404 Jews from Skopje, Macedonia, to Treblinka, which left on March 29 at 1230 hours, after being loaded for four and a half hours from 0600 hours. The train passed through Albanian territory, reaching its final destination on April 5, 1943, at 0700 hours. It was unloaded the same day between 0900 hours and 1100 hours. Superficially, there is nothing interesting about this transport. However, a train from southern Europe to Treblinka, completing its journey on the eighth day, could have made almost two trips during that period with supplies for the troops on the Eastern Front, or at least made a return trip to the old Reich. In addition, it occupied a route that could have been used for military traffic. Shorter journeys, too, had an impact on the exclusive needs of the troops on the front. The Starachowice labor camp, for instance, was in the Lower Silesian district of Poland. Although the camp was only 225 kilometers from Auschwitz, it took the Jewish deportees thirty-six hours to get there. Thus, a journey that should have lasted a maximum of four hours occupied this route for three days.[22]

Dieter Wisliceny, who worked in Eichmann's IV-A4 department in the Reich Main Security Office, was in Greece from February to December 1943. According to Wisliceny, between mid-March and the end of May 1943, some twenty-four transports carrying 60,000 Jews from Salonika and its surroundings, as well as from Athens, headed for Auschwitz, with an average of 2,500 Jews per transport. The majority, 55,000, came from Salonika. In April alone, almost 25,000 Greek Jews were transported to Auschwitz. Because the entire area was under military rule, Eichmann's request from March 10 for the evacuation of the Jewish communities in Greece had to go through the army group commander, who at that time was Colonel General Alexander Löhr, a former Austrian air force major and a friend of Göring's.

The sole condition made by the military was that the Todt Organization[23] would get 3,000 male Jewish workers for railroad construction work. The transports from Greece began on Eichmann's order in mid-March 1943. Three thousand workers were provided to Todt Organization, but they were returned by the end of May and dispatched to Auschwitz. Wisliceny claims that there was always a close connection between the IV-A4 representatives and the army. The IV Department, including the Gestapo and the secret police, was headed by Gruppenführer Heinrich Müller. It was subdivided into several groups, designated by capital letters. Group A, to which Eichmann's sector belonged, had one head. Section IV-A4 was one of several sections belonging to group IV-A. Section IV-A4 was headed by Obersturmbannführer Eichmann. This section had two subdivisions. Subsection IV-A4a dealt with questions of the church and subsection IV-A4b with Jewish questions.[24]

During 1943–1944, Heinz Guderian was appointed inspector general of the armored troops. As such, he made repeated tours of the tank production factories and of occupied Europe. This role makes it unthinkable that the Panzer leader remained ignorant of the inhuman crimes and brutal reality of the Nazi occupation. He visited steel manufacturing factories and tank plants, all of which made extensive use of slave labor drawn from the concentration camp system based on European Jewry. In 1942–1943, Alfred Krupp built the Berthawerk factory (named after his mother) near Auschwitz for the production of artillery fuses. Jewish women were used as slave labor there, leased from the SS for 4 reichsmarks per head a day. Later in 1943, it was taken over by Union Werke. When Guderian toured these factories, he could not have been unaware of the brutal exploitation of slave labor, which was responsible for the dramatic increase in war production in 1943–1944.[25]

The army participated in preparing and providing the transports with freight cars that had to be delivered for the evacuation by the German transport command. All the orders went through Eichmann and Dr. Max Merten, chief of the military administration in Greece, and the task itself was supervised by Wisliceny and SS-Hauptsturmführer Alois Brunner, when two transports of 2,500 people each were shipped from Athens in July 1944. The requests for train cars for these transports came from SS-Hauptsturmführer Franz Novak in subsection IV-A4b, who was in charge of all transportation matters related to the evacuation of Jews, and these were transmitted to department counselor Otto Stange in the transport ministry in Berlin, then through various channels to the area transport command. Wisliceny stated in his testimony, "All transports used in effecting the final solution of the Jewish problem in Greece and anywhere else it has worked in Europe, including Slovakia, Slovenia, Hungary and even Thrace and Macedonia, commanded a sufficiently high priority to take preference over other freight movements. All shipments were made on schedule, even in 1944 when the Germans were evacuating

Greece and the rail transport needs were critical."[26] The military administration cooperated in every request made by subsection IV-A4b, and there was no serious opposition to deal with.[27] All the Jews from Greece were transported by trains that went via Marawska–Ostrawa to Auschwitz. Upon the departure of each transport, a message was sent to Eichmann in Berlin stating the number of heads sent. On completion of the evacuation of the Jews from northern Greece, Brunner made a summary report to Eichmann.[28]

In addition to prioritizing transport of the Jews over troop movements, food supplies were diverted to concentration and death camps. According to Hans Frank, governor of the General Government, food requisitions for Majdanek (or, as it was referred to, the Lublin concentration camp) were decided by the SS or the police but were actually debited from the armed forces budget in accordance with the population distribution. Thus, not only did the SS use military transports within the 140,000 square kilometers of the General Government, but it also used military food supplies to keep the concentration camps running. The entire General Government covered a huge area. It was a night's journey from Kraków to Warsaw and from Kraków to Lemberg (Lvov). The distance from east to west was approximately 600 kilometers, similar to that between Munich and Berlin. Approximately 500 kilometers separated the southern and northern parts of the General Government, which was run by a total of 5,000 officials working directly under Hans Frank. The police and SS battalions were under Himmler's authority and were administered, together with the concentration camps, directly from Germany. According to Frank (who insisted to his investigators that he was not governor of all of Poland but of the much smaller geographical area of the General Government), the General Government consisted of the area not occupied in 1939 by the Russians but the other half, which was also divided into two. The larger part was incorporated into the German Reich and included Upper Silesia, Pozen, Danzig, West Prussia, and the southern part of East Prussia. The remaining area was called the General Government. Because the General Government was not a self-sufficient area but relied on German rations coming from the Reich, the entire food supply of the Polish population there was based on supplies carried by the Reichsbahn's trains. They frequently amounted to

400,000 meals a day, including rations for staff at the death camps and prisoners.[29]

According to Rudolf Höss, commandant of Auschwitz, Himmler told him that when an action was being carried out in one of the countries under German occupation, it was not to be stopped or delayed because of inadequate facilities. Auschwitz was chosen by Himmler for dispatching the major portion of European Jews because it had good rail connections and could be enlarged; it was also sufficiently far from population centers and could be isolated.[30]

On June 10, 1943, an order from the transport ministry was sent to the general directors of the Reichsbahn in Warsaw, Kraków, Lemberg, Prague, and Berlin. It dealt with the use of express trains in all four districts in connection with the actions that were taking place at that time. The most significant action was the liquidation of the Warsaw ghetto and the transportation of some 56,000 Jews to all the districts — Treblinka, Auschwitz, Belzec, and Terezín. According to the order, people in the wagons should be treated more courteously, and women should perhaps be used for escorting the transports. Anti-Bolshevik propaganda should be hung on billboards in the wagons and on the windows in order to combat Soviet propaganda against the Reich.[31] This order from June 1943 was in line with another fact concerning the handling of deportees. Since July 1943, people destined to be transported from the Drancy camp in France to Auschwitz were organized into groups of fifty to sixty to be loaded onto a single train wagon.[32] This number was lower than the transports sent to the Soviet territories or the deportations from various parts of Poland to the General Government, which consisted of an average of 100 per wagon. The former amount was not much higher than the number of soldiers the Wehrmacht transported per wagon, which was about forty. The only possible explanation is that because there was a lack of decent wagons for troops and supplies, the Reichsbahn was now trying to return the trains in a condition fit for transporting Wehrmacht troops immediately. When 100 people were crammed into a single wagon, the results were devastating to them as well as to Reichsbahn property.

The nature of the war was such that everything connected to it was dependent on the logistics of Reichsbahn trains. References to Jewish transports can therefore be seen in almost every action taken in regard to the military. For instance, in April 1943, 36,000 head of cattle were transported from a very limited wagon fleet aboard eighty trains from the Paris district to Essen in West Germany. It was no secret that Essen had the biggest industrial war plants, owned by the Krupp family, which supplied the military.[33] The train routes point to a strong connection between trains that carried ammunition, food supplies, and "Jew supplies" going from west to east, with stops on the way that fed "different industries."

On July 2, 1943, SS-Hauptsturmführer Alois Brunner, one of Eichmann's assistants, whom Eichmann referred to as his "best man," was appointed commander of the Drancy internment camp near Paris. In the summer of 1943, the Germans estimated that some 60,000 Jews were still living in Paris, and their clear destiny was deportation as soon as possible to Auschwitz. On August 15, 17, and 19, three trains were about to transport 400 trucks for the Wehrmacht from the industrial motor park in Strasbourg via the Alsace region to Zhytomyr in the southern Ukraine. These trains consisted of sixty wagons each, the same number used for the special trains that went to Treblinka.[34] It seemed that nothing at the front really interested Himmler, Eichmann, and their associates, for despite the German defeats, the persecution and deportation of French Jews were not suspended; rather, with so many enthusiastic French collaborators, they were intensified.[35]

In order to transport a full German division to the front during that period, the Reichsbahn had to supply forty to forty-five trains. For a Panzer and motorized division the number was fifty trains, and for a Romanian division forty-seven trains. Each train consisted of thirty-six to fifty-two wagons, the average being forty wagons with a total weight of 850 tons. The average speed of these trains was twenty-five kilometers per hour, which in the summer allowed them to travel 350 kilometers daily and during winter 250 to 300 kilometers. Thus, transporting an infantry division from Paris to Smolensk in the eastern theater would take ten days. Remarkably, out of four main routes through which these trains would pass, two would begin the trip at odd stations: the Lemberg–Zhytomyr–Kiev–Bachmatsch route and the Kraków–Lemberg–Proskuros–Umjani–Dnjepropetrowsk–Stalino route. Both left from the SS death camps. Lemberg was the station closest to Belzec, where some Jewish deportees were sent, and Kraków was the station closest to Auschwitz.³⁶ This demonstrates that the SS and the Wehrmacht used the same locomotives and wagons supplied by the Reichsbahn, sometimes shipping human stock to the death factories and at other times delivering military supplies to the troops at the front. However, the trains that left Lemberg or Kraków had apparently completed an entirely different mission.

Assessment of the Battle of Kursk

For years, the Battle of Kursk and the subsequent counteroffensive by the Red Army, launched on July 12, 1943, was overdramatized and overpraised by Soviet historians and commentators. Nevertheless, this was the only example in the war of a carefully prepared Wehrmacht offensive that failed within such a short time. On the other hand, the losses suffered by the attacking armies were far lower than Soviet literature claims. The truth thus lies somewhere in between. Total losses in tanks in July, August, and September were almost completely made good by new production. The failure of the German summer offensive in the Kursk area buried the Nazi propaganda myth about the Soviet troops' ability to attack in winter conditions only. The Soviet armed forces showed that they could smash the enemy in any season—in summer as well as in severe winter.³⁷

The eventual victory of Soviet arms in 1943 and 1944 has usually been portrayed as a consequence of the Soviet Union's overwhelming resources—their huge superiority in men and matériel. The German defeat has also been commonly interpreted as a result of strategic error and wrong decision making by Hitler as supreme commander of the armed forces, as well as poor intelligence and logistical overstretch. However, neither of these interpretations does justice to the historical reality. In the decisive battles from Stalingrad to the autumn of 1943, the balance of power in favor of the Soviets was much less marked than it was to become in the final stages of the German defeat. The Germans were not overwhelmed by sheer numbers; nor did the Red Army win the war simply because of the decline of the enemy. The operational experience and technological assets of the German forces in 1943 improved their fighting ability from 1940.[38] Even in numbers, the Germans built up their armed forces in 1943 to a total of 10.3 million soldiers, almost to the level it was at in the summer of 1942 when it reached its height.[39]

Another misleading interpretation that became a myth was that the Soviet Union won the war because it had endless space in the East from which to absorb manpower. True, in the East there was more space than people. However, the Soviet Union survived because it mobilized two-thirds of its women to run the factories and farms, and it modernized its armed forces so that it no longer had to rely purely on manpower but, like the American army, on mass-produced weapons. In addition, Soviet forces were not as fearsome as the Germans portrayed them. The numbers of men and tanks were much reduced after Kursk. Pavel Rotmistrov's 5th Guards tank army was reduced from 500 tanks to fifty. As he advanced toward the Dnieper, he divided them into three units, then set up a phantom radio communications net to persuade German eavesdroppers that he had an entire tank army behind him. In the south, German forces faced large infantry armies with a weak sprinkling of Soviet armor. Red Army divisional strength was approximately half the number it had been in 1942. Soviet weakness prevented a more decisive attack, and although much of the Donbas industrial region was recovered, German forces eluded capture and reformed a powerful Panzer group to defend the lower reaches of the river from Zaporozhye to the Black Sea.[40]

The belief that the German armies conquered Europe because of overwhelming motorized-based strength is untrue even in the case of the blitz campaigns. Even in 1939 the Germans had no clear lead in the area of tank production. The French, for instance, had more tanks than the Germans in May 1940, and they were boosted by British forces. The British, in fact, were producing more tanks than the Germans did in 1939, although they were not committed to such an extensive land war. Germany's victory in the West was gained not by overwhelming superiority in numbers but because the French General Staff failed to understand the new tactics of mechanized warfare and had reduced motorized strength by allocating tanks and vehicles among a large number of divisions, even those guarding the Maginot line.[41] In many ways the eastern campaigns between 1941 and 1943 were similar until the Soviets revised their strategy from defensive retreat to offensive attacks.

The Soviet victories of 1943 were won at an extremely high price in manpower. Stalingrad cost the lives of 586,834 soldiers and air men. The Battle of Kursk was won after 70,000 soldiers had been killed and the German line was broken, with the loss of another 183,000. In two months of fighting, the Red Army lost almost as many men as the United States or the British did in the entire war. The level of sacrifice imposed on the Soviet people might have destroyed any other society. In two years of fighting, more than 4.7 million men were killed, even though at Kursk the casualty rate was half that at Moscow. So severe was this toll that by the autumn offensives of 1943, Soviet divisions were down to as few as 2,000 men.[42] Thus, it is hard to blame the German army for being incompatible or ill-prepared for Soviet warfare. It seems that in terms of Soviet casualties on the battlefield, the German generals were achieving much better results than Eichmann and his gang of SS officials were in the death camps of the General Government. Operation Reinhard, apparently, was as tough as fighting at Stalingrad and Kursk in terms of mission completion. If the German army still managed to inflict such huge enemy casualties, perhaps without the logistical burden of Operation Reinhard they would have had a better chance of winning a war of attrition against the Soviets.

The German defeat at Kursk and the Red Army's advance to the Dnieper River in the summer–fall campaign of 1943 left a legacy of major historical controversies, the most contentious of which regarded the wisdom of Hitler's decision to launch Operation Citadel, Stalin's strategy, and the degree to which the Battle of Kursk represented a turning point in the war. Many historians have questioned Hitler's decision to launch Operation Citadel. Others have argued that he should have begun the offensive on the heels of von Manstein's counteroffensive in March; still others have criticized his decision to terminate the offensive before it achieved its full potential. In retrospect, the imposing strength of the Red Army field forces and strategic reserves in the summer of 1943, their powerful defenses in the Kursk bulge, and the predictability of a German offensive against them seemed to have ensured a Russian victory.[43]

Within the context of Operation Barbarossa and Operation Blue,

Hitler and his generals had every reason to expect success at Kursk because the Wehrmacht had always won in summer campaigns and the Red Army had never before experienced a concentrated Wehrmacht offensive before it had reached strategic, much less operational, depth. This grim reality explains why Stalin and the Stavka began the Battle of Kursk with a premeditated defense. Although the Battle of Stalingrad was the most significant turning point in the war, the Battle of Kursk was also decisive in several important respects. First, it presented the Wehrmacht with its final opportunity to achieve any sort of strategic success. Second, the battle's outcome proved conclusively that the war would end in Germany's total defeat. After Kursk, a Red Army victory was inevitable.

Throughout 1943, assessments and inventories of looted Jewish property became frequent at all levels of the system. In 1942, forty-five shiploads of goods looted from Dutch Jews arrived in Hamburg alone. They represented a net weight of 27,227 tons. The total value of Jewish belongings secured during Operation Reinhard up to December 15, 1943, was estimated at the operation's headquarters in Lublin as 178,745,960.59 reichsmarks. These items collected by the SS in early January 1944 from Lublin and Auschwitz filled 825 railway freight cars.[44] In other words, they occupied approximately another forty trains. On March 3, 1943, the head of the SS and police in the Lublin district reported booty worth 100,047,938 reichsmarks, including cash in banknotes, gold, silver, and jewelry. These were sent to the Reich's bank in Berlin in trucks. The victims' clothing from Lublin district alone was loaded onto 1,000 wagons—the equivalent of about fifty trains.[45]

Calculating the combined number of trains the Reichsbahn operated in connection with the Final Solution during the months of March to August 1943, including deportees, booty, and food supplies to the concentration camps, one arrives at a figure of some 250 trains: 120 trains for deporting Jews from the Reich, as well as from France, Belgium, and the Netherlands; another thirty trains for transferring Greek Jewry to Auschwitz; and some thirty trains for transporting the 56,000 Jews remaining in the Warsaw ghetto to Treblinka. Deferring implementation of the Final Solution would have supplied the Reichsbahn with enough trains to transfer another six full Wehrmacht divisions either to the Kursk salient or to southern Italy, or to both sectors of the three-front war the German army was then conducting.

In a pamphlet distributed among Communist Party members from July 11, 1943, Martin Bormann, head of the party chancellery and Hitler's private secretary and close associate, wrote that Hitler had asked him to state that there would be no public debate or any future discussion in regard to the Jewish question for which there was a comprehensive solution. Nevertheless, some Jews could be deployed for work purposes, and therefore, any reference to them was to be made in this framework. The word *Endlösung* (final solution) was not used but *Gesamtlösung* (total solution), further emphasizing the severe nature of Jews' fate at this period of the war.[46] Back in April 1943 there had been visits by Axis and pro-Axis leaders to Berlin, such as Benito Mussolini, Romanian prime minister Ion Antonescu, Hungarian leader Miklós Horthy, head of the Slovak puppet state Jozef Tiso, Vichy France prime minister Pierre Laval, Croatian fascist leader and head of the Croatian puppet state under Axis-occupied Yugoslavia Pavelić, Norwegian minister-president Quisling, and Japanese ambassador to Germany Hiroshi Ōshima. The German foreign minister, Ribbentrop, accused Horthy of dragging his feet over the Jews in Hungary. Some 800,000 Hungarian Jews were to be transported to the East, but Horthy would not be easily persuaded.[47]

By the time the Battle of Kursk was over and the Allies were already advancing from southern Italy to the north in autumn 1943, the OKW intended to recruit an additional 500,000 men for dispatch to the front lines.[48] At the same time, Eichmann was already planning for the same number of Hungarian Jews to be transported the following summer to Auschwitz.

The longer the fighting in Russia continued, the greater became Hitler's hatred of the Jews. In his conversations with Himmler and Goebbels, he left no room for doubt that he was not in the least concerned about what was happening to them.[49] Nor did he seem in the least troubled by the impact their deportations to the death camps had on the war effort.

July 18, 1942. Himmler's visit to IG Farben factory (Monowitz, near Auschwitz) where Ziclon-B was manufactured. Himmler is in the first row second from left. To his right are engineer Maximilian Faust and Auschwitz commandant Rudolf Höss. Note the freight wagons behind them. (Courtesy of Yad Vashem Archives)

Moscow, December 8, 1942. The face of "The Grand Alliance." Churchill arriving for a conference, overlooking Red Army soldiers that would defeat Hitler on the eastern front. First row from left General Shaposhnikov, Molotov, Stafford Cripps (British ambassador to Moscow) and Winston Churchill. (Courtesy of Yad Vashem Archives)

USSR, January 23, 1942. Marshal Semyon Timoshenko visiting the front. Timoshenko commanded the Soviet retreats to Smolensk in 1941 and was witness to the Wehrmacht's strength at its height. (Courtesy of Yad Vashem Archives)

Warsaw, Poland, April 1943. SS General Jürgen Stroop during the Warsaw Ghetto Uprising with SS men fit and armed for combat in the Soviet territories. Stroop's force was equivalent in numbers to a Wehrmacht division. (Courtesy of Yad Vashem Archives)

Kiev, Ukraine, 1942. Alfred Rosenberg, Reich Minister for the eastern occupied territories, arriving in an airplane. In his post, Rosenberg promoted the Germanization of Eastern peoples under brutal conditions, arranged the extermination of Jews in the Soviet Union, supervised slave labor, and carried responsibility for rounding up quotas of workers and sending them to the Reich. (Courtesy of Yad Vashem Archives)

Southern Soviet Union, end of 1941. General Friedrich Paulus (center), commander of the 6th Army, with his officers at 6th Army headquarters. As they have cake and wine, they seem relatively calm in planning their next operational maneuvers. Exactly one year later they would all be in a completely different situation at Stalingrad. (Courtesy of Bundesarchiv)

Stalingrad, USSR, December 12, 1942. Exhausted German soldiers retreating. (Courtesy of Yad Vashem Archives)

Julius Dorpmüller, General Director of the Reichsbahn from 1925 to 1945, and Reich Transport Minister in parallel from 1937 to 1945. (Courtesy of Yad Vashem Archives)

Wolf's Lair, Eastern Prussia, September 15, 1943. Discussing the military situation. From right to left: Generaloberst Kurt Zeitzler (OKH Chief of Staff), Hitler, General Erich von Manstein (commander of Army Group South), and Theodor Busse (von Manstein's Chief of Staff). (Courtesy of Yad Vashem Archives)

Bielefeld, Germany, December 13, 1941. Jews boarding a deportation train at Bielefeld railway station to the ghetto in Riga. The coaches used are regular third-class passenger cars. (Photo courtesy of "Stadtarchiv Bielefeld")

German soldiers in a train on their way to the front. One train had a capacity of transporting 750 men with full combat gear. (Courtesy of Yad Vashem Archives)

Lodz, Poland. Deported Jews with their belongings boarding a train in Radogoszcz railway station in Marysin. Note the sealed windows of a regular passenger car. (Courtesy of Yad Vashem Archives)

1942/1944. General Friedrich Fromm, Commander in Chief of the German reserve army and Wehrmacht chief of Armament; two sailors; Albert Speer, minister of armament and war production; Grand Admiral Karl Doenitz; and Hans Kehrl, head of planning division at the armament ministry, before a ship's hull. It is no exaggeration that these two men—Speer and Fromm, one supplying the means and the other the manpower—were together responsible for keeping the German war machine operational for so long. (Photo courtesy of Bundesarchiv)

France, June 1944. Transport by train of camouflaged Panzer V tanks still operating regardless of the heavy Allied bombing. Note the freight car that is carrying the ammunition is the same as the ones used for Jewish deportations. (Courtesy of Bundesarchiv)

Normandy, France, June 6, 1944. Germans bombing American troops with 88mm guns on the beach, D-Day. (Courtesy of Yad Vashem Archives)

Normandy, France, 1944. An aerial photo of a bombed railway station.
(Courtesy of Yad Vashem Archives)

Riga, Latvia. Soviet campaign against "Army Group North" and Waffen SS Divisions German Soldiers defending a railway bridge from sabotage. (Courtesy of Yad Vashem Archives)

Marshal and hero of the Soviet Union, Georgi Zhukov, commander of the central forces of the Red Army. In the winter of 1941, Zhukov was responsible for the counterattack during the Battle of Moscow and acted as coordinator of the Soviet forces during the Battle of Kursk. (Courtesy of Yad Vashem Archives)

Courland, Latvia, May 1945. Horses turned over to Soviet forces after the surrender of German military forces. During the war the Germans used over 2,750,000 horses for military operations and invaded the Soviet Union with around 750,000. (Courtesy of Yad Vashem Archives)

Part 4

The Extermination of Hungarian Jewry and the Allied Invasion of Normandy

The summer of 1944 was another turning point in the chronicles of World War II for two major reasons. The first was the opening of a second front on the European continent by the Allied invasion of western France, and the second was the final phase of the Jewish deportations by Reichsbahn-owned trains as a systematic means of eliminating European Jews. Transports of Hungarian Jews were conducted intensively in terms of both numbers and time. Meanwhile, dramatic developments were occurring on the Western Front: the Allied invasion of Normandy and the advance of Soviet forces from the east toward the German Reich.

The perpetration of the Final Solution in Hungary, which consisted of the dispatch of some 438,000 Jews to Auschwitz between May 15 and July 1944 aboard some 220 Reichsbahn trains,[1] occurred in parallel with the extreme difficulties of renewing supplies via the rail net to German divisions in the West. These transportation problems influenced the outcome of the Allied invasion of Western Europe. Although Germany had fifty-eight divisions in the West, the majority were not mobile, so the infantry divisions and even the Panzer units were solely for local use and static defense.[2] The outcome of events thus depended on which side would succeed in bringing additional forces to the battlefield in Normandy more quickly—Germany or the Allies.[3]

12

A Long and Winding Road

This chapter reviews the state of the German army during the months between the Battle of Kursk and the spring of 1944. The German invasion of its puppet ally, Hungary, was a turning point in the fate of the largest Jewish community still living in Europe, which was in a status quo with the authorities of the Hungarian state. That is, they continued to live a relatively regular and safe life despite increasing restrictions on their civil rights and economic possibilities. The Hungarian authorities continued to reject the repeated demands by the Germans to apply the Final Solution to the Jews living within their borders. Operation Margarethe (the occupation of Hungary) would pave the way for the destruction of almost the entire community in just a few weeks but would also raise a debate as to whether this action was in German interests.

The months from August 1943 until June 1944—from the Battle of Kursk until the Allied landings in Normandy—are occasionally referred to as the forgotten year of the war, or in Soviet literature as the third period of the war, when both forces had reached full maturity.[1] By now, both sides were in a stage of attrition, with the intention of bringing the clash of titans to a showdown. The German generals were aware of their desperate situation. They continued to ask Hitler for freedom of action so that they could use the vast open spaces of Russian territory to perform large-scale tactical maneuvers, in hopes of cutting off the advancing Soviet armies and demolishing them. Hitler saw this as a pretext for defeatism and a state of mind aimed at overall retreat; as time passed, he became even more fanatical about holding the lines. This meant that increasingly, German withdrawals were not integrated into any overall strategy; rather, they took place suddenly,

in reaction to a threat of encirclement by Soviet forces. Nevertheless, the German armies withstood the reckless assaults of the Soviets,
whose repeated frontal attacks caused them to suffer five times the
losses of their enemy and sometimes even more.[2]

In late August 1943, the Soviet High Command assessed that the
Germans still held substantial forces for continuing the war, despite
the Allies' advances. The landings in Sicily did not lead to any critical
changes in the Germans' strategic layout, although the Nazi leadership had to cope with the additional stress and pressure laid upon it.
Still, the Soviet High Command, and Zhukov in particular, believed
that after Kursk, the strength and combat effectiveness of the German armies in the East had entered a period of almost continuous decline. In any event, it was predicted that on the Eastern Front the
Wehrmacht was unable to conduct another major military assault. On
the other hand, the Soviets knew that the enemy had enough supplies and manpower to conduct active defensive operations.[3] For instance, with the addition of substantial forces from the Axis states,
the Waffen-SS alone had in 1943—despite some personnel shortages—250,000 men, with the potential to double the amount to half
a million.[4] In late March 1944, the Waffen-SS, which was the best-
equipped, though militarily not always the most effective, part of the
Wehrmacht reached a strength of 400,000 men.[5]

The third phase of the war marked the full development of the Soviet force in structure, equipment, and operational and tactical concepts, but like the Germans, they too suffered from severe manpower
shortages. The huge civilian and military casualties of the war, the
large factories needed to maintain weapons production, and the demands of rebuilding a ruined economy reclaimed from a German rule
of more than two years—all strained the supposedly inexhaustible
supply of Soviet labor. The manpower needed to build new, special-
ized units could come only by reducing the number of replacements
provided to existing front-line units. Moreover, because the Soviets
were almost continuously on the offensive, they inevitably suffered
heavier casualties at the tactical level than the German defenders. By
1944, the Red Army faced a manpower crisis that in its own way was
as serious as that confronting the Wehrmacht. Many rifle divisions
had an effective strength of 2,000 men or less, just as the German

six-battalion division became a standard one. The resulting disparity between the official and actual size of manpower in Soviet units goes a long way toward explaining the seemingly amazing performance of some German counterattacks. The ability of a full strength Waffen-SS division to halt a Soviet corps or army probably resulted more from the numerical weakness of the Soviet units than from the tactical superiority of the German attackers.[6]

At the start of 1944, Germany was on the strategic defensive, but the Nazi leadership still believed, not without reason, that the war could be concluded successfully. On January 4, 1944, Hitler held an armaments conference at the Wolf's Lair attended by Erhard Milch, Wilhelm Keitel, minister of food and agriculture Herbert Backe, Himmler, and Fritz Sauckel, the general plenipotentiary for labor deployment, the main theme of which was the labor program. Sauckel pledged to procure four million workers, for which Hitler promised his full support. Ironically, by the time this meeting took place, over four million European Jews had already been exterminated with the approval of this forum, although at least three million of them—excluding infants, the sick, and the old—could serve Sauckel's purpose.[7]

Hitler knew that the Americans and the British were committed to an assault on northern Europe; he believed that the German army could defeat an invasion on the beaches. The plan, then, was to concentrate German forces on the Eastern Front and stem the relentless advance of the Red Army. Therefore, if the Reich could control its resources, it might still prevail.[8] At this point in the war, Germany's main problem was that when it conquered such vast territories, it had no way of defending them against enemy attacks for long. The Wehrmacht had changed its tactics and its arms. From an army typically known for its blitzkrieg campaigns in 1940 and 1941, with a fast and light tank mobility as well as a quick and mobile infantry, it had turned into an awkward force with heavy armor and an entrenched infantry. Ever since the Battle of Kursk, Hitler had no illusions about winning a military campaign against the Soviet Union, but he was not desperate. He still possessed enormous spaces that enabled the German army to gain time on the Eastern Front and then wait until the strange alignment between Great Britain, the United States, and the Soviet Union fell apart.[9]

The war in Russia dragged on, with Hitler continuing to demand that they hold onto Nikopol and the Crimea; both, however, were lost in the course of the next few weeks, Nikopol in February and the Crimea during the second half of May. The Russians kept sending new units into battle, while the same old German troops were gradually being worn down. There were no replacements in Germany, and fresh divisions had to be brought up from the south of France. Hitler had to accept that time was running out, but he was not the type of leader who sat around waiting for something to happen. On April 10, Odessa fell, but by the end of the month, the Russians had halted along the Tarnopol–Kovel line when the muddy season arrived. In the meantime, the Wehrmacht was breaking new ground.

The Hungarian Adventure

On March 16, 1944, Nicolaus von Below, Hitler's Luftwaffe adjutant, was granted leave by the Führer to attend his uncle's funeral. During the service, he had a chance to speak to his son-in-law, Major Harald von Borries. The latter was quartermaster of an army corps that was part of Army Group North. Von Borries complained bitterly about the miserable supply situation, claiming that he had lodged repeated complaints with the appropriate bureau of the High Command, without success. This seemed inexplicable to von Below, and upon his return to the Berghof, he initiated inquiries regarding the matter, to no avail. At their next meeting, however, at the end of July, Borries told his father-in-law that supplies had been mysteriously restored.[10] This anecdote illustrates the essence of what the Wehrmacht had to deal with in 1944 between the months of March and July.

At the beginning of 1944, there were 825,007 Jews on Hungarian territory, including 100,000 Christians of Jewish origin who, racially, were considered Jews, and some 309,000 in areas Hungary had annexed between 1938 and 1941. Although Hungary's Jews had suffered from a series of harsh anti-Jewish laws passed since 1938, they had been spared the ravages inflicted on the Jews of neighboring Poland and Slovakia. Ironically, it was the attempt of the Hungarian regime to shake off its alliance with Germany and make peace with the Allies that put the Jews of that country in jeopardy. Hitler was infuriated when he learned about the feelers of peace that Miklós Horthy's regime was putting out. In his mind, there was a connection between this perceived treachery and the presence of a large Jewish community in Hungary.[11]

On March 15, 1944, Admiral Horthy received an invitation from Hitler to meet with him at Schloss Klessheim near Salzburg.[12] Instead of talking to Horthy about the repatriation of Hungarian troops from the Soviet front, Hitler opened the conversation with the Italian "betrayal" that had put Germany in a difficult position. Because according to his information Hungary was also contemplating a change of alliance, he felt obliged to take precautionary measures to avoid being caught unawares for a second time. Once Horthy realized from the discussion with Hitler that everything had been decided upon, he wanted to leave immediately. He was unaware that precautionary measures had already been set in motion and orders given, in the event that Horthy proved to be stubborn, to arrest him in Vienna on his way back to Budapest.

The scene then became almost farcical. In an attempt to prevent Horthy's departure, an air raid alarm was sounded, and Schloss Klessheim was put under a smoke screen. The Hungarian entourage was informed that bombs had severed the telephone communication lines and that it was best to stay there at least until evening. After a tense lunch with Hitler, Horthy was told that his special train could leave Klessheim at 2000 hours that night. After further delays in Salzburg and Linz, Horthy was finally on his way back to Hungary. On the night of March 18–19, while he was still on the train, German troops marched into Budapest.[13] By the time he arrived in the morning, Horthy found two German sentries at the gate of his palace in Budapest. During the train journey, Horthy was introduced to Dr. Edmund Veesenmayer, who was to bear not only the title of minister but also plenipotentiary of the Reich in Hungary.[14]

The chance to implement the Final Solution on Hungarian Jewry was now at hand, and consequently, the German supply system, based on the Reichsbahn's trains, was reburdened. The fate of Hungarian Jews, as well as other remnants of Jewish communities, and the efforts to save them as the war neared its inevitable end with the upcoming Allied landing in Europe, would provide the focus for developments in the Final Solution during the remaining year of the global conflict. These events would be greatly complicated by two closely related aspects of the collapsing Third Reich. The first was the determined advance of the Allies, which was met by equal German determination not only to hold on to as much territory as possible but also to evacuate to other camps thousands of prisoners still in their hands, most of whom did not survive the journey. The second aspect was the resolve to keep the trains carrying the Jewish transports rolling, regardless of the situation at the front.[15]

Just over a fortnight before the Wehrmacht entered Hungary, on March 4, 1944, Hermann Göring, acting in accordance with his appointment as Hitler's plenipotentiary for the Four Year Plan, circulated a memorandum to the supreme Reich authorities, among them Himmler, Albert Speer, and the chiefs of the three military services. This memorandum was to become the basis for the Jäger plan. It dealt with ensuring the paramount importance of armaments production for the military and air industry, on three conditions: that Allied bomb damage to existing plants be repaired; that updated products be produced to meet the threats Germany was now facing; and that bombproof manufacturing facilities be created. It was up to Himmler to see that the construction work was begun immediately. This meant that Oswald Pohl had to supply the workforce for the task. Minister Speer was to be in charge of construction, and the war production companies were to supply the facilities and raw materials and see to swift implementation.[16]

Speer confirmed during his interrogation that in 1944 Hungarian Jews were used for the building program. According to Speer, in the fall of 1943, Hitler had intended to build great underground aircraft factories. Although he gave an order to that effect, it was not executed immediately. In March 1944, the director of the central Todt Organization submitted plans to Hitler for the building of six factories. There were several major differences over this issue between Göring and Speer, as well as between Hitler and Speer. As a result, Speer received a written order from the Führer that Bosch should build the six factories and that the construction work should be completed within six months. Bosch also received a direct order to build these facilities outside the normal sphere of Speer's armaments ministry.

On March 17, Hitler demanded that Horthy supply the German war industry with 100,000 Hungarian Jews for the construction of the underground factories. Hungarian Jews were made available for building through direct negotiations carried out with Bosch officials. Some 100,000 Hungarian Jews were obtained for this project and were to be transported to Germany. However, Speer denied having ordered their deportation and his participation in the discussions concerning it, because from April until mid-May 1944, he had been ill and had spent time recovering, first near Salzburg and then in Nerano (northern Italy).[17]

On April 14, Veesenmayer reported to Joachim von Ribbentrop that Döme Sztójay, the former Hungarian ambassador to Berlin who was appointed prime minister of Hungary after its occupation by German forces, had given his approval for 50,000 Hungarian Jews to be made available to the Reich for forced labor, and that he anticipated that a further 50,000 would be on hand in May.[18] The German industrial situation was deteriorating, and the Wehrmacht was about to reach its limit in the drafting of new recruits. By mid-September, Martin Bormann would send an order in the Führer's name to Field Marshal Keitel drafting all able-bodied men between sixteen and sixty years of age for the German people's militia.[19] There was no question, then, of Germany needing the support of forced labor, and at this time, Hungarian Jews were the most accessible. This, in fact, correlates with the plea of Fritz Bracht, the governor of Upper Silesia, to Himmler, in a letter dated March 6, to increase food rations for Polish workers in his region, explaining that it was in German war interests that the 120,000 Poles working at the Auschwitz facilities in Upper Silesia be preserved as a workforce. As a result of poor nutrition, the Polish workers were becoming physically and mentally unfit, leading to a dramatic drop in their performance. On March 20, Bracht sent a second letter to Himmler demanding that his request be fulfilled, but Himmler was already awaiting the Hungarian workers he would soon receive.[20]

Operation Margarethe, the occupation of Hungary by eleven German divisions, including several armored ones, progressed without serious incident. The Gestapo arrested nine members of the Upper House and thirteen of the Lower House in the Magyarian Parliament. They seized the police headquarters and requisitioned the Hotel

Astoria in Budapest for their use.[21] On March 19, immediately following the army troops, the SS marched into Hungarian territory as well,
closing all Jewish shops and warehouses and boycotting their wares.[22]
The Germans claimed that Jewish elements in Hungary were involved in disseminating propaganda about atrocities and sowing uncer-
tainty among the civilian population against the German–Hungarian
partnership.[23]

Transports May 15–June 7, 1944

The decision Hitler made in March 1944 to occupy Germany's puppet ally and institute a pro-Nazi government that would continue the
war provided the opportunity to deal with Hungary's Jews. However,
the actual invasion of Hungary was not driven by the Final Solution;
nor was it an irrational strategic act. The Germans entered Hungary
with various rational objectives that meshed with their strategic ones.
The primary goal was to keep their untrustworthy ally in the Axis
coalition and to ensure that the Hungarian armies would remain in the
battlefield with the Wehrmacht. In addition, Hungary had tempting
reserves of food, fuel, and raw materials, which were essential to the
German war effort since it had lost the Ukraine to the Soviets.[24] The
Soviet army had almost reconquered the Ukraine and was getting close
to the Carpathian Mountains. There was serious concern among the
Nazi perpetrators of the Final Solution that if they did accelerate the
annihilation process, it would be too late, and the opportunity of making Europe *Judenfrei* would be lost forever. Thus, all Nazi Germany's
military means and the entire bureaucratic system of the Hungarian
state were to be used for this purpose.[25]

   The German concern for prioritizing a solution to Hungary's Jewish problem was shared by Albert Ganzenmüller, who by then was
virtually acting executive director of the Reichsbahn. Ganzenmüller
cooperated fully with Adolf Eichmann's *Sonderkommando*, and especially with Franz Novak, Eichmann's chief transportation expert, by
providing the rolling stock needed for the scheduled deportations.
The schedule for deporting thousands of Hungarian Jews, as well as
the route plan, was finalized at a conference in Vienna on May 4 to 6,

which was attended by representatives of the railroad, the Hungarian gendarmerie, and the Sicherheitspolizei.

Three alternative deportation routes were considered before the conference. The first, which was generally preferred, led through eastern Slovakia; the other two went via Lemberg and via Budapest–Vienna. The problem with the last two routes was that while the Lemberg one was the shortest militarily, it had become extraordinarily difficult, while the Budapest route raised objections because it was claimed that the Jews of that city who were still untouched would become restless and prepare for an uprising such as the one in Warsaw the previous year. The direction finally decided on was through eastern Slovakia, following the Kassa, Pres'ov, Muszyna, Tarnow, and Kraków route to Auschwitz.[26] However, the German planners did not take into consideration that on June 22, the Soviets would start a major offensive, rendering the entire debate fruitless because military obstacles and needs were mounting.

On April 22, Eberhard von Thadden, the German foreign office official in charge of Jewish affairs and the intermediary between the foreign office and the SS, confirmed to Ribbentrop's office that an agreement had been reached with Admiral Horthy on the first installment of Jews to be deported. Von Thadden also informed the foreign minister that deportations, and in particular timetables and ordering of railway carriages, would be dealt with by the head office for Reich security. The trains began moving on May 15, and arrangements were made to deliver 3,000 Jews daily to Auschwitz. Every effort had been made to avoid disrupting the war effort, and for this reason, it was decided not to deport 50,000 Jews from Budapest in the first wave of forced labor in Germany: the roundup of the Jews had to be total. Von Thadden also objected to Jews being sent to the already *Judenfrei* Reich unless they were under heavy SS guard. Overall, it was better to get rid of them all by deportations to Auschwitz, and the labor force should be forgotten. Von Thadden considered that transport problems prevented them beginning the *aktion* in Budapest, with his message echoing Eichmann's preference for starting in eastern Hungary.[27]

The evacuation was carried out by rail transport to Kaschau (Kosice) near the Slovakian border. The evacuees were guarded by Hungarian field gendarmes, who were replaced at the border by Waffen-SS men—

the guard battalion of the commander of the security police in Budapest. This battalion traveled with the transports to Auschwitz and returned with the empty wagons. It took three to four days for the trains
from Hungary to reach the Upper Silesia region, where the death camp
facilities were awaiting the arrival of their new freight. The deportation schedule called for four trains per day, with each trainload carrying
3,000 to 3,500 Jews.[28]

Like the rest of the German economy, the Reichsbahn was heavily dependent on coal. Its locomotives consumed over thirty-two
million tons of hard coal in 1943, and stock levels were maintained at
twenty days. Coal was purchased by the central office directly from
the syndicates. Only certain types of coal were acceptable, and engineers went to the mines to select them. The chief supplier was the
Rhenish–Westphalin Cal Syndicate, which provided about 43 percent
of the Reichsbahn's needs; Upper Silesia satisfied about 40 percent.
The German locomotives pulled a total of 1,208,438 freight cars, of
which the Reichsbahn owned 937,045. There were two basic types.
Boxcars—about a third of the total—were used to move perishable
or high-unit-value freight. Open cars—comprising the other two-
thirds—were used to ship bulk commodities such as coal. Both types
had an average capacity of twenty tons. However, as of 1942, they were
regularly overloaded with an additional one to two tons.[29]

The wagons used for transporting the Hungarian Jews were all
closed freight cars. No passenger cars were used except sometimes for
the guards, but even they traveled mostly in closed freight cars. This
procedure was repeated four times daily on average, although at times
there were five transports a day.[30] A broad range of services were offered and adapted to the dictates of running trains that stopped only
at major distribution centers and not at smaller stations. Almost a
third of all trains ran empty because return cargoes could not always
be arranged, despite energetic efforts to do so. Trains carrying mixed
freight averaged thirty-nine cars in length with an average load of
about 300 tons. The exact amount of tonnage was carried by the same
trains when they were deporting Hungarian Jews to Auschwitz. Coal
trains were about forty cars long and carried about 800 tons. Most
freight trains traveled at about fifty kilometers per hour.[31]

The SS administration of Auschwitz was well prepared for the anticipated arrival of 12,000 to 14,000 Jews from Hungary daily.[32] Comparing these numbers to the military forces results in a rather distorted picture of German priorities. Instead of transporting two or three divisions daily from the Eastern Front to the western sector, which, almost all the German High Command agreed, would be invaded sooner or later that year, every day, Germany brought two or three divisions' worth of deportees to the platform at Birkenau. Had this activity anything to do with increasing the odds of repulsing an upcoming military invasion of Western Europe by the Allies, there is every reason to believe that logistically, such an operation, which was even bigger than Operation Overlord in terms of mobilizing personnel, would have been rational. However, nothing concerned with the Hungarian tragedy even came close to sound military strategy or logistics.

The first trains were packed to capacity, and von Thadden reported that 116,000 Jews were deported in nine days. Every day, they were loaded onto four trains of forty-five boxcars each, which meant there were more than sixty-five passengers per wagon. When Eichmann was negotiating over his scheme with Dr. Rudolf Kastner for facilitating the departure of Jews out of Hungary, he explained that if ninety people were sometimes loaded into one wagon, it was because Ruthenian Jews had plenty of children who took up very little room. "Besides, the Jews of those regions were not pretentious."[33]

When the war began, the cruising speed of the Reichsbahn's locomotives, whether they were on operational journeys transporting troops or only troop supplies, was thirty kilometers an hour on average, which was about 700 kilometers per day. However, that rate fell as a result of partisan activity. The locomotives could up their pace to seventy-two kilometers an hour, but usually the speed would decline again to about thirty-six kilometers per hour. The longest transport route ran from Hendaye in France to Arnavie in Russia and was over 4,000 kilometers long. As of 1943, and through Operation Citadel, Operation Margarethe I, and the Ardennes offensive, the troop transports comprised trains of forty-nine to fifty-three wagons, depending on the type of locomotive that pulled them.[34] This was approximately the amount of wagons used for the Hungarian deportations by the SS, which was around forty-five.

While the Hungarians were busy with the technical-organizational details of the deportations, the Germans were settling the problem of transportation, including the acquisition of freight cars, and determining the route. Because of the high priority attached to building the aircraft factory and other military-related projects, in which able-bodied Jews were to be employed, the Wehrmacht was cooperative in releasing the rolling stock demanded by the SS. The single-mindedness with which the Nazi leaders pursued their objective of the Final Solution seemed to override even the military requirements of the Reich. They continued to attach greater priority to the deportation of the Jews than to the transportation needs of the Wehrmacht, even when Soviet troops were rapidly approaching the Carpathians.[35]

The Hungarian Jews were crammed into freight wagons in groups of sixty-five to eighty per wagon. This was actually less than the SS used to shove into the rail wagons when the numbers in one car reached 100 and in some cases even more.[36] The only reason for this could have been technical, because the Hungarian Jews were taken to Auschwitz straight from their regular lives. There was no time to turn them into walking corpses, as with the Jews taken from the ghettos, who were much thinner as a result of malnutrition. Each deportee was allowed to take fifty kilograms' worth of luggage and food for fourteen days, which in most cases was never consumed. By June 7, some 289,357 Jews were deported aboard ninety-two trains of forty-five wagons each, with a daily capacity of up to 14,000 deportees.[37]

In 1944, Reichsbahn passenger traffic rose steadily, reaching a peak of 3.7 billion people in total. Still, this had nothing to do with the fact that the trains used for Jewish deportations were part of the operational apparatus of the rail net that served the Wehrmacht in parallel with serving the German population in general. Because in 1944 there was an increase in freight traffic—as well as difficulties caused by developments on the fronts and air attacks on the railways—the total number of trains used daily had no real impact on the perception that the Final Solution transports were a drop in the ocean compared to the enormous amount of traffic the Reichsbahn operated daily.[38]

A German army group was formed from a number of armies that were under the command of a field marshal. As a result of the circumstances, there was a major difference between the number of men that comprised each group—250,000 to more than a million—but such a force could hold an entire front. Each German army usually numbered from 40,000 to 100,000 troops. A Panzer division had approximately sixty-five tanks.[39] One could assume, then, that until June 7, the number of Hungarian Jewish deportees traveling on board the trains was equivalent to that of an army group. On the basis of the capacity of a troop transportation (750 men per train), the amount of trains used for those ninety-two deportations could have borne some 207,000 German troops to Western Europe; these could have reinforced the so-called Atlantic Wall built by General Erwin Rommel and even driven a potential Allied invasion into the sea.

13

Risk and Fear of Invasion

Challenges and risks confronted the German commanders when deciding on the strategic route they would pursue in spring 1944, as well as the balance of power between the Wehrmacht and the Western Allied armies. Despite Operation Overlord—the code name for the Normandy landings on D-day—the Germans still had opportunities to reinforce their divisions in western France using the railway routes that were still operating. The Hungarian transports to Auschwitz were at an advanced stage before the Normandy landings. Here I focus on their procedures after the Allied forces had already landed on the beaches of Normandy and created a bridgehead, the priorities of the Reichsbahn, and the needs of Gerd von Rundstedt's armies, along with SS objectives.

In April and May 1944, it seemed that luck and time were still on Hitler's side. If an invasion from the West were defeated, Germany could turn its full strength east. The chances for a victory in the West appeared relatively good, and by the end of April, new Panzer divisions had filled the gap in the western defenses created when the 2nd SS Panzer Corps was transferred east. The southern half of the Eastern Front was a nightmare for the Germans, but at the center, 467 kilometers west of Moscow, between Vitebsk and Orsha, the passage to the Soviet capital was still in German hands. At the closest point, the Russians were still 885 kilometers from Berlin; therefore, the end of the war was not yet in sight. Although in spring German army strength reached a new low, in other respects it had actually risen. Industrial production was rising, and the Luftwaffe's quota stood at 5,585 planes in January 1944, compared to 3,995 the year before. Synthetic oil production reached a peak in April 1944, and stocks of aviation fuel were larger than at any time since 1941. Although the British and American air forces resumed daylight bombing in March, German fighter plane production rose every month in 1944 between March and September.[1]

Hitler's Directive 51 from November 3, 1943, was issued in order to freeze operations in the East because the Germans could no longer lose the chance of weakening the West in favor of other theaters of war. It was therefore decided to reinforce defenses in the West, particularly in those places from which long-range bombardment of England would begin. Hitler specified in his order that in order to deliver a counterattack in the event of an enemy landing, the entire weight of the German army should be turned to the Western theater. However, the problem was to concentrate adequate forces and matériel in order to form large units that would be available for a reserve offensive of high fighting quality and mobility. Only a force at that level could prevent the enemy from exploiting the landings and push them back into the sea.[2]

The successes of the Allied forces in the Mediterranean and the ever-increasing heavy bombing raids on the Reich left no doubt as to the matériel superiority of the Western Allies. The German generals, while agreeing with the rumors that an invasion would come, nevertheless limited the possible landing areas to Belgium and northern France. However, the distraction of the other fronts and the false sense of security that Hitler's highly exaggerated Atlantic Wall gave him ensured that the divisions assigned to the West were deficient both in numbers and in quality, leaving them in no condition to meet a determined invasion of Normandy.[3]

By June 3, the German army command in the West had about fifty-eight divisions in France, Belgium, and Holland, covering 2,600 kilometers of coastline. Ten were Panzer divisions, with a total of 1,143 tanks, and the rest were infantry, with extra divisions that could be transferred from the East if Hitler would give the order to withdraw to key strategic positions. Instead, he was committed to holding every acre until the last breath of his last miserable soldier. Of these divisions, thirty-six infantry and six Panzer divisions were located in the general coastal area facing England, from Holland to Lorient in western France. In the immediate area of the Normandy assault, the Germans had concentrated only nine infantry divisions and one Panzer division, while their greatest strength, the 5th Army, remained in the Pas-de-Calais area.⁴ These forces, which included the Luftwaffe, and which amounted to 1,873,000 men, 950,000 of whom were combat soldiers, constituted about one-quarter of the field force of the entire German army.⁵ For several years, the Germans had been developing the coastal defense organization known collectively as the Atlantic Wall. They assumed that an invader would have to secure a port either in the initial assault or very soon afterward in order to land the heaviest types of equipment and organize their defenses. By 1944, the Atlantic Wall had become virtually invulnerable to seaward assault. After the ports, attention was turned to the Pas-de-Calais, which bordered the narrowest part of the Channel and was considered the most likely area the Allies would choose for the assault. Elsewhere, defenses were less organized, for by the beginning of 1944, the Germans had not possessed the transport resources to put the entire coastline in a uniform state of defense.⁶ It was the policy of the Supreme German Command to transfer exhausted, often decimated divisions from the Eastern Front to the West for rest and rehabilitation. As soon as the divisions had been reformed and reequipped, they returned to Russia. Thus, the battle order, which frequently showed numerous divisions that were in fact only skeletons, was misleading.⁷

As well as securing the occupied western territories against enemy landings, von Rundstedt was responsible for reconstructing exhausted divisions from other theaters, especially the Soviet Union, and returning them to the front. According to the instructions of the Army General Staff, his mission was to make the strongest forces possible available for the East in the shortest possible time while maintaining defensive capability in the West. By early 1943, after the severe losses sustained by the Wehrmacht at Stalingrad, the remains of a total of thirteen divisions of the 6th Army had been transferred to the West as backup strength in manpower and equipment.⁸

The combined strength and combat readiness of the German armed forces in the West underwent great fluctuations in the period from mid-1943 to the invasion. It was estimated that there were twenty-five static divisions under the German army command from October 1943 onward, mostly deployed near the coast. As a rule, the units sent to the West as replacements were completely worn out and often needed many weeks to become relatively fit for action. In many cases, their operational redeployment was not resumed until the end of May or even later. The increase in divisions in the West from mid-1943 up to the invasion to a total of approximately sixty did not necessarily mean they had reached combat strength. The absolute figures are nevertheless impressive. In the area of Army Group B, there were over 468,000 men, although their combat value as operational divisions was nothing like they had been in earlier years.[9]

The Germans never really used a standard divisional organization. Ideally, the division should have included between 13,500 and 14,000 officers and men and about 160 tanks, but that was rare. The inability of the German economy to produce the necessary numbers of vehicles—and more importantly the fuel needed to run them—forced the German army to remain heavily dependent on horses for the bulk of its transport. In this respect, the Wehrmacht was conducting a nineteenth-century-style war rather than modern twentieth-century mobilized operations.[10] However, a distinction should be made between what Germany could not produce and what in fact was being manufactured and simply could not be transported on time to its destination. As the artillery was drawn by horse, it had little mobility.

Thus, even toward the end of the war, the German army was still based largely on horse-drawn traffic. The number of horses needed for each division did not change and was ultimately set at 3,000. However, as a result of exhaustion of the horses and malnutrition of the troops, many animals were slaughtered on the spot for food, which meant that there was a constant need for new horses on the front. The total number of horses used by the Wehrmacht on all fronts was around one million, with only 650,000 to 700,000 operational on the Eastern Front. Most of the horses came from breeding farms in East Pomerania, but at the beginning of 1944, the Germans also bought horses in northern Italy. The use of train wagons to transport the Hungarian Jews was equivalent to transporting some 35,000 animals, which could support almost twelve divisions with sufficient horse-drawn transportation.[11] The horses were of such dominance in the transport apparatus that it was even necessary to determine the insurance premiums per horse because losses were extremely high; in addition, the regulations limiting the burdens they were permitted to carry were not enforced.[12]

Thirty-eight of the sixty German divisions in Normandy were infantry. Five were static formations comprising nine battalions. The others were divisions established in 1944 consisting of six infantry battalions each. The transport of supplies was provided by 615 motor vehicles and 1,450 horse-drawn vehicles. Because each of the latter needed at least two horses, almost 3,000 horses were used in the West for moving each division, similar to the number used on the Eastern Front.[13]

By the end of 1943, both Rommel and von Rundstedt, as well as other commanders, agreed that the Allied invasion was certain to take place within the coming year. They thought that it was a matter of months, perhaps six at the most, before the Allies would try to make a breakthrough in the conflict and invade Western Europe by sea.[14] The Germans greatly overestimated Allied forces in the United Kingdom at the New Year. Their view was that fifty-five divisions were waiting across the Channel, when in fact there were only thirty-seven.[15] The Germans thus estimated that these amounted to a total of some 220,000 men, based on 4,000 men per division. In fact, both armies standing on either side of the Channel were equally matched, but the Germans were overwhelmingly superior in troops, guns, and tanks. The Allies had only 175,475 men available for crossing the Channel and 20,111 vehicles. There was a difference of 45,000 troops between the German assessment and actual Allied strength.[16]

Before the situation in the East deteriorated, German reinforcements consisted of newly formed units from the Reich, but in March 1944, Hitler approved transfers from the commander in chief of the West, including several infantry divisions, an entire SS armored corps, and several assault gun battalions. In exchange, the General Staff were ordered to send some units to complement forces in the West. However, the organization branch argued that this was impossible because of equipment shortages. At the end of March, High Command chief General Kurt Zeitzler ordered the transport branch to prepare to transfer the 1st Mountain Division to Hungary in order to guard the passes through the Carpathian Mountains, although this division was nominally under the control of the supreme command of the Wehrmacht (OKW). The 1st Mountain Division was the last unit that the OKW had at its disposal. Nevertheless, despite the extensive Allied aerial campaign, Wehrmacht forces in the West actually managed to narrow the gap between their own strength and that of the invasion force before D-day.[17]

As German intelligence began to evaluate more and more information concerning Allied intentions in the West, it became evident that the main attack would be in the spring of 1944 somewhere along the Channel. Because they had no clear indication, the German generals continued to speculate throughout the spring months. The consensus was that it would probably come between the mouth of the Seine and the Pas-de-Calais area, but they did not rule out at least small-scale operations on the Contentin and Brittany peninsulas.[18] Consequently, the area between Le Havre and Cherbourg on the Normandy coast consisted of only four infantry divisions, each stretched over an area of forty-five kilometers, while in military theory, an effective division operated over a range of five kilometers.[19] Only Admiral Theodor Krancke, the German naval commander in the West, consistently held a different view. Krancke and his staff based their assessments on tidal considerations, the availability of a major harbor, and the pattern of enemy mine laying activity in the Channel. They concluded from 1942—correctly, as it turned out—that the region between Cherbourg and Le Havre was the most logical spot for an Allied invasion.[20] The city of Caen was a vital road and rail communications center through which the main routes from the east and southeast passed. Because the bulk of German mobile reserves were located north of the Seine, they had to approach Normandy from the east and were thus expected by Bernard Montgomery's army to converge on Caen. Hence, if a major threat to the German containing forces could be developed and sustained in the Caen sector, then their reserves would probably be engaged there first.[21]

There was no sign of an economically efficient strategy on the German side to meet an invasion. No changes were made in the interference of outside influences in the transport system, such as the Jewish deportations. This was of valuable assistance to the enemy. Similarly, the shunting system only remained workable where it was left untouched by enemy attacks. New ways and methods more suited to the war situation were never considered. The goods transport side of the railways, including the Jewish transports, operated without close contact with the military traffic side—in fact, they even refused to have anything to do with it. When in 1944 Albert Ganzenmüller tried to save the rapidly deteriorating situation by *Ganz-Zügen* (single-purpose trains), this idea, which in itself was a good one, was stymied by railway bureaucracy and fell prey to the conflict between traffic management and goods transport services.[22]

In April 1944, the 2nd Panzer Division (Das Reich) was brought to Montauban near Toulouse. After providing grueling service on the Eastern Front, the division was supplied with new Tiger tanks, which were the best and also the largest tanks the German war industry had ever manufactured. Because the Tiger was a large fuel consumer as well as a heavy machine—it weighed sixty-three tons—with steel tracks that wore out quickly if driven for long distances on paved roads, the Germans transferred it from one place to another aboard freight wagons. The Tigers were concentrated in Montauban under heavy guard, and the freight wagons were concealed as much as possible from air raids.[23]

The rail facilities that served the OKW were the same ones used by the SS for its Jewish transports needs, some of which were freight wagons. The only benefit from the SS transports was that a substantial part of the booty from the Jewish deportees was immediately distributed among combat divisions. Waffen-SS divisions Das Reich and Totenkopf each received 500 wristwatches as well as 300 fountain pens. U-boat fighters received 3,000 watches and 2,000 pens.[24] Strategically, these benefits meant little except as bribes to the army to remain patient with the SS's Jewish enterprise; however, in the long run, the cost was much higher.

Operation Overlord

When Winston Churchill and Theodore Roosevelt met with Joseph Stalin at the Tehran conference on November 28, 1943, it was obvious that Churchill was less keen on the plan for Operation Overlord—the invasion of Western Europe—than Roosevelt and his advisers were. He kept arguing that such an offensive could not be mounted the following spring, when Stalin wanted it.[25] After lengthy debates in the

Allied forces' High Command, and contrary to what Churchill believed was the right move, the Allies reached a decision. In order to distract the Germans from preparations for possible landings, the Allies launched an operation code named Frantic. This was a bomb shuttle system by which the United States forces flying either from Britain or Italy could use the Soviet air base at Poltava in order to extend their range and blanket areas previously outside their target limit. Frantic remained operational for more than four months. Field Marshal Montgomery was optimistic in regard to Frantic and Overlord; he believed that the war with Germany could end by December 1944. However, the Germans frustrated them by continuing it until May 1945.[26]

In the preparatory phase for the invasion, the tactical air strikes conducted by the Allies were to be directed against railways, bridges, and airfields in the vicinity of the assault area. The attack program on rail centers and bridges was intended to deprive the enemy of means for rapidly concentrating men and matériel and to hinder its efforts to maintain an adequate flow of reinforcements and supplies. It was designed to force it to move by road with resultant delay, increased wastage in road transport and fuel, and increasing vulnerability to air attack by the 2,434 fighters and 700 light and medium bombers.[27] The planners of Operation Overlord were aware that the success of an eventual Allied invasion on the Normandy beaches would depend above all on their ability to pour in troops and equipment more quickly than the Germans.[28]

The Allied concepts for the landing and the campaign were relatively straightforward. The initial amphibious attack of five divisions, supported by three airborne divisions, would achieve a beachhead from which Allied forces would drive inland. Of the beaches, only Omaha Beach, positioned between Utah Beach in the west and the British beaches in the east, was essential if the Allies were to succeed. In fact, the Omaha Beach landing was almost a failure, largely as a result of the unwillingness of General Omar Bradley, commander in chief of the American ground forces, to address essential tactical problems confronted by an amphibious assault on prepared defenses, as well as lack of fire support from navy vessels and significantly underestimated ammunition allocations for the upcoming battles.

The Normandy countryside, with its thick hedges, stone walls, and farmhouses, proved ideal for the Wehrmacht to conduct its tactics of in-depth defense, in which German strengths of machine guns and antitank weapons extended far into the rear while reserve forces were deployed deep in the defensive zone to counterattack and destroy any Allied penetrations.[29] Hitler's basic theory was that the enemy should be defeated on the beaches and thrown back into the sea—hence the building of the Atlantic Wall. As the months of 1944 passed, these tactics were reinforced by a simple consideration. As a result of the heavy losses in Russia, only inadequate mobile forces were available in the West to fight a battle of maneuver. There was therefore no choice but to stick to Hitler's theory of stiff linear defense. Therefore, in theory, all that von Rundstedt could assemble for action against the Allies was a single immobile defensive system consisting of ground troops without air support.[30] This is why Pas-de-Calais was not eventually chosen for the invasion but rather Normandy: it was more fortified than any other area, and the Germans were able to reinforce it with an excellent rail network. Because it was clear that there was a balance of forces, it came as no surprise that heavy German resistance, especially on the beaches of the American sector, repulsed the initial invading forces.[31] Any mistake on the part of the Wehrmacht, then, was to originate from poor strategic decision making, which placed an extra burden on the logistics sphere.

Allied weaknesses were especially glaring in the areas of weaponry, tactics, and training. Despite the mass production of Anglo-American industry, much of the equipment, such as weapons, machine guns, and tanks, proved to be far inferior to German matériel. The Sherman tank, although in some respects more reliable than anything the German inventory possessed, had a low-velocity gun that could not penetrate the armor of the German Panzers and Tigers, or even the Mark IV, at close range. A more serious weakness lay in the tactical level of the British and Canadian troops. Although they had four years to prepare for an eventual invasion of Western Europe, the British troops, especially at the lower levels, possessed no common doctrine. As a result, training rarely reached a high level of consistency and effectiveness; even basic infantry tactics seemed problematic. The British relied too much on their artillery, which they believed would smash the Germans before they came to shore, and were less prepared for face-to-face combat—something that the Germans were more than familiar with after three years of fighting against the Red Army. The Americans also had their fair share of problems, owing primarily to the fact that they were the last to enter the war. In contrast to the Germans, who had prepared for war six years beforehand, the Americans had barely three years to prepare their soldiers for combat in Normandy. Consequently, like their British allies, many units that fought during the invasion displayed a lack of tactical sophistication.[32]

Operations in Europe in 1944 demonstrated more strikingly than ever the extent to which logistic forces entered into all strategic and tactical planning. This was true for both the Germans and the Allies. The very nature of Allied cross-Channel operations implied a vital role for logistical considerations. According to the plan for Operation Overlord, the objective was "to secure a lodgment on the continent from which further offensive operations can be developed." Once the invading forces had secured a foothold, the most important single strategic goal was the capture and development of major ports, beginning with Cherbourg. Similarly, the German planners of strategic operations in Western and Eastern Europe were supported by logistical considerations involving the Reichsbahn and the entire European rail net. Nothing could be done without trains, especially when the Final Solution entailed major logistics.[33]

To carry out the mission of invading Western Europe, the Allies had available for D-day thirty-seven divisions awaiting orders in Great Britain from the headquarters of the combined chiefs of staff of the supreme Allied command for the Channel crossing. These divisions—twenty-three infantry, ten armored, and four airborne—were to be used in the assault and subsequent buildup period in France. As the campaign progressed, the flow of divisions to the Continent was to be maintained at a rate of three to five per month, to be augmented by divisions entering the European theater for the assault against southern France from the Mediterranean. These divisions, with attachments of antiaircraft, antitank, and tank units, had an average combat strength of 17,000 men.[34]

No single factor in itself assured victory for the American and British forces. The tactical and strategic bombing campaigns played an important role, but the transportation plan had only limited success. German coastal defenses were not seriously damaged by the aerial attacks that preceded the landings on D-day. Germany enjoyed no superiority other than the abilities of its fighting men and the quality of its equipment; the Allies had no overwhelming advantages with respect to either men or equipment.[35]

The Western Rail Network

On June 2, dive bombers dropped over a thousand bombs on the railway marshaling yards at Debrecen, Hungary. These actions caused severe damage to the rail system. All tracks in the main marshaling yards were cut, according to air intelligence reports, and large quantities of rolling stock were destroyed. However, these bombings had only a limited effect because they only severed Debrecen's gas and electricity supply but did not save the Jewish community, which was still deported to Auschwitz. Although Debrecen was a railway junction, linking several deportation routes, the object of the raid was to harm German communications in such a way as to help Soviet forces which were then in the Carpathians. In northwestern Europe, these bombings were the least effective because the railways formed a crowded network, and within a few hours or days of repairs, the Germans were able to open an alternative route, thus avoiding a blockage. The Allied High Command thought that southeastern Europe was a much better objective for such bombings and that dislocating rail traffic there would be more effective. The disruptions caused by raids on Hungary, Romania, Serbia, and Bulgaria seemed to be of longer duration than in northwestern Europe because there were fewer alternative routes and little in the way of repair facilities.[36]

From mid-May 1944 until the day of the invasion on June 6, Allied planes dropped over 76,000 tons of bombs on the French railway system. This was about seven times the amount of explosive material dropped on Hiroshima. The results were devastating for the bridges over the River Seine in western Paris. Railway traffic was reduced from sixty-nine trains in mid-May to thirty-eight on the day of the invasion. On June 3, 1944, the intelligence department of the Allied High Command reported that the German-controlled rail net absorbed and continued to absorb an attack that no transportation system in the world had ever known, either in strength or length. About 1,700 locomotives and 25,000 rail wagons were demolished and thus put out of service. Although these numbers seem impressive, they were only 8 to 13 percent of the railway layout before the air bombing. Moreover, the Germans managed to fill up the gaps from the French civilian sector. Those who suffered most were the French themselves, whose transportation system was already curtailed because of German needs; hence, the French economy, which was already in ruins, experienced another blow. The destruction therefore was not such that would prevent the Germans from transporting supplies and reinforcements, even though traffic movement was less efficient.

In addition to the plan for destruction of locomotives and rail wagons, the bombings were directed at replacement warehouses. Some 58,000 tons of bombs were dropped over ninety targets, causing great damage, but the Germans exhibited tremendous skill and talent in repairing them. In many cases, the debris was quickly removed, and lines were operating again within twenty-four to forty-eight hours. The Allied forces' High Command intelligence department was gloomy. Evidence showed that the impact of the heavy bombing on the mobility of German forces was still only limited. Years later, these bombings were reassessed and their effectiveness questioned on the strategic level, taking into account the cost as well as the damage they did to French and Belgian cities.[37]

Still, the logistical situation the Germans faced was one of drastic shortages that handicapped the units. Panzer Group West, for instance, was equipped with only 400 to 900 tons of supplies per day throughout July.[38] On June 5, the chief quartermaster, General Eduard Wagner, signed a decree demanding top priority for the Wehrmacht's needs over all others. Monetary and troop requisites, including fuel and coal, and even pocket money for the soldiers, would be determined by the chief director of each sector or country. All priorities were to be considered according to the principles of economic efficiency and the local situation in each area and sphere of fighting. The indirect implication was that traffic movement was now in an extremely delicate situation—and this without knowing that D-day was just a day away. However, Hungarian transports were already well on their way.[39]

In 1944, the Wehrmacht was in a strange situation. The three Panzer divisions under General Rommel's command were accompanied by fairly well-equipped mobile forces, with updated firearms but with no fuel to conduct strategic operations. As a result of the Allied bombing campaign in the Romanian oil fields, Germany faced a desperate fuel crisis. This meant that in France, training of Panzer divisions had to be cut drastically. Examination of the infantry divisions portrayed an army that was almost identical to the Kaiser's army in 1918. The Wehrmacht was dependent on freight trains and horses for supplies, as well as the infantry corps for mobilization. All these were bound primarily by railway transport, which had to be at full capacity.[40] With the German railways suffering ever-increasing difficulties resulting from air bombardment, shortages, inadequate repair facilities, destruction, and breakdown, in 1944, the Reichsbahn, which was once known to operate like clockwork, fell into total confusion. The jurisdiction of the central rail directorate no longer reached every nook and cranny of the system, and the full use of potential forces still at the Germans' disposal was rendered impossible by bureaucracy and a lack of competent managers. In addition, military rail transport was managed with a marked lack of inspiration because the supply lines to the front were controlled by weak, bureaucratic officers.[41]

The loss of the western and a large part of the eastern occupied territories led to a considerable reduction in the output of iron and steel. At the same time were new demands in other critical spheres. These could only be met by a parallel reduction in quotas allocated to other products, and Reichsbahn quotas were consequently cut. From the third quarter of 1943 to the end of the first quarter of 1945, the output of the wagons industry fell by 11.4 percent as a result of heavy bomb damage and by 47.5 percent as a result of loss of territory. Although the supply question had always been difficult, it was not so much the lack of supplies themselves as the impossibility of transporting and delivering the material from the plants to the front. During 1944, nearly half of all iron and steel quotas were needed to meet rail requirements. Normal requirements of the Reichsbahn alone were stated to be in the neighborhood of 90,000 tons per quarter. However, the supply of necessary superstructure material was getting very low indeed. For instance, after deducting the locomotive quotas of about 735,000 tons, all that the Reichsbahn had left in 1943 for the construction of wagons, plus all the repair shops, amounted to about 260,000 tons—that is, 65,000 per quarter when the normal requirements for rails alone amounted to 90,000 tons. It is evident, therefore, that by the end of the war, the Reichsbahn had no reserve stock left, and this undoubtedly intensified the initial difficulties that it faced in restarting and maintaining normal rail traffic.[42]

The shortages of matériel reinforced the effects of reduced troop strength. Forces at the front required 1,100 tons of munitions, 1,000 tons of fuel, and 250 tons of supplies per day—needs that were satisfied for a time from depots established before D-day. On June 6, the German armies had a sixty-day supply of rations, and the Panzer divisions had enough fuel to travel 483 kilometers. Supplying the troops with adequate provisions required thirty-six trains a day. However, only nine were able to reach the Seine–Loire triangle daily between June 10 and August 11. In the northeast area of the triangle, through which 98 percent of the military traffic passed, the volume of trains entering dropped in May by 50 percent compared to January–February; it rose again to 80 percent of this level in the last three weeks of June, but then fell steeply to 39 percent in July. In the Seine area, rail traffic fell from 213 trains during the first week of April to fifty in the last week of May, then almost vanished, averaging only a single train per week in the months that followed. The shortage of gasoline at the front had especially dramatic consequences. At the end of June, the commanders of the 7th Army complained that their Panzers were unable to counterattack southwest of Caen as a result of a lack of fuel. Back in the East, however, four trains per day with approximately 600 tons of human flesh traveled efficiently from Hungary to Auschwitz from May 15 until July 8, with halts in this traffic only to concentrate extra human freight.

The lack of matériel became truly critical for the Germans only in August, when stocks, which had been at their highest levels between May and July, were finally exhausted. The Allies' transportation plan involving heavy bombing did not seriously disrupt German logistics until the beginning of July, after which German movement became increasingly disorganized and locomotives were more urgently needed. Damaged engines, for the most part hastily repaired, were by then more likely to be immobilized by mechanical failure, hampering rail traffic still further.[43]

On the eve of the Normandy invasion, the railways in Europe were organized nationally but were coordinated into a network that enabled the Germans to operate an efficient transportation system freely in all directions. This meant that in June 1944, the Germans could run frequent services of freight and passenger trains from Cherbourg on the Normandy coast to Constantsa or Budapest, or from Rotterdam to Fiume on the Yugoslav coast, as well as to Odessa and Smolensk. There were fewer difficulties in that respect in Western Europe because of the density of the railway system there. France, Belgium, and Holland were all well served by their railways. Moreover, after the damage done in 1940 during the German invasion, the railways were sufficiently repaired to provide skeleton services on the main lines. In the case of Belgium and Holland, rail routes were for the most part extensions of the German system, providing a link to all of Europe. The most serious difficulties were the dislocation by air bombings and shortages in trains resulting from the large-scale requisitioning by the Germans of locomotives, coaches, and wagons for use in Germany and Eastern Europe. Their effect was already evident in the strenuous and costly efforts made to revive coastal traffic along alternative sea routes.[44]

Bombing of the French railways was becoming routine by June. However, Wehrmacht regulations on how to act during air raids were issued as early as mid-April 1944, and Wehrmacht transportation continued, despite frequent delays. There were even widespread rumors regarding the high cost in human life and matériel.[45] In 1944, the French railways had a capacity of 2,938 wagons per day, amounting to approximately seventy trains. The trains were concentrated in the Paris area and, until the Allied bombing began, were capable of reaching Le Havre, Cherbourg, Brest, and Caen, carrying between forty and 120 wagons of building materials to western and southern France.[46] In Hungary, too, the railways were bombed, but they were immediately fixed in order to sustain traffic. Over 200 troops from the

Hungarian state railways and the Hungarian transport network were deployed with the information and matériel they needed in order for the Hungarian Jewish transports to keep functioning.[47]

Overall, by the time the Allied troops were headed for the beaches of Normandy on June 6, the air forces had dropped 56,930 tons of bombs on transportation targets in support of Operation Overlord in France, Belgium, and West Germany.[48] The increased intensity of air attacks, both by day and night, demonstrated the relative importance of the Luftwaffe. The French and Belgian rail networks, as well as the Luftwaffe's own instillations, were the main targets. Troop movement by train became increasingly difficult, until finally reinforcement of the coast had to be carried out almost entirely by road. When the Seine and Loire bridges were destroyed systematically, even road movement grew difficult and very slow.[49] The breakdown of travel in certain sections of France threatened to hold up the arrival of matériel, and it became necessary to set up bicycle couriers because the Allies could no longer rely on the railroads. However, it also worked to their disadvantage. Sometimes Allied bombing caused the main transportation divisions in Brussels and Paris to send locomotives and freight cars out of Germany to compensate for the decline in marshaling capacity they suffered. By the time the landings began, air raids on the German and French rail net may have sabotaged it but did not bring rail traffic to a halt, as intended.[50]

The fact remains that before the landings in Normandy on June 6, the Germans were suffering from severe fuel and transport difficulties throughout Europe. However, it was not the paralysis of the French railway and road network that isolated the Wehrmacht completely at the front after June 6. Despite round-the-clock air attacks from heavy and medium fighter bombers, augmented by the sabotage of rail and cable communication by guerillas, results were not absolute. Air attacks rarely destroyed bridges, trains continued to run, albeit with extreme difficulty, and marching columns continued to filter through by night.[51]

Communications with Germany via the Cologne–Jeumont–Paris route were rendered uncertain. Communications along the lines to the south of the Ardennes did not suffer too greatly, however. Communications by way of Strasbourg were also not gravely hindered, and even the line from Dunkirk to Basel continued to operate despite countless air raids. There was no significant effect on communications in the Loire area or toward the west, and although the lines between Marseille and Paris suffered damage, traffic was not halted. Only in northern France was the rail net close to utter paralysis, with the Paris area suffering extensive damage. However, the Germans charged the Todt Organization with repairing the railroads using special trucks—a task they performed quite efficiently, even impressing local French workers. To halt the traffic from Germany to France, it was urgent that the bridges on the north and south rivers be demolished.[52] Because this was mostly not done, the Germans had almost a free hand, at least with the railways, to bring troops to the front. As with the Eastern Front, the problem lay with the number of locomotives and wagons they had at their disposal.

By June 4, every railroad bridge across the Seine between Rouen and Paris had been knocked out. By June 6, not only had the northwestern corner of France been isolated, but the bombing campaign had disrupted the French railway system, reducing rail traffic to 60 percent of capacity. This meant that some divisions had to walk the last hundred kilometers into combat. Still, the Germans managed to move a total of fifty-eight divisions into France during spring 1944, despite the success of the Allied air bombings of the French railways.[53]

Therefore, the effects of the Allied bombings should not be overestimated. At the beginning of April, the Germans accelerated delivery of supplies and equipment to armored formations in France. However, German military needs absorbed only a third of the French railway capacity, not two-thirds, as the Allied experts had believed. At least at the outset, the bombing disrupted the lives of French civilians more than those of their occupiers. The 12th SS Panzer and Panzer Lehr divisions were delayed in reaching the front by only twenty-four hours. German armed forces were strengthened further by the recall of the 2nd SS Panzer Corps from Galicia in June—a disturbing sign that the likelihood of a Soviet offensive was not enough to stop the transfer of units to Normandy.[54]

Because the rail net to Auschwitz was never bombed by the Allies, the route from Germany to Upper Silesia, Kraków, and Budapest was always open. Therefore, despite all the difficulties, the Hungarian deportees carried daily to the crematoriums on four trains could have been replaced with new reserves for Normandy.

Normandy or Upper Silesia

As long as the D-day attack remained limited to three assault divisions, General Bradley foresaw difficulties in the capture of a major port soon after the landing. The cross-Channel invasion planning staff had banked on an eventual lodgment force of twenty-six to thirty Allied divisions. To supply such a huge force would require a major port in addition to the beaches. Meanwhile, time would be against the Allies as they came ashore. Unless a port was taken before the arrival of bad weather on the Channel, the beach buildup would be slowed down. According to the cross-Channel invasion planning staff, the nearest port, that of Cherbourg, lay dangerously far from the beachhead. The tentative point for attack had been located on a forty-kilometer stretch of the shingled Normandy beach, almost midway between Le Havre and Cherbourg.[55]

Only one day after the landings in Normandy, the Germans completed the first phase of the Hungarian deportation plan when the last train from Ruthenia and Transylvania reached Auschwitz. This brought the number of Hungarian Jews deported, parallel to the preparations for the Allies landings, to a total of 289,357, most of whom were removed in just twenty-three days.[56] In logistical terms, this translates into 145 trains that were used for the deportation of Jews instead of transporting at least seven divisions of infantry or Panzers that could have been used for the layout in the West in order to help repulse the imminent enemy invasion. In other words, these trains could have brought about 108,750 combat soldiers, amounting to almost a full army.

On June 7, after evaluating the amount of supplies arriving from the beaches and the units identified in the buildup, including the 82nd Airborne Division and the US 1st and British 67th armored divisions, von Rundstedt, commander in chief of the German army in the West, decided that Normandy would be the area where the main effort should be concentrated in repelling the invaders. Meanwhile, the

Germans had recovered a briefcase full of VII Corps plans chained to the corpse of an American officer near Carentan. That same day, near Pointe du Hoc (closer to Omaha Beach), the Germans found a briefcase containing the entire scheme of maneuvers and the US order of battle prepared by Lieutenant General Fredrick Morgan. It seemed odd that documents stamped "Destroy before embarkation" were taken ashore, and the Germans suspected a trap. However, von Rundstedt accepted the discovery as being authentic and informed Hitler on June 8, thus obtaining the OKW's permission to commence the movement of eight Panzer divisions.[57]

By the evening of June 7, the Germans were on the move. Twenty-four hours after the landings, the German High Command had virtually written off the Bay of Biscay and southern France as the focal points of major Allied action and had instead shifted all attention toward the Channel coast. Positions south of the Loire and on the Mediterranean coast were stripped of all but garrison troops to concentrate the full weight of the field divisions in northwest France.[58] This also indicates that by June 7, the German General Staff already knew that the immediate need was to move as much manpower and armor to the Normandy sector as possible. By June 12, every bridge across the Seine south of Paris, as well as the principal bridges across the Loire River, were destroyed. Most of the reinforcements had to use roads and railways running through the passage between Paris and Orleans. On July 8, the Germans reported that all rail communications from Paris to the west and southwest had been cut.[59] On the same day, the last transport of Hungarian Jews left for Auschwitz. Thus, there was a rail service in Western Europe at least until the beginning of July, and the reason for not using it seemed to lie in the southeastern part of the European continent.

Erwin Rommel's efforts were dedicated to repelling the Allied flow, throwing into the line every new unit as it reached the battlefront. Above all, he was compelled to use his armored forces as brake drums, and he was thus unable to concentrate them in the rear of a major counterattack. The armored divisions reached Normandy first because they possessed far greater mobility than the infantry, many of whom traveled the last eighty or 160 kilometers to the front on foot.[60]

On Omaha Beach, the Normandy invasion almost foundered.

Virtually everything went wrong, beginning with the weather, which did not favor the American forces because the clouds were obscuring the beaches, and the bombing contributed little to softening the targets. Out of thirty-four tanks dropped by the navy, only five made it to the beach, and most of the 29th Infantry Division's tanks were destroyed by German antitank guns as soon as they landed. Worst of all, however, was the failure of Allied intelligence to learn that the Germans had already moved their first-class 352nd Infantry Division into the area in May. Interestingly, from May 15, the Hungarian operation began with 14,000 people a day being transferred to Auschwitz, using the same trains that could have mobilized about three infantry divisions daily to Western Europe, just as the 352nd Infantry Division was being transferred. Because the rail net in northern France was under continuous bombing by the Allies, the line from Hungary to Auschwitz could have carried troops without disruption.

When the German defenders at Omaha Beach saw through their binoculars the American landers approaching them, they could not believe their eyes. It looked as though the Americans were literally about to swim to the beach in front of the German guns.[61] Five or six hundred yards from the shore, the assault force became the target of small arms, mortar, antitank gun, artillery, and machine gun fire. Some of the landing craft received direct hits and sank, leaving the survivors no choice but to jump into the water and swim as best they could. The German machine gunners fired patterns that killed or wounded the first four or five men coming down the ramps, with fire converging from multiple automatic weapons and causing the American forces heavy casualties. Some soldiers jumped overboard to avoid the lethal fire and lost much of their equipment in the process. Because the tides and winds caused boats to land east of the designated beaches, most of the teams encountered terrain they could not identify. Some boats landed as far as 915 meters from their destinations. Weak swimmers were unable to disentangle themselves from their gear, and those carrying heavy equipment such as flamethrowers drowned. Many of the soldiers who made it to the shore arrived without weapons and were too exhausted to advance.[62] However, the assault troops' worst disappointment of the day was when they found the beach untouched by air bombardment and soon realized that it had had little effect on the beach defenses.

Not only were the German squads and platoons capable of generating greater firepower but they were also better trained than most of the American formations. The 29th Infantry Division entered the war for the first time on June 6. It fought its first battle against the veteran 352nd Infantry Division on the shoreline of Omaha Beach. The German soldiers and formations had already fought for five years, with tactical doctrine being refined on the Eastern Front in hard-fought campaigns. The German soldiers understood much better how to fight and survive on the battlefield.[63]

When planning the assault, the Americans originally counted on a thin German lineup of two static divisions between Caen and Cherbourg. Rommel was known to have concentrated his best reserves behind the beach. Among them was the 352nd Infantry Division, which had been assembled at Saint-Lô. Just before boarding the *Augusta* in Plymouth harbor, Bradley's chief intelligence officer, Colonel Benjamin A. "Monk" Dickson, learned that the 352nd German division had been moved from Saint-Lô to the assault beaches for a defense exercise and had been in position for over a month. He promptly forwarded this information to the 1st Division but was unable to give it to the troops, who were already sealed aboard their craft. At about noon, Bradley even thought of evacuating Omaha Beach, clearly more concerned with operations after the assault than with the assault itself.[64] According to American intelligence, troops defending the Omaha Beach strong points amounted approximately to a reinforced battalion — 800 to 1,000 — most of whom were manning the beach defenses. The local reserves of these forces were thought to be part of the 716th Infantry Division and were estimated at three battalions, two of them near enough to Omaha Beach to reach it within two to three hours. Counterattacks by these units were not regarded as likely to be effective against penetrations of the beach defenses, and major counterattacks would depend on the arrival of mobile reserves.[65]

For much of June 6, the Americans who survived the slaughter that morning on Omaha Beach barely made it to the dunes below the cliffs. The devastation was so great that the German commander of fortifications overlooking Omaha Beach reported to his superiors that the American landing had failed. Similar reports reached General Bradley, who considered shutting Omaha Beach down and directing all reinforcements to Utah Beach. However, gradually naval gunfire by the destroyers took an increasing toll on the German defenders. The 352nd Infantry Division received no reinforcements, probably because of the favorable reports on developments and the deteriorating situation on the other beaches. Still, it could have been possible to reinforce the 352nd with supplies and backup forces by rail. Until June 7, an average of seven or eight trains transported approximately 290,000 people to Auschwitz daily. Aid for the Western Front thus had to wait for a halt in the Hungarian operation from June 8 to 11.

The cost was terrible for the Americans. On the first day of the invasion, 2,500 men perished at Omaha Beach alone. Nevertheless, by sunset on June 6, the Allies had secured a successful lodgment on the coast of Western Europe and managed to land over 155,000 men—eight divisions and three armored brigades—on French soil. The most important aspect of D-day was that the Allies were finally in a position to push the Germans inland so that the buildup of Allied forces and supplies could begin.[66] By the end of the day, on June 6, the Allies could thus look back on the first day of the invasion as a major military success. They had managed to gain a foothold in all five landing zones and to bring ashore 16,000 motorized vehicles. Against all expectations, their losses remained fairly low—6,000 men for the Americans and 3,000 for the British and Canadians.[67]

However, despite these early successes, the Allies did not manage to achieve the planned objective for the day. In particular, they could not take Caen, and therefore they were unable to gain access to the area south of the town, which was suitable for armored vehicles. The main factors responsible for this failure were that once the Allies had broken through the first German lines north of Caen, the broad advance southward announced by General Montgomery did not happen. The British armored units were not aggressive enough, thus enabling the Germans to bring parts of the nearby 21st Panzer Division into battle. Montgomery and his staff mistakenly assumed that this division would only be deployed once all its units were fully assembled. They therefore thought the British corps would have enough time to reach the southern edge of Caen before the German Panzer units could attack. The poor weather conditions and inadequate coordination among the various forces also weakened the momentum of the

Allied offensive. Accordingly, how the situation would develop over the next few days remained an open question. The decisive factor was which side would be faster in bringing in motorized forces and heavy weapons. This would determine whether the Allies managed to break through rapidly or were forced into a lengthy positional battle that would cost them dearly.[68] It is clear that the Americans grossly underestimated the capabilities of the German army and did not believe that German soldiers were as competent as their own men.[69]

At Omaha Beach, the Germans were reinforced by only one new division, a detail that escaped Allied intelligence. The result was that the losses among the landing forces were the highest of all the Normandy sectors. Had the Germans sent just a few more divisions, the other landing sectors might have met even greater resistance and might have been suppressed as well. The devastation on the beach was huge, as was the waste in manpower, ammunition, tanks, mobile artillery guns, grenades, and other armor that was either demolished or drowned by the Germans. The huge number of young lives lost there without ever firing a single shot bordered on the outrageous; it seemed a far cry from the days of Dunkirk in June 1940. The sight of military gear sent from factories in California, Illinois, Michigan, and the Deep South to East Coast ports of the United States, then across the Atlantic Ocean to England and aboard trains and trucks to Portsmouth, then finally sinking to the bottom of the Channel opposite Omaha Beach, did not bode well for the American army.[70] Still, the German reaction to the landings was even more outrageous than the landings in Omaha itself. By the end of the first day, the Allies had had major military success, but nevertheless, they did not manage to achieve their planned objective of taking the city of Caen, and they therefore could not gain access to the area south of the town, which was suitable for armored vehicles. Accordingly, the situation would be determined by a single decisive factor: which side would be faster in bringing in motorized forces and heavy weapons.[71]

The overall plan prepared by the Allied High Command had failed. The success of the Western Campaign was more the result of improvisation and the failure of the German formations in defending the Atlantic Wall. The Allied forces' need to integrate two very different practices of war, two very different military traditions, and two very different amphibious doctrines in operations worked together to cause the near disaster at Omaha Beach. Unlike the Americans, the British were not trained for deliberate defense; they won their battles with manpower, while the Americans won them mainly with firepower. However, Britain's lack of resources militated against the development of a firepower-based doctrine. Both US and British armies also lacked battle experience, a problem that Montgomery tried to deal with by integrating the veterans of his 8th Army with the Green formations.[72] In a noble act of leadership, Montgomery managed until mid-May 1944 to inspect every formation in Great Britain. He made it his business to be seen in person by almost every soldier and officer who would participate in the Normandy landings, which he hoped would boost their confidence in him as their commander. Monty must have reviewed over one million men including Canadians, Americans, Belgians, Poles, Dutch, and French. The American troops were overwhelmed by this gesture of leadership from a field marshal, and this gave them a major boost before their almost suicidal mission.[73]

The Wehrmacht 15th Army remained immobile in Pas-de-Calais until late July. After the war, high-level interrogations of German generals revealed that what kept this army (the Germans' greatest strength in the West) in place was the threat of attack by the Allied forces. However, this does not correspond to what was already known by the German military High Command on June 7 from the captured plans of Operation Overlord: that Normandy was the main landing spot and not Pas-de-Calais. It was not until July 25 that the first division of this army advanced westward in a late and fruitless attempt to reinforce the crumbling Normandy front.[74] The Hungarian deportations had come to a standstill as of July 9 and would not be resumed. After the invasion began, the Germans still used another fifty-eight trains to deport Hungarian Jews. This number would have been enough to help the 15th Army reinforce the Normandy sector with two infantry divisions, or at least one full Panzer division. Because the 12th Panzer Division had been so successful against the invaders at Omaha Beach, one can only imagine what another Panzer division from the 15th Army could have achieved on the Normandy battlefield.

The landing situation appeared in a quite different light at Utah Beach, where the terrain was less hostile to the Allies. The beach rose toward the shore in a gentle slope, and the absence of reefs deprived the defenders of the advantage they enjoyed at Omaha Beach, although flooded areas inland threatened to slow the advance of the troops. Successful as it was, the assault on Utah Beach was not free of complications. Losses of landing craft were relatively high; indeed, the commander of Force U, Rear Admiral Don P. Moon, considered suspending landing operations at night.[75]

From the beginning of the invasion until June 25, the Germans lost 43,080 men. Three weeks later, by mid-July, the number had risen to 97,000, while they received only 6,000 replacements and seventeen new tanks in place of the 225 that had been destroyed.[76] The Americans, on the other hand, had 100,000 casualties in June alone, 85 percent of them infantrymen. The infantry losses and the turnover of officers and men were far more serious than the planners of Operation Overlord had allowed for; they eventually reached crisis proportions for the American and British armies, just as they did for the Germans.[77] Despite the extreme difficulties, which no other army had had to face during World War II, Hitler's new front was actually not far from reaching a balance of power. That he had chosen to leave the reserves out of the initial battle and move forward with his Hungarian enterprise was another matter.

From the moment the landings began, it was obvious that Rommel was short of infantry and artillery reserves. Even General Bradley agreed that each German unit that reached the Normandy front bore scars that had been inflicted on it by hazardous movement across France. However, while the air attacks could harass the reserves, it could neither halt nor destroy them. The result was that each evening at sunset, when the Allied fighters returned to their base, the Germans began moving reserves on the roads under cover of darkness. Difficult and dangerous though these movements were, the Germans showed astonishing creativity and resourcefulness in getting their troops to the front.[78] However, these attempts to transfer troops to Normandy also encountered difficulties. The Allied air force and resistance fighters had managed to block many of the German troop routes to Normandy during daylight hours, so men and supplies could be brought in without too much risk only under cover of darkness or in bad weather. Because the railway network had been partly destroyed, motorized units often had to disembark 100 kilometers from the front and then continue by road. These actions cost time and fuel—a serious matter given the growing shortage of resources. When Hitler decided on June 12 to move two Panzer divisions—the 9th and 10th—from the Ukraine to France, they managed to reach the allotted assembly area northwest of Paris on June 26. However, the first sections of the corps were not deployed in Caen until three days later, just in time to halt the British advance west of Caen. Only by using all their remaining antiaircraft backup and repair units did the Germans manage to keep a few main supply lines open from the Reich to France, thus leaving them with some capability of supporting the troops attempting to counter the Allied forces.[79]

Because marching in daytime was out of the question for the German forces, it was therefore necessary to make the most of the short summer nights. However, the troops had to be prepared for low-level attacks at any time. Rail transport could reach no nearer than 150 to 200 kilometers from the front, making it necessary for the routes to be changed hourly.[80] Yet it was a march of only three or four days, and the reserves would eventually relieve the exhausted divisions. By June 12, a decision was made to transfer two SS armored corps, the 9th and 10th, from the East. However, from the point of view of the OKW High Command supreme headquarters, by June 9, the first phase of the battle against the invasion was over, and the intention to defeat the Allies on the coast and on the beaches before they could develop superior strength had failed. Moreover, the problem from then on was no longer that of moving in additional reinforcements but of reexamining the entire basis of future German strategy.[81]

Despite German difficulties in building up their forces, the Americans had not abandoned the notion of a powerful counteroffensive. Bradley and Montgomery had become increasingly uneasy over two troublesome soft spots in their line of action. Each was marked by a seam where two sectors had been stitched together, but so loosely that it was tempting for the Germans to tear them apart. The first of these seams followed the boundary between the American and British sectors. The second ran through Carentan, where Omaha Beach and Utah Beach met. Wherever a pair of Allied armies joined up, a weak point was created that the Germans could easily exploit to their advantage.[82]

This only strengthens the argument that had the Germans acted more swiftly in bringing more reserves to the Normandy sector—a feasible move despite the problems of the damaged rail system—the Allied landings might have been repulsed and the confrontation between the armies restricted to the beaches, as Rommel had hoped. The fact that the Eastern Europe rail net was busy until June 7 with the first phase of transporting Hungarian Jews to Upper Silesia and the second phase from June 11 did not help the crippled rail system in Western Europe.

During the four days after the successful landing, the Allies strengthened the bridgeheads and poured in more troops and supplies. By June 11, some 326,000 soldiers and 45,000 vehicles, with 104,000 tons of supplies, were on the beaches of Western Europe.[83] At the same time in Eastern Europe, between June 7 and 16, another twenty-three trains with some 50,805 Jews were deported from northern Hungary to Auschwitz, bringing the total to 340,162 Jewish deportees from May 15.[84] Thus, instead of preparing means of transport and reserves to aid the forces along the Normandy beaches in their efforts to repulse the invasion, the SS were preparing shipments of Jews. Those twenty-three trains used by the SS could certainly have come in handy for any purpose, from transferring extra regiments and tanks as well as fuel to any type of ammunition that would help repel the invading forces. Bombing raids, together with action by the French Resistance, had increased the difficulties of supplying German units. Only a few days after the landings, they found themselves short of fuel and munitions. The only time the Germans could bring in extra supplies was during periods of bad weather, but even then, they did not have enough trucks or trains. In light of these conditions, the general quartermaster concluded as early as late June that supplies to the 7th Army, now numbering 420,000 men and 45,000 horses, could no longer be guaranteed.[85] This number was almost as high as that of Hungarian Jews sent by train to the Auschwitz gas chambers.

By the end of June, it was far too late to execute von Rundstedt and Rommel's original plan to launch a massive armored counterattack and throw the Allies into the sea. However, they were about to shift their battle strategy from a static to a more flexible one. They placed their hopes in Panzer attacks in the direction of Bayeux, a move initiated by Hitler on June 29 in order to split the Allied bridgehead.[86] Between

June 19 and 22, the weather in the Channel deteriorated, making Allied efforts almost impossible. The British forces, too, were in need of new divisions to keep going according to plan and hold the initiative, and four divisions were aboard two American and two British ships anchored just opposite the Normandy beaches without any way of landing. The American 1st Army suffered the most and was forced to withdraw from Mulberry harbor at Omaha Beach, delaying Bradley's schedule.[87] Nevertheless, the delay served the Germans in regard to transport for reinforcements. Between June 16 and 25, there were no transports of Hungarian Jews. These days were used for concentrating the remnants of Hungarian Jewry in the southeastern and southwestern part of the country, as well as from the suburbs of Budapest.

The German commanders in the West thought that by rapidly bringing in Panzer divisions, they would be able not only to withstand the attackers but also to drive them back and out of that part of the mainland. Because of German resistance, the Allies had to rethink their original plans. By June 11, the same day the second phase of Hungarian transports to Auschwitz began, it had become clear that the Allies now intended to amass their armored forces, especially in the Caen area, by means of continuous attacks, and thereby give the US 1st Army more room for maneuver in the west. First, however, they wanted to capture the great port of Cherbourg in order to step up the flow of matériel and personnel into France. Nevertheless, by the end of June, the Allies had gained only modest strips of terrain in the eastern part of the bridgehead where the British 2nd Army was, in spite of the massive deployment of tanks, artillery and aircraft.[88] Rommel discovered that any counterattack that he considered was impossible to execute as a result of local tactical difficulties, fuel shortages, or enemy fighter-bomber attacks. Each effort to move troops west to meet the threat to Cherbourg was thwarted by more desperate needs closer at hand.[89]

The strategic bombing policy of the pre-D-day period was at that point yielding good dividends, and the growing paralysis of German communications was beginning to give the Allies a tremendous advantage. This was well illustrated in one of von Rundstedt's reports, in which he admitted that marching during the daytime in good weather was definitely excluded, and therefore, it was necessary to make the most of the short summer nights. As noted, rail transport could not be brought closer to the front than 150 to 200 kilometers without a definite schedule.[90] This, however, was the same distance the troops were used to marching during battle in the Soviet territories, so in that respect, combat in the West was turning out to be quite similar to the eastern campaigns, when the trains could reach only a certain point in the rear of the battlefield. Still, this was a distance that the Panzers could cover from the furthest rail junction to the combat area. Yet from June 25 until July 8, another 121,240 deportees were dispatched to Auschwitz aboard forty trains. Rail transport to Upper Silesia seemed as reliable as ever.

14

The Destruction of Army Group Center

The Russians launched a new offensive at the end of June 1944, three years after Operation Barbarossa. The second phase of the Hungarian deportations occurred at the same time as the Russian assault and the advancing stages of the Allied armies after the landings in the West. Normandy harkened back to the nerve-racking days of Dunkirk in 1940, as well the deportations from the Lodz ghetto, the last attempt to complete the task of the Final Solution. Throughout the fateful days of June 1944, the Western Allies naturally focused on the fighting in Normandy and on the hope that the war could be brought to a rapid conclusion. However, little attention was paid to the momentous events that were taking place simultaneously on the Eastern Front. While the German army deployed fifty-nine divisions in the West, 165 divisions were still engaged on that front.[1]

The existence of other fronts where Germany had to keep substantial forces or deliberately run great risks was a key factor in rendering the invasion in the West feasible. A few German divisions were in Italy and in the Balkans, but in mid-1944, about half of all German divisions were on the Eastern Front. Any landing in the spring or summer of 1944 in the West was conditional on the amount of military pressure the Soviets put on the Wehrmacht. The summer Soviet offensive was expected to keep the Germans from moving any large units from the Eastern Front to the West once the Allied forces smelled victory. The main problem was that Hitler was simply not prepared to make a major sacrifice of territory in the East in order to send massive reinforcements to the western sector, where a successful defense was needed because the Atlantic Wall had proved useless in that respect.[2]

Nevertheless, matters on the Eastern Front were not quite at a standstill. On June 22, 1944, one of the largest campaigns of the entire war was about to begin in Belorussia. One hundred eighteen Soviet infantry divisions and another forty-three armored divisions began a combined offensive on the Wehrmacht's Army Group Center.[3] Planned for early summer, Operation Bagration, the Soviet campaign launched to drive the German army out of Belorussia, was delayed by disputes over supplies and logistics. The only reason Operation Bagration escaped the kind of epic treatment that Stalingrad and Kursk were given in the history books was because it was overshadowed, especially in Western Europe and the English-speaking world, by the drama that took place on the beaches of northern France.[4]

The Red Army had managed to liberate some 330,000 square meters, but the German formations were still hard to break. In July 1944, German industry reached a peak in war production: steel production was three times higher than that of the Soviet Union, and in the second half of 1944, Germany produced over 17,000 planes and over 9,000 heavy tanks. The German Wehrmacht had a total of 324 divisions; 179 of them faced the Red Army in the summer of 1944. An additional forty-nine divisions belonging to the Axis powers brought the total to four million men on the Eastern Front, with 49,000 artillery guns, 5,250 tanks, and almost 2,800 airplanes. The Red Army possessed 6.4 million men with 92,000 artillery guns, 7,700 tanks, and 13,400 airplanes.[5] Nevertheless, the Soviets, like the Germans, suffered from severe manpower shortages. By 1944, the Red Army faced a manpower crisis that was in its own way as serious as that confronting the Wehrmacht. Many rifle divisions had an effective strength of 2,000 men or less. The resulting disparity between the official and actual sizes of many Soviet units goes a long way toward explaining the seemingly amazing performance of some German counterattacks. The ability of a full-strength Waffen-SS division to halt a Soviet corps or army probably resulted more from the numerical weakness of the Soviet units than from the strength of the German attackers.[6]

At the beginning of 1944, the Red Army was still fighting the Wehrmacht and its partners from the Axis countries alone. During the winter of 1943–1944, the Germans were defeated on the Soviet front when thirty divisions were simply destroyed: 142 divisions lost 50 to

70 percent of their military strength, which meant that in order to reinforce the German lines, the German High Command had to move forty divisions from Germany and other West European countries to the Eastern Front. In order for this reinforcement to be formed as rapidly as possible, a new double bypass rail route, Vitebsk–Orsha, intended to serve as an alternative to the main Moscow–Minsk route, was constructed beginning on April 6. Some 1,000 civilians were employed to carry out the work, which progressed at a pace of 350 to 500 meters a day. Work ended on April 23. The line spanned about twenty-six kilometers, including a two-track bridge thirty-four meters long and nine meters high.[7] On June 22, 1944, the Soviet Belorussian operation was about to take place on a 1,000-kilometer front and would engage some 800,000 German soldiers equipped with 900 tanks and 1,300 planes.[8]

Operation Bagration entailed five separate coordinated strikes along the Soviet Western Front, with Minsk the strategic prize liberated on July 3. Within three weeks, the troops of General Konstantin Rokossovsky's 1st Belorussian Front had crossed the border into Poland. In just twelve days, German Army Group Center lost twenty-five divisions and more than 300,000 men. In the following week, it lost more than 100,000 men. The Soviet drive finally slowed toward the end of the month, as its armored spearheads had become worn down and dulled.[9] The cost to the Red Army ran to tens of thousands of lives. To claim that this was a huge Soviet military success would be an exaggeration. Joseph Stalin's regime waged war in a special manner that was eventually the key to Soviet victory. Human life counted for little in the scale of history compared to the interests of the state. Georgi Zhukov explained this strategy to Dwight D. Eisenhower simply: "When we come to a minefield our infantry attacks exactly as if it were not there. The losses we get from personnel mines we consider equal to those we would have gotten from machine guns and artillery had the Germans chosen to defend that particular area with strong troop forces instead of with minefields." Some Soviet divisions, including those that fought near Mogilev, were so battered that they were forced to withdraw and regroup in late July.[10]

After five days of the offensive, the 12th Panzer Division was still on its way. Because with only 11,600 personnel it was not yet a full division in summer 1944, it needed only fifty-three trains to move it to its new position. Having passed trainloads of administrative troops and civilians with their baggage, all traveling westward, the division's first train arrived in the Marina Gorka area at the rear of the 9th Army, forty-eight kilometers southeast of Minsk. While attempting to hold open an escape route for the 4th Army, it was halted by a railway official with the news that the line ahead had been demolished in order to prevent its use by the Soviets, and that because the unloading ramp was about to be blown up, they needed to unload quickly.[11]

Hitler seemed encouraged because the front was now shortened. On July 7, he ordered the formation of fifteen new Panzergrenadier divisions and ten Panzer brigades. Composed of men from decimated divisions, the new forces absorbed all the replacements intended for the Eastern Front for July and August 1944 and 45,000 troops released from hospitals. Despite the Germans' need to direct new divisions and equipment eastward, throughout June and July, the Wehrmacht was still able to contain the Allied bridgehead in Normandy.[12] It is impossible that the measures in Hungary against the Jews were congruent with the immediate needs of the army when even 45,000 troops newly released from hospitals were used to form the new German divisions.

On June 28, more trains carrying troops of the 12th Panzer Division arrived throughout the day and were unloaded in Marina Gorka. In other words, the entire process of moving the 12th Panzer Division from the northern sector to the Belorussian sector in order to relieve the 9th Army lasted eight days. Hitler reluctantly released the 12th Panzer Division from Army Group North to stem the advance of the right wing of Rokossovsky's 1st Belorussian Front, which was already threatening to cut off the entire 9th Army east of Bobruysk, a situation sufficiently critical to break Army Group Center. One division could have changed the fate of an entire army group.[13] Once the Red Army troops began storming toward the German forces, on June 22, 1944, they left the commanders of the Wehrmacht in no doubt that within a few weeks, they would create a situation that would lead to a fundamental change in circumstances on the ground. More than the invasion of Normandy, then, the beginning of Operation Bagration had a strong impact that would bring the Nazi High Command to the events of July 20, 1944.[14]

On the night of June 19–20, 1944, Belorussian partisans launched a wave of attacks against railroad junctions, bridges, and other key traffic points at Army Group Center's rear. Although local German defenses repulsed many of the attacks, more than a thousand traffic junctions were put out of action, rendering a German retreat, resupply efforts, and lateral troop movements impossible.[15] The planners of the Hungarian deportations were no doubt aware of these difficulties, but they did nothing to delay them in order to release extra trains for supplies. Until June 22, when Operation Bagration was launched, the SS used 115 Reichsbahn trains to deport Jews from Hungary. Up to June 16, a total of 340,162 Jews were deported from Carpathian Ruthenia, North Transylvania, and northern Hungary to Auschwitz. The next phase of deportations would begin on June 25 and end only on July 8, when Army Group Center collapsed. The 115 trains that carried them could each have fitted 750 German troops and at least one Panzer division. As in the western sector, they could have been used for military purposes rather than deporting innocent civilians.[16] Theoretically, if the Wehrmacht had used these trains for transferring the extra divisions needed in Belorussia on the eve of Operation Bagration, some 86,250 troops could have been transported, comprising twenty-one infantry divisions—a full German army.[17] This was half the strength needed to reinforce the entire front, according to Marshal Zhukov.[18] Such a major shift in the balance of power could have changed the scenario between the Wehrmacht and the Red Army in June 1944.

Judging by experience, when the Russians reached Minsk, Army Group Center assumed that they had attained their first major objective, and having gone about 200 kilometers more than their usual limit on a single issue of supplies, they would pause for a few days in order to regroup and resupply. They were wrong, however. The Soviets continued their offensive, forcing the 9th Army to retreat toward Białystok and the east Prussian border. The Soviets, who by July 13 had covered more than 320 kilometers without a pause, had for the time outrun their supplies. They were now deep in territory destroyed by recent fighting, where bridges had to be rebuilt and rails relaid after the Germans turned long stretches of the railway lines into tangles of twisted tracks and broken links.[19] Even at this late stage of the war, the Red Army forces opposing Army Group Center were still too weak to achieve overall superiority. When the Stavka first began to plan the battle, it discovered there were forty-two German divisions, totaling 850,000 men, facing approximately one million men in seventy-seven divisions and five mobile corps on the Baltic and Belorussian fronts.[20]

Transports: June 7–July 7, 1944

In late June 1944, the deportations from the Hungarian provinces were virtually completed. The attention of the de-Jewification squads turned next to the Jews of Budapest—the largest Jewish community still relatively intact in Nazi-dominated Europe. However, behind the scenes, doubts about the deportations were reaching a head.[21] In early January 1944, Dr. Heinrich "Heinz" Josef Philipp Müller, president of the audit office of the German Reich in Potsdam, launched an inquiry into the Ostbahn. The purpose was to examine whether the operational, economic, and financial management of the Ostbahn (which still operated as an independent body under General Government regulations) was maintaining the interests of the Reich. Müller was determined to ensure that auditing was carried out in accordance with the standards and regulations of the National Railroad Act.[22] Thus, the train routes operating under the Ostbahn were checked by the committee. Among these were the routes to five extermination camps: Warsaw–Małkinia (Treblinka), Kraków–Plaszow (forced labor camp)–Skewina–Auschwitz, the latter being the last stop of the Ostbahn, Cholm–Sobibor, Lukow–Lublin (Majdanek), and Rejowiec–Belzec. The routes to Hungary, Slovakia, and Romania were also now under scrutiny, although, as noted, they were not part of the Ostbahn but a regular service of the Reichsbahn.[23]

Apparently, these reviews and assessments of the Ostbahn's management and accounting had begun in June 1942, with Hans Frank, the governor of the General Government, in cooperation with the audit committee. Correspondence on the issue exists between Dr. Winzerling, director of the audit office, and Dr. Busch, ministerial director from July 17 to December 21, 1943.[24] These letters reveal that the management and financial statements of the Reichsbahn and the Ostbahn were to be investigated, and that this inquiry was in the interests of the transport ministry and the war effort. It was suggested that the Reich transport minister submit to the finance minister the annual accounts of the eastern railways, together with the opinion of the main examination board of the German railway authority and an expert opinion on the accounts.[25]

Finally, on June 6, 1944, the very day the Allies invaded Western Europe, the Reich audit office issued a new set of regulations. This was no coincidence: by then, no more trains were to be used solely for military requirements. The new instructions were forwarded to the secretariat of the General Government. The bottom line was that from then on, the Ostbahn, which was considered a fundamental asset of the General Government, was no longer to have external rights on the eastern railways. Any train operation would have to get permission from the transport minister and the Reich finance court. This meant that men like Rudolf Gercke, Franz Novak, and Adolf Eichmann were no longer free to obtain and coordinate trains without questions being asked. However, the routes via Małkinia, Auschwitz, Belzec, and Lublin examined by the audit office did not seem to make any sense at the strategic level. Regulations concerning the railway system of the General Government and economic and financial auditing were issued on June 6. The decree dealt with the operation and management of the eastern railways, while the Reich minister of transport, Julius Dorpmüller, was expected to see that the interests of the Reich and its overall traffic be taken into consideration when dealing with permits for rail traffic around the General Government. It included financial statements and a balance sheet showing profit and loss.[26]

Examinations under the accounting regulations for the German state railway were conducted from July 11, 1939, almost two months before the war began, taking into consideration the special position of the eastern railway, the German Reich rail system, the ministry of transport, and the auditors of the Reich. The financial statements of the Ostbahn were also scrutinized under the same regulations. Their balance sheets were to be available for the transport and finance ministers within six months from the end of the year.[27] Interestingly, these regulations were written on May 15, 1944, the day the first transports of Hungarian Jewry departed for Auschwitz. However, it was no coincidence; only the timing was bad, and it was already too late. By July 8, the Reichsbahn had used 147 trains for this mission.

On July 31, 1944, Himmler sent Albert Ganzenmüller at the transport ministry a telex message stating that SS-Obergruppenführer Hans-Adolf Prützmann was coming to Berlin from the Ukraine and southern Russia, where he was responsible for internal security and combating partisans. Prützmann, who was also notorious for the murder of thousands of Jews in Latvia and for establishing the Riga ghetto, was now about to make sure that the railroads in the southern part of the Reich were protected against attacks by partisans and air raids. Himmler asked Ganzenmüller to cooperate with Prützmann in order to ensure that the next phase of deportations, which was in fact the last round of deportations to Auschwitz, would not run into delays or resistance from the army.[28]

The deportations from Hungary to Auschwitz continued throughout the first week of July, as did deportations from Holland and France. Despite the pressure of the Allied forces in Normandy, even the Drancy camp in France was still being used to deport Jews from Paris to the East. Deportations began whenever the number of inmates reached 1,000 to 1,500. On June 30, a train carrying 1,153 Jews left Paris for Auschwitz, traveling through eastern France, the Rhineland, Saxony, and Silesia, without interference, at the time Allied armies were battling in Normandy, less than 240 kilometers away.[29] By July 9, 1944, 437,402 Jews out of a total of 800,000 living in Hungary since 1938, before the Germans entered the country, had been sent to Auschwitz. The remaining planned deportations from Hungary, and in particular the swift removal of the Jews of Budapest, were stopped by Admiral Miklós Horthy in mid-July 1944.[30]

On July 20, Horthy published a statement declaring that the Hungarian government had decided to halt the Jewish deportations. Horthy's announcement stemmed from a number of reasons. First, extensive media reports had begun to circulate in June and July 1944 about the extermination of Hungarian Jews in Auschwitz. Second was the response of neutral governments, above all the king of Sweden and his ministers, to proposals regarding the possibility of Jewish refugees going to Sweden. President Franklin Roosevelt, who was quick to condemn the German occupation of Hungary and the threat of deportations, addressed Horthy personally on June 26. He demanded a cessation of the deportations and threatened retribution against those responsible. On June 25, Pope Pius XII's appeals to Admiral Horthy to stop the deportations, in addition to calls from the International Red Cross and the War Refugee Committee, probably had some influence on the fate of the surviving Jews. However, the main reason for Horthy's decision was doubtless the knowledge he received that the gendarmerie units, which were responsible for concentrating the Jews before their deportation, were plotting a coup against him. In addition, the Hungarians had intercepted a telegram originally sent by Richard Lichtheim (a Jewish Zionist of German origin responsible for news messages passed to the heads of the Yishuv in Palestine from the occupied territories) to the Jewish Agency, proposing that the Allies bomb the rail line from Hungary to Auschwitz and government buildings in Budapest. When the train station in Budapest was bombed by the Americans on July 2, Horthy was convinced that it was a result of Jewish pressure on the Allies; a day later, he notified the Germans of his decision to halt the deportations, although they soon resumed. When the train station in Budapest was bombed by the Americans on July 2, Horthy was convinced that it was a result of Jewish pressure on the Allies, and the day after, July 3, he notified the Germans about his decision to halt the deportations, which went into action only on July 7.[31] Horthy would later claim in his memoirs that only in August 1944 did secret information reach him about the truth of the extermination camps. Horthy's explanation was that for a long time he was helpless in the face of German influence in Hungary. As the defeat of the Reich drew nearer, he slowly regained a certain freedom of action, which enabled him in the summer to at last "succeed" in preventing the deportations.[32]

Although the mission was not complete and there was some contact between SS representatives, such as Kurt Becher and Dieter Wisliceny, not to mention Eichmann himself, with some Jewish bodies, represented by Dr. Rudolf Kastner, one of the leaders of the Jewish Aid and Rescue Committee in Budapest, and Joel Brand (in a plan to offer the lives of the 700,000 Jews of Greater Hungary against the payment of 10,000 trucks, to be delivered by the Allies at the port of

Salonika), eventually, it was Admiral Horthy who refused to cooperate with Himmler further, and he issued the order himself to halt the deportations of the remaining 250,000 Hungarian Jews.[33]

It is almost certain that the Germans were not really interested in liberating the Jews of Hungary in large numbers, as the Eichmann–Kastner negotiations suggest. The speed and scope of the unprecedented deportations and extermination at Auschwitz leave no doubt as to their true intentions at the time. The contacts with the Jewish representatives were simply a ploy to deceive them and keep all options open. German considerations were guided by the notion that if the Allies rejected the German offer, it would be easy to blame them for assisting the mass extermination of Hungarian Jewry, similar to after the 1938 Evian conference, when the Germans claimed of the Jews that "nobody wants them." On the other hand, if by chance, according to German thinking, the Allies began negotiating with the Germans and the negotiations came to Stalin's attention, the Great Alliance might collapse — an event that Hitler was eager to see happen.[34]

Eichmann, recollecting and organizing events in his favor, would later claim that the 10,000 trucks exchanged for one million Hungarian Jews were for the use of the 8th and 22nd SS cavalry divisions.[35] Between June 25 and 28, seven trains carrying 18,000 to 20,000 Jews were sent from Hungary to Vienna and the Strasshof concentration camp; 12,000 of them survived the war. Eichmann was ordered to ship Jews to Vienna because the mayor of the city, who was a friend of Ernst Kaltenbrunner, head of the Reich security office, had prevailed upon the head of the Reich Main Security Office to supply him with slave labor for the local arms industry.[36] The extra 1,684 Jews who left Hungary on the so-called Kastner train amounted to eight more trains used between July 25 and 30. Their transport was portrayed by Eichmann to Kastner as a gesture of goodwill in their so-called negotiations. The Jews sent to Vienna were apparently not at immediate risk of being gassed at Auschwitz.

In 1944, about 35,000 locomotives were available in Germany, of which, after deducting the number of damaged ones, some 28,000 were in working order. With a monthly average of 6,000 locomotives at repair workshops, this meant a standing total of 22,000 locomotives in running order. In other words, Germany had considerable reserves, as the traffic network had meanwhile been further reduced.[37] Albert Speer would claim many years later that according to his calculations, it took forty to sixty train wagons a day to supply the Auschwitz death facilities, out of 150,000 train wagons a day that were under his direction as minister of armaments. Speer spoke of approximately 5,000 trains that the Reichsbahn operated daily across the entire European continent. This included civilian transportation within Germany as well as trams. He claimed, therefore, that the perpetration of the Final Solution was not such a difficult task to carry out. Speer's calculations, however, were wrong. In August 1944, the number of trains under his direction was only 130,000 wagons per day, while the number of wagons used for Auschwitz was at least 120 wagons daily—twice as many as Speer cited.[38] Further, he stressed that the bombing of the railways based on the Allies' transport plan was inefficient. The track, he said, was a piece of metal a few centimeters wide. It could be bent or broken by massive bombing, but then it was simply a matter of two Polish forced laborers with large pliers who would quickly repair the damaged part so that the trains could continue to run. The myth surrounding the Allied bombing in Germany and France carried no real weight, then, in changing the tide of the war in the West before the end of 1944. Although at the beginning the bombings were a substitute for opening a second front in Europe, they had no real impact on the progress of the war, except perhaps a psychological one.[39]

On July 25, 1944, Governor Martin Mutschmann of Saxony sent a telegram to Himmler at Prinz-Albrecht-Strasse 8, in Berlin, telling him of a recent press memo that he had read. It stated that in the occupied parts of Normandy, which the American and British forces had liberated, a fair number of Jews still existed. Mutschmann reminded Himmler that just a few years before, he had told Martin Bormann that as long as the Jews of Europe were still at large, partisans and saboteurs were bound to strike fiercely against the Wehrmacht. He was therefore keen that a cleanup be carried out, and he noted that there was plenty of enthusiasm to do so.[40] On July 31, Himmler replied in a brief letter that he welcomed his suggestions, as they corresponded to his own experience. Himmler confirmed that in Hungary this policy had been activated, and that 450,000 Jews, half of all Hungarian Jewry, had already been exterminated.[41]

By early July, the struggle for Normandy was inflicting misery almost equally on the German, British, and American armies. The German generals knew that their forces were being inexorably ground down and that they could not hope for adequate replacements. Many of the difficulties of manpower, armor, and ammunition were known to senior Allied commanders, although not to their subordinates. On the battlefield, the effectiveness of the German resistance seemed undiminished. Meanwhile, the men of the invading forces were growing weary. Summer was slipping away, and the disturbing prospect of autumn weather in the Channel lay ahead. The problem of infantry casualties, which was a matter of concern for the Americans, had become a crisis for the British. General Bernard Montgomery was personally warned about the shortage of replacements. British battalions had already been broken up to fill the ranks of others, but now came the possibility that entire divisions might have to be disbanded.[42]

The last mass transport of deportees that could actually interfere with military needs took place in August 1944, when some 67,000 Jews from the Lodz ghetto were dispatched daily to Auschwitz. The last transport, which left Lodz on August 30, was on its way when the Red Army was on the banks of the Visla River in Poland, only 100 kilometers from Lodz.[43] By the beginning of September, the Germans estimated that the Allies had fifty-three divisions in the West. Theoretically, the same number could be counted on the German side, but their combat strength seldom amounted to much more than a third of an Allied division—the equivalent of some twenty-seven German divisions facing fifty-three Allied ones.[44] Because the successful Ardennes offensive was imminent, in mid-December, allocating fresh divisions would indeed have been feasible. Thus, instead of the Lodz transports, the Reichsbahn again could have transferred at least another division, if not two or three, depending on combat strength, either to the western sector or to the East.

The attack on the German forces after the landings in Normandy was successful; it turned out to be a chase after the retreating German forces. However, during the pursuit, the commanders of the Allied armies—George Patton, Omar Bradley, Courtney Hodges, and Montgomery—forgot to take into account the time-consuming logistical operation around it. There was no synchronicity between the swift operational tempo and the far slower logistical one, which created a breakdown in the operational effectiveness of the campaign. The logistical support system was unable to keep up with the fast maneuvers, and as a result, the Allied assault was slowed down and eventually halted when General Patton's forces simply ran out of fuel.[45] August 29 was a critical day in the Battle of Normandy. It was evident that there was no real threat from the Germans to Patton's 3rd Army, and the Americans were unstoppable in their advance toward the Siegfried Line. Everything seemed to be going well when suddenly Patton was told that 140,000 gallons of fuel that were supposed to be supplied to his army that day had not arrived. The XII Corps, which estimated that it used between 200,000 and 300,000 gallons of gasoline to move eighty kilometers, had only 31,000 gallons at hand on August 24 and 75,000 gallons for the next day. By August 29, they were virtually out of gasoline. It was not until September 3 that the XII Corps at Ligny-en-Barrois captured 100,000 gallons of aviation gasoline and so could move on.[46]

On August 31, the last transport from Lodz to Auschwitz left the city. With Paris in Allied hands on August 25, and with Patton's crossing of the Meuse halted on August 29, this is another example of Germany's strange priorities at such a crucial time. At this juncture, there were perhaps only 100 German tanks on the entire Western Front against over 2,000 Allied ones.[47] Had Patton's 3rd Army met one or two Panzer divisions (albeit shrunken ones) transferred from the East after it was halted by a lack of supplies, it would not have been able to resume mobility on September 4, and casualties would have been much higher. What seemed to be certain victory in the West after the breakthrough from Normandy and the collapse of the German army in France during August 1944 turned into an improvised retreat—albeit an efficient one—to the borders of Germany and the Netherlands. As a result, Germany's Western Front stabilized during summer, autumn, and winter of 1944–1945. The Germans were sufficiently rehabilitated in early winter that fighting was almost static until the Wehrmacht received enough reinforcements to renew combat on all fronts. Some assaults cost the Allies dearly because of the difficult terrain, the mud and rain, and the skillful German enemy.[48]

By the end of 1944, the Germans had little left it could do

strategically other than try and reach a peace agreement with the West. However, even before December 1944, the Soviet offensive had lost its momentum as a result of logistical difficulties. When Hitler launched the Ardennes offensive in the West, the Soviet front was unusually quiet.[49] The only front left that no one was paying too much attention to because of the bad topography was the Ardennes. Surprisingly, this was precisely the site from which Hitler launched his last major offensive in the West, better known as the Battle of the Bulge, in December–January 1944–1945. This assault, which initially caused much concern among the Allies, was suppressed only after harsh fighting and heavy losses on both sides. Matters reached a point where General Eisenhower asked Stalin to begin the planned Soviet attack in the East earlier in order to ease the plight of the Western armies.[50]

Surprisingly, when preparing the offensive in the Ardennes, the supreme command of the Wehrmacht used sixty-four trains for carrying ammunition for what would be their last successful offensive. This gives an idea as to how much effort and rail resources the Nazis used, for instance, when they transported 67,000 Jews from the Lodz ghetto to Auschwitz using some fifty-two trains. One can only imagine how much ammunition and determination would result from a similar mission in late August against Patton's stationary tanks.[51]

In terms of tactics and communications, the Germans were far in advance of the Western Allies; in addition, coordination on the battlefield between Allied tanks and infantry was still in its infancy compared to the experience the Germans had accrued during the campaigns in Russia and North Africa. With regard to equipment, it is clear that in all cases except aircraft, the Germans enjoyed clear advantages. This was particularly true in regard to tanks. Allied tanks could be knocked out by any German tank at a range of up to 1,000 meters and often more, while it was a matter of luck if Allied gunners disabled a German tank. In most cases, the Tiger was invulnerable, even at close range, to anything other than a British Sherman tank or a rocket fired from an aircraft.[52]

In contrast to previous campaigns, during the Ardennes offensive, code named Operation Autumn Mist (Herbstnebel), which began on December 16, 1944, and which initially went well for the Germans, there were no transports to the death camps. The only camp that still functioned during this period was Auschwitz; however, in December 1944, no transports arrived there. Apart from a small number of Jews sent there in January 1945, just before the Russians liberated it, there were no mass-murder activities. This raises questions yet again concerning the burden the Final Solution placed on German resources and its impact on the tactical capabilities of the Wehrmacht.

There were some sporadic transports to Auschwitz at the end of 1944 in addition to the Lodz *aktion*. In October 1944, some 14,403 deportees from Theresienstadt were dispatched to Auschwitz in eleven transports, and between August and November, transports of 7,936 people arrived from Slovakia.[53] The transports from Greece, which Eichmann's subordinate Wisliceny claimed were pursued fanatically even in summer 1944, when the Germans were evacuating the Greek islands and needed all the railway services available, were another example of Nazi priorities. The wagons the Germans used for transporting the Jews of Thessaloniki and Athens to Auschwitz in July 1944 were taken from the military transport command. The appeals came, as usual, from Franz Novak to Otto Stange, a consultant to the transport ministry. However, according to Auschwitz records, there were no more than 1,500 Greek deportees in April, 2,000 in June, and 2,500 in July. Therefore, their impact on the military effort could not have been too serious, although methodologically, it was the same pattern that followed Hungary and Lodz.[54]

By the time Admiral Horthy was deposed and Ferenc Szálasi had taken over power, by mid-October, the Final Solution as an organized systematic operation was coming to a halt. The war in Hungary was approaching its end, and no trains at all were allocated for the transportation of Jews to Auschwitz or any other extermination site. Moreover, Himmler was no longer interested in the deportations. Himmler, it seems, was acknowledging that his end, as well as that of the war, was approaching. Although he was unable to take any serious steps to stop the killings because of his fear of the Führer, as of early 1945 onward, he tried to find ways to appeal to the Western powers, for which he was willing to spare a few small groups of Jews in order to prove his earnest intentions.[55]

On April 23, 1945, Himmler approached Count Folke Bernadotte, vice president of the Swedish Red Cross, to mediate between him and the Allies, offering to lay down arms in the entire Western theater, including Denmark and Norway, in return for letting the German army continue fighting on the Eastern Front for just a little longer in order to save the civilian population from the Soviets. Himmler's appeal was rejected by Winston Churchill and Harry S. Truman on the grounds that he was trying to drive a wedge between the Western Allies and the Soviet Union. They demanded unconditional surrender of all three major powers on all fronts.[56]

The desperate labor shortage in Germany now led to plans to deploy Hungarian Jews as slave laborers in the underground assembly sites of V-2 rockets. The V-2 rockets fired against Britain were morale dampening, but most German generals were skeptical about the long-term effects of this long-range weapon because its aim was imprecise. Moreover, British bases and production facilities in southern England were about to take further retaliatory action.[57] Therefore, the risk was great enough to use the remaining Hungarian Jews for labor, although without trains to transport them, they would have to walk in order to work in Germany. These would turn out to be notorious death marches that killed many of them. Subsequent SS attempts to move more Jews by rail were stymied by a lack of transport, leaving 70,000 Budapest Jews cramped into a ghetto within range of Soviet guns until the surrender of the city in February 1945.[58] Given the determination of the Germans to fight on till the bitter end, along with their equally fierce determination to slaughter Jews until the last moments of the Third Reich, there were thousands of deaths daily until the final days of the war. However, the Reichsbahn was out of the picture by then.[59]

Conclusion

German historiography and the status of the Final Solution in historical discourse has varied over the years after the surrender of the Third Reich. Before reunification, German historiography relating to the war were influenced by the postwar geopolitical situation that developed. In East Germany, history was shaped by the Soviet approach and in West Germany by the Western one. The profound impact of the Nuremberg trials on the German population created an apologetic attitude in German historical writings; Basil Liddell Hart's interviews with German officers also had some effect. The generals' memoirs and diaries served as primary material for the first wave of West German writing. In most cases, these writings were unilateral in their approach, with the entire blame for the failure of the war put on Hitler, who was branded an amateur strategist.[1] Only at the beginning of the 1980s, with the publication of the Militärgeschichtliches Forschungsamt (MGFA) (Germany and World War II) series, did an official German approach take shape. Lack of preparation for the war in Russia, underestimation of Soviet power, Soviet production capability, and Soviet endurance in fighting a long war of attrition that eventually won them victory over the Nazi regime became the principal motifs in German historical writings.[2] However, the Germans were also forced to deal with an unconventional reading of World War II in which they had a leading role, and which was inseparable from the historical narrative. The unique character of the war in the Soviet Union was partly a result of the close relationship between conquering new "living space" in the East and the Final Solution of the Jewish question. Yet German public opinion has always tended to emphasize German tragedy and suffering at the expense of the Jewish and Russian experience.[3]

German historiography connected to the Holocaust and the Final Solution were also a direct outcome of the political changes and national developments that occurred in West Germany during the second half of the twentieth century. After a period of almost complete ignorance in the first years after 1945—an ignorance related to rehabilitation efforts and reshaping a national identity—a need arose among Germans to deal with the legacy that Nazi Germany had left in general, as well as with the place of the Holocaust in historical, political, and civil discourse in particular. The German people have come a long way, beginning with the silence of embarrassment and the treatment of the national past as a moral no-man's-land, through the distinction in the Adenauer era between war crimes, crimes against humanity, and crimes against the Jews, and up to the abandonment of guilty feelings in everything connected to dealings with the state of Israel in favor of normalization of relations. The process undergone by the German people was comprehensively reflected in a passionate discourse that eventually led to a historical controversy (now known as the historians' debate) that began in 1985 in the pages of two important newspapers in Germany, *Frankfurter Allgemeine Zeitung* and *Die Zeit*.[4] The philosopher Jürgen Habermas expressed it best when he wrote an article claiming that the argument among historians was not over historical detail but was connected to political changes that imposed contemporary writing of revisionist history.[5]

Since then, a profound historical debate regarding the academic conception of the Final Solution has been going on between two schools of thought—one that has long since crossed the borders of the Republic of Germany.[6] According to the intentionalist school, from his early days, Hitler conformed to initial ideological patterns, calculating his steps meticulously, driven mainly by his desire to annihilate the Jewish people. The Final Solution, therefore, was an inevitable outcome of the anti-Semitic racial ingredient in his worldview. The intentionalist school emphasizes the autonomy of will of the person standing on top of the pyramid as a decisive factor in the course of history; it sees the anti-Semitic line as connected integrally and organically to Nazi policy, which moved consistently and in defiance of all logic toward the Final Solution. There is a direct line of continuity, then, from the anti-Jewish boycott and anti-Jewish legislation in 1933 to the gas chambers of Auschwitz and Treblinka. Lucy David-owicz, who was among the first in the 1970s to hold such a position, claimed that the Final Solution took root in Hitler's mind as early as 1918 while he was recuperating in the hospital from his World War I injury. In her view, this long-held ideological basis led over time to the murder of Russian Jews and later to the annihilation of the vast majority of European Jewry. There was no deviation from this line of thought throughout the years; nor was there any hesitation in deci-sion making. Only questions of opportunity and timing would serve to implement the ideology. According to Davidowicz, "The Final So-lution grew out of a matrix formed by traditional anti-Semitism, the paranoid delusions that seized Germany after World War I, and the emergence of Hitler and the National Socialist movement. Without Hitler, the charismatic political leader, who believed he had a mission to annihilate the Jews, the Final Solution would not have occurred."[7] Another basic assumption can be found in Gerald Fleming's research from the 1980s, which goes back even earlier than Davidowicz's start-ing point. Fleming presents Hitler's anti-Semitism in his years at Linz as a prelude to his joining the Viennese anti-Semitic association in April 1908: "Much later but, still to be ranged along the same contin-uum, were the first shootings of German Jews in . . . Kovno and Riga on November 1941."[8] Fleming argues repeatedly that a direct connec-tion exists, with its origins lying in Hitler's personal hatred toward Jews. It ends with the orders given during the war for their annihila-tion. This approach is summed up by Jäckel Eberhard, who points out that although the perpetration of genocide faced no opposition and Hitler never lacked enthusiastic assistants up to the very end, the an-nihilation policy was an outcome of his will and his decisions.[9]

On the other hand, historians representing the functionalist school of thought, which grew out of the historians' debate, emphasize the lack of a systematic policy, which in their eyes points to an improvised one. Although these improvisations eventually led to extremes in anti-Semitic policy, the objectives and the steps leading up to them were not foreseen or planned in advance. This approach tends to underesti-mate Hitler's personality and his role in creating such a policy, as well as putting it into action. Hans Mommsen, who holds the most radical view, claims that the Final Solution was not based on a program that developed over a long period of time but that the bureaucratic mechanism created by Reinhard Heydrich and Adolf Eichmann functioned more or less automatically. Because no explicit order for murder was given by Hitler, only vague declarations spoken aloud to his men, the process had an interior dynamic of its own. Therefore, direct responsibility cannot be placed on Hitler, Himmler, Heydrich, and Martin Bormann alone. According to Mommsen's interpretation, ideological factors, the effect of anti-Semitic propaganda, and the despotic element in the traditional political culture of Germany are insufficient to explain how the Holocaust became a reality.[10] A chaotic administrative situation led to improvised bureaucratic initiatives that held within them a destructive internal momentum. Such a reality led to the increasing extremism of anti-Semitic policy.[11] The German historian Martin Broszat offered a similar explanation. Accordingly, the expulsion of the Jews remained the main objective of the regime until autumn 1941. The governors, police commanders, and SS heads did not succeed in coping with the huge number of Jews transferred to their administrative district because of the failed blitz in Russia. As a result, local initiatives, sometimes driven by individuals, were born and then were later adopted retroactively by the higher echelons. According to this approach, murdering the Jews was an escape of sorts from a blind alley, which the Germans had reached as a consequence of their failures in Russia. These sporadic initiatives became a general solution along the way.[12] Philippe Burrin agrees that there was no blueprint and instead claims that physical annihilation was proposed as a solution only during Operation Barbarossa. However, contrary to Mommsen and Broszat, Burrin emphasizes that Hitler was at the center of the debates; it was he who made the decision around mid-August 1941 regarding the genocide of Russian Jewry, and he who a month later extended it to the complete annihilation of European Jewry.[13]

My work here has dealt with the Jewish question in the operational context of the German campaigns along the war's fronts. In the framework of the historical discourse, my research has examined a possible position that is characteristic of Jürgen Förster's and Christopher R. Browning's writings in that it attempts to serve as a bridge between the functionalists and intentionalists by moderating both approaches. According to this perception,

Nazi racial policy was radicalized in quantum jumps between 1939 and 1941, with war acting as a stimulant. . . . But at the same time, Hitler must be credited with making the key decisions in the summer of 1940 and in the spring and summer of 1941. The symbiosis between ideology and strategy was realized with the vernichtungskrieg against the Soviet Union, when the concept of destruction was declared a military necessity and formed an integral part of the strategic and tactical planning.[14]

Hitler, then, was behind the scenes regarding all decisions taken at all levels, even if he only gave permission for actions presented to him after the fact.[15] Ian Kershaw can be placed among advocates of this school in the center of the debate, although he reached that point after originally supporting the functionalist approach. Over a quarter of a century ago, Kershaw claimed that Hitler did not plan liquidation; that during the 1930s there was no clear policy regarding the Jewish question; and that it was not Hitler who came up with the initiatives in the field.[16] By the end of the 1990s, when he published the first part of his biography of Hitler, Kershaw presented a more moderate line, which approached that of Förster and Browning. Kershaw points in the first part of his biography to 1919 as the year in which for the first time there is documentation regarding the Jewish question. In a letter to an acquaintance, Hitler wrote that "anti-Semitism . . . must lead to the systematic removal of the rights of Jews . . . and its final aim must unshakably be the removal of the Jews altogether."[17] Kershaw claims that this letter exposed for the first time the basic elements that were inherent in Hitler's worldview and that remained unchanged till his last day in the Berlin bunker.

A relatively new approach, one that is somewhere in the middle, has been proposed by Tobias Jersak. According to Jersak, it was Hitler who reached the decision to carry out the annihilation of the Jews, but only after he had recognized the failure of his strategy to defeat the Soviet Union in a blitzkreig; it was not necessarily as part of a blueprint. Jersak claims that the declaration of the Atlantic Treaty by Franklin D. Roosevelt and Winston Churchill on August 14, 1941, played a part in his resolution because its meaning was that Germany would soon be at war with the United States.[18]

In the past two decades, various studies have raised doubts as to whether the outcome of World War II should be taken for granted. These publications, well represented by Richard Overy, Kenneth Macksey, Heinz Magenheimer, and Russel H. S. Stolfi, examine key strategic decisions taken by Hitler and the German High Command and emphasize the deployment of field forces, air and naval superiority, industrial production, and logistics on both the Axis and Allied sides.[19] The focus of these studies is the strategic blunders Hitler made while he conducted the war as the only decision maker for most of the time.[20] There is agreement among historians that Hitler indeed made serious mistakes that cost Germany the war; however, it is hard to determine why these decisions were taken, in what frame of mind, and what the main assumption was regarding the advantages and goals Germany would achieve. In this context, the approach of the so-called revisionist discourse is that the Allied victory was due less to the superiority of forces and more to the tactical and strategic management of the war. The central claim of this research is that Germany's defeat was an operational and organizational failure and that the effort and resources invested in the Final Solution were detrimental to the army.

There is no doubt that Germany faced severe logistical problems that hampered the army's performance and played no less a major part in the defeat than strategy. However, the reasons for those difficulties are not at all clear, and they raise several questions. Because the mechanism of annihilating European Jews faced no logistical problems and operated meticulously, the conclusion of this research is that the Wehrmacht's logistical problems resulted from the decentralization of logistics, while the ideological mechanism that dealt with the annihilation and that was not necessarily equal to the military one sabotaged the normal function of the Wehrmacht, especially in its battles with the Russians, but also with the rest of the Allies on the other fronts as well. Decentralization caused a conflict of interests in the Reich High Command between the officers of the Wehrmacht and the heads of the SS, with each functionary of these branches reflecting a different element in Hitler's dual worldview: the Wehrmacht as the body responsible for *Lebensraum*, and the SS as the body responsible for the territories intended to serve the racist National Socialist doctrine.

Some of the points raised in this research have been dealt with by other scholars, and it is important to note here a few studies that discuss the connection between the war and the Holocaust. The barbarization of warfare that broke borders in Hanoch Bartov's studies about the German army, the euphoria of victory on which Christopher Browning bases his claims, and the frustration following failures in the battlefield portrayed by Arno J. Mayer all arguably influenced the extermination process in one way or another.[21] Unlike these studies, the emphasis in the current work has been on how the search for a solution to the Jewish question and ideological fanaticism sometimes influenced decision making, operational maneuvers, logistics, the order of priorities, and the outcome of campaigns. Studies to date have dealt with the fertile soil that war created for performing mass executions. What passes as a connecting thread in most cases is that a general situation of chaos during the campaigns provided cover for the execution of war crimes and crimes against humanity. Yet until now, no research has specifically examined the cost incurred by those behind the persecutions, genocide, and transfer of populations from one place to another—in other words, how the Final Solution influenced military operations, such as the movement of supplies and troop replacements to the front lines. The assumption that the operational capabilities of the Wehrmacht were weakened as a result of Germany's decentralization of logistics had not been examined in depth. This study is an attempt to fill this gap and to shed light on the impact the resources invested in annihilating European Jewry had on the Wehrmacht and its operational abilities.

In retrospect, it appears that the occupation of Poland served as a test case for Nazi racial policy. It is clear that there was a turnabout in the treatment toward the Jews and their persecution, but the Final Solution was not yet a concrete aim from 1939 to 1941. The difference between the Polish campaign, code named Case White, including the occupation of Poland, and the events of 1941 during Operation Barbarossa, was that during this operation, the line between a war fought on the basis of military doctrine alone and ideological war was erased even before the first shot was fired on June 22, 1941.[22] In Poland there was still a red line that was not crossed—at least on the official level. Time and again, the meticulousness of German planning and perfectionism raises astonishment: everything, down to the smallest detail, was considered and scrutinized. However, the bottom line was that it was impossible to operate on multiple fronts and be successful at all of them. Conducting a world war and finding a suitable solution for a huge-scale ideological problem, which from the German point of view was indeed acute, was simply too much even for a nation as large and powerful as Germany.

Notably, while in the West there were very few military clashes between September 1939 and May 10, 1940, one result of the *Sitz-krieg* (phony war)[23] was that the main casualty was the policy against the Jews, which came up against countless difficulties. As it turned out, a suitable solution was not found during that period. However, while the campaign against the USSR during the second half of 1941 was in progress, the entire mechanism began to crack. A lack of focus on truly important objectives was a crucial issue during the war Nazi Germany conducted against the Soviet Union from then on. The question that thus should be asked is why it was so urgent to deal with this ideological project in the midst of the war. The answer lies somewhere within the comprehension shared by Hitler and his fellow bearers of Nazi ideology: when an armistice came and the guns fell silent across Europe, there would be no way to solve the racial problem.[24] Hitler recognized an opportunity, and he was not about to let it slip away. This insight made him try and adjust his future foreign policy and military strategy to fit these ideological opportunities.

On June 12, 1944, General Field Marshal Alan Brooke, along with Churchill, boarded the destroyer *Kelvin* at Portsmouth to approach the French coast. The sea was blanketed with ships of all shapes and sizes in continuous activity. It was striking how this scene resembled another one in different circumstances only four years previously, during the British Operation Dynamo in June 1940. Brooke and Churchill met Bernard Montgomery on the beach, escorted by a convoy of jeeps, which took them to Montgomery's headquarters in France. Brooke would recall in his diary how during lunch his thoughts wandered back four years when he was at Le Mans with Pierre Laval, waiting for Montgomery and his 3rd Division to join him: "I knew then that it would not be long before I was kicked out of France, if I was not killed or taken prisoner. But if anybody had told me then that in four years time I should return with Winston and Smuts to have lunch with Monty commanding a new invasion force, I should have found it hard to believe it."[25]

It is hard to forget that four years before the Allied invasion of Normandy, close to the same Channel coast, the same Wehrmacht was facing more than twice as many British forces at Dunkirk than it did on D-day—and it still managed to bring the British to their knees and force them to evacuate their entire expeditionary force on June 3, 1940, and the French to sign an armistice at Compiègne on June 22. Nevertheless, there was one striking element that made the entire difference between D-day and Dunkirk. It is quite certain that in June 1944 the German army in Western Europe was still stronger and more powerful than the army that invaded France in May 1940. In June 1944, it still had a good chance of repelling the Allied landings and turning the situation around while inflicting on the British and Americans a Dunkirk-style defeat. Lieutenant General Frederick E. Morgan, the mastermind behind the plan for Operation Overlord, admitted after the war that Adolf Hitler had been the most effective commander produced by the war: "His successes however were scored by his enemies against his own side."[26]

Back in 1940, the Germans had to prepare themselves before they attempted to overcome one of Europe's strongest military forces. Only after he had ensured an iron ore supply from Sweden's mines and conquered Norway and Denmark, which secured Germany's northern flank, did Hitler return to his main program to deal with the French and British threats. He still did not possess the French resources he would have in 1944, however. On May 10, 1940, German infantry and Panzer divisions invaded along the French, Dutch, and Belgian borders. In just over six weeks, the French army, which until then was considered the mightiest military force in all of Europe, was literally destroyed. The defeat of these three countries, and especially France, shook the world, mainly because of the speed with which the Germans achieved their objective.[27]

Fedor von Bock's Army Group B crossed the French frontier on May 10 with only thirty-two divisions, compared to the fifty-eight divisions that were in Normandy on D-day. In the course of the May 1940 campaign, Army Group B gave up eleven divisions to other army groups and fought against eleven Dutch, twenty-two Belgian, twenty-five French, and elements of 14 to 15 British divisions—an opposing force with more than twice its superiority in numbers. More than half of these divisions were captured; the rest were smashed, with heavy losses.[28] The German soldiers who charged across France and the Low Countries, and who were much less skilled and experienced than the Wehrmacht veterans of the Eastern Front who faced the Allies in 1944, continued to close in on the French and British forces until they finally managed to trap the enemy in a small beach town. Pushed slowly into an enclave around the town of Dunkirk with a port on the banks of the English Channel, the British forces were trapped sixteen kilometers from the Belgian border. On the morning of May 24, General Paul Ludwig Ewald von Kleist's army, which included three Panzer divisions under General Heinz Guderian's command, and two more motorized infantry divisions suddenly appeared some twenty-five kilometers from Dunkirk. Von Kleist's forces, who were within sight of Dunkirk, estimated that the town and port could be in their hands within less than twenty-four hours.[29]

It should be emphasized that the German victories of May 1940 were due primarily to the skillful application of two principals of war: surprise and concentration. The German army was actually inferior to the Allied armies, not only in numbers of divisions but also in tank numbers. While the combined French and British forces had about 4,000 tanks, the German army had only 2,800. Nor did the German army have any real advantage in quality. The Allied tanks, and especially the British Matilda, had stronger armor than the Panzer Mark III; its 37mm gun was inferior to the British two-pounder. The Wehrmacht won the campaign in the West in May–June 1940 because it reintroduced the decisive factor of mobility, in contrast to its operational strategy in June 1944. In 1940, the German divisions achieved mobility through a combination of firepower, mobility, and surprise, as well as expert handling of the latest modern arms.[30]

There were various explanations for the events of Dunkirk. Most importantly, in a single campaign, thirty-two German divisions managed to bring an Allied army force of four nations to its knees—an army that faced a combined enemy force four times bigger than the one it would confront on June 6, 1944. Oddly, just as Hitler let the British evacuate Dunkirk unharmed, he allowed the landing forces of

Operation Overlord to reach the continent without real resistance—
or at least not of the kind that it was within his power to use. I refer
to Dunkirk because of the similarities to the Normandy landings
but mostly because of the difference in logistical operations of the
Third Reich. When conducting the French campaign, the German
army faced no competition over rail transport. In contrast to D-day,
all transportation needs were focused on military objectives alone.
During the French campaign, there were no large-scale population
transfers demanding transport. In addition, because in May 1940 the
Wehrmacht could not rely on the French railways for supplies, the
German performance in Normandy in 1944 should have been far superior to that in Dunkirk. The French rail net in June and July 1944
was not functioning, but it was not because of damage; it simply lacked
enough trains to mobilize supplies and reinforcements because they
were being used for the Hungarian deportations. The evidence clearly
shows that the masses deported to the extermination camps in Poland
on a daily basis were using the logistics of approximately one division, whether armored or infantry. Whatever the number of trains
dispatched daily, they could have been used to send troops to reinforce
a beaten division or to supply a Panzer division with fuel, horses, and
ammunition—or simply food and winter clothing.

Although on the Eastern Front there were 160 divisions in June
1944, they were divided among three sectors. In military theory, an
effective division operates within a range of five kilometers. Terrain
is also a factor because in mountainous areas, range has no effectiveness. If the ground is flat, there can be wide deployment. Depth has no
meaning in this case because it is always a matter of fire depth, which
could have been up to five kilometers then—or in modern terms of
tank warfare, even ten kilometers. An armored regiment would com-
prise some thirty-six tanks deployed over two kilometers. If, for instance, one examines a sector in which at any point in time two or
three divisions were fighting a battle in one of the Russian pockets of
resistance, the effectiveness of an extra division integrated into the
battle could have been crucial for the outcome. An extra division sent
from the rear could have injected new life into a battle of attrition and
possibly could have created new challenges for the Red Army around
the *Kessel*.[31] In this respect, it did not matter that in July 1942 General

Friedrich Paulus had over 700 tanks scattered along the southern sector, because when eventually he was about to be encircled by Vasily Chuikov's forces, he was left with only sixty. Another Panzer division, or even twenty tanks, could have helped the 6th Army survive. Because the Rostov railway station was only sixty kilometers from Stalingrad, the tanks could easily have been driven along the tank tracks.

To take another military case: during the 1973 Yom Kippur War, Division 146 was sent as a relief force to the Golan Heights in order to help repulse the Syrian assault on the Israel defense forces. Division 210 and Division 36 were on the brink of losing the battle to a massive Syrian army. On the morning of October 7, chief of staff General David "Dado" Elazar made a crucial decision that changed the entire strategic balance in the war on the northern front. Elazar ordered Division 146 (the last reserves the Israel Defense Force High Command had left) to move toward the northern sector from Central Command. Originally, Division 146 was supposed to be ready to fight a possible Jordanian offensive if they were to join the attack on a third front. However, this was a unique example of decisive decision making and mobilization of forces that would bring about a turn of the tide, despite the Syrians' ruthless surprise attack. After Division 146's counteroffensive in the Golan Heights, it was recalled to reinforce units fighting in Sinai against the Egyptians. Movement of this division from the Golan to Beer-Sheba in the south was managed by tank transporters, but from Beer-Sheba up to fifteen kilometers from the Suez Canal, the tanks traveled some 200 kilometers or more on tracks. In 1944, the Wehrmacht could have sent extra divisions from the Eastern Front to reinforce Gerd von Rundstedt's deployment in the West. This was not done, however, as a result of a lack of trains, which should have been mobilized in time to meet the Normandy landings. There is no doubt that an extra division in a second-line offensive at Omaha Beach could have made a difference. The most crucial element in tank warfare was—and to this day remains—fuel supply, because after fourteen to twenty hours, the operational effect is lost.[32]

Tanks could move on a flat surface up to approximately 200 kilometers. The 19th Armored Corps under General Guderian's command was supported by a supply line that could move an average of 160 kilometers per day. This included 262 tons of ammunition, 1,600 tons of fuel, 160 tons of food supplies, 140 tons of booty, and sixty tons of POWs.[33] If we put the weight of an average person aboard a Jewish deportation train of twenty wagons at fifty to eighty kilograms, this would amount to 160 tons in human freight.[34] The German Panzer Mark III and Mark IV consumed 300 liters of fuel every 100 kilometers. On good ground, movement of 200 tanks in a German armored division consumed 60,000 liters of fuel, but over harsh terrain, the volume of fuel required could more than double. Therefore, it was planned that every armored division would expend fuel worth four supply convoys. Because there were almost no motor vehicles in the Soviet Union, four supply trains per day was the amount a division needed to survive as a fighting force; this was the equivalent of the average number of trains sent on a daily basis to the death camps in the General Government.

It is clear that when the Germans invaded the Soviet Union, they did not pay enough attention to the supply aspect of an operation on that scale. As soon as they sent armored units into enemy territory, they should have had enough supply bases for renewal of stocks, spare parts, and workshop repairs. This was not the case, and on July 20, 1941, the 18th Armored Division, which began the operation with 210 tanks, lost fifty-nine because of enemy attacks, as well as another 103 tanks because of a shortage of spare parts. Only thirty tanks remained battle worthy. Because the production of new tanks was not a problem (even in 1944 Germany managed to manufacture an average of 500 tanks per month), all that was needed was an extra four trains with another thirty to forty tanks in order to change that scenario. On November 12, 1941, the 18th Armored Division had only eighteen tanks in operational usage.[35] Therefore, it is evident that even a single train with ten new Panzers could have kept it in combat-operational status.

The Wehrmacht, which proved to be the most powerful army in World War II, was led by a man who had served as a lance corporal and messenger, or runner, in World War I. That war had made an indelible impression on Hitler—but spiritually, not strategically or tactically, and still less administratively. He understood maintenance problems but nothing at all about naval operations. Yet sometimes he exhibited flashes of genius, especially in the earlier stages of the war, and these led to plans and blows that proved extremely successful, although they scared his military commanders and advisers. There was no room in his mind, however, for the unspectacular but valuable ingredient of common sense, any more than there was for humanitarianism. Above all, he thought in grandiose terms, owing largely to new-found military mobility and range of aircraft.[36]

The first formal definition of the term *logistics* was suggested by Antoine-Henri Jomini in 1838. Logistics, according to Jomini, was the art of mobilizing armies. It consisted of arrangements and details related to movement (originally marching), parking, and storage and supply of troops, and it was equivalent to the execution of strategic and tactical initiatives. Logistics was one of the fundamentals of Jomini's art of war. He argued that logistics comprised "arranging and supervising the march of trains of baggage, munitions, provisions, and ambulances, both with the columns and in their rear, in such a manner that they will not interfere with the movements of the troops and still be near at hand. Taking precautions for order and security both on the march and when trains are halted and parked."[37] In that respect, the Germans should have stuck to nineteenth-century military theory because the logistics behind the Jewish deportations apparently interfered with troop movement. Mobilizing troops, in Jomini's view, was part of the surprise element. Intelligence efforts had always been directed at guessing where the enemy would strike. Jomini regarded logistics as one of the surest ways of forming good combinations in the art of war. Ordering movements would only come after obtaining perfect information of the enemy's plans.[38]

On June 22, 1941, the Germans relied too heavily on the nineteenth-century East European railroad system to sustain a mechanized campaign, which outran its logistical support in the first seventy-two hours of battle. Behind the mechanized spearheads slogged the infantry, and behind them the horse-drawn support of the Wehrmacht.[39] One of the main logistical problems that the German forces had to deal with during Operation Barbarossa was the lack of spare parts for armored vehicles. This shortage was due mainly to Hitler's preference for investing in arms expansion rather than in logistical support of the matériel already available.[40] Tanks broke down frequently, but the mean time between failure, or MTBF, varied from one vehicle to another (failure being defined as any repair that could not be made by the crew in half an hour; a track link replacement, for instance, was not counted). The MTBF of the Panzer Mark III was 175 to 247 kilometers and was responsible for the initial successes in the Soviet Union in 1941. The Panzer Mark IV, which went into operation in 1942, served the German armored corps until the end of the war, with an MTBF of 210 to 320 kilometers, exactly like the Russian T-34. However, most of all, fuel shortages were the problem, not tank reliability, and less in weight terms than in capacity. One of the conclusions of the Agranat Commission's inquiry into the ill-prepared situation the Israel Defense Force found itself in before the Yom Kippur War was that there were not enough tank transporters; in other words, there was a massive transport problem.[41]

Because there was no definitive approach to the strategic developments chose as test cases for my research, the contribution of this book is in its examination of the events in a different light and as an alternative to existing interpretations. What is important is not whether Germany really had a chance of winning the campaigns dealt with here, but the abilities Hitler believed the Wehrmacht possessed before he took a strategic decision and issued an operational directive. In addition, the German generals' opinion about the capabilities of their armies and the way they presented matters before their supreme commander are also central. I have presented an unconventional approach that perceives the Final Solution as an integral part of the configuration of World War II in terms of logistical and operational considerations. My approach also views the Final Solution as a criterion in every military interpretation, just as economic and logistical interpretations of warfare on all fronts, and physical-topographical conditions of war in general, have been taken into account in every work dealing with that period. An attempt has been made here to offer an alternative approach to the mismanagement of some of the most important campaigns of World War II and to shed new light on operations in which Germany had a strategic-logistical ability to take different decisions and operate in a different way from the ones that it did.

Much has been written on almost every possible aspect of World War II, and it is doubtful that the last word has been said. The events I describe here are not new; they are based on the annals of World

War II. On June 22, 1941, the German army invaded Russia; it was not the Red Army that invaded western Poland. Joseph Stalin did not intend to be the aggressor in the summer of 1941 (an argument that has aroused a dispute in recent years), and in Stalingrad, it was Paulus's forces that were encircled and not those of Chuikov, the commander of the 62nd Soviet Army. These are facts and cannot change. However, the innovation of this work lies in its presentation of the emergence and execution of the Final Solution as an integral part of military operations. After detailing Germany's military needs in parallel with the deliberate policy of using the railways to transport Jewish populations to death camps, as well as negating alternative explanations for military events, one may deduce that carrying out the Final Solution had a profoundly negative influence on the German military effort during the war, as well as on the course of modern history in general and on modern Jewish history in particular.

On August 24, 1960, fourteen years after he had begun his incarceration in Spandau prison, and after apparently coming to terms with his notorious past, Albert Speer admitted:

> Perhaps I can forgive myself for everything else: having been his [Hitler's] architect is excusable, and I could even justify my having served as his armaments minister. I can even conceive of a position from which a case could be made for the use of millions of prisoners of war and forced laborers in industry—even though I have never taken that position. But I have absolutely nothing to say for myself when a name like Eichmann's is mentioned. I shall never be able to get over having served in a leading position a regime whose true energies were devoted to an extermination program. . . .
>
> Hatred of the Jews was Hitler's central conviction; sometimes it even seems to me that everything else was merely camouflage for this real motivating factor. That perception came to me in Nürnberg . . . when Hitler was even prepared to risk his plans of conquest for the sake of that mania for extermination.[42]

Notes

Acknowledgments

1. The reference is not to the late prime minister, Yitzhak Rabin, but to the former IDF chief of the Armored Corps, 1990–1993.

Introduction

1. The research assumption is based on an interview with General Jacob Amidror, then head of the IDF military colleges and previously head of the research division at the IDF's intelligence department.

2. Förster, "Operation Barbarossa," MGFA 4:1251–1253; Müller, "Failure of the Economic 'Blitzkrieg Strategy,'" MGFA 4:1141.

3. Brandt, "Germany's Vulnerable Spot," 230.

4. Robbins, "Third Reich and Its Railways."

5. Schüler, *Logistik Im Russlandfelzug;* Creveld, *Supplying War;* Williamson and Millett, *War to Be Won;* Brandt, "Germany's Vulnerable Spot," 230.

6. Schüler, *Logistik Im Russlandfelzug,* 637.

7. Haupt, *Die Schlachten,* 16.

8. Keegan, *History of Warfare,* 279.

9. DiNardo, *Mechanized Juggernaut,* 50, 117.

10. Müller, "Failure of the Economic 'Blitzkrieg Strategy,'" MGFA 4:1109.

11. Mierzejewski, *Most Valuable Asset,* 162.

12. Ibid., 127–128; Attorney General against Adolf Eichmann, *Verdict,* 141–148; Reder, *Belz'ec,* 109.

13. Sereny, *Into That Darkness,* 152. Stangel, the commandant of Treblinka, claimed that each car had the number of people chalked on its doors, usually 150 to 180. Scheffler and Schulle, *Die ins Baltikum deportierten deutschen,* 52, 89.

14. Schüler, *Logistik Im Russlandfelzug,* 237–238; Rohde, *Deutsche Wermachttrasportwessen,* 151–152.

15. Wegner, "Global War," MGFA 6:1092.

16. Williamson and Millett, *War to Be Won,* 180–182.

17. The optimal number of men in one German division was around 15,000; Ose, *Entscheidung im Westen 1944,* 72. However, in practice, and during the

critical periods of each campaign that I deal with here, only about a third of this number was deployed. Divisions in the Red Army and the Wehrmacht varied greatly in size. A Soviet rifle division in theory should have mustered 11,780 men, but most had between 3,000 and 7,000 men. German infantry divisions were often even more under strength, especially in the last phase of each operation. The math in general is based on an assumption of an average of either 7,000 men per one German division or 750 German soldiers in one train, although at certain places divisions had only 4,000 or 5,000 men. See also Beevor, *Berlin*, 27.

18. Blatman, *Death Marches*, 526–527.
19. Ibid., 528.
20. Kershaw, *The End*, 6, 10, 76.
21. Ibid., 24–26.
22. Fritz, *Endkampf*, 3–5.
23. Ibid., 7–9.
24. Bessel, *Germany, 1945*, 2.
25. Herf, *Jewish Enemy*, 265.
26. Ibid., 12.
27. Ibid., 236–237.

Part 1. Operation Typhoon and German Deportations to the East

1. Browning, *Road to the Final Solution*, 428–429.
2. Gallagher, *Soviet History of World War II*, 158, 160–161.
3. Ibid., 3.
4. Ibid., 177–178.
5. *History of the Great Patriotic War of the Soviet Union.*
6. Gallagher, *Soviet History of World War II*, 3. For the Japanese defeat, see Alperovitz, *Decision to Use the Atomic Bomb.*
7. Zhukov, *Marshal Zhukov's Memoirs.*
8. Roberts, *Victory at Stalingrad*, 172–173.

Chapter 1. Operation Barbarossa

1. Glantz and House, *When Titans Clashed*, 30.
2. Bullock, *Hitler and Stalin*, 783–784.
3. Trevor-Roper, *Hitler's War Directives;* Führer's Directive 21, December 18, 1940.
4. Halder, *Halder War Diary*, January 28, 1941.
5. Hillgruber, "German Military Leader's View of Russia," 171–172.

6. By December 10, 1941, after the failure of the Wehrmacht to take Moscow, Hitler had relieved von Brauchitsch from his post, becoming Germany's warlord himself and responsible for most of the military decision making until the end of the war.

7. Reinhardt, *Moscow: The Turning Point*, 11.

8. Glantz and House, *When Titans Clashed*, 31.

9. Ibid., 33.

10. Geyer, "German Strategy," 588.

11. Ibid., 588–590.

12. Gorodetsky, *Grand Delusion*, 305–330.

13. Arad, "Great Patriotic War," 21–22.

14. Stahel, *Operation Barbarossa*, 306.

15. Morell, *Secret Diaries of Hitler's Doctor*, 82–83.

16. Glantz and House, *When Titans Clashed*, 76.

17. Ibid., 60–61.

18. Bullock, *Hitler and Stalin*, 790.

19. Arad, "Great Patriotic War," 30.

20. Weinberg, *Germany, Hitler, and World War II*, 165.

21. Weinberg, *World at Arms*, 274.

22. Guderian, *Panzer Leader*, 248.

23. RH2/1327/30-134, Bundesarchiv-Militärarchiv/Freiburg, Oberkommando Des Heeres, February 18, 1942, "Übersicht über die meteorologicschen verhältnisse bei Ausgang des Winters im Ostraum übersandt."

24. Cooper, *German Army*, 333–334; Overy, *Russia's War*, 119; Reinhardt, *Moscow: The Turning Point*.

25. Orenstein, *Soviet Documents on the Use of War Experience*, 2:38–39.

26. Guderian, *Panzer Leader*, 249.

27. Schüler, *Logistik Im Russlandfelzug*, 519–520.

28. Ibid., 516–517.

29. Liddell Hart, *Other Side of the Hill*, 190.

30. Zhukov, *Marshal Zhukov's Memoirs*, 167.

31. Reinhardt, "Moscow 1941," 213.

32. Golikov, "To Moscow's Rescue," 314–317.

33. Schüler, in *Logistik Im Russlandfelzug*, his study of the logistics of the German army, deals with the role of the railroad in planning and preparing Operation Barbarossa and its execution up to the winter crisis at the gates of Moscow during Operation Typhoon. Although Schüler's research sheds light on major problems of German logistics, it does not deal with those of carrying out the Final Solution. Moreover, it covers the war only up to winter 1942; Stalingrad and Kursk are left out of the picture. A similar limitation

exists in Rohde's extensive research on German army transport, *Deutsche Wermachttrasportwessen*, because it fails to mention the transports to the death camps used from the same train reserve.

34. Müller, "Failure of the Economic 'Blitzkrieg Strategy,'" MGFA 4:1107.

35. Macksey, *For Want of a Nail*, 115.

36. Kroener, *Generaloberst Freidrich Fromm*, 404.

37. Müller, "Failure of the Economic 'Blitzkrieg Strategy,'" MGFA 4:1109–1110.

38. Blumentritt, *The Soldier and the Man*, 117.

39. Megargee, *Inside Hitler's High Command*, 123.

40. Kroener, *Generaloberst Freidrich Fromm*, 429.

41. Yad Vashem Archives, Jerusalem, "Divisions-Befehl No. 22/41v. 26.10.41," "Kraftfahrzeuge," Armee-Oberkommando 2, October 24, 1941, Records of the Reich Ministry for the Occupied Eastern Territories, 1941–1945, No. 28.

42. Brandt, "Germany's Vulnerable Spot," 230.

43. Schulte, *German Army and Nazi Policies*, 50.

44. Müller, "Failure of the Economic 'Blitzkrieg Strategy,'" MGFA 4:1111.

45. EDS/AL-1403, Imperial War Museum, London, Zustand der Eisenbahnen in den Baltischen Staaten während des Vormarsches des 18. Army nach Leningrad, 12.

46. Ibid., 21.

47. Schulte, *German Army and Nazi Policies*, 89.

48. Ibid., 90; Hoffmann, "Attack on the Soviet Union," MGFA 4:99.

Chapter 2. Operation Typhoon

1. Reinhardt, "Moscow 1941," 210.

2. Ibid.

3. Guderian, *Panzer Leader*, 81.

4. Overy, *Russia's War*, 112–113; Glantz and House, *When Titans Clashed*, 81.

5. Reinhardt, *Moscow: The Turning Point*, 81.

6. *Rasputitza* is the term used for the autumn rains, which turned the ground into mud. See Shirer, *Rise and Fall*, 711.

7. Clark, *Barbarossa*, 121–122.

8. Glantz and House, *When Titans Clashed*, 83.

9. Overy, *Russia's War*, 114–116.

10. Ibid., 117; Glantz and House, *When Titans Clashed*, 162.

11. Ripley, *Wehrmacht*, 154.

12. Brigadier General Benny Michalson (former head of the IDF historical division), "Operation Barbarossa and the Invasion of the Soviet Union" (unpublished paper, November 2006).

13. Kraunsnick, "Persecution of the Jews," 68. The directives to solve the Jewish question have undergone countless historical interpretations and debates, including their ascription as the blueprints for the eventual comprehensive Final Solution.

14. The geographical borders of the General Government are dealt with elsewhere in this book.

15. Aly, *Final Solution*, 161.

16. Ibid., 171.

17. Burrin, *Hitler and the Jews*, 129.

18. Aly, *Final Solution*, 196–197.

19. Ibid., 199.

20. Hans Frank interrogation, November 14, 1945, Box 156, Imperial War Museum, Duxford.

21. Adolf Eichmann, Memorial Text, Shofar FTP Archive File, 325.

22. Ibid., 329–330.

23. Von Below, *At Hitler's Side*, 112.

24. Jackel, *Hitlers Weltanschaung und Herrschaft*, 139.

25. Adolf Eichmann, Memorial Text, Shofar FTP Archive File, 211.

26. Ibid., 214.

27. Arad, *Soviet Union*, 2:625.

28. R5-3349, Bundesarchiv/Berlin, Reichsverkehrsministerium.

29. Attorney General against Adolf Eichmann, *Verdict*, 95.

30. EDS 545, AL-1520, Imperial War Museum, London, Der Reichsprotektor in Böhmen u. Mähren, Parg, December 15, 1941. Betrifft: Evakuierung der Juden: Durchführungsbestimmungen, Betrifft: Durchführungsbestimmungen.

31. Scheffler and Schulle, *Buch der Erinnerung*, 50.

32. Browning, *Origins of the Final Solution*, 372–373.

33. Erickson, *Road to Stalingrad*, 218.

34. Ibid., 269.

35. Each train contained approximately 1,000 people compressed into ten to twenty cars.

36. Browning, *Ordinary Men*, 9–11.

37. These figures refer to trains loaded with troops but not necessarily fully equipped because they were arriving to relieve exhausted men. Of course, the same number of trains could just as well be used for supplies and logistics.

The main point is that seventy-five Reichsbahn trains were used for executing ideological tasks rather than military ones in a critical phase of Operation Typhoon.

38. Attorney General against Adolf Eichmann, *Verdict*, 95.

39. Hans Frank interrogation, September 1, 1945, Box 156, Imperial War Museum, Duxford.

40. *Hitler's Table Talk*, October 25, 1941, evening, No. 52, 87.

41. RH2-1326, Panzer Nachschub ost vor Beginn der Operation de H. Gr. Mitte; BM, N-119/3. Zuführungsstraßen Hgr. Mitte, Bundesarchiv-Militärarchiv/Freiburg.

42. Gottwaldt and Schulle, *Die Judendeportationen aus dem Deutschen Reich*, 444–445.

43. N119-18, Bundesarchiv-Militärarchiv/Freiburg, Vortrag Über die Bearbeitung und Durchführung von Landmärchen.

44. R5-22299, Bundesarchiv/Berlin, Reichsverkehrsministerium.

45. Browning, *Origins of the Final Solution*, 427–429.

46. Von Bock, *War Diary*, November 12, 1941, 356.

47. Ibid., November 11, 1941, 354.

48. Hoffmann, "Attack on the Soviet Union," MGFA 4:99; Müller, "Failure of the Economic 'Blitzkrieg Strategy,'" MGFA 4:1108.

49. Heusinger regarded Nazi ideology as useless and the anti-Semitic campaign as "a military imbecility that needlessly added to the difficulties in fighting the enemy." Sinder, *Encyclopedia of the Third Reich*.

50. Franz Halder, Kriegstagebuch, November 17, 1941, Alfred Wiener Collection, Tel Aviv University.

51. Breitman, *Architect of Genocide*, 214–215.

52. Kroener, *Generaloberst Friedrich Fromm*, 404.

53. Franz Halder, Kriegstagebuch, 1939–1942, Alfred Wiener Collection, Tel Aviv University; see also DiNardo, *Mechanized Juggernaut*, 38.

54. DiNardo, *Mechanized Juggernaut*, 45.

55. Schulte, *German Army and Nazi Policies*.

56. Von Bock, *War Diary*, 426.

57. DiNardo, *Mechanized Juggernaut*, 43.

58. Scheffler and Schulle, *Buch der Erinnerung*, 49.

Chapter 3. The German War Economy

1. Gorodetsky, *Grand Delusion*, 109.

2. *Trials of War Criminals before the Nuremberg Military Tribunals under Control Council Law No. 10*, NID-1344, 12:541–542.

3. Noakes and Pridham, *Nazism*, 4:203.

4. Macksey, "Smolensk Operation," 347; Ose, "Smolensk," 350.

5. Creveld, *Supplying War*, 58.

6. Wegner, "Global War, Stalingrad," MGFA 6:1109.

7. Abelshauser, "Germany," 170.

8. Reinhardt, *Moscow: The Turning Point*, 27.

9. Milward, *War, Economy, and Society*, 164.

10. Ibid., 222.

11. Die Deutsche Zivilverwarltung in den Ehemeligen Bezsetzten, Ostgebie-ten 22/40/I–II, Wiener Library, Documents Section No. 582, Nos. 216, 132, 315.

12. Ibid., No. 115, 10.941.

13. Reinhardt, *Moscow: The Turning Point*, 39.

14. Overy, *War and Economy*, 255–256.

15. Ibid., 256.

16. Ibid., 352.

17. Milward, *German Economy at War*, 45.

18. Sherwood, *Roosevelt and Hopkins*, 336–339.

19. Weinberg, *World at Arms*, 286.

20. Ibid., 286, 288–289.

21. Sherwood, *Roosevelt and Hopkins*, 336.

22. Ibid., 339.

23. Ciano, *Ciano's Diplomatic Papers*, 448.

24. Ibid., 448–449.

25. *Documents on German Foreign Policy*, vol. 13, no. 372, 5083/E29281719, 596, memorandum, October 1941, by Hans Lammers, head of the Führer's office and one of his most trusted associates.

26. Heer and Naumann, *Vernichtungskrieg*, 90.

27. Dallin, *German Rule in Russia*, 376–377.

28. Aly, *Final Solution*, 201.

29. Office of the United States Chief of Counsel for Prosecution of Axis Criminality, *Nazi Conspiracy and Aggression*, EC-126, 7:303–304.

30. Ibid., 7:304.

31. Liddell Hart Centre for Military Archives, King's College, London, 15/15/137, Liaison Staff of Supreme Headquarters Armament Procurement Office with the Reich Marshal, Re: Economic Notes for the Reporting Period of August 15 to September 16, 1941, September 18, 1941.

32. *Hitler's Table Talk*, November 5, 1941, evening, No. 63, 14.

33. Lazowick, *Hitler's Bureaucrats*, 2.

34. Scheffler and Schulle, *Buch der Erinnerung*, 662–663.

35. Ibid., 91–94.

36. Arad, *Soviet Union*, 2:626.

37. Megargee, *Inside Hitler's High Command*, 118.

38. Ibid., 118–122.

39. Mierzejewski, *Most Valuable Asset*, 100–101.

40. Attorney General against Adolf Eichmann, *Verdict*, 95.

41. Ibid., 96.

42. EDS-AL-1403, Imperial War Museum, London, Zustand der Eisen-bahnen in den Baltischen Staaten während des Vormarsches des 18. Army nach Leningrad.

43. Müller, "Failure of the Economic 'Blitzkrieg Strategy,'" MGFA 4:1116.

44. Ibid., 4:1119–1120.

45. Ibid., 4:1123.

46. Franz Halder, Kriegstagebuch, September 27, 1941, Alfred Wiener Collection, Tel Aviv University.

47. Von Bock, *War Diary*, November 14–15, 1941, 357–358.

48. N-1497/67, Bundesarchiv/Koblenz, Nachlaß Adolf Eichmann, Band 69.

49. Cooper, *German Army*, 333.

50. Yad Vashem Archives, Jerusalem, Ministry for the Occupied Eastern Territories, No. 28: Records of the Reich, 1941–1945, "Divisions-Befehl No. 22/41v. 26.10.41," "Kraftfahrzeuge," Armee-Oberkommando 2, October 24, 1941.

51. Evidence regarding this phone call was found in Himmler's handwriting in a phone memo; see Fleming, *Hitler and the Final Solution*, 76.

52. Von Bock, *War Diary*, November 16, 1941, 359; November 19, 1941, 363; December 1, 1941, 376.

53. Schüler, *Logistik Im Russlandfelzug*, 513.

54. Ibid., 516–517.

55. Skorzeny, *My Commando Operations*, 112.

56. Ibid., 115.

57. RH2-1327/63, Bundesarchiv-Militärarchiv/Freiburg, Oberkommando des Heeres, December 8, 1941, Wisung Für Aufgaben des Ostheeres im Winter.

Chapter 4. Soviet Capabilities

1. Volkogonov, *Stalin*, 368–369.

2. Khrushchev, *Khrushchev Remembers*, 160.

3. Glantz, *Soviet Military Operational Art*, 119–120.

4. Zhukov, *Memoirs of Marshal Zhukov*, 186.

5. Ibid., 164–171.

6. Ibid., 186.

7. Ibid., 187.

8. Ibid., 197, 201.

9. Glantz and House, *When Titans Clashed*, 55.

10. Zhukov, *Memoirs of Marshal Zhukov*, 204.

11. *Hitler's Table Talk*, night of July 11–12, 1941, No. 4, 8.

12. Stahel, *Operation Barbarossa*, 401, 438–439.

13. Ulam, *Stalin*, 544.

14. In the beginning of August, Moscow was still 250 kilometers east of Guderian's Panzer group after the battle of Roslavl. Between October 2 and 10, the Army Group Center gained forty-eight kilometers a day. The advance then fell to three to eight kilometers a day. By the first two weeks of November, they remained practically at a standstill on the Kalinin–Tula line, eighty-seven kilometers west of Moscow. Still, by November 28, the German 7th Panzer Division had seized a bridgehead across the Moscow Volga Canal—the last major obstacle before Moscow—and stood less than thirty-five kilometers from the Kremlin. Just northwest of Moscow, the Wehrmacht reached Krasnaya Polyana, a little more than twenty kilometers from Moscow. On November 27, German scouts reached the small town of Khimki and its railway station on the Moscow–Leningrad line. Half a dozen motorcyclists from Panzer Group 4 and a couple of light trucks were only eighteen kilometers from the center of Moscow; see Mawdsley, *December 1941*, 86; Glantz and House, *When Titans Clashed*, 80; Clark, *Barbarossa*, 79; Ziemke, *Stalingrad to Berlin*, 13.

15. Grigorenko, *Memoirs*, 123–124.

16. Zhukov, *Memoirs of Marshal Zhukov*, 168.

17. Maisky, "Struggle for the Second Front," 90.

18. Churchill, *Second World War*, 2:393–395.

19. Duffi, *Hitler Slept Late*, 83.

20. Halder, *Halder War Diary*, July 3, 1941, 446.

21. Megargee, *Inside Hitler's High Command*, 132.

22. Guderian, *Panzer Leader*, 190.

23. Liddell Hart Centre for Military Archives, King's College, London, 15/15/150/12, notes on the interrogation of Generaloberst Franz Halder, October 1945.

24. Reinhardt, *Moscow: The Turning Point*, 27.

25. Glantz and House, *When Titans Clashed*, 58–61.

26. Overy, *Russia's War*, 91.

27. Liddell Hart, *Other Side of the Hill*, 191.

28. Cooper, *German Army*, 300.

29. Guderian, *Panzer Leader*, 195.

30. Schramm, *Kriegstagebuch Des Ober*, Besprechung gelegentlich Anwesenheit des Führers und Obersten Bewfelshabers der Wehrmacht bei Heersgruppe Mitte, August 4, 1941, 1041 (88). See Guderian, *Panzer Leader*, 189–190.

31. Gat, *Sources of Modern Military Thought*, 99–100.

32. AL-1426, Imperial War Museum, London, "Der Marks Plan und der Feldzug Gegen Russland, 1941," Allgemeine Schweizerische Militaer Zeitschrift, October 1950.

33. Hart, *Guderian*, 69.

34. Ibid., 76.

35. Liddell Hart Centre for Military Archives, King's College, London, 15/15/149/13, August 9, 1945, first talk with Field Marshal von Kleist.

36. Klink, "Conduct of Operations," MGFA 4:574.

37. Ose, "Smolensk," 351.

38. Halder, *Halder War Diary*, July 26, 1941, 485.

39. Mierzejewski, *Most Valuable Asset*, 97.

40. Franz Halder, Kriegstagebuch, December 4, 1941, Alfred Wiener Collection, Tel Aviv University.

41. Von Bock, *War Diary*, December 9, 1941, 376.

42. Browning, *Origins of the Final Solution*, 428.

43. R5-2094, Bundesarchiv/Berlin, Reichsverkehrsministerium Eisenbahnabteilungen, August 18, 1941.

44. Hilberg, "Reichsbahn," 33–34.

45. Scheffler and Schulle, *Buch der Erinnerung*, 49.

46. Ibid., 574, 631.

47. Skorzeny, *My Commando Operations*, 111.

48. Boelcke, *Secret Conferences of Dr. Goebbels*, November 18, 1941, 191.

49. Cooper, *German Army*, 340.

50. Creveld, *Supplying War*, 176.

51. Ibid., 176–178.

52. Jackel, *Hitlers Weltanschauung und Herrschaft*, 139; Mayer, *Why Did the Heavens Not Darken*, 293.

53. Cooper, *German Army*, 333.

54. Liddell Hart Centre for Military Archives, King's College, London, 15/15/149/13, January 7, 1946, third talk with Field Marshal von Kleist.

55. Müller, "Failure of the Economic 'Blitzkrieg Strategy,'" MGFA 4:1125.

56. EDS/AL-1403, Imperial War Museum, London, Zustand der Eisenbahnen in den Baltischen Staaten während des Vormarsches des 18. Army nach Leningrad, 1–2.

57. Saul Friedländer, "Ideology and Extermination" (paper presentation, 1999), 19.

58. Glantz and House, *When Titans Clashed*, 92.

59. Friedländer, "Ideology and Extermination," 17.

60. Cholavsky, "Jews of the Reich in Ghetto Minsk," 221–222.

61. Breitman, *Official Secrets*, 81.

62. Creveld, *Supplying War*, 176–178.

63. Scheffler and Schulle, *Buch der Erinnerung*, 59.

64. The first transports were sent to Chełmno on December 7, 1941, and on December 8, the camp began operating its facilities. See Karkowski, "Chelmno," 504.

65. Burrin, *Hitler and the Jews*, 126.

66. Mawdsley, *December 1941*, 205–207.

67. Ibid., 265.

68. Von Bock, *War Diary*, December 1, 1941, 376.

69. Hilberg, "Reichsbahn," 39; see also Mierzejewski, *Most Valuable Asset*, 113.

70. Schulte, *German Army and Nazi Policies*, 50.

71. Macksey, *For Want of a Nail*, xiii.

Part 2. Operation Reinhard and the Downfall at Stalingrad

1. Weinberg, *World at Arms*, 458–459; Clark, *Barbarossa*, 225.

2. Anders, *Hitler's Defeat in Russia*, 231, 232.

3. Ziemke, *Stalingrad to Berlin*; Erickson, *Road to Stalingrad*; Kehrig, *Stalingrad*.

4. Harrison, *Accounting the War*, 171–172.

5. Geyer, "German Strategy," 588–591; see also Reinhardt, "Moscow 1941," 103; Naveh, *In Pursuit of Military Excellence*, 129, 131, 138, 144.

Chapter 5. The Wehrmacht and the SS

1. Wette, *Wehrmacht Feinbilder*; see also Heer and Naumann, *Vernichtungskrieg*.

2. Schulte, *German Army and Nazi Policies*, 228.

3. Westermann, *Hitler's Police Battalions*, 163; Aly, *Final Solution*, 140.

4. Browning, "Hitler and the Euphoria of Victory," 140.

5. Breitman, *Architect of Genocide*, 163, 169.

6. Liddell Hart Centre for Military Archives, King's College, London, von Manstein files, 6/7/B1, GB99 KCLMA.

7. Goldensohn, *Nuremberg Interviews*, 374–375.

8. Testimony of Erich von dem Bach Zelewski taken at Nuremberg, October 26, 1945, FO 645, Box 155, Imperial War Museum, Duxford.

9. Liddell Hart Archives 6/6/B2/253, reports Liddell Hart Archives of Einsatzgruppen and Sonderkommandos, military situation report on the Leningrad front, and the activity of Einsatzgruppe A.

10. Westermann, *Hitler's Police Battalions*, 166–167.

11. Kroener, *Generaloberst Friedrich Fromm*, 443.

12. N-1340/513, Bundesarchiv/Koblenz, Nachlaß Albert Speer, September 7, 1942, "The Speer Plan in Action—Mobilizing Reserves of Men and Materiel, Hitler's New Drive for Victory," 28.

13. Fritz Todt died in a mysterious plane accident at Rastenburg, near the Führer's headquarters on the Eastern Front. The possibility that the accident was an assassination ordered by Hitler and the SS was not discounted.

14. Müller, "Die Mobilisierung der Deutschen Wirtschaft für Hitlers Kriegführung," 5:677–679.

15. N-1340/513, Bundesarchiv/Koblenz, Nachlaß Albert Speer, "A Clash of Views," 30–33.

16. Robbins, "Third Reich and Its Railways," 85.

17. Wegner, "War against the Soviet Union," MGFA 6:977.

18. Halder, *Halder War Diary*, 670.

19. Liddell Hart Centre for Military Archives, King's College, London, 15/15/150/4, notes on the interrogation of Speer, October 1945, Speer on Hitler.

20. Megargee, *Inside Hitler's High Command*, 181.

21. Wegner, "War against the Soviet Union," MGFA 6:1057.

22. Megargee, *Inside Hitler's High Command*, 183.

23. Liddell Hart Centre for Military Archives, King's College, London, 15/15/150/43, notes on the interrogation of Zeitzler, May 19, 1946.

24. Black, *Ernst Kaltenbrünner*, 127–129.

25. Weinberg, *World at Arms*, 233.

26. Black, *Ernst Kaltenbrünner*, 152–155.

27. Megargee, *Inside Hitler's High Command*, 187.

Chapter 6. From German Blue to Russian Uranus

1. Beevor, *Stalingrad*, 54.

2. Clark, *Barbarossa*, 150; Weinberg, *World at Arms*, 294–295.

3. Chuikov, *Beginning of the Road*, 270–271.

4. Ibid., 364–365.

5. RH2/1327, Bundesarchiv-Militärarchiv/Freiburg, Richtlien für organisatorische Kaßnahren, 12.2.42.

6. RH2/1327, Bundesarchiv-Militärarchiv/Freiburg, Übersicht über die meteorologischen Verhältnisse bei Ausgang des Winters im Ostraum übersandt February 8, 1942.

7. Zhukov, *Memoirs of Marshal Zhukov*, 273.

8. Ibid., 270.

9. See Citino, *Wehrmacht Retreats*, 207–209.

10. Ibid., 295–296.

11. Glantz and House, *When Titans Clashed*, 116.

12. Zhukov, *Memoirs of Marshal Zhukov*, 276–278.

13. Glantz and House, *When Titans Clashed*, 118; Zhukov, *Memoirs of Marshal Zhukov*, 279.

14. Krohner, *Starke Mann*, 435.

15. Wegner, "War against the Soviet Union," MGFA 6:860–863.

16. Overy, *Interrogations*, 246.

17. Citino, *Death of the Wehrmacht*, 157.

18. Von Below, *At Hitler's Side*, 163.

19. Mawdsley, *World War II*, 170.

20. Citino, *Death of the Wehrmacht*, 163.

21. Overy, *Russia's War*, 165.

22. Overy, *Why the Allies Won*, 113.

23. Zhukov, *Memoirs of Marshal Zhukov*, 276.

24. Liddell Hart Archives 15/15/150/2, Notes on the Interrogation of Generaloberst Franz Halder, CW, October 1945.

25. Weinberg, *World at Arms*, 434–435.

26. Chuikov, *Beginning of the Road*, 61.

27. Ibid., 280.

28. Von Below, *At Hitler's Side*, 149.

29. Zhukov, *Memoirs of Marshal Zhukov*, 280.

30. Ibid., 281–289.

31. Chuikov, *Beginning of the Road*, 16.

32. Erickson, *Road to Stalingrad*, 387–392.

33. MGFA 6:866; Zhukov, *Memoirs of Marshal Zhukov*, 293–294.

34. Zeitzler, "Stalingrad," 139.

35. Beevor, *Stalingrad*, 185–186.

36. Chuikov, *Beginning of the Road*, 367.

37. Citino, *Death of the Wehrmacht*, 153.

38. Ibid.

39. Beevor, *Stalingrad*, 189.

40. Weinberg, *World at Arms*, 432; von Below, *At Hitler's Side*, 157; Beevor, *Stalingrad*, 192.

41. Beevor, *Stalingrad*, 220.

42. Göeritz, *Paulus and Stalingrad*, 69.

43. Glantz and House, *When Titans Clashed*, 133–134.

44. Zhukov, *Memoirs of Marshal Zhukov*, 309–311; MGFA 6:1134–1137.

45. Zeitzler, "Stalingrad," 170–171.

46. Franz Halder interrogation, 1946 MS C-067a, Imperial War Museum, Duxford.

47. Kershaw, *Hitler: Nemesis*, 545.

48. Von Below, *At Hitler's Side*, 161.

49. Zhukov, *Memoirs of Marshal Zhukov*, 299.

50. Glantz, *Zhukov's Greatest Defeat*, 308. Glantz, one of the few historians provided with access to the Russian archives, writes scholarly texts that are less broadly popular than those by Antony Beevor. Glantz's extensive account of Operation Mars was published in 1999, a year after Beevor's book on Stalingrad.

51. Eden, *Eden Memoirs*, 275.

52. Churchill, *Second World War*, 2:394.

53. Harrison, "Soviet Union," 268.

54. Roberts, *Victory at Stalingrad*.

55. Zhukov, *Memoirs of Marshal Zhukov*, 272.

56. Müller "Alber Speer," MGFA 5:650; Hillgruber, *Kriegstagebuch*, 2:1385–1390.

57. Chuikov, *Beginning of the Road*, 94.

58. Ibid., 246.

59. Ibid., 235–236.

60. Kehrig, *Stalingrad*, 407.

61. Beevor, *Stalingrad*, 366.

Chapter 7. Jewish and Military Proportions

1. Liddell Hart Archives 6/6/B2, von Manstein, May 16, 1942.

2. Liddell Hart Archives 15/15/139/15, Attachment of the Inspectorate of the Concentration Camps to the SS–Main Office Economics and Administration, April 30, 1942.

3. N119/11, Bundesarchiv-Militärarchiv/Freiburg, Nachlaß der Friedrich Kuzbach.

4. Ostbahn was the railway of the General Government and its special property, financially separate from the Reichsbahn but still subordinate to the Reichsbahn's operating and administrative procedures. Traffic priorities were organized in Berlin along the same lines as the German railway.

5. Arad, *Soviet Union*, 1:509–512.

6. Reder, *Belz'ec*, 81; Arad, *Soviet Union*, 1:518.

7. Reder, *Belz'ec*, 90–91.

8. Arad, *Soviet Union*, 1:516.

9. Ibid., 1:516–518.

10. Rudolf Höss interrogation, Box 157, 29, Imperial War Museum, Duxford.

11. Yehil, *Holocaust*, 490.

12. Zhukov, *Memoirs of Marshal Zhukov*, 295–296.

13. Arad, *Treblinka, Loss and Uprising*, 95–96.

14. Rohde, *Deutsche Wermachttrasportwessen*, 120. Arad, *Treblinka, Loss and Uprising*.

15. Hilberg, *Destruction of the European Jews*, 2:489–493.

16. Kehrig, *Stalingrad*, 286.

17. NS4Anh./9, Bundesarchiv/Berlin; this assumption of fifty kilograms per person is also based on the weight allowed per car destined for Treblinka, which was 2,500 kilograms, whether loaded with horses for the Wehrmacht or with civilians for the SS.

18. Mierzejewski, *Most Valuable Asset*, 121; Sereny, *Into That Darkness*, 152.

19. Demjanjuk Trial, *State of Israel vs. Ivan (John) Demjanjuk*, 47–51.

20. Glantz and House, *When Titans Clashed*, 136–138; Beevor, *Stalingrad*, 225.

21. N119/12, Bundesarchiv-Militärarchiv/Freiburg, Anhalt Für Beladung der Nachschubkolonnen des Inf. Divisionachubführers.

22. N119/15, Bundesarchiv-Militärarchiv/Freiburg, Zahlenangaben über Transportraumbedarf des Versorgungsgutes, July 5, 1942.

23. Wegner, "War against the Soviet Union," MGFA 6:1151.

24. Arold, *Technische entwicklung*, 92, 93.

25. Wegner, "War against the Soviet Union, 1942–43," MGFA 6:1035–1037.

26. Beevor, *Stalingrad*, 259, 266.

27. Kehrig, *Stalingrad*, 74; Wegner, "Global War," MGFA 6:1092.

28. Orgill, *Tank*, 160–161.

29. Müller "Alber Speer," MGFA 5:568.

30. Beevor, *Stalingrad*, 186.

31. RW4/604; Bundesarchiv-Militärarchiv/Freiburg, N119/12, Kriegsgliederung der Versorgungstruppen einer Panzer Division; N119/11, Anhalt fur die mögliche Kreigsliederung einer Panzer Division.

32. RH2/2580, Bundesarchiv-Militärarchiv/Freiburg, Auszug aus der täglichen kurzen Feinbeurteilung, October 25–November 20, 1942.

33. N601/8, Bundesarchiv-Militärarchiv/Freiburg, Notizen zur 6. Armee, December 7, 1942.

34. N601/8, Bundesarchiv-Militärarchiv/Freiburg, Fs—Gesprach Gen. Feldmarschall v. Manteib—Gen. Oberst Paulus, December 19, 1942, 18.15–18.30 Uhr.

35. Göeritz, *Paulus and Stalingrad*, 252–254.

36. Ibid., 199, 210. The total number of Soviet tanks assembled before Operation Uranus (the Soviet counterattack and encirclement of the 6th Army) was 979; see Overy, *Russia's War*, 177.

37. Citino, *Death of the Wehrmacht*, 250–252.

38. Von Bock, *War Diary*, 426.

39. RH2/43, Bundesarchiv-Militärarchiv/Freiburg, Beurteilung der versorgungslage für Aufmarsch Blau, June 10, 1942.

40. N601/8, Bundesarchiv-Militärarchiv/Freiburg, Fernschreiben von Gen. Schmidt–Gen. Schulz, December 22, 1942, 1710–1745.

41. Hilberg, "Reichsbahn," 35.

42. Author interview with Carel Eijkenaar (May 4, 2007, Tel Aviv), International Federation for Equestrian Sports, international dressage judge, trainer, instructor, and coach; DiNardo, *Mechanized Juggernaut*, 11, 44.

43. NS4nh./9, Bundesarchiv/Berlin, 229 Konzentrationslager, Laufzeit 1942; Rohde, *Deutsche Wermachttrasportwessen*, 32.

44. DiNardo, *Mechanized Juggernaut*, 12.

45. Ibid., 61–62.

46. Schüler, *Logistik Im Russlandfelzug*, 151–152.

47. Wegner, "Global War," MGFA 6:1092.

48. Williamson and Millett, *War to Be Won*, 180–182.

49. Zeitzler, "Stalingrad," 152.

50. Wegner, "Global War," MGFA 6:1091–1092.

51. Ibid., 6:1151.

52. Beevor, *Stalingrad*, 175.

53. RH2/733, Bundesarchiv-Militärarchiv/Freiburg, Tätigkeitsbericht, January 1943.

54. Von Manstein, *Lost Victories*, 335–336.

55. Piper, *Auschwitz: Estimating the Number*.

56. Von Manstein, *Lost Victories*, 348–350.

57. Piper, *Auschwitz: Estimating the Number*, table.

58. Kehrig, *Stalingrad*, 300.

59. RH2/733, Bundesarchiv-Militärarchiv/Freiburg, OKH/Gen st d H/Gen Qu, November 4, 1942, Betr.: Winterbekleidung für winterbewegl. Verbände.

60. RH2/733, Bundesarchiv-Militärarchiv/Freiburg, General der Pioniere und Festungen, November 27, 1942, Betr: Winterbevorratung.

Chapter 8. The State of Reichsbahn in Winter, 1942–1943

1. Richard Fiebig, head of the main committee for railway vehicles, Report 84, Part 2, July 27, 1946, written at the request of the economic branch, "Dustbin," FD 3063/49 (Speer 3668), Imperial War Museum, London.

2. N-1340/508, Bundesarchiv/Koblenz, Nachlaß Albert Speer, "The Speer Era—organization, collaboration and competition, control of raw materials and reorganization of Reich Offices in 1942–1943."

3. N-1340/513, Bundesarchiv/Koblenz, "The Role of the Occupied Territories in Raw Material Production—1943," 24.

4. N-1340/513, Bundesarchiv/Koblenz, "Finished Armament Production," 29.

5. R5/023128, Bundesarchiv/Berlin, Der Prasident, der Generaldirektion der Ostbahn, September 16, 1942; BAB R5/023128, Regierung des Generarslgouvernement der Letter der Hauptabteilung Eisenbahnen.

6. N-1340/244, Bundesarchiv/Koblenz, Abschrift: Lublin, July 1942, An den Höheren SS- und Polizeifuehrer Ost SS Gruppenführer Kruger; N-1340/244, Bundesarchiv/Koblenz, Wehrkreisbefehlshaber im Generalgouvernement, September 18, 1942, An das Oberkommando der Wehrmacht, Betr.: Ersatz der Judischen Arbeitskrafte durch Polen.

7. Mierzejewski, *Most Valuable Asset*, 130–131.

8. Ibid., 138–139.

9. Kurt Weissenborn (deputy chief of the main committee for weapons in the Speer ministry), "Dorpmüller, Ganzenmüller and Wartime Inefficiency of the German Railway," "Dustbin," February 1946, EDS/1160, Report 77, Part 16, Imperial War Museum, Duxford.

10. RH4/67, Bundesarchiv/Berlin, Besprechung im Führer—Hauptquartier, May 24, 1942; Bestelt um 16 Uhr: Minister Speer, Feldmarschal Milch, Herr Ganzenmüller.

11. Weissenborn, Report 77, Imperial War Museum, Duxford.

12. MGFA 7:496–499.

13. Keitel and Gorlitz, *Memoirs of Field Marshal Keitel*, 176–177.

14. Piper, *Auschwitz: Estimating the Number*, 68–70.

15. Richard Feissig (head of the main committee for railway vehicles), "The Main Committee for Railway Vehicles," 5, report written at the request of the economic branch, July 27, 1946, FD 3063/49 (Speer 3668), No. 84, Part 2, Imperial War Museum, London.

16. Hilberg cites 20,000 trains daily. Hilberg, "Reichsbahn," 34.

17. FD 3063/49 (Speer 3668), No. 84, Part 1, Imperial War Museum, London.

18. Liddell Hart Centre for Military Archives, King's College, London, 15/15/142/75, Die Beschäftigung von ausländischen Arbeitskäften in Deutschland.

19. Liddell Hart Archives 15/15/142/76, Erlass des Generalbevolmächtigten von Arbeitertransporten; hier Beschadigungen und Verunreiinigungen der Personnenwagen der Deutchen Reichsbahn und ihrer Einrichtungen, July 20, 1942.

20. N-118/122, Bundesarchiv/Koblenz, Nachlaß Joseph Goebbels, September 30, 1942 (Mittwoch), 480.

21. RH2/940, Bundesarchiv-Militärarchiv/Freiburg, October 8, 1942, Geheim! Grundlegender Befehl Nr. 1 (Hebung der Gefechtsstärke).

22. RH2/940, Bundesarchiv-Militärarchiv/Freiburg, October 9, 1942, Geheim! Grundlegender Befehl Nr. 2 (Kampf- und Verlegungstransporte).

23. Brandt, "Germany's Vulnerable Spot," 233.

24. Ibid., 232.

25. N-1340/250, Bundesarchiv/Koblenz, Staatliche Pressestelle Hamburg, April 19, 1979, Anhang II (Einleitung).

26. Hilberg, "Reichsbahn," 34.

27. RH20-6/928, Bundesarchiv-Militärarchiv/Freiburg, Tätigkeitsbericht des Bv. T. O. beim A. O. X. 6 für Monat, June 1942.

28. N1497/17, Bundesarchiv/Koblenz, Nachlaß Adolf Eichmann, Band 18, 3.

29. RH19-I/156, Bundesarchiv-Militärarchiv/Freiburg, General des Transportwesens H. Gr. B, Transportlagemeldung October 9–14, 1942; RH 19-I/261, Zugeleitung im monat Februar 1942—Heeresgruppe Sud.

30. N119/13, Bundesarchiv-Militärarchiv/Freiburg, 1942 Transportwesen Maj. I. G. Kutzbach, 3. Vortrag über das Transportwesen der Wehrmacht.

31. Nh/9-225-236, Bundesarchiv/Berlin, Lichterfelde, Wehrmachtfahrschein, Teil 1, Der Transport Fahrt nummer Osten 24/0627967, August 22, 1942.

32. RH4/725, Bundesarchiv-Militärarchiv/Freiburg, Die Reichsbahn Amtliche Nachrichtenblatt der Deutschen Reichsbahn. Herausgegeben im Reichsverkminsterium, Berlin, May 6/13, 1942.

33. Kehrig, *Stalingrad*, 84.

34. Wegner, "Global War," MGFA 6:1091–1092.

35. RH2/940, Bundesarchiv-Militärarchiv/Freiburg, Der Chef des Generalstabes des Heeres Generalquartiermeister, November 14, 1942.

36. N 119/12, Bundesarchiv-Militärarchiv/Freiburg, Generalstabslehrgänge Heeresversorgung, Umdruck Nr. 6 Gang des Verpflegungsnachschubs, March 1942.

37. N601/7, Bundesarchiv-Militärarchiv/Freiburg, Betr. Funkverkehr Stalingrad 22/11/42–23/1/1943.

38. Friedrich Kuzbach was a German official serving in Warsaw as head of the office dealing with transportation for the Wehrmacht within the Soviet territories. The office served as the main coordinating organization between

all bodies responsible for the transport issue. Allegedly, in an attempt to ease the logistical difficulties connected to combat deep into enemy lines on Soviet soil, the army formally enjoyed top priority.

39. N119/13, Bundesarchiv-Militärarchiv/Freiburg, Beispiel für die Bearbeitung des Land marsches der B = Staffel einer Division. Bearbeitung des E Transportes durch Feldtransportabteilung I, December 20, 1941.

40. RH-4/309, RH-4/308, Bundesarchiv-Militärarchiv/Freiburg, Chef des Transportwesens (mit karten).

41. Hans Frank interrogation, Box 156, 10–11, Imperial War Museum, Duxford

42. RH51/10, Bundesarchiv/Berlin, Stammtafel der pferde—Marsch—Stafel G/1-2, April 25, 1942, auf gestellt.

43. N1340/511, Bundesarchiv/Koblenz, Juden Berlin, Protocoll vom September 20/21/22, 1942, Nr. 44, Seite 189.

44. Goebbels, *Goebbels Tagebucher*, 183.

45. Ibid., 189.

46. Overy, *Interrogations*, 253.

47. Reitlinger, *Final Solution*, 273–274.

48. Hans Frank interrogation, September 7, 1945, 11, Imperial War Museum, Duxford. During his long trial in Nuremberg before the International Military Tribunal, Frank wrote his thoughts on the defeat of the Third Reich, ruled and destroyed by Hitler, portraying him as the dominant figure and blaming him for everything. The only responsibility he took upon himself was for being part of those who helped Hitler to reach a position where he could put in motion the entire machinery of the Reich without having to consult anybody. See Stanislaw Piotrowski, *Hans Frank's Diary*, 146–149.

49. RH2/2581, Bundesarchiv-Militärarchiv/Freiburg, Brief aus dem Kessel bei Stalingrad.

50. Göeritz, *Paulus and Stalingrad*, 283.

51. Ibid., 88–89.

52. Overy, *Interrogations*, 481, testament of Robert Ley, August 1945.

Part 3. The Battle of Kursk and the Height of the Final Solution

1. Kroener, "Management of Human Resources," MGFA 2:1008–1014.

Chapter 9. On the Road to Another Disaster

1. Zhukov, *Memoirs of Marshal Zhukov*, 319.
2. Zetterling and Frankson, *Kursk*, 1–4.

3. Glantz, *Colossus Reborn*, 59, 62.

4. Hitlers Lagebesprechungen, *Die protokollfragmente seiner militärischen Konferenzen*, 122.

5. Vasilevsky, "Strategic Planning," 62–63.

6. Glantz and House, *Battle of Kursk*, 21.

7. Ziemke, *Stalingrad to Berlin*, 124.

8. Rokossovsky, "On the Central Front," 78.

9. Vasilevsky, "Strategic Planning," 64–66.

10. Glantz and House, *When Titans Clashed*, 165.

11. Hart, *Guderian*, 90, 92.

12. Von Below, *At Hitler's Side*, 166–167.

13. Zetterling and Frankson, *Kursk, 1943*, 139–140.

14. Von Mellenthin, *Panzer Battles*, 262.

15. Glantz and House, *Battle of Kursk*, 21.

16. Wegner, "War against the Soviet Union," MGFA 6:1081.

17. Kreidler, *Eisenbahnen im Machtbereich*, 158–159.

18. Cooper, *German Army*, 457.

19. Ibid., 456.

20. Kershaw, *Hitler: Nemesis*, 588.

21. Hans Frank testimony, November 2, 1945, Box 156, Imperial War Museum, Duxford, 24–25.

22. Piotrowski, *Hans Frank's Diary*, 94.

23. NS-19/2774, Bundesarchiv/Berlin, January 20, 1943, "Herrn Staatssekretär Dr. Ing. Ganzenmüller, Berlin W 8." Karl Wolff was Himmler's chief of personal staff and SS liaison officer to Hitler until his replacement in 1943, when Hitler assigned him as SS adjutant to Mussolini's Italian government, personally granting him a rank equivalent to general in the Waffen-SS. When Italy surrendered to the Allies, Wolff became the supreme SS and police chief of Italy, and he served as military governor of northern Italy from February to October 1943.

24. *The Protocols of the Elders of Zion* is a fraudulent anti-Semitic text purporting to describe a Jewish plan for achieving global domination. It was first published in Russia in 1903. Adolf Hitler and his close circle were major proponents of this text. The *Protocols* purport to document the minutes of a late nineteenth-century meeting of Jewish leaders who discuss the goal of global Jewish hegemony by subverting the morals of Gentiles and by controlling the press and the world's economies.

25. Goebbels, *Tagebücher*, April–June 1943, 283–291.

26. Stroop and Milton, *Stroop Report*.

27. Goebbels, *Tagebücher*, July–September 1943, 582–583.

28. Weinberg, *World at Arms*, 370–374.

29. Rahn, "War at Sea," MGFA 6:343, 348.

30. Hilberg, "Reichsbahn," 35.

31. RH4/175, Bundesarchiv-Militärarchiv/Freiburg, Algemeine Transport-möglichkeitenp, 8.

32. RH4/725, Bundesarchiv-Militärarchiv/Freiburg, Reiseverkehr in der Sowjetunion (Ernst Timma), 155–156.

33. N22/16, Bundesarchiv-Militärarchiv/Freiburg, Tagebuchnotizen, July 16, 1962 (Osten III.), General Feldmarschal von Bock.

34. N1340/513, Bundesarchiv/Koblenz, Speer Private Papers, "Importance of the Occupied Territories for Supplies of Consumer Goods—1943," 21–22.

35. Ibid., N1340/513, 23–26.

36. Konev, "Great Battle at Kursk," 29.

37. N1340/313, Bundesarchiv/Koblenz, Speer Private Papers, "Importance of the Occupied Territories for Supplies of Consumer Goods—1943," 56.

38. Herbert, *Hitler's Foreign Workers*, 296–297.

39. Robbins, "Third Reich and Its Railways," 88.

40. Herbert, *Hitler's Foreign Workers*, 82–83, 102.

41. Rokossovsky, "On the Central Front," 79.

42. Overy, *Russia's War*, 196–197.

43. RH4/175, Bundesarchiv-Militärarchiv/Freiburg, Aus die russische transportlage zu wasser und lande unter betrachtung der sich aus ihr ergebenden opertativen und wehrwitschftlichen Möglichkeiten; BAMA/Freiburg, RH4/706, Sits und Liege-Einrichtung in Gedeckten Guterwagen fur 40 Mann.

44. Antipenko, "Logistics," 236–237.

45. Ibid., 242.

46. RH4/725, Bundesarchiv-Militärarchiv/Freiburg, Transport des Feindes an der Sowjetische-deutschen Front. aus handbuch der deutsche Wehrmacht 1943, October 9, 1943.

47. Mierzejewski, *Collapse of the German War Economy*, 76–79.

48. Goebbels, *Goebbels Tagebucher*; Goebbels, *Goebbels Diaries*, 274.

49. NS-19/649, Bundesarchiv/Berlin-Lichterfelde, June 3, 1943.

50. Müller "Alber Speer," MGFA 5:494–495.

51. Ibid., 498.

Chapter 10. The Warsaw Ghetto Uprising

1. Friedländer, *Years of Extermination*, 525.

2. Goebbels, *Tagebücher*, April–June 1943, 189–193 (May 1, 1943).

3. Kermish, *General Jürgen Stroop's Report*, 237.

4. Kershaw, *Hitler: Nemesis*, 589; see also Broszat, *Nationalsozialistische Plenpolitik*, 166–169.

5. Gutman, *Jews of Warsaw*, 377–381.

6. Zetterling and Frankson, *Kursk, 1943*, 18–21.

7. Kroener, "Management of Human Resources," MGFA 2:1022.

8. NS-19/1570, Bundesarchiv/Berlin-Lichterfelde, Der Inspecteur für Statistik, Berlin W 35, April 19, 1943.

9. NS-19/1570, Bundesarchiv/Berlin. The entire list of "Juden in dem Konzentrationslagern" also included camps such as Gross-Rosen, Lichtenburg, Neuengamme, Flossenburg, Sachsenburg, Esterwegen, Niederhagen, and Natsweiler. However, their inmates numbered only a few dozen to a few hundred Jews.

10. NS-19/1570, Bundesarchiv/Berlin, Der Reichsführer SS Personlicher Stab, April 20, 1943.

11. Gutman, *Jews of Warsaw*, 397–401.

12. Goebbels, *Tagebücher*, April–June 1943, 349–355 (May 23, 1943).

13. Gutman, *Jews of Warsaw*, 408–410.

14. Goebbels, *Tagebücher*, April–June 1943, 101–105 (April 14, 1943).

15. NS-18/0225, Bundesarchiv/Berlin-Lichterfelde, Betrifft: Rundschreiben uber die Propaganda-kampagne gegen das Judentum, May 19, 1943, June 9, 1943.

16. Friedländer, *Years of Extermination*, 527.

17. NS-19/1740, Bundesarchiv/Berlin, July 23, 1943, Betrifft: Errichtung eines KL im ehemaligen Ghetto in Warschau. Besug: Befel, June 11, 1943.

18. The number of 180,000 men comes from multiplying the average of 3,000 forces used daily under General Stroop's command by approximately sixty days of fighting, although Stroop's official report indicates less.

19. NS-19/1740, Bundesarchiv/Berlin-Lichterfelde, Betr.: Abbruch Ghetto Warschaw, October 29, 1943; Kermish, *General Jürgen Stroop's Report*, 76.

20. Zhukov, *Memoirs of Marshal Zhukov*, 330–332.

21. Ibid., 350.

22. Citino, *Wehrmacht Retreats*, 144.

23. Kermish, *General Jürgen Stroop's Report*, 207.

24. Zetterling and Frankson, *Kursk, 1943*, 22.

25. Ibid., 136–139; von Mellenthin, *Panzer Battles*, 277.

26. Citino, *Wehrmacht Retreats*, 119.

27. Hans Frank interrogation, September 7, 1945, Box 156, 20–23, Imperial War Museum, Duxford.

28. N1340/243, Bundesarchiv/Koblenz, SS und Polizei-Führer im District

Warschau an den Reichsführer SS und Deutschen Polizei H. Himmler, February 2, 1943.

29. N1340/247, Bundesarchiv/Koblenz, Reichsführer SS, Posen, October 6, 1943.

30. Goldhagen, "Albert Speer."

31. Warlimont, *Inside Hitler's Headquarters*, 333–334.

32. Von Below, *At Hitler's Side*, 173.

33. Glantz and House, *When Titans Clashed*, 160.

34. Evans, *Third Reich at War*, 485–486.

35. Konev, "Great Battle at Kursk," 25.

36. Zetterling and Frankson, *Kursk, 1943*, 37–38.

37. Ibid., 39–41.

38. See Stroop and Milton, *Stroop Report*, for forces used on average per day.

39. Evans, *Third Reich at War*, 487–488.

40. Zetterling and Frankson, *Kursk, 1943*, 138–139.

41. Zhukov, *Memoirs of Marshal Zhukov*, 382–384; for erroneous statements on German tank losses, see Zetterling and Frankson, *Kursk, 1943*, 120–123.

42. Glantz and House, *Battle of Kursk*, 18.

43. Evans, *Third Reich at War*, 490.

44. Shirer, *Rise and Fall*, 828.

Chapter 11. The Allied Invasion of Sicily

1. Evans, *Third Reich at War*, 489.

2. Warlimont, *Inside Hitler's Headquarters*, 332–333.

3. Churchill, *Second World War*, 5:40.

4. "Chronologie der Deportationen aus dem Deutschen Reich," Bundesarchiv/Berlin, http://www.bundesarchiv.de/gedenkbuch/chronicles.html?page=1; "Chronologie der Deportationen aus Frankreich," Bundesarchiv/Berlin, http://www.bundesarchiv.de/gedenkbuch/chronicles.html?page=3; "Chronologie der Deportationen aus den Niederlanden," Bundesarchiv/Berlin, http://www.bundesarchiv.de/gedenkbuch/chronicles.html?page=4.

5. RW4/710, Bundesarchiv-Militärarchiv/Freiburg, August 1, 1943.

6. Montgomery, *Memoirs*, 158–161.

7. Weinberg, *World at Arms*, 593–594.

8. Liddell Hart, *Other Side of the Hill*, 349–350.

9. Blumentritt, *The Soldier and the Man*, 167–168.

10. NS-19/1577, Bundesarchiv/Berlin-Lichterfelde, Betrifft Juden fremder Staatsangehörigkeit.

11. Weinberg, *World at Arms*, 484–485.

12. Ibid., 595, 597, 599.

13. Von Neurath was a former foreign secretary who acted as Sonderführer —a title used for certain civilian experts who were given temporary military status.

14. Churchill, *Second World War*, 5:19–30; Warlimont, *Inside Hitler's Headquarters*, 319–320.

15. Churchill, *Second World War*, 5:24–28.

16. Skorzeny, *My Commando Operations*, 185. Skorzeny would later be the one to rescue Mussolini from exile.

17. Kroener, "Management of Human Resources," MGFA 2:1018–1019.

18. "Chronologie der Deportationen aus dem Deutschen Reich," Bundesarchiv/Berlin, http://www.bundesarchiv.de/gedenkbuch/chronicles.html?page=1.

19. Cesarani, *Becoming Eichmann*, 129, 133.

20. After the uprising in Yugoslavia, when the German divisions had to be transported back to the Eastern Front from there and from Greece in spring 1941 in order to get ready for Operation Barbarossa, they failed to make it on time as a result of the harsh terrain.

21. Cesarani, *Becoming Eichmann*, 146–148.

22. See Friedländer, *Years of Extermination*, 493–494.

23. The Todt Organization was a semimilitary governmental unit set up in 1938 for the purpose of constructing military installations and special highways suitable for armored vehicles. It was administered by Dr. Fritz Todt until his death in 1942 and then by Albert Speer.

24. Testimony of Dieter Wisliceny taken at Nuremberg, November 15, 1945, Box 162, 18–19, Imperial War Museum, Duxford.

25. Hart, *Guderian*, 91.

26. Testimony of Dieter Wisliceny taken at Nuremberg, November 24, 1945, Box 162, 5, Imperial War Museum, Duxford.

27. Ibid., November 14, 1945, 1–18, Imperial War Museum, Duxford.

28. Ibid., November 17, 1945, 9.

29. Testimony of Hans Frank taken at Nuremberg, November 13, 1945, Box 156, 110–113, Imperial War Museum, Duxford. In further testimony provided on September 1, 1945, Frank claimed that the size of the General Government was much smaller than 140,000 square kilometers—only 90,000 square kilometers, with 10.5 million inhabitants.

30. Testimony of Rudolf Höss taken at Nuremberg, April 1, 1946, Box 157, Imperial War Museum, Duxford.

31. R5/20236, Bundesarchiv/Berlin-Lichterfelde, Deutsche Reichsbahn,

Eisenbahnabeilung des Reichsverkehrministeriums, Berlin W8, June 10, 1943, Betre: Aushange in Personenwagen.

32. Bergman, *Drancy*, 174.

33. RW18/18, Bundesarchiv-Militärarchiv/Freiburg, Der Militarbefehlshaber in Frankreich, Paris, March 31, 1943.

34. R5/3643, Bundesarchiv/Berlin-Lichterfelde, Betr. Kfz. Transporte ab Strassburg nach Shitomir fur Wirtschafts-Strassensportdienst Ost, Berlin–Wilhemsdorf, August 12, 1943.

35. Bergman, *Drancy*, 138–145.

36. RH4/175, Bundesarchiv-Militärarchiv/Freiburg, Transport des Feindes an der Sowjetische-deutschen Front, 2–5.

37. Konev, "Great Battle at Kursk," 30.

38. Overy, *Russia's War*, 186–187.

39. Konev, "Great Battle at Kursk," 15.

40. Overy, *Russia's War*, 217.

41. Overy, "Transportation and Rearmament," 406–407.

42. Overy, *Russia's War*, 212.

43. Glantz, *Colossus Reborn*, 59.

44. Friedländer, *Years of Extermination*, 500–501.

45. NS-19/2234, Bundesarchiv/Berlin-Lichterfelde, Der SS und Polizeiführer im District Lublin, 3 März 1943.

46. NS-19/1577, Bundesarchiv/Berlin-Lichterfelde, Führerhauptquartier, July 11, 1943, Rundeschreiben Nr. 33/43.

47. Von Below, *At Hitler's Side*, 168–169.

48. Kroener, "Manpower Resources," MGFA 7:907.

49. Von Below, *At Hitler's Side*, 180.

Part 4. The Extermination of Hungarian Jewry and the Allied Invasion of Normandy

1. Yad Vashem Archives, Jerusalem, Die Staatsanwaltschaft Wien erhebt gegen Franz Novak. Prozeß, November 16, 1964, 48–49.

2. Overy, *Why the Allies Won*, 168–169.

3. Weinberg, *World at Arms*, 687.

Chapter 12. A Long and Winding Road

1. Evans, *Third Reich at War*, 492; see also Glantz and House, *When Titans Clashed*, 179. According to Glatnz and House, this period lasted, with brief pauses, until May 1945 with the surrender of the German armed forces to the Allies.

2. Evans, *Third Reich at War*, 492.

3. Zhukov, *Memoirs of Marshal Zhukov*, 369.

4. Kroener, *Generaloberst Friedrich Fromm*, 662.

5. Ziemke, *Stalingrad to Berlin*, 312.

6. Glantz and House, *When Titans Clashed*, 179–180.

7. Von Below, *At Hitler's Side*, 190–191.

8. Cesarani, *Becoming Eichmann*, 162.

9. Ambrose, *D-Day*, 25–26.

10. Von Below, *At Hitler's Side*, 195–196.

11. Cesarani, *Becoming Eichmann*, 160–161; Karkowski, *Encyclopedia of the Holocaust*, 2:355; Braham, "The Jews in Hungary"; Braham, "Holocaust in Hungary," 432.

12. Schloss Klessheim was a Baroque palace situated four kilometers west of Salzburg. It was an estate belonging to Archduke Louis Victor, brother of the late Austrian-Hungarian emperor. When staying at his nearby Berghof residence, Hitler used Schloss Klessheim for conferences and to host official guests like Mussolini, Horthy, Antonescu, Tiso, and Pavelić.

13. Horthy, *Ein Leben für Ungarn*, 211–214.

14. Ibid., 215–216.

15. Weinberg, *Germany, Hitler, and World War II*, 244.

16. R50-II/46a, Bundesarchiv/Berlin-Lichterfelde, Der Reichsmarshal des Grossdeutschen Reichs der Beauftragte Für den Vierjahresplan, C.U., March 4, 1944.

17. Speer interrogation, October 18, 1945, Box 369, Imperial War Museum, Duxford.

18. Cesarani, *Becoming Eichmann*, 161; Lazowick, *Hitler's Bureaucrats*, 195.

19. RW4/494, Bundesarchiv-Militärarchiv/Freiburg, Betrifft: Bildung der Deutschen Volkswehr, Führerhauptquartier, dem 14 Sept. 1944.

20. NS-19/1743, Bundesarchiv/Berlin-Lichterfelde, Der Gauleiter und Oberpräsident von Oberchlesin, Kttowitz den 20.März 1944, An dem Reichsführer SS und Reichsminister Innern Parteigenossen Heinrich Himmler.

21. Horthy, *Ein Leben für Ungarn*, 215–216.

22. NS-9/2067, Bundesarchiv-Militärarchiv/Freiburg, Auszüge aus den Berichten aus Ungarn (Vermerk Für den Volksgruppenführer, Betrifft: Dr. Franz Schibera Weissbrunn).

23. NS-9/2067, Bundesarchiv-Militärarchiv/Freiburg, Auszüge aus den Berichten aus Ungarn (Lagebericht der Gebietsbeauftragten des Gebiets Ost., Berlin, April 24, 1944).

24. Cesarani, *Becoming Eichmann*, 161–162.

25. Attorney General against Adolf Eichmann, *Opening Address*, 106.

26. Braham, *Politics of Genocide*, 2:604.

27. Cesarani, *Becoming Eichmann*, 169.

28. Braham, *Politics of Genocide*, 2:675.

29. Mierzejewski, *Collapse of the German War Economy*, 45.

30. Testimony of Dieter Wisliceny taken at Nuremberg, November 17, 1945, Box 162, Imperial War Museum, Duxford.

31. Mierzejewski, *Collapse of the German War Economy*, 45. The deportation trains contained 3,000 people crammed into wagons of seventy to ninety passengers, each weighing an average of fifty to sixty kilograms, plus fifty kilograms of luggage.

32. Braham, *Politics of Genocide*, 2:674.

33. Reitlinger, *Final Solution*, 459; for Kastner, see 360–361.

34. Kreidler, *Eisenbahnen im Machtbereich*, 300–303.

35. Braham, *Politics of Genocide*, 2:603.

36. Yad Vashem Archives, Jerusalem, TR-10/621, Krumey–Hunsche Prozeß, September 30, 1965, wegen gemeinschaftlichen Mordes und gemeinschaftlicher räuberischer erpressung, 30.

37. Yad Vashem Archives, Jerusalem, TR-10/515, Die Staatsanwaltschaft Wien erhebt gegen Franz Novak. Prozeß beginn November 16, 1964, 45–50.

38. Mierzejewski, *Most Valuable Asset*, 145.

39. Beevor, *Berlin*, 27.

Chapter 13. Risk and Fear of Invasion

1. Ziemke, *Stalingrad to Berlin*, 311–312.

2. Trevor-Roper, *Hitler's War Directives*, Directive 51, November 3, 1943, 218–219.

3. Cooper, *German Army*, 493–494.

4. Eisenhower, *D-Day to V-Day*, 66; Ose, *Entscheidung im Westen 1944*, 97–98.

5. Ose, *Entscheidung im Westen 1944*, 98.

6. Montgomery, *Normandy to the Baltic*, 17–18.

7. Zimmerman, "France, 1944," 202.

8. Vogel, "German and Allied Conduct," MGFA 7:472.

9. Ibid., 7:521–522, 526.

10. DiNardo, *Germany's Panzer Army*, 116, 125–126.

11. RH40/27, Bundesarchiv-Militärarchiv/Freiburg, Kavallerie—Regimnt Mitte, March 21, 1944, Major V. Amsberg OKH; RW4/688, Betr.: PferdeanKauf in Oberitalien, January 11, 1944; RW4/711a, Vortragsnotiz, March 22, 1945.

12. NS-3/1191, Bundesarchiv/Berlin-Lichterfelde, Betrifft-Vieh und Pferdeversicherungen bei Wämtern, June 16, 1944.

13. Hastings, *Overlord*, 349.

14. Wilt, *Atlantic Wall*, 116.

15. Hesketh, *Fortitude*, 169.

16. Eisenhower, *D-Day to V-Day*, 47; Weinberg, *World at Arms*, 688.

17. Megargee, *Inside Hitler's High Command*, 209–211.

18. Wilt, *Atlantic Wall*, 132.

19. Ose, *Entscheidung im Westen 1944*, 88; author interview with Brigadier General (Ret.) Yitzhak Rabin (March 15, 2011, Tel Aviv), IDF chief of the Armor Corps, 1990–1993.

20. Wilt, *Atlantic Wall*, 132.

21. Montgomery, *Normandy to the Baltic*, 16.

22. Kurt Weissenborn, Report No. 77, FD-3063/49, Imperial War Museum, London.

23. Ambrose, *D-Day*, 91–92.

24. NS-19/1918, Bundesarchiv/Berlin, SS-Wirtschafts-Verwaltungshauptamt, Betr: Verwertung des Jüdischen hehler und diebesguts, Berlin (Lichterfelde West), May 13, 1943.

25. Overy, *Russia's War*, 220–221.

26. Montgomery, *Memoirs*, 217.

27. Eisenhower, *D-Day to V-Day*, 42.

28. Creveld, *Supplying War*, 211.

29. Williamson and Millett, *War to Be Won*, 418–420.

30. Zimmerman, "France, 1944," 209–210.

31. Creveld, *Supplying War*, 213–214.

32. Williamson and Millett, *War to Be Won*, 416–417.

33. Ruppenthal, "Logistic Planning," 87–89.

34. Eisenhower, *D-Day to V-Day*, 35–36.

35. Wieviorka, *Normandy*, 357–359.

36. Gilbert, *Auschwitz and the Allies*, 220–221.

37. Ambrose, *D-Day*, 85–86.

38. Wieviorka, *Normandy*, 241.

39. RW4/711a, Bundesarchiv-Militärarchiv/Freiburg, June 5, 1944, Abgrenzung der Befugnisse der Chef bzw. Wehrmacht intendanten gegenüber den für die Versorungsführung zuständigen Dienststellen des Generalquartermeisters des heeres.

40. Ambrose, *D-Day*, 100.

41. Kurt Weissenborn (deputy chief of the main committee for weapons in the Speer ministry), "Dorpmüller, Ganzenmüller and Wartime Inefficiency of the German Railway," "Dustbin," February 1946, EDS/1160, Report 77, Part 16, Imperial War Museum, Duxford.

42. Richard Fiebig, head of the main committee for railway vehicles, Report 84, Part 2, July 27, 1946, written at the request of the economic branch, "Dustbin," FD 3063/49 (Speer 3668), Imperial War Museum, London.

43. Wieviorka, *Normandy*, 245–246.

44. Francis, *Battle for Supplies*, 119.

45. RS/6-2, Bundesarchiv-Militärarchiv/Freiburg, Der Wehrmacht befehlshaber in den Niederlanden, April 14, 1944, Tagesbefehl Nr. 20/44. Wehrmachtreisegepäck, Verhalten auf Transporter.

46. RW18/14, Bundesarchiv-Militärarchiv/Freiburg, "Hauptverkehrsdirktion Paris-Transportleitstelle West und Sudfrankreich: Wagengestellungsubersicht, 29.2.1944."

47. RH66/173, Bundesarchiv-Militärarchiv/Freiburg, Deutcher Transportbevollmachtigter Ungarn und Slovakei, Budapest, May 20, 1944.

48. Mierzejewski, *Collapse of the German War Economy*, 86.

49. Zimmerman, "France, 1944," 208.

50. Petersen, *From Hitler's Doorstep*, document 3-138, telegram 688-89 to London, June 5, 1944; Dulles corresponded with General Donovan and Davis Bruce concerning order-of-battle reporting, 299; see also Mierzejewski, *Most Valuable Asset*, 139.

51. Macksey, *For Want of a Nail*, 133.

52. Petersen, *From Hitler's Doorstep*, document 3-140, telegram 3722-26, June 6, 1944; report sent on D-Day on the status of German transportation and communications in France, 300–301.

53. Bradley, *Soldier's Story*, 245–246.

54. Wieviorka, *Normandy*, 242.

55. Bradley, *Soldier's Story*, 212–214.

56. Gilbert, *Auschwitz and the Allies*, 223.

57. Eisenhower, *Eisenhower at War*, 285.

58. Ibid., 280.

59. Churchill, *Second World War*, 6:18.

60. Hastings, *Overlord*, 172.

61. Ambrose, *D-Day*, 283–284.

62. Lewis, *Omaha Beach*, 18–22.

63. Lewis, *American Culture of War*, 43.

64. Bradley, *Soldier's Story*, 272; Lewis, *Omaha Beach*, 29, 182.

65. War Department, Historical Division, *Omaha Beachhead*, September 20, 1945, 26 (assault plan).

66. Williamson and Millett, *War to Be Won*, 422–423.

67. Vogel, "German and Allied Conduct," MGFA 7:595.

68. Ibid., 7:595–596.

69. Lewis, *Omaha Beach*, 290.

70. Ambrose, *D-Day*, 316–317.

71. Vogel, "German and Allied Conduct," MGFA 7:594–595.

72. Lewis, *Omaha Beach*, 32, 56, 291, 302.

73. Montgomery, *Memoirs*, 198–199.

74. Eisenhower, *D-Day to V-Day*, 53–54, 66.

75. Wieviorka, *Normandy*, 195–196.

76. Zimmerman, "France, 1944," 223.

77. Hastings, *Overlord*, 210.

78. Bradley, *Soldier's Story*, 292.

79. Vogel, "German and Allied Conduct," MGFA 7:598.

80. Montgomery, *Normandy to the Baltic*, 61.

81. Warlimont, *Inside Hitler's Headquarters*, 428.

82. Bradley, *Soldier's Story*, 292.

83. Overy, *Why the Allies Won*, 175.

84. Lazowick, *Hitler's Bureaucrats*, 203.

85. Vogel, "German and Allied Conduct," MGFA 7:605–606.

86. Ibid., 7:600.

87. Montgomery, *Memoirs*, 229.

88. Vogel, "German and Allied Conduct," MGFA 7:596.

89. Hastings, *Overlord*, 174.

90. Montgomery, *Normandy to the Baltic*, 60–61.

Chapter 14. The Destruction of Army Group Center

1. Adair, *Hitler's Greatest Defeat*, 7.

2. Weinberg, *World at Arms*, 679.

3. Clark, *Barbarossa: The German War*, 278.

4. Merridale, *Ivan's War*, 263, 264.

5. Zhukov, *Memoirs of Marshal Zhukov*, 383–384.

6. Glantz and House, *When Titans Clashed*, 179–180.

7. RH66/397, Bundesarchiv-Militärarchiv/Freiburg, Kommandeur es Eisb. Pionier-Btl. II/1, May 11, 1944, Erfahrungsbericht Über den Bau der Umgehungsstrecke (Strecke Witebsk—Orscha).

8. Zhukov, *Memoirs of Marshal Zhukov*, 389.

9. Glantz and House, *When Titans Clashed*, 209.

10. Merridale, *Ivan's War*, 226, 275, 276.

11. Adair, *Hitler's Greatest Defeat*, 133–134; Ziemke, *Stalingrad to Berlin*, 322.

12. Glantz and House, *When Titans Clashed*, 214–215.

13. Adair, *Hitler's Greatest Defeat*, 134, 139.

14. Kroener, *Generaloberst Freidrich Fromm*, 662.

15. Glantz and House, *When Titans Clashed*, 204.

16. RH19II/327, Bundesarchiv-Militärarchiv/Freiburg, Transportleistungen in Monat, May 1944.

17. See Braham, *Politics of Genocide*, 2:607.

18. Zhukov, *Memoirs of Marshal Zhukov*, 383.

19. Ziemke, *Stalingrad to Berlin*, 326–328.

20. Glantz and House, *When Titans Clashed*, 198.

21. Braham, *Politics of Genocide*, 2:743.

22. R5-3273, Bundesarchiv/Berlin-Lichterfelde, Abschrift: Der Präsident des Rechnungshüfs des Deutschen Reichs, Anlage zum Schreiben, January 10, 1944. Betrifft: Prüfung der wirtschafts und Rechnungs führung der Ostbahn.

23. R5-3273, Bundesarchiv/Berlin-Lichterfelde, Warschau–Praga–Deblin–Lublin–Cholm–Dorohusk, Warschau–West Abstellbf Hbf–Ost–Prage–Małkinia (Treblinka last station)–Osbahngerenze, Krakau–Plazow–Skewina–Ostbahgerenze (last stop)–Auschwitz, Siedlce–Małkinia–Ostbahgerenze–Scharfonwiese, Tschentochau Gbf Hbh–Stradon–Ostbahngrenze–Lublinitz, Rewiec–Zawada–Belzec, Cholm–Sobibor–Bug Wiodawski–Wlodawa, Lemberg Hbf–RawaRuska–Belzec, Lemberg Hbf–Samber–Sianki–Gerenze gegen Ungarn., Nowy Zegorz–Lupkow–Gerenze gegen die Slowakei, Biala Czottkowska–Zaleszczyki–Gerenze gegen Rumän.

24. R5-3273, Bundesarchiv/Berlin-Lichterfelde, An den Herrn Reichsverkehrsminister Eisenbahabteilungen, Betrifft: Prüfung der Wirtschafts und Rechnungs fürung der Ostbahn.

25. R5-3273, Bundesarchiv/Berlin-Lichterfelde, An den Herrn Reichsverkehrminister, January 8, 1944, Betr.: Entwurf einer Verordnung über des Eisenbahnwesen im Generalgouvernements.

26. R5-3273, Bundesarchiv/Berlin, An die Regierung des Generalgouvernements. Staatssekretariat Leiter des Amtes für Gesetzgebung—Krakau; R5-3273, Verordnung über das Eisenbanwesen desr Generalgouvernemnets. Gegentwurf des Rechnungshofs des desr Generalgouvernements, June 6, 1944. Wirtschafts- und Rechnungsprüfung.

27. R5-3273, Bundesarchiv/Berlin-Lichterfelde, An die Regierung des Generalgouvernements Staatssekreteriat Leiter des Amtes für Gesetzgebung, Krakau, June 6, 1944, Betr: Eisenbahnverordung des Generalgouvernements, Bezug: Schreiben, May 15, 1944.

28. NS-19-3351, Bundesarchiv/Berlin-Lichterfelde, Fernschreiben, Herrn Staatssekretär Dr. Ganzenmüller—Reichsverkilometersinisterium, July 31, 1944, RF/M.

29. Gilbert, *Auschwitz and the Allies*, 260.

30. Yad Vashem Archives, Jerusalem, TR-10/621, Krumey–Hunsche Prozeß, September 30, 1965, wegen gemeinschaftlichen Mordes und gemeinschaftlicher räuberischer erpressung, 30–33.

31. Porat, *Entangled Leadership*, 379, 24–26; Cesarani, *Becoming Eichmann*, 183–194.

32. Horthy, *Ein Leben für Ungarn*, 219–220.

33. Lazowick, *Hitler's Bureaucrats*, 211; Friedländer, *Years of Extermination*, 580; Reitlinger, *The SS*, 356.

34. Friedländer, *Years of Extermination*, 582.

35. N1497/96, Bundesarchiv/Koblenz, Nachlaß Adolf Eichmann, Private Papers, Correspondence, and Literary Works, 39.

36. Cesarani, *Becoming Eichmann*, 182.

37. Richard Fiebig, head of the main committee for railway vehicles, Report 84, Part 2, July 27, 1946, written at the request of the economic branch, "Dustbin," FD 3063/49 (Speer 3668), Imperial War Museum, London.

38. N1340/250, Bundesarchiv/Koblenz, Nachlaß Albert Speer, Private Papers.

39. Aronson, *Hitler, the Allies, and the Jews*, 424–425.

40. NS-19/1872, Bundesarchiv/Berlin-Lichterfelde, Der Reichsminister in Sachsen, Dresden, July 25, 1944, An Herrn Reichsführer SS und Chef der Deutschen Polizei Reichsminister Heinrich Himmler.

41. NS-19/1872, Bundesarchiv/Berlin-Lichterfelde, Ihr Schreiben, July 25–July 31, 1944, An Gauleiter und Reicsstatthalter in Sachsen Pg. Martin Mutschmann.

42. Hastings, *Overlord*, 221.

43. Unger, *Lodz*, 535, 538, 557.

44. Zimmerman, "France, 1944," 234–235.

45. Keress, *Operational Logistics*, 79.

46. Patton, *War as I Knew It*, 119–126; Blumenson, *Duel for France*, 378–379.

47. Hastings, *Overlord*, 320.

48. Aronson, *Hitler, the Allies, and the Jews*, 350.

49. Glantz, *Belorussia, 1944*, 187–191; Weinberg, *World at Arms*, 759–760, 765–770.

50. Aronson, *Hitler, the Allies, and the Jews*, 350–351.

51. Warlimont, *Inside Hitler's Headquarters*, 485.

52. Reynolds, *Men of Steel*, 22–23.

53. Piper, *Auschwitz: How Many Perished*, 57; Friedländer, *Years of Extermination*, 638.

54. Testimony of Dieter Wisliceny, November 24, 1945, Box 162, Imperial War Museum, Duxford.

55. Lazowick, *Hitler's Bureaucrats*, 214; Friedländer, *Years of Extermination*, 604.

56. Truman, *Memoirs*, 100–101.

57. NS-22/16, Bundesarchiv-Militärarchiv/Freiburg, Tagbuchnotizen von Generalfeldmarschall von Bock, July 1944, 49.

58. Kershaw, *Hitler: Nemesis*, 736.

59. Weinberg, "The Allies and the Holocaust," 489.

Conclusion

1. Weinberg, *Germany, Hitler, and World War II*, 308; Kershaw, *Nazi Dictatorship*, 197.

2. Messerschmidt, "Der Angriff auf die Sowjetunion," MGFA 4:xiii–xix.

3. Förster, "Operation Barbarossa," MGFA 4:1245.

4. Rabinbach, "Jewish Question," 62–65.

5. Habermas, "Vom Öffentlichen Gebrauch der Historie."

6. See *Historiker-Streit*.

7. Davidowicz, *War against the Jews*, 201–208, 218–219.

8. Fleming, *Hitler and the Final Solution*, 2–3.

9. Eberhard, *Hitlers Weltanschauun*, 142.

10. Mommsen, *From Weimar to Auschwitz*, 250–253.

11. Bankier, "Hitler's Part," 149–150.

12. Broszat, "Genesis of the Final Solution," 404–405.

13. Burrin, *Hitler and the Jews*, 142–144.

14. Förster, "Jewish Policies of the German Military," 68.

15. Ibid.; Browning, *Path to Genocide*.

16. Kershaw, *Nazi Dictatorship*.

17. Kershaw, *Hitler: Hubris*, 125.

18. Jersak, "Entschidungen zu mord und Lüge, Die Deutsche Kriegsgesellschaft und der Holocaust," MGFA 9:304–306.

19. Overy, *Why the Allies Won*; Macksey, *Military Errors*; Roberts, *Victory at Stalingrad*.

20. Magenheimer, *Hitler's War*; Stolfi, *Hitler's Panzers East*.

21. Bartov, *Eastern Front*. See also Browning, "Hitler and the Euphoria of Victory"; Mayer, *Why Did the Heavens Not Darken*.

22. Förster, "Relation between 'Operation Barbarossa,'" 87, 89.

23. The Sitzkrieg was a stage in the war during which, despite threats from the British and French to implement the guarantees they gave Poland, they did not clash militarily with Germany until Winston Churchill was appointed prime minister in May 1940.

24. Overy, *Göring*, 129.

25. Brooke, *War Diaries*, June 12, 1944, 557.

26. Morgan, *Overture to Overlord*, 112.

27. Duffi, *Hitler Slept Late*, 23.

28. Von Bock, *War Diary*, June 1, 1940, 161.

29. Duffi, *Hitler Slept Late*, 26–27.

30. Von Mellenthin, *Panzer Battles*, 16, 30.

31. Author interview with Brigadier General (Ret.) Yitzhak Rabin (March 15, 2011, Tel Aviv), IDF chief of the Armor Corps, 1990–1993.

32. Ibid.; see also Bartov, *Dado*.

33. Steiger, *Panzer Taktikum*, 124–125.

34. Author interview with Major General (Ret.) Amiaz Sagis (February 4, 2011, Tel Aviv), former head of the technology and logistics division in the IDF.

35. Steiger, *Panzer Taktikum*, 133–135.

36. Falls, *Art of War*, 179–180.

37. Jomini, *Art of War*, 134.

38. Ibid., 140–141.

39. Lynn, *Feeding Mars*, 265.

40. Keress, *Operational Logistics*, 91.

41. Interview with Sagis.

42. Speer, *Spandau*, August 22, 1960, 353–354.

Works Cited

Bundesarchiv-Militärarchiv/Freiburg

Contains a comprehensive collection of material related to the high command of the German armed forces. Includes various operation commands, official war diaries of the Wehrmacht, maps, and a wide variety of documents ranging from 1867.

Oberkommando des Heeres/Generalstab des Heeres (Teil 1)

Heeresgruppen der Ostfront, p. 394
RH3/2552 zg. 12–81
RH3/2575 zg. 12/81
RH3/743 (H32/246) (III H 437)
RH3/744 (34171) (H32/213)
Chef sachen 1942 (mit karten) (H32/235) (III H 435), p. 237 RH 2/429
RH 2/noch 427 (H32/234) (III H 434), p. 236
RH 2/300k Taifun—schlacht um Moskau, lagekarten box 11/17, 11/18
RH 2/744, Operation Siegfried 1942 (34171) (H 22/213), p. 395
RH/2 (H 22/276)
RH/2 733 (34140) (H 22/277) Übersicht der kampfhandlungen der heersgruppe süd, January 31–May 31, 1942

Oberkommando des Heeres/Generalstab des Heeres (Teil 2)

Chef des Truppenamtes
RH3-1327/63
RH3/1327/30-134
RH3-1326
RH3/733
RH3/940
RH3/2580
RH3/940
RH3/43
RH3/2581
RHD 46/2

RH 2/1424 (H 1/426)
Grundsätze für aufstellung und verwendung von ost truppen, January 1943
Kriegsgefangene
RH 2/RH 53-23/58
Fern sprech verzeichnis des oberkommando des heeres/generalstab des heeres, stand; October 15, 1942

Oberkommando des Heeres/Generalstab des Heeres (Teil 3)
RH/2 H 3/48 p. 525, Durchbruch der roten armee bei Stalingrad. Deutche Untersuchungen über das RH/2, p. 295
Verhalten der Rumänen, December 1942–March 1943
Heeresgruppe Don–Heeresgruppe B

Oberkommando des Heeres/Generalstab des Heeres (Teil 4)
Waffen merkblätter enthält bei den amtsduck sachen
RH 53-17/144, p. 9, Technische beschreibung sowie einsatz möglichkeiten von meinen, brükkengerät, raupen schlepper ost und lastkraftwagen— maultier January 1943
RH 4 — Chef des Transportwesens
RH4/725
RH4/67
RH4/175
RH4/308
RH4/309
RH 2/Teil
RH 2/365 Arbeitslager
RH 2/73 Arbeitszeit im Kriege
RH 3/168 Blomber Werner von General Fieldmarshal
RH 1/221 Brauchitsch Walther von General Fieldmarshal
RH 2/215 2/321 Ordungspolizei
RH 3/35 3/259 Sicherheit polizei und des sicherheitsdienstes
RH 2/43 Wehrmacht — Ordungstruppen
RH 1/101 2/351 Chef des zivilverwaltung
RH 1/119 2/161 2/162 Chef der oberkomandos der Wehrmacht
RH 1/90, 1/97, 1/99, 1/100, 1/101 Chef des transportwesens
RH 1/89 1/101 Chef des wetterdienstes

Oberkommando der Wehrmacht/Wehrmacht Fuhrung stab
RW 4/663, p. 196
RW 4/894, p. 241
RW 4/674
RW 4/35
RW 4/711a
RW 4/604
RW 4/688
RW 4/710, 47
RW 4/821
RW 4/494
RW 19/687, p. 244
RW 19/687, p. 257
RW 19/687, p. 229
RW 4/717, p. 230
RW 5/v. 327, p. 241
RW 19/686, p. 237
RW 19/687
RH 24-200/97, p. 261

RW18 Wehrmacht — Transport- und Verkehrsdienststellen
RW18/14
RW18/18
RH 1/243, 2/51, 2/52 Eisenbahnartillerie
RH 2/294, 2/298 Eisenbahntruppen
RH 2/52, 4/8, 4/10, 4/54 Eisenbahn-Panzerzüge
RH 2/162 Führer und oberster befehlshaber der wehrmacht
Führer gehilfen

Private Papers
N 372 Paulus Friedrich
N 28 Beck Ludwig
N 252 Blumentritt Günther
N 22 Bock Fedor von
N 236 Dönitz Karl
N 220 Halder Franz
N 503 Hoth Hermann
N 69 Jodl Alfred
N 54 Keitel Wilhelm
N 179 Milch Erhard

N 245 Reinhardt Hans
N 145 Leeb Wilhelm Ritter von
N 53 Wienskowski Hellmuth von

N119 Nachlaß der Kuzbach Friedrich (Transportkommandantur Warschau)
N 119/11
N 119-18
N 119/12
N 119/15
N 119/13
N 119/12
N 601/7 Betr. Funkverkehr Stalingrad
N 601/8, Notizen zur 6. Armee
N 601/8, Fs
N 601/v. 3
N 601/6 Grundsätzliche Feststellungen zur Operation der 6. Armee bei
  Stalingrad
RH40/27 Kavallerie–Regiment Mitte

RH66, General der Eisenbahntruppen
RH66/173
RH66/397
RH66/180
RH66/732

**RH19-I/156, Heeresgruppe Süd/Oberbefehlshaber Ost/Heeresgruppe A/
Oberbefehlshaber West/Heeresgruppe Süd**
RH29I/261
RH29II/324
RH29II/325
RH29II/327
RH29VI/26

RH30-6/928, 6. Armee (AOK 6)
RS/6-2, Befehlshaber der Waffen-SS
NS-22/16, Tagebuchnotizen von Generalfeldmarschall von Bock
NS-9/2067

Bundesarchiv/Berlin-Lichterfelde

Contains material on the Nazi Party, SA, and SS, as well as files on members of these three organizations. The archive also contains files of various ministries, including those of transport and armaments. Until 1994, the collection had been in the possession of the US Department of the Interior. A large part of the documents was microfilmed and is kept at the National Archives in Washington, DC.

R5 Reichsverkehrsministerium

R5/3273
R5/3274
R5/3643
R5/22299
R5/2094
R5/3349
R5/20236
R5/023128
R5/2228
R5/2092
R5/9167
R5/22635
R5/6669
R5/7254
NS3/1191

R50-II Transporteinheiten Todt/Speer

R50-II/46a

NS-19 Persönlicher Stab Reichsführer-SS

NS-19/1570
NS-19/649
NS-19/1740
NS-19/1577
NS-19/1743
NS-19/1872
NS-19/3351
NS-19/1918
NS-19/2234

NS-18 Reichspropagandaleiter der NSDAP
NS-18/0225
NS-18/592
NS-18/1132
NS-181126
NS-18/1133
NS-18/1134
RH51/8 Armee-Pferdelazarett
RH51/10
NS4nh./9, 229 Konzentrationslage

Bundesarchiv/Koblenz

Persönliche Papiere, Korrespondenzen und Literarische Texte

NACHLASS ALBERT SPEER, N 1340
N 1340/201, N 1340/208, N 1340/211, N 1340/227, N 1340/231, N 1340/233,
    N 1340/243, N 1340/244, N 1340/247, N 1340/519, N 1340/508, N 1340/241,
    N 1340/511, N 1340/513, N 1340/276, N 1340/275, N 1340/273, N 1340/260,
    N 1340/256, N 1340/255, N 1340/50, N 1340/258, N 1340/253, N 1340/502,
    N 1340/501, N 1340/499, N 1340/505, N 1340/299, N 1340/459, N 1340/250,
    N 1340/313, N 1340/2

N 1110 — NACHLASS HANS FRANK
N 110/17, N 110/18

N 1497 — NACHLASS ADOLF EICHMANN
N 1497/27, N 1497/90, N 1497/11, N 1497/64, N 1497/17, N 1497/182, N 1497/96,
    N 1497/91, n 1497/67, N 1497/48, N 1497/44

N 1118 — NACHLASS JOSEPH GOEBBELS
N 1118/122

N 1126 — NACHLASS HEINRICH HIMMLER
N 1126/3

N 1171 — NACHLASS FREIDRICH EARNST MORITZ SAEMISCH
N 1171/182, N 1171/184, N 1171/183

KLE 750 — JULIUS HEINRICH DORPMÜLLER
KLE 750

KLE 848 — FRITZ SAUCKEL
KLE 848/1, KLE 848/3

KLE 525 — Hitler Adolf
KLE 525/2

N 1128 — Nachlass Adolf Hitler
N 1128/26, N 1128/25

N 1163 — Nachlass Joachim von Ribbentrop
N 1163/3a

IWM — Imperial War Museum (London)

The Imperial War Museum Archives contains copies of documents seized in Germany after the war by the British and American forces. Some are stored in the National Archives in Washington, DC. Most of the original documents were returned to Germany after being microfilmed or copied. Collections related to World War II and war crimes were taken from various government offices in the Reich and are an important source on the military and economic history of Germany during the war.

EDS (Captured Enemy Documents Section), B1–E5
FD-3063/49 (Speer)
FO-645/161 (Speer)
AL-1426, AL-175-14/823, A-1397, A-1491, AL-1520 WB, AL-1403, AL-1391
    (1 + 2), AL-761, AL-1652/1, AL-1652/2, AL-1481 (2), AL-1048, AL-2569/2
MI (Military Intelligence Branch, British): MI-14/13, MI-14/15, MI-14/21,
    MI-14/22, MI-14/24, EDS/D-232

IWM — Imperial War Museum (Duxford Air Field)

Interrogation Files
Bach Zelewski, Box 155
Becher Kurt, Box 155
Wisliceny Dieter, Box 162
Funk W., Box 156
Frank Hans, Box 156
Höss Rudolf, Box 157
Halder Franz Interrogation File, MS#C-067a
Speer Albert Interrogation Box
EDS/1160, Report 77 Part XVI

PRO — Public Record Office, Kew, London

British state archives. Contains a vast collection of documents related to judicial and state records beginning from the "Doomsday Book" of William the Conqueror in 1086 to the present. British repository operates in collaboration with governmental ministries, and official documents are open to public inspection after thirty years from its storage at the archive.
CAB 121 Cabinet War Papers
CAB 106
FO 371 Foreign Office Documents
MN 353

Liddell Hart Centre for Military Archives, King's College, London
The archive contains primarily the private library of Sir Basil Liddell Hart, with its entire collection of documents, as well as about 600 private papers of veteran British military personnel starting from 1900.

GB99 KCLMA von Manstein — Documents related to the trial of Erich von Manstein held in Hamburg between August and December 1949 for charges on war crimes
Von Manstein—6/6/B2-237; 6/6/B2-240; 6/6/B2-249; 6/6/B2-253; 6/6/B2-254; 6/6/B2-258; 6/6/B2-260; 6/6/B2-262; 6/6/B2-231; 6/6/B2-276; 6/6/B3-251; 6/7/B1-315; 6/6/B1-316; 6/6/B1-245; 6/6/B1-323; 6/6/B1-341; 6/6/B1-317; 6/6/B2-237; 9/3a;11;2b; 6/12; 6/5/A-233; 6/8/B3-341/21; 6/8/B3-341/22; 6/8/B3-341/19; 6/8/B3-341/372; 6/8/B3-341/373; 6/8/B3-341/369

LH 15/15 — Notes taken by Liddell Hart during his interviews with German officers from 1945 to 1948, reports and memorandums relating to the investigation of captured German officers, 1944–1950
LH 15/15/149/9, 15/15/149/13, 15/15/139/15, 15/15/139/40, 15/15/139/41, 15/15/139/42, 15/15/139/44–45, 15/15/139/1, 15/15/137, 15/15/141/34, 15/15/141/38, 15/15/141/39, 15/15/40, 15/15/41, 15/15/42, 15/15/43, 15/15/142/34, 15/15/142/35, 15/15/142/36, 15/15/142/LH: 15/15/142/34, 15/15/142/35, 15/15/142/36, 15/15/142/39–44, 15/15/142/75, 15/15/142/159, 15/15/142/98, 15/15/142/91, 15/15/150/4, 15/15/150/5, 15/15/150/10, 15/15/150/2, 15/15/50/3

Yad Vashem Archives, Jerusalem

TR-10/515, Die Staatsanwaltschaft Wien erhebt gegen Franz Novak, Prozeß
beginn November 15, 1964

TR-10/621, Krumey-Hunsche Prozeß, September 30, 1965
M9/355, M9/356, M9/357, M9/360, M9/361, M9/363
Periodic status reports of the Einsatzgruppen and the Security Police
JM/4319–5911

Guides to German Records Microfilmed at Alexandria, Virginia
Records of the Reich Leader of the SS and the Chief of the German Police,
no. 32 (parts 1–4)
Records of the Reich Ministry for the Occupied Eastern Territories, 1941–
1945, no. 28

Alfred Wiener Collection, Tel Aviv University
Die Deutsche Zivilverwarltung in den Ehemeligen Bezsetzten Ostgebieten
(UdSSR), 22/40/I–II, Wiener Library Documents, Section 582
Franz Halder-Kriegs Tagbuch, Kommando Stab, RFSS Nachrichtenkompa-
gnie: Ost—1941
Wiener Library Documents, Section 568 (Collection of documents related
to the Einsatzgruppen operating in the occupied territories of the Soviet
Union in the summer of 1941)

Internet Source
Eichmann, Adolf, *Die Memoiren Text*, http://www.nizkor.org/ftp.cgi/people/e
/eichmann.adolf/memoire/Eichmann.txt. Full transcript in German of Eichmann's memoirs written in Ramla prison, Israel, during his trial. The material was released to the public to help strengthen the defense in the *Irving v.
Lipstadt* trial.

Books and Articles

Abelshauser, Werner. "Germany: Guns, Butter, and Economic Miracles."
In *The Economics of War: Six Great Powers in International Comparison*, ed-
ited by Mark Harrison, 122–176. Cambridge: Cambridge University Press,
1998.
Adair, Paul. *Hitler's Greatest Defeat: The Collapse of Army Group Center, June
1944*. London, 1994.
Alperovitz, Gar. *The Decision to Use the Atomic Bomb and the Architecture of an
American Myth*. London: Fontana Press, 1996.
Aly, Götz. *Final Solution: Nazi Population Policy and the Murder of the European
Jews*. London: Arnold, 1999.
Ambrose, Stephen E. *D-Day* [in Hebrew]. New York: Simon & Schuster,
1994.

Anders, Władysław. *Hitler's Defeat in Russia*. Chicago: Henry Regnery, 1953.

Antipenko, Lieutenant General Nikolai. "Logistics." In Parotkin, *Battle of Kursk*, 236–237.

Arad, Yitzhak. "The Great Patriotic War: The Price of Victory from the Ribbentrop Molotov Pact to Battle for Stalingrad" [in Hebrew]. *Michael Journal* 13 (1993): 17–38.

———. *The Soviet Union and the Annexed Territories* [in Hebrew]. 2 vols. Jerusalem: Yad Vashem, 2004.

———. *Treblinka, Loss and Uprising*. Am Oved: Tel Aviv, 1983.

Arold, Stefan. *Die Technische entwicklung und rüstungswirtschaftliche bedeutung des lokomotivbaus der deutschen reichsbahn im dritten reich, 1933–1945*. Stuttgart: Franz Steiner Verlag, 1997.

Aronson, Shlomo. *Hitler, the Allies, and the Jews* [in Hebrew]. Be'er Sheva, Israel: Ben Gurion University, 2008.

Attorney General against Adolf Eichmann. *The Opening Address* [in Hebrew]. Read in Jerusalem, 1962.

———. *The Verdict*. Read in Jerusalem District Court on December 11–13, 1962.

Bankier, David. "Hitler's Part in Shaping the Policies on the Jewish Question and the Extermination Process" [in Hebrew]. *Yalkut Moreshet* 16 (1973): 149–170.

Bartov, Hanoch. *Dado — 48 Years and Another 20 Days*. Vol. 2, *The War Diary, 6.10.1973–25.10.1973* [in Hebrew]. Tel Aviv: Maariv, 1978.

Bartov, Omer. *The Eastern Front, 1941–1945: German Troops and the Barbarization of Warfare*. Oxford: Macmillan, 1985.

Beevor, Antony. *Berlin: The Downfall, 1945* [in Hebrew]. Tel Aviv: Yavneh, 2003.

———. *Stalingrad* [in Hebrew]. Tel Aviv: Yavneh, 1999.

Below, Nicholaus von. *At Hitler's Side: The Memoirs of Hitler's Luftwaffe Adjutant, 1937–1945*. London: Greenhill, 2001.

Bergman, Miriam. *Drancy: A Transit Camp from France to Auschwitz, 1941–1944* [in Hebrew]. Tel Aviv: The Goldstein-Goren Diaspora Research Center, 1998.

Bessel, Richard. *Germany, 1945: From War to Peace*. London: Simon & Schuster UK, 2009.

Black, Peter R. *Ernst Kaltenbrünner: Ideological Soldier of the Third Reich*. Princeton, NJ: Princeton Unviersity Press, 1984.

Blatman, Daniel. *The Death Marches, 1944–1945* [in Hebrew]. Jerusalem: Yad Vashem, 2010.

Blumenson, Martin. *The Duel for France, 1944: The Men and Battles that Changed the Fate of Europe*. Washington, DC: Da Capo Press, 2000.

Blumentritt, Günther, *Von Rundstedt: The Soldier and the Man.* London: Odham, 1952.

Bock, General Field Marshal Fedor von. *The War Diary, 1939–1945.* Atglen, PA: Schiffer, 1996.

Boelcke, W. A., ed. *The Secret Conferences of Dr. Goebbels, October 1939–March 1943.* London: Weidenfeld & Nicolson, 1967.

Bradley, Omar N. *A Soldier's Story.* New York: Henry Holt and Company, 1951.

Braham, Randolph L. "The Holocaust in Hungary: A Retrospective Analysis." In *The Holocaust and History: The Known, the Unknown, the Disputed, and the Reexamined,* edited by Michael Bernbaum and Abraham J. Peck for the United States Holocaust Museum, 427–438. Bloomington: Indiana University Press, 1998.

———. *The Politics of Genocide: The Holocaust in Hungary.* 2 vols. New York: Columbia University Press, 1981.

Brandt, Karl. "Germany's Vulnerable Spot: Transportation," *Foreign Affairs,* January 1943. http://www.foreignaffairs.com/articles/70226/karl-brandt/germanys-vulnerable-spot-transportation.

Breitman, Richard. *The Architect of Genocide: Himmler and the Final Solution.* Hanover, NH: Brandeis University Press, 1991.

———. *Official Secrets: What the Nazis Planned, What the British and Americans Knew.* New York: Hill and Wang, 1998.

Brooke, Field Marshal Lord Alan. *War Diaries, 1939–1945.* London: Weidenfeld & Nicolson, 2001.

Broszat, Martin. "The Genesis of the Final Solution." In *Aspects of The Third Reich,* edited by H. W. Koch, 73–125. London: St. Martin's Press, 1985.

———. *Nationalsozialistische Plenpolitik, 1939–1945.* Frankfurt am Main: Fischer Bücherei, 1965.

Browning, Christopher R. "Hitler and the Euphoria of Victory." In *The War and the Final Solution,* edited by David Cesarani, 137–150. London: Routledge, 1994.

———. *Ordinary Men.* New York: Harper Collins, 1998.

———. *The Origins of the Final Solution: The Evolution of Nazi Jewish Policy, September 1939–March 1942* [in Hebrew]. Jerusalem: Yad Vashem, 2004.

———. *The Path to Genocide: Essays on Launching the Final Solution.* Cambridge: Cambridge University Press, 1992.

———. *The Road to the Final Solution* [in Hebrew]. Jerusalem: Yad Vashem, 2004.

Bullock, Alan. *Hitler and Stalin: Parallel Lives.* London: Fontana Press, 1993.

Burrin, Philippe. *Hitler and the Jews: The Genesis of the Holocaust.* London: Arnold, 1994.

Cesarani, David. *Becoming Eichmann: Rethinking the Life, Crimes, and Trial of a "Desk Murderer."* Essex: SX Composing DTP, 2004.

Cholavsky, S. "The Jews of the Reich in Ghetto Minsk." *Yad-Vashem* 17 (1987): 219–245.

Chuikov, Vasily I. *The Beginning of the Road.* London: MacGibbon & Kee, 1963.

Churchill, Winston S. *The Second World War.* Vols. 1–6. Boston: Houghton Mifflin, 1948–1953.

Ciano, Count Galeazzo. *Ciano's Diplomatic Papers.* London: Odham Press, 1948.

Citino, Robert M. *Death of the Wehrmacht: The German Campaigns of 1942.* Lawrence: University Press of Kansas, 2007.

———. *The Wehrmacht Retreats: 1943.* Lawrence: University Press of Kansas, 2012.

Clark, Alan. *Barbarossa* [in Hebrew]. Tel Aviv: Ministry of Defence, 1970.

Cooper, Matthew. *The German Army, 1933–1945.* London: MacDonald and Jane's, 1978.

Creveld, Martin L. van. *Supplying War: Logistics from Wallenstein to Patton.* Cambridge: Cambridge University Press, 1977.

Dallin, Alexander. *German Rule in Russia, 1941–1945: A Study in Occupation Policies.* Boulder, CO: Westview Press, 1981.

Dawidowicz, Lucy S. *The War against the Jews, 1933–1945.* New York: Bantam, 1975.

Demjanjuk Trial. *The State of Israel vs. Ivan (John) Demjanjuk in the District Court of Jerusalem.* Tel Aviv: Israel Bar Publishing, 1991.

DiNardo, R. L. *Germany's Panzer Army.* Westport, CT: Greenwood Press, 1997.

———. *Mechanized Juggernaut or Military Anachronism? Horses and the German Army of World War II.* Westport, CT: Greenwood Press, 1991.

Documents on German Foreign Policy, Series D (1937–1945). Vols. 9–13. London, 1957–1964.

Duffi, James P. *Hitler Slept Late.* New York: Praeger, 1991.

Eden, Anthony. *The Eden Memoirs: The Reckoning.* London: Casell, 1965.

Eisenhower, David. *D-Day to V-Day, 1944–45: General Eisenhower's Report on the Invasion of Europe.* London: Her Majesty's Stationery Office, 2000.

———. *Eisenhower at War, 1943–1945.* New York: Random House, 1986.

Erickson, John. *The Road to Stalingrad.* London: Weidenfeld & Nicolson, 1975.

Evans, Richard J. *The Third Reich at War: How the Nazis Led Germany from Conquest to Disaster.* London: Allen Lane, 2008.

Falls, Cyril. *The Art of War from the Age of Napoleon to the Present Day.* Oxford: Oxford University Press, 1961.

Fleming, Gerald. *Hitler and the Final Solution.* Oxford: Oxford University Press, 1986.

Förster, Jürgen. "Jewish Policies of the German Military, 1939–1942." In *The Shoah and the War*, edited by Asher Cohen, Yehoyakim Cochavi, and Yoav Gelber. New York: Peter Lang, 1992.

———. "Operation Barbarossa as a War of Conquest and Annihilation." In MGFA 4:481–524.

———. "The Relation between 'Operation Barbarossa' as an Ideological War of Extermination and the Final Solution." In *The War and the Final Solution*, edited by David Cesarani, 85–102. London: Routledge, 1994.

Francis, E. V. *The Battle for Supplies.* London: Jonathan Cape, 1942.

Friedländer, Saul. *The Years of Extermination, 1939–1945.* New York: Harper-Collins, 2007.

Fritz, Stephen G. *Endkampf: Soldiers, Civilians and the Death of the Third Reich.* Lexington: University Press of Kentucky, 2011.

Gallagher, Matthew P. *The Soviet History of World War II: Myths, Memories, and Realities.* London: Praeger, 1963.

Gat, Azar. *The Sources of Modern Military Thought* [in Hebrew]. Tel Aviv: Ministry of Defence, 2000.

Geyer, Michael. "German Strategy in the Age of Machine Warfare, 1914–1915." In *Makers of Modern Strategy: From Machiavelli to the Nuclear Age*, edited by Peter Paret, 527–597. Princeton, NJ: Princeton University Press, 1986.

Gilbert, Martin. *Auschwitz and the Allies.* New York: Henry Holt and Company, 1981.

———. *The Dent Atlas of the Holocaust.* London: Buler & Tanner, 1993.

Glantz, David M. *Colossus Reborn: The Red Army at War, 1941–1943.* Lawrence: University Press of Kansas, 2005.

———. *Soviet Military Operational Art: In Pursuit of Deep Battle.* London: Frank Cass and Company, 1991.

———. *Zhukov's Greatest Defeat.* Lawrence: University Press of Kansas, 1999.

Glantz, David, and Jonathan M. House. *The Battle of Kursk.* Lawrence: University Press of Kansas, 1999.

Glantz, David, ed. *Belorussia, 1944: The Soviet General Staff Study.* London: Frank Cass Publishers, 2001.

Glantz, David, and Jonathan M. House. *When Titans Clashed.* Lawrence: University Press of Kansas, 1995.

Goebbels, Joseph. *Die Tagebücher von Joseph Goebbels.* Teil 2, Band 8, April–June 1943. Munich: K. G. Saur, 1992.

———. *The Goebbels Diaries, 1939–1941.* Translated by Louis P. Lochner. New York: Putnam, 1983.

————. *Goebbels Tagebücher; aus den Jahren 1942–43*. Zurich: Atlantis Verlag, 1948.

Goldensohn, Leon. *The Nuremberg Interviews* [in Hebrew]. Jerusalem: Ivrit and Keter, 2006.

Goldhagen, Erich. "Albert Speer, Himmler, and the Secrecy of the Final Solution." *Midstream*, October 1971, 43–50.

Golikov, Marshal F. I. "To Moscow's Rescue." In *Stalin and His Generals: Soviet Military Memoirs of World War II*, edited by Severin Bialer, 311–318. Boulder, CO: Westview Press, 1969.

Gorlitz, Walter. *Paulus and Stalingrad: The Life of Field Marshal Friedrich Paulus*. New York: Citadel Press, 1963.

Gorodetsky, Gabriel. *Grand Delusion: Stalin and the German Invasion of Russia*. Cambridge, MA: Yale University Press, 1999.

Gottwaldt, Alfred, and Diana Schulle. *Die Judendeportationen aus dem Deutschen Reich, 1941–1945: Eine Kommentierte Chronologie*. Weisbaden: Marixverlag, 2005.

Grigorenko, P. *Memoirs*. London: Norton, 1983.

Guderian, Heinz. *Panzer Leader*. London: Michael Joseph, 1952.

Gutman, Ysrael. *The Jews of Warsaw, 1939–1943: Ghetto–Underground–Uprising* [in Hebrew]. Jerusalem: Yad Vashem, 1977.

Habermas, Jürgen. "Vom Öffentlichen Gebrauch der Historie." In *Historiker-Streit: Die Documetation der Kontroverse um die Einzigartigkeit der national-sozialistichen Judenvernichtung*. Munich: Piper Verlag, 1987.

Halder, Franz. *The Halder War Diary, 1939–1942*. Edited by Charles Burdic and Hanes-Adolf Jacobsen. London: Greenhill, 1988.

Harrison, Mark. *Accounting the War: Soviet Production, Employment, and the Defence Burden, 1940–1945*. Cambridge: Cambridge University Press, 1996.

————. "The Soviet Union: The Defeated Victor." In *The Economics of World War II: Six Great Powers in International Comparison*, edited by Mark Harrison, 206–301. Cambridge: Cambridge University Press, 1998.

Hart, Russel A. *Guderian: Panzer Pioneer or Myth Maker?* Dulles, VA: Potomac Books, 2006.

Hastings, Max. *Overlord: D-Day and the Battle for Normandy*. New York: Simon & Schuster, 1984.

Haupt, Werner. *Die Schlachten der Heersgruppe Süd*. Friedberg: Podzun-Pallas, 1985.

Heer, Hannes, and Klaus Naumann, eds. *Vernichtungskrieg: Verbrechen der Wehrmacht 1941 bis 1944*. Hamburg: Hamburger Institut für Sozialfor-shung, 1996.

Herbert, Ulrich. *Hitler's Foreign Workers: Enforced Foreign Labor in Germany under the Third Reich*. Cambridge: Cambridge University Press, 1997.

———. "Vernichtungspolitik: Neue Antvorten Und Fragen zur Geschichte des Holocaust." In *Nationalsozialistische Vernichtungspolitik, 1939–1945: Neue Forschungen und Kontroversen*. Frankfurt: Fischer Taschenbuch, 1998.

Herf, Jeffrey. *The Jewish Enemy: Nazi Propaganda during World War II and the Holocaust*. Cambridge, MA: Belknap Press, 2006.

Hesketh, Roger. *Fortitude: The D-Day Deception Campaign*. London: St. Ermin's, 1999.

Hilberg, Raul. *The Destruction of the European Jews*. Rev. ed. 3 vols. New York: Holmes and Meier, 1985.

———. "The Reichsbahn and Its Part in the Extermination of the Jews" [in Hebrew]. *Yalkut Moreshet* 24 (1977): 27–50.

Hillgruber, Andreas. "The German Military Leader's View of Russia Prior to the Attack on the Soviet Union." In *The War and the Final Solution*, edited by David Cesarani, 169–186. London: Routledge, 1994.

Hillgruber, Andreas, ed. *Kriegstagebuch des Oberkommandos der Wehrmacht*. Vol. 2, *1. Januar 1942–31. Dezember 1942*. Frankfurt: Bernard & Graefe, 1963. https://archive.org/details/kriegstagebuchdeo2halbrich.

History of the Great Patriotic War of the Soviet Union. Moscow, 1960–1963.

Hitlers Lagebesprechungen. *Die protokollfragmente seiner militärischen Konferenzen, 1942–1945*. Stuttgart: Deutsche Verlags-Anstalt, 1962.

Hitler's Table Talk, 1941–1944. Translated by Norman Cameron and R. H. Stevens. Oxford: Oxford University Press, 1988.

Hoffmann, Joachim. "The Attack on the Soviet Union." In MGFA 4:99.

Horthy, Admiral Miklós. *Ein Leben Für Ungarn (Memoirs)*. Essex: Hutchinson, 1956.

Jäckel, Eberhard. *Hitlers Weltanschauung und Herrschaft*. Stuttgart, 1981. Hebrew-language translation, Tel Aviv: Hakibbutz Hameuchad–Sifriat Poalim, 1990.

———. *Hitlers Weltanschaung und Herrschaft* [in Hebrew]. Tel Aviv: Hakibbutz Hameuchad–Sifriat Poalim, 1990.

Jersak, Tobias. "Entschidungen zu mord und Lüge, Die Deutsche Kriegsgesellschaft und der Holocaust." In MGFA 9: 273–355.

Jomini, Antoine-Henri. *The Art of War*. Harrisburg, PA: J. B. Lipincott, 1947.

Karkowski, Shmuel. "Chelmno." In *Encyclopedia of the Holocaust* [in Hebrew], edited by Israel Guttmann, 504. Jerusalem: Yad Vashem, 1990.

Keegan, John. *A History of Warfare* [in Hebrew]. Tel Aviv: Dvir Publishing, 1996.

Kehrig, Manfred. *Stalingrad: Analyse und Documentation einer schlacht*. Stuttgart: Deutsche Yerlags-Anstalt, 1974.

Keress, Moshe. *Operational Logistics* [in Hebrew]. Tel Aviv: Ministry of Defence, 2002.

Kermish, Joseph. *General Jürgen Stroop's Report* [in Hebrew]. Jerusalem: Yad Vashem, 1966.

Kershaw, Ian. *The End: Hitler's Germany, 1944–45*. London: Allen Lane, 2012.

———. *Hitler: Hubris, 1889–1936*. London: Penguin, 1998.

———. *Hitler: Nemesis, 1936–1945*. London: Arnold, 2000.

———. *The Nazi Dictatorship: Problems and Perspectives of Interpretation*. London: Arnold, 1993.

Khrushchev, Nikita. *Khrushchev Remembers*. London: Andre Deutch, 1971.

Klink, Ernst. "The Conduct of Operations." In MGFA 4:525–762.

Konev, Marshal Ivan. "The Great Battle at Kursk and Its Historic Significance." In Parotkin, *Battle of Kursk*.

Krausnick, Helmut. "The Persecution of the Jews." In *Anatomy of the SS State*, by Helmut Krausnick, Martin Broszat, and Hans-Adolf Jacobsen. London: Collins, 1968.

Kreidler, Eugen. *Die Eisenbahnen im Machtbereich der Achsenmächte während des Zweiten Weltkrieges: Einsatz und Leistung für die Wehrmacht und Kriegswirtschaft*. Frankfurt: Musterschmidt, 1975.

Kroener, Bernhard R. *Der Starke Mann im Heimatkriegsgebiet: Generaloberst Friedrich Fromm*. Paderborn: Ferdinand Schöningh, 2005.

———. *Generaloberst Friedrich Fromm: Der Starke Mann im Heimatkriegsgebiet; Eine Biographie*. Paderborn: Ferdinand Schöningh, 2005.

———. "Management of Human Resources, Deployment of the Population and Manning the Armed Forces in the Second Half of the War (1942–1944)." In MGFA 5:833–1070.

Lazowick, Yaacov. *Hitler's Bureaucrats: The Nazi Security Police and the Banality of Evil* [in Hebrew]. Jerusalem: Hebrew University Magnes Press, 2001.

Lewis, Adrian L. *The American Culture of War*. New York: Routledge, 2007.

Lewis, Adrian R. *Omaha Beach: A Flawed Victory*. Chapel Hill, NC: University of North Carolina Press, 2001.

Liddell Hart, B. H. *The Other Side of the Hill*. London: Pan Books, 1983.

Lynn, John A. *Feeding Mars: Logistics in the Western Warfare from the Middle Ages to the Present*. Oxford: Westview Press, 1993.

Macksey, Kenneth. *For Want of a Nail: The Impact of Logistics and Communications*. London: Brassey's, 1989.

———. *Military Errors of World War II*. London: Cassell, 1998.

———. "The Smolensk Operation: 7 July–7 August 1941." In *The Initial Period of War on the Eastern Front, 22 June–August 1941*, edited by David Glantz, 347. London: Frank Cass, 1993.

Magenheimer, Heinz. *Hitler's War: Germany's Key Strategic Decisions, 1940–1945*. London: Cassell, 2000.

Maisky, Ivan. "The Struggle for the Second Front." In *Main Front: Soviet Leaders Look Back on World War II*. London: Brassey's Defence, 1987.

Manstein, Erich von. *Lost Victories: The War Memoirs of Hitler's Most Brilliant General*. New York: Presido Press, 1994.

Mawdsley, Evan. *December 1941: Twelve Days that Began a World War*. Reprint ed. Cambridge, MA: Yale University Press, 2012.

———. *World War II: A New History*. Cambridge: Cambridge University Press, 2009.

Mayer, Arno J. *Why Did the Heavens Not Darken*. New York: Pantheon, 1990.

Megargee, Geoffrey P. *Inside Hitler's High Command*. Lawrence: University Press of Kansas, 2000.

Mellenthin, F. W. von. *Panzer Battles: A Study of the Employment of Armor in the Second World War*. Norman: Oklahoma University Press, 1956.

Merridale, Catherine. *Ivan's War: Life and Death in the Red Army, 1939–1945*. Reprint ed. New York: Picador, 2007.

Messerschmidt, Manfred. "Der Angriff auf die Sowjetunion." In MGFA 4.

[MGFA]. Research Institute for Military History, ed. *Germany and the Second World War*. 7 vols. to date. Oxford: Clarendon, 1990–present.

Mierzejewski, Alfred C. *The Collapse of the German War Economy, 1944–1945: Allied Air Power and the German National Railway*. Chapel Hill, NC: University of North Carolina Press, 1988.

———. *The Most Valuable Asset of the Reich*. Chapel Hill, NC: University of North Carolina Press, 2000.

Milward, Alan S. *The German Economy at War*. London: Athlone Press, 1965.

———. *War, Economy, and Society, 1939–1945*. Berkeley: University of California Press, 1979.

Mommsen, Hans. *From Weimar to Auschwitz*. Princeton, NJ: Princeton University Press, 1991.

Montgomery, Bernard L., Field-Marshall the Viscount of Alamein. *The Memoirs of Field-Marshall Montgomery* [in Hebrew]. Tel Aviv: Ministry of Defence, 1960.

———. *Normandy to the Baltic*. London: Hutchinson, 1946.

Morell, Theodor. *The Secret Diaries of Hitler's Doctor*. New York: Macmillan, 1983.

Morgan, Lieutenant General Sir Fredrick. *Overture to Overlord*. New York: Doubleday, 1950.

Müller, Rolf Dieter. "Alber Speer und die Rüstungspolitik im Totalen Krieg." In MGFA 5: 275–770.

———. "Die Mobilisierung der Deutschen Wirtschaft für Hitlers Kriegführung." In MGFA 5:405–786.

———. "The Failure of the Economic 'Blitzkrieg Strategy.'" In MGFA 4:1081–1188.

Naveh, Shimon. *In Pursuit of Military Excellence: The Evolution of Operational Theory.* London: Frank Cass, 1997.

Noakes, J., and G. Pridham, eds. *Nazism, 1919–1945: A Documentary Reader.* Vols. 2–4. Exeter: University of Exeter Press, 1998.

Office of the United States Chief of Counsel for Prosecution of Axis Criminality. *Nazi Conspiracy and Aggression: A Collection of Documentary Evidence and Guide Materials for Presentation before the International Military Tribunal at Nuremberg, Germany.* Nuremberg, Germany, 1945–1946. 8 vols., 12 books. Washington, DC, 1946. http://www.loc.gov/rr/frd/Military_Law /NT_Nazi-conspiracy.html.

Orenstein, Harold S., trans. and ed. *Soviet Documents on the Use of War Experience.* 2 vols. New York: Frank Cass, 1991.

Orgill, Douglas. *The Tank: Studies in the History and Development of Tank Warfare* [in Hebrew]. Tel Aviv: Ministry of Defence, 1980.

Ose, Dieter. *Entscheidung im Westen 1944: Der Oberbefhlshaber West und die Abwehr der alliierten Invasion.* Stuttgart: Deutsche Verlags-Anstalt, 1982.

———. "Smolensk: Reflections on a Battle." In *The Initial Period of War on the Eastern Front, 22 June–August 1941,* edited by David Glantz, 349–353. London: Frank Cass, 1993.

Overy, Richard. *Göring: The Iron Man.* London: Routledge, 1984.

———. *Interrogations: The Nazi Elite in Allied Hands, 1945.* London: Penguin, 2001.

———. *Russia's War.* London: Penguin, 1997.

———. "Transportation and Rearmament in the Third Reich." *History Journal* 16 (1973): 389–409.

———. *War and Economy in the Third Reich.* Oxford: Oxford University Press, 1994.

———. *Why the Allies Won.* London: W. W. Norton, 1995.

Parotkin, Ivan, ed. *The Battle of Kursk.* Moscow: Progress Publishers, 1974.

Patton, George S., Jr. *War as I Knew It.* Boston: Houghton Mifflin, 1947.

Piotrowski, Stanislaw. *Hans Frank's Diary.* Warsaw: PWN Polish Scientific Publishers, 1961.

Piper, Franciszek. *Auschwitz: How Many Perished—Jews, Poles, Gypsies.* Oświęcim: Frap-Books, 1996.

———. "The Number of Victims." In *Anatomy of the Auschwitz Death Camp,* edited by Yisrael Gutman and Michael Bernbaum, 61–80. Bloomington: Indiana University Press, 1994.

Porat, Dina. *An Entangled Leadership: The Yishuv and the Holocaust, 1942–1945* [in Hebrew]. Tel Aviv: Am Oved, 1986.

Rabinbach, Anson. "The Jewish Question in the German Question." *New German Critique* 44 (1988): 159–192.

Rahn, Werner. "The War at Sea in the Atlantic and in the Arctic Ocean." In MGFA 6:301–468.

Reder, Rudolf. *Belz'ec.* Kraków: Fundacja Judaica, 1999.

Reinhardt, K. "Moscow 1941: The Turning Point." In *Barbarossa,* edited by John Erickson. Edinburgh: Edinburgh University Press, 1994.

———. *Moscow: The Turning Point—The Failure of Hitler's Strategy in the Winter of 1941–1942.* London: Bloomsbury Academic, 1992.

Reitlinger, Gerald. *The Final Solution: The Attempt to Exterminate the Jews of Europe, 1939–1945.* London: A. S. Barnes & Co., 1961.

———. *The SS: Alibi of a Nation, 1922–1945.* 1956. Reprint, New York: Norton, 1973.

Reynolds, Richard. *Men of Steel—I SS Panzer Corps: The Ardennes and Eastern Front, 1944–1945.* Oxford: Casemate Publishers, 1999.

Ripley, Tim. *The Wehrmacht: The German Army in World War II.* New York: Fitzroy Dearborn, 2003.

Robbins, Michael. "The Third Reich and Its Railways." *Journal of Transport History* 5 (1979): 83–90.

Roberts, Geoffrey. *Victory at Stalingrad: The Battle that Changed History.* London: Pearson Education, 2002.

Rohde, Horst. *Das Deutsche Wermachttrasportwessen im Zweiten Weltkrieg.* Stuttgart: Deutsche Verlags-Anstalt, 1971.

Rokossovsky, Marshal Konstantin. "On the Central Front in the Winter and Summer of 1943." In Parotkin, *Battle of Kursk.*

Ruppenthal, Ronald G. "Logistic Planning for Overlord in Retrospect." In *D-Day: The Normandy Invasion in Retrospect,* edited by the Milton S. Eisenhower Foundation, 87–103. Lawrence: University Press of Kansas, 1971.

Scheffler, Wolfgang, and Diana Schulle. *Buch der Erinnerung: Die Baltikum deprotierten deutschen, Osterreichischen und tschechoslowakischen Juden.* Munich: Saur, 2003.

Scheffler, Wolfgang, and Diana Schulle, eds. *Die ins Baltikum deportierten deutschen, österreichischen und tschechoslowakischen Juden.* Munich: Saur, 2003.

Schüler, Klaus A. Friedrich. *Logistik im Russlandfeldzug: Die Rolle der Eisenbahn Bei Planung, Vorbereitung und Durchfurung des Deutschen Angriffs auf die Sowjetunion bis zur Krise vor Moskau im Winter 1941/42.* Frankfurt: Peter Lang, 1987.

Schulte, Theo J. *The German Army and Nazi Policies in Occupied Russia.* New York: Berg, 1989.

Sereny, Gitta. *Into That Darkness: An Examination of Conscience.* New York: Vintage, 1983.

Sherwood, Robert E. *Roosevelt and Hopkins: An Intimate History.* New York: Harper & Bros., 1948.

Shirer, William L. *The Rise and Fall of the Third Reich* [in Hebrew]. Tel Aviv: Schocken, 1985.

Sinder, Louis L. *Encyclopedia of the Third Reich.* Kent: McGraw-Hill, 1976.

Skorzeny, Otto. *My Commando Operations: The Memoirs of Hitler's Most Daring Commando.* Atglen, PA: Schiffer, 1995.

Speer, Albert. *Spandau: The Secret Diaries.* London: Collins, 1976.

Stahel, David. *Operation Barbarossa and Germany's Defeat in the East.* Cambridge: Cambridge University Press, 2009.

Steiger, Rudolf. *Panzer Taktikum im Spiegel Deutscher Kriegs-Tagebücher* [in Hebrew]. Tel Aviv: Ministry of Defense, 1995.

Stolfi, R. H. S. *Hitler's Panzers East: World War II Reinterpreted.* Norman: University of Oklahoma Press, 1992.

Stroop, Jürgen, and Sybil Milton. *The Stroop Report.* 1960. Reprint, London: Secker & Warburg, 1980.

Trevor-Roper, Hugh. *Hitler's War Directives.* London: Pan, 1966.

Trials of War Criminals before the Nuremberg Military Tribunals under Control Council Law, No. 10. Nuremberg, October 1946–April 1949. 15 vols. http://www.loc.gov/rr/frd/Military_Law/NTs_war-criminals.html.

Truman, Harry S. *Memoirs of Harry S. Truman.* Vol. 1, *1945 — Year of Decisions* [in Hebrew]. Tel Aviv: Am Oved, 1955.

Ulam, Adam. *Stalin: The Man and His Era.* New York: Viking Press, 1973.

Unger, Michal. *Lodz: The Last Ghetto in Poland* [in Hebrew]. Jerusalem: Yad Vashem, 2005.

Vasilevsky, Marshal Aleksandr. "Strategic Planning of the Battle of Kursk." In Parotkin, *Battle of Kursk.*

Vogel, Detlef. "German and Allied Conduct of the War in the West." In MGFA 7:459–702.

Volkogonov, Dimitry. "The German Attack and the Soviet Response, Sunday, 22 June 1941." In *Barbarossa*, edited by John Erickson, 76–94. Edinburgh: Edinburgh University Press, 1994.

———. *Stalin: Triumph and Tragedy.* London: Weidenfeld & Nicolson, 1991.

War Department, Historical Division. *Omaha Beachhead.* Washington, DC: War Department, Historical Division, 1945. http://www.history.army.mil/books/wwii/100-11/100-11.HTM.

Warlimont, Walter. *Inside Hitler's Headquarters, 1939–45.* London: Weidenfeld & Nicolson, 1964.

Wegner, Bernd. "The Global War: Widening the Conflict into a World War and the Shift of the Initiative, 1941–1943." In MGFA 5: 843–1206.

———. "The War against the Soviet Union, 1942–1943." In MGFA 6:843–1216.

Weinberg, Gerhard L. "The Allies and the Holocaust." In *The Holocaust and History: The Known, the Unknown, the Disputed, and the Reexamined,* edited by Michael Bernbaum and Abraham J. Peck for the United States Holocaust Museum, 480–491. Bloomington: Indiana University Press, 1998.

———. *Germany, Hitler, and World War II.* Cambridge: Cambridge University Press, 1995.

———. *A World at Arms.* Cambridge: Cambridge University Press, 1994.

Westermann, Edward. *Hitler's Police Battalions: Enforcing Racial War in the East.* Lawence: University Press of Kansas, 2007.

Wette, Wolfram. *Die Wehrmacht Feinbilder, Vernichtungskriege, Legenden.* Frankfurt: Fischer Taschenbuch, 2002.

Wieviorka, Olivier. *Normandy: The Landings to the Liberation of Paris.* Cambridge, MA: Harvard University Press, 2008.

Williamson, Murray, and Allan R. Millett. *A War to Be Won: Fighting the Second World War.* Cambridge, MA: Belknap Press, 2000.

Wilt, Alan F. *The Atlantic Wall: Hitler's Defenses in the West, 1941–1944.* Ames: Iowa State University Press, 1975.

Yehil, Leni. *The Holocaust: The Fate of the European Jews, 1932–1945* [in Hebrew]. Jerusalem: Yad Vashem, 1987.

Zeitzler, Kurt. "Stalingrad." In *The Fatal Decisions,* edited by Seymour Freidin and William Richardson, 113–172. New York: William Sloane Associates, 1956.

Zetterling, Niklas, and Andres Frankson. *Kursk, 1943: A Statistical Analysis.* London: Frank Cass, 2000.

Zhukov, Georgi K. *Marshal Zhukov's Memoirs* [in Hebrew]. Moscow: Ministry of Defense, 1968.

———. *The Memoirs of Marshal Zhukov* [in Hebrew]. Tel Aviv: Ministry of Defense, 1981.

Ziemke, Earl F. *Stalingrad to Berlin: The German Defeat in the East.* Washington, DC: U.S. Army Center of Military History, 1968.

Zimmerman, Lieutenant General Bobo. "France, 1944." In *The Fatal Decisions,* edited by Seymour Freidin and William Richardson, 173–214. New York: William Sloane Associates, 1956.

Index